THE GOOD LORD WILLING AND
THE CREEK DON'T RISE

"The story of the thousands of men and women in the military who resisted the Vietnam War was buried for decades following the war. Robert Norris was one of those brave resisters, and his deeply personal story of finding his conscience when ordered to Vietnam, and both the struggle and joy of that one moment that altered the course of his life, is told here with direct, powerful prose. An important, fascinating read."

—David Zeiger, documentary filmmaker, director of *Sir, No Sir*

"A most impressive achievement by a highly talented writer. An emotionally powerful memoir that spans nearly a century and several continents. Riveting and rich in detail with passages that evoke Hemingway and Maugham, it draws you in and doesn't let up. For Japanophiles, the sections on life in Osaka and Kyushu offer important lessons on cultural assimilation. You come away from this book with gratitude to the author for having written it and respect for a life well lived."

—Robert Whiting, author of *Tokyo Junkie, Tokyo Underworld*, and *You Gotta Have Wa*

"A sweeping epic of a memoir told by a Vietnam War-era serviceman who risked his all by declaring himself a conscientious objector. Encompassing a lifetime of tragedy amid achievement, the story is both memoir and philosophical treatise. Make no mistake, it is also a snapshot of a significant slice of history. As such, this book will be widely appreciated. Norris writes his vast narrative with clarity and thoroughness."

—Alan Samson, retired journalist and author of *Me. And Me now: A 1970s' Kiwi Hippie Trail Adventure*

"A memoir that spans well over a hundred years in the trials and tribulations of the Norris family. The heart lies in Norris's own story, from his troubled upbringing in Northern California to his fight for conscientious objector status during the Vietnam War to teaching English in Japan. Norris is an accomplished yarn spinner, from childhood adventures to experiences in uniform to the intimate connection he has with his mother. A wide-ranging, fascinating ramble of a tale that has you rooting for the characters every step of the way. [It] invites you to reflect on American culture, family, duty, home, and what it means to live a full life."

—Rosa del Duca, author of *Breaking Cadence: One Woman's War Against the War*

"Heartfelt and ever-alive, inspired by a constant wonder with all the world can offer."

—Sharif Gemie, co-author of *The Hippie Trail: A History*

"A bumpy coming-of-age tale set in the logging country of the Pacific Northwest, dosed with a mother's love, transforms an alienated young man into an expat and ultimately an emeritus professor in Japan. Robert W. Norris crafts the stages of this extraordinary journey—punctuated with a turn as a Vietnam War resister—in a narrative style that is both graceful and seamless."

—Michael Uhl, author of *Vietnam Awakening* and *The War I Survived was Vietnam*

Norris's story should be 'must reading' for today's students who think that the Sixties was all about Woodstock and 'high times.'"

—Thom Nickels, journalist and author of *Literary Philadelphia* and *Out in History*

The Good Lord Willing and the Creek Don't Rise

Pentimento Memories of Mom and Me

Robert W. Norris

A Tin Gate book

For Terri, the Fredericks, and the Murphys

Published by Tin Gate

83 Ducie Street, Manchester, M1 2JQ United Kingdom

www.tingatebooks.com

Copyright © 2023 Robert W. Norris.

ISBN   978-1-80100-000-0

The moral right of the author has been asserted.

Set in 12 pt Libertinus Serif.

Contents

Illustrations

Preface

O N January 11, 2021, my seventieth birthday, Mom fell into a coma. Three days later and four days short of her ninety-fifth birthday, she died peacefully. My sister Terri was at her side. I felt a deep emptiness and loneliness that still lingers. I was once again a lost little boy who couldn't find his mama to run to for warmth and comfort.

Terri and a close cousin asked me to write the obituary. I had to keep it fairly short as newspapers now charge for the service. Here's how it turned out.

Catherine Caroline (Murphy) Schlinkman

Catherine Caroline (Murphy) Schlinkman, 94, passed away at her home in King City, Oregon on January 14, 2021. Kay, as she was known to all, was born in Grand Forks, North Dakota to Lorna (Frederick) Murphy and Patrick Murphy on January 18, 1926.

Kay grew up in White Salmon, Washington, where she attended Columbia High School and was active as a cheerleader and majorette in the marching band. After graduating high school, she attended a business school for two years in Portland, Oregon, then married Bill Norris in 1946 and moved to Humboldt County, California.

Kay had a full and active life. She enjoyed music,

painting, golf, writing, traveling, and dancing. For a time in the 1950s, she became a roller skating instructor. In the 1960s and 1970s, she learned to fly, got a private pilot's license, worked at the Truckee Tahoe Airport, and flew fire patrol for the Division of Forestry for two summers. She spent most of her working career as a legal secretary. Her travels took her to Japan seven times and once to Ireland in 2003 to trace her father's family roots on a three-week journey with her son Robert and his wife Shizuyo. Her warmth and good cheer made her many friends from around the world. Beginning in her 60s, she began studying the Japanese language and continued into her 90s.

Kay is survived by her three children: Richard C. Norris, Robert W. Norris, and Terri M. Norris.

Everyone was pleased with it. A local newspaper ran the obit with a wonderful picture from Mom's high school days. I felt empty. Could Mom's life, her vitality, her entire essence be reduced to four paragraphs of dry, dreary prose? Was that how people would remember her?

She was so much more than that. In many ways, Mom's is the story of a remarkable American woman, a fighter, and a survivor of the time in which she lived. As a child, her experience of traveling across the United States with her family in the early days of the Great Depression was not unlike that of the Joad family in Steinbeck's *The Grapes of Wrath*. Being ostracized by a small logging community in the late 1950s for her divorce and later being kicked out of the Catholic Church when she remarried were symbolic experiences. When I became a conscientious objector, refused my order to fight in the Vietnam War, got court-martialed, and spent time in a military prison, Mom bravely defended me against patriotic and conservative friends, colleagues, neighbors, and family members who considered me a coward and a traitor. This courage also exemplified her life.

At heart, she was a feminist ahead of her time who fought against sexual and power harassment in the home and workplace. After her second divorce, in addition to her main day job as a legal secretary, she took on two hourly-wage jobs—one wrapping presents at a mall and one splitting time between night clerking and cleaning rooms at a hotel—in order to pay off thousands of dollars in gambling debts her second husband left behind. She didn't have money for gas, so she bicycled to work in the snow. In her forties, when she was a licensed pilot flying for the Department of Forestry as a forest fire spotter, she became chairperson of the Reno chapter of Ninety-Nines, the women pilots' organization whose first president was Amelia Earhart. Later, she took night classes to qualify as a legal secretary, worked at three law firms in that capacity, and finally retired at seventy-eight. In the end, she'd gained a hard-earned independence and a pension to pay for living expenses for herself and Terri, who could not work because of disability caused by multiple sclerosis.

Mom was an artistic soul who painted oil and *sumi-e* scenes of animals and nature, wrote haiku poems, and played the piano for social gatherings. She played the Catholic church organ for seven years of Sunday sermons before her priest refused to administer Communion one Sunday after her divorce. When he bypassed her at the Communion rail, she grabbed him and gave him a piece of her mind in front of the whole congregation.

She was an adventurer who traveled to Japan, Ireland, Costa Rica, and Canada. She made friends with people in all those countries and kept up a lifelong correspondence with many of them. She was an athlete who, in addition to her high school cheerleading and majorette activities, played golf, umpired Little League games, bowled in a city league, water-skied, roller-skated, practiced aerobics, and did a lot of mountain trekking. In short, she was a ball of energy.

Her hug was the strongest and best in the world. Her love was true, and you knew she meant it when she hugged you. The last time I got one of those hugs was in August 2015 when I chaperoned some Japanese university students to a Portland, Oregon homestay-study program that I'd arranged through the Japanese university where I taught. I treasure the memories of those times with Mom and Terri.

Memories, however, fade quickly. After Mom's death, I was left with a lot of pictures, copies of our e-mail correspondence dating back to 1998, dozens of actual letters dating back to the late 1980s, a couple of videos of Mom, and about five hours of audio files I recorded of stories Mom told during a 2010 trip I took to Portland. I have a multitude of images in my head from childhood, adolescence, hippie ramblings, the times she visited Japan, our journey to Ireland, and much more, but these images are forever changing.

I've always been interested in Lillian Hellman's usage of the word "pentimento." In the introduction to *Pentimento: A Book of Portraits*, Hellman wrote:

> Old paint on canvas, as it ages, sometimes becomes transparent. When that happens it is possible, in some pictures, to see the original lines: a tree will show through a woman's dress, a child makes way for a dog, a large boat is no longer on an open sea. That is called

pentimento because the painter "repented," changed his mind. Perhaps it would be as well to say that the old conception, replaced by a later choice, is a way of seeing and then seeing again.

Don't we all handle our memories that way? In the end, do our memories preserve the truth, or do they hide it? Or is the truth always changing? Did all those things in the past really happen? Were they merely dreams, figments of the imagination? Timothy Dow Adams in *Telling Lies in Modern American Autobiography* wrote that for Hellman, "pentimento becomes a metaphor for memory, an analogy to the particular difficulty of artistically remembering a life, telling the truth despite the mendacity of memory."

What I do know is that the feelings these memories evoke are entirely real. I want to preserve them. This book is a pentimento journey into the memories that came to me while going through Mom's letters and tapes—and a journey into the memories of my own life. It's a telling of a decades-long conversation I have constantly in my head: the two of us sitting at Mom's dining room table, sipping cups of coffee, and discussing our lives and experiences.

During the last month of Mom's life, she often fretted about her loved ones forgetting her. "Please don't forget me," she implored Terri and me several times. It was hard to convince her that we wouldn't. If Mom is up there in heaven and still worried about that, here's what I'd like to say to her: Mom, no one who ever met you could possibly forget you. Believe me, we'll always remember, love, and cherish you. We'll always remember your infectious laugh, your warmhearted hug, and your family stories. Oh, those stories. That's why I wrote this book!

THE GOOD LORD WILLING AND THE CREEK DON'T RISE

BOOK ONE

1

Grapes of Wrath,
Frederick-style

FAMILY was everything to Mom. She had an endless supply of stories about parents, cousins, aunts, uncles, grandparents, and assorted other characters too numerous to count. Chief among these relatives was her grandfather on her mother's side. The number of stories about Granddad Frederick dwarfed the number about the others. Her Granddad Frederick stories created a mythical character. He was the patriarch of a large family, and his word was final.

Not much is known about Granddad Frederick's early years, but he was born Charles F. Frederick on January 11, 1880, to a Pennsylvania Dutch family in Hartleton, Union County, Pennsylvania. When he was a young man, he hopped a ride on a freight train, got off somewhere in Minnesota, and found his way to a Swedish family's farm. That's when he met his wife. Mom's story of this union goes like this:

"When Granddad Frederick was somewhere around twenty, he left his home in Pennsylvania and rode a freight train toward the Midwest lookin' for work and that is, of course, how he met Grandma Frederick. When I was a little girl, I asked him several times about experiences he had durin' those times, but he wouldn't talk about those days. They weren't very good days for him and he chose to completely wipe them from his memories. Anyway, he stopped at the Minnesota wheat farm to get work. They rode the train out like hobos. They just jumped on the freight train and headed north and if they saw a farm that looked like it had a lot of wheat—and of course those fields were so flat you could see for miles—then they'd jump off and go to the nearest farm and say, 'Do you need any help today?' That's when my grandmother's mother said, 'Now if you're gonna go to the fields to take these workers a meal, you carry a can of pepper in your pocket. And if they get fresh with you, the rule is you don't go to the haystack and you just use the pepper and throw it at them.'

"My grandma told me when she saw my granddad, she said, 'Whoa! I don't think I'll take the pepper with me today.' She didn't go into any detail, but my mother was born nine months later. So I guess they had a good time in the haystack! He was a hobo. She slept with a hobo in a haystack and started eight children."

Mom's mother, Lorna (Grandma Murph when I was growing up), was born on March 29, 1901. She was followed by Olive in 1905, Nina in 1907, Stella in 1909, Alfred Thomas in 1911, Alan William in 1915, and twins Dorothy and Doris in 1917.

Over the years, Granddad Frederick and his family moved a lot. Lorna was born in Minnesota; Olive, Nina, and Stella in Idaho; Alan William and the twins back in Minnesota; and there's no record of where Alfred Thomas was born. For some reason, everyone referred to Alan William as either A.W. or Jack, and Alfred Thomas as Tommy. At one point in their years of moving from job to job and place to place, they ended up in

North Dakota. Patrick Murphy entered the story. Lorna had grown into an attractive young woman and was working as a waitress in a diner. Patrick Murphy stopped in for a meal and was smitten. He and Lorna got married in 1921. Mom was born in 1926. He and three brothers shared a farm, but his portion of the land wasn't fertile. He was ready to move when Lorna's family decided to head west.

I think Mom's whole story really begins with the trek west with the Frederick family, led by Granddad Frederick. Of course, Mom also had her father's Irish ancestry and his large family background (eight brothers and sisters), but she didn't know much about the Murphys except that originally some had left Ireland during the potato famine of the 1840s and settled in the United States with Patrick's father, eventually starting a farm in North Dakota. The Frederick's tight-knit family and their stories became the foundation of her own life history.

Around 1928, the Fredericks loaded their belongings in two beat-up trucks and headed west from North Dakota. They'd travel until they found work farming, picking fruit, or any kind of labor. They sometimes became scattered, with some members staying in one place working while others moved on ahead. Granddad Frederick and some of his clan finally settled in White Salmon, Washington in 1932. Not long after, Mom, her mother, father, brother Jack (born in 1928 in Montana), and maybe a couple of cousins or aunts and uncles also made the journey. Mom didn't remember much about that, but stories handed down from her mother and grandparents were repeated to her own children. A family legend was created.

One story has stayed with me through the years—Grandma Murph's tale of the egg truck that tipped over on the road. No doubt this story has mutated many times, but it's one that gives me great satisfaction to recall. I can still visualize her telling it. After her husband (Grandpa Pat to me) died in 1958, Grandma Murph came to stay with Mom, Dad, brother Dick, sister Terri, and me. We were living outside of Arcata, California, a place out in the country called Jacoby Creek. Grandma Murph radiated warmth and good humor. She was always singing, chuckling, and hugging the people around her.

It's all still in my head. There I am, a little country boy who loves his grandma dearly. I never tire of listening to her tell the story of that journey across the country. Dick and I pester her continually to tell it again. "C'mon Grandma Murph, please. Please tell us about when you went from North Dakota to Oregon and Washington and that time you had to eat all those eggs."

She's in the kitchen baking something. She wipes her hands with a towel, puts it down, and says, "Bobby, you've heard that story a hundred times."

"Just once more, please."

We move to the front room. Grandma Murph sits down in her favorite chair, begins knitting a sweater she seems forever working on, rocks gently back and forth, and begins her tale with Dick and me at her feet.

"Well, my family the Fredericks and your Grandpa Pat's family the Murphys were all farmers. It was all any of us knew. We'd lived and worked in different parts of the country—Minnesota, North Dakota, Montana, Idaho—always farmin', but then the Great Depression came along and it clean wiped everybody out. By that time, I was married to your Grandpa Pat and we had your mother and your Uncle Jack.

"We all decided to head to Oregon. We'd heard the land was rich and there was farms, loggin' camps, fruit orchards, and the like for able-bodied people to work in. At first, my dad and some of my brothers and sisters—the ones who weren't married—went ahead of us to find work and get settled. When we heard they'd found work, some of the rest of us banded together and loaded what we could into two beat-up jalopy trucks. Now if that wasn't a sight to beat all—what with kids and fryin' pans and old suitcases and tools and the like hangin' from every end of those trucks. It's a wonder they could move at all."

She smiles to herself for a moment, then looks at us again. "I remember your Grandpa Pat lookin' at the trucks, shakin' his head like he was in a dream or somethin', then takin' one last look at the old North Dakota farm. He never shed a tear, not like the rest of us. He just told everyone, 'Load up. We're headin' to Oregon,' then climbed up into the driver's seat.

"Well, we made it about two miles down the road and everyone was whoopin' and hollerin' like we was on a circus ride, tryin' to be in good spirits and forget about the farm we'd left behind. Oh, by the way, I forgot to mention your great-uncle John and Aunt Stella had stayed behind to manage the farm best they could—there wasn't no more room for more than the twelve people we had anyway—and if they could sell the place, they'd catch up to us later in Oregon and Washington. As I was sayin', we got about two miles down the road when suddenly POW the rear tire of the truck Grandpa Pat was drivin' popped and went about as flat as my old breasts!"

Grandma Murph can't contain the laughter welling up inside of her. She breaks into a fit that is so infectious Dick and I fall to our sides laughing at the image of Grandma Murph's breasts as tires on an old jalopy truck stranded on a road in North Dakota in the 1930s. With tears sliding down her cheeks, Grandma Murph continues.

"Yes sir, that old tire went flat as a pancake, and with the weight of all our belongings shifted to the flat side, that old truck looked like a leanin' tower of Pisa stranded in the middle of the road. And in all the excitement of movin', your Grandpa Pat had plumb forgot to load the jack and pump. He was mad as a wet hen when he realized this. You should've seen the look on his face when he realized he had to walk all the way back to the farm. He didn't say a word to anyone, just stood there lookin' all in a tiffy. Of course, we all thought it was the funniest thing that ever happened, but we saved our laughter till later cause if anyone had said anything to him, he might've had a stroke right on the spot."

Grandma Murph waves her right hand in the air as if to dismiss any worries Dick and I might have. "It wasn't exactly a glorious beginnin', but we was lucky it happened at the beginnin' cause there's no tellin' how we would've got that tire fixed if we'd been a hundred miles down the road instead of just a couple."

Grandma Murph takes a deep breath. "Well, the trip to Oregon took us nearly two months. Often we'd camp out on the side of the road near the hobo camps. There was many people driftin' across the country then lookin' for work, and often we'd meet up with another group and travel in a caravan.

"Now, I remember one time shortly after we arrived and were livin' in a tent in White Salmon right next to the Columbia River and down the road a bit was a hobo camp. We'd told the kids to stay away from the hobos cause there was no tellin' what kind of men was there, you know, robbers and desperadoes and the like. But your mother and Uncle Jack was like any other kids in that they was curious as could be about them camps. The two of them sneaked down by that hobo camp just to get a peek at what kind of people was there. It happened that the hobos had skinned a cat and was cookin' it up. They was takin' some snorts off a bottle of cheap whiskey while they was cookin' the cat. One of them spotted your Uncle Jack and mother and decided to play a trick. He sneaked up behind the two of them and growled like a big bear and shouted to the other hobos, 'Look what we got here, boys. We got a couple tender young morsels. What say we cook 'em up for dinner?' which of course scared the livin' daylights out of your Uncle Jack and mother. Good Lord, if that wasn't a sight to see them two youngsters come skeedaddlin' as fast as they could fly back to our camp! Why, they looked as if they'd witnessed the return of Lazarus. There was no need to scold them for those hobos had put the fear of God into their young hearts. Not once after that did they stray far from our own place."

Grandma Murph stops to think a moment and get her bearings in the story. Dick and I move closer to her, knowing the climax is coming.

"Now all durin' that time, we had precious little money, and what little we had went mainly for gasoline to keep us movin' along the road. Providence was watchin' over us though and somehow we managed to occasionally catch some fish out of a river or stream or land a two-day job pickin' fruit where all of us, kids and older folks alike, would pick till our hands was bleedin', all for a few dollars, which we'd pool together to buy flour and milk and whatever else we could buy. We didn't have much, but we shared what we had. I remember another time there in White Salmon when we was camped out and there wasn't any food and we was all wonderin' where the next meal would come from. Well, suddenly we heard a bang and a clatter over a hill about half a mile away and we all rushed to see what'd happened. Lord have mercy if we wasn't all surprised to find that a big truck carryin' eggs had gone around a bend in the road too fast and tipped over. The driver wasn't hurt and we got permission to gather as many eggs as we could. It was a godsend. If you can imagine it, there we was the whole lot of us on that lonely stretch of road pickin' and gatherin' eggs like it was the last of the great Easter egg hunts. I'll tell you one thing—we all thanked the good Lord for our good fortune.

"For a solid two weeks we ate nothin' but eggs, eggs cooked every way you can imagine: fried eggs, hard-boiled eggs, soft-boiled eggs, scrambled eggs, egg salad, eggs sunny side up, eggs over easy, eggs over medium, eggs over hard. Why we ate them blessed eggs every way but raw. We ate them till they was comin' out of our ears. Why it got so bad I thought your Uncle Jack and mother would turn into eggs. And you know somethin', children? To this very day your mother cannot eat an egg cause of that awful time. Lord have mercy if she should ever have to eat nothin' but eggs again!"

Grandma Murph slaps her leg, drops her knitting, and lets loose with such a flood of laughter, tears again streaming down her cheeks, that she's rendered incapable of continuing the story. I still think of that whenever I eat an egg.

2

White Salmon Days

DURING Mom's years of growing up in White Salmon, Granddad Frederick and her father had the most influence on her. Their guidance and protection helped forge her strength, moral character, perseverance, fortitude, stubbornness, pride, and mischievous sense of humor. Of course, her entire family contributed to her acquisition of survival skills, family loyalty, an independent spirit, and a strong sense of self-worth, but to me, the stories about Granddad Frederick and Grandpa Pat stood out the most because, whether Mom intended it or not, there was always something allegorical about them.

Take for instance the story about the Indians who fished at Celilo Falls before The Dalles Dam was built on the Columbia River. Terri, Mom, and I are seated at Mom's King City apartment dining table in 2010.

"I have always related to the Indians and Indian history," Mom says. "There were several Indian families that lived right on the banks of the Columbia River when I was growin' up. Dad and Granddad always told me I must always respect the Indians. Granddad took me and my cousin Larry Gernaat. You remember him, don't you, Bob? He and Terry were Aunt Stella's boys. Anyway, Granddad took Larry and me up to Celilo Falls in his little Model T truck one time before the dam was built so we could watch the Indians fish for salmon with nets while standin' out on the edge of wooden platforms—right over the falls—as the fish were migratin' up those falls. It was quite a sight. I think I was probably nine or ten at the time.

"Granddad said to me, 'I want you to see how the Indians fish.' They didn't have any safety ropes tied to them or anything. They were right at the foot of those falls. If they fell in, it was goodbye. Many of the fish that couldn't jump all the way up the falls would fall back down and the Indians would catch them in their nets. I just kept thinkin', 'Oh my' and the fish were huge! I don't remember exactly, but if they'd catch one, they'd have to get it back up to the platform and it was wigglin' all over—the fish was—and get it out of the net into maybe a box or something. Boy, they were clever with that. I really appreciated the fact Granddad did that because you'd never have a chance to see it again."

Mom looks into her cup of coffee as if lost for a moment. The memory retrieved, she looks up at Terri and me and smiles. "There were also four Indians in high school when I was goin' to school in White Salmon and they were great athletes. Quaempts was their name. Mitchell and John Quaempts. Johnny was my age and Mitch was older. And they lived right on the Columbia River in a tent. Johnny's grandfather fished off of those platforms. And these two kids were so strong and wonderful athletes and somehow durin' that time the government gave the Indian families along the Columbia River—the Yakima Indians and the Klickitat Indians and maybe some others, too—gave them some sort of a settlement. Maybe it was from when the Bonneville

Dam was constructed—I don't remember exactly. Anyway, they got a pretty good settlement and Mrs. Quaempts had all of her front teeth capped in gold. If she knew you and you passed her on the sidewalk in downtown, she'd give you a big smile and oh boy how those teeth would shine! And she always wore her buckskin clothes. Granddad Frederick told us kids—my brother, me, and my cousins—that we must never, ever make fun of Mrs. Quaempts. Her people were here long before the white man came. He said we should respect her culture and feel very privileged that she would smile at us."

I remember that Mom often reminisced about Kyoko Nakagawa, a Japanese-American girl who was her best friend for several years until World War II broke out and the government put her family and others in internment camps. I ask Mom to tell that story again.

She looks pleased that I've remembered. The sun is going down, so Terri gets up to turn on the overhead light. Mom says, "Thanks, honey" and returns to the story. "I was in high school at that time and remember well the events of that day and the days and months that followed. There were so many things I didn't learn about until many years later. One of my very best friends in high school was Kyoko and we spent many lunch hours together gigglin' and talkin' about our futures. We'd usually exchange sandwiches because mine were on homemade bread and hers were on the store bread put out by Wonder Bakeries. We thought we were being so sneaky and clever to exchange our sandwiches. How young and naive we both were. I think when I was a junior in high school, I went to school one mornin' and couldn't find Kyoko. I didn't know what happened to her. I was very hurt to think she left and didn't say goodbye.

"I thought all her family were so nice. They had a home down on the river and I remember I got permission to walk down there to see if she was sick and there was nobody home. Everything was gone. I found out a long time later that she and her family had been transported to an internment camp for Japanese in Idaho. I did try very hard and seriously to track her down and finally did only to find out that she died in childbirth just after her family was released from the camp after the war. I felt very sad for a long time after that."

Mom plays with her napkin for a bit before speaking again.

"And that makes me think about Granddad's neighbor who was Japanese—Ken Kida. Ken and Kay Kida. Ken must've been a short nickname. After they disappeared, Granddad kept up their yard and their garden and swept the sidewalks and plowed the snow from there. He didn't buy up the property after they were taken away. He just kept it up. Actually, Ken Kida owned the property and the little house, which was pretty rare in those days. But, you know, in those days White Salmon was kind of in the boonies, so maybe the government or whoever didn't come and take his property. They did take the property of some of the Japanese who were truck farmers in Hood River, but Mr. Kida just had a little piece of property with his house and a little garden.

"In fact, he and my granddad shared a garden. They shared a little plow that a little goat pulled. And so my granddad just kept up the yard and then when they were released and came back to see what happened to their property—I don't think they expected anything—but there it was and my granddad met them and said, 'I tried to keep your place clean for you.'"

Mom beams with pride.

"I know they really appreciated what he did, but you know he was kind of one of the settlers just in that area, so I think if anybody would've been mean to the Kidas, they would've had to put up with my granddad. He was a staunch believer in 'treat people nicely so that you'll be treated nicely' and 'if you want to learn to do something, you learn the right way.'"

Mom closes her eyes, perhaps to get a clearer picture of that memory. A slight grimace crosses her face before opening her eyes, which light up again. She says, "You know, thinkin' about Granddad and that time reminds me now of the time he went to Pennsylvania and one of his calves started grievin' and wouldn't eat."

Mom shifts in her chair to get more comfortable. "After everyone came to White Salmon and got settled, Granddad'd often say, 'Gosh, I was born in Pennsylvania and that's way across the U.S. I don't think I'll ever see Union County, Pennsylvania again.' One Christmas, everyone in the family decided to pitch money into the pot for him to take a trip to Pennsylvania. We raised enough money for an airplane ticket, which in those days was very excitin'.

"I remember specifically I had four dollars in my piggy bank. Wow! That was like havin' five hundred dollars now. And for me, that took weeks of savin'. I was earnin' seventy-five cents an hour at the theater usherin' and that was a lot of money. I got thirty-five cents an hour at the Feed and Seed store keepin' their books and I also worked in the fruit orchards pickin' when it was harvest time. So we all put money in the pot."

"That must've created a huge family discussion," I say.

Mom's eyes get wider. "Oh, it did. Grandma had a table about half again longer than the usual. Anyway, we collected enough money. Then the big decision was Granddad not wearin' a tie on the plane." Mom acts out the conversation between Granddad and Grandma Frederick. "'But you have to wear a suit and a tie.' 'I don't have to do anything I don't want to.' And he wasn't sarcastic. And he wasn't condescendin'. He was just content within himself, I think. He said, 'I'm gonna get on the plane. It's a long ride. I'm goin' clear to Pennsylvania and you want me to wear a tie?'"

Mom waves her hand in front of her imitating Granddad Frederick's dismissal of the others' concerns. "So off he went and he was gonna spend maybe a week there. About the third day he was gone, Uncle Jack and my dad got together with the rest of the family for another meetin'. You see, the cow had had a calf before Granddad left and Granddad was with those animals all the time. He'd go out and sit with them. He had a little stool to sit on in the corner of the stall until the cow had her calf and then he'd baby it and feed it. Well, the calf wouldn't eat while he was gone. And the calf kept gettin' thinner and thinner. Granddad was hopin' to sell one of the cows and then he'd still have two cows, the mom and the baby, because that's where we got our milk. Everybody got their milk from him.

"So we had to call. It was very expensive to call. Aunt Doris and Uncle Wes were the only ones that had a telephone. There were about five of us there. I don't remember exactly, but definitely my dad and Uncle Jack. Everybody wrote down what they were gonna say because they didn't want to take up a lot of minutes."

Mom sits up straight, pretends to hold a phone, and leans forward to speak into it. "You're gonna have to come home because if you don't, we think the calf's gonna die."

I bust out laughing and say, "Oh no, on the biggest trip of his life!"

"That's right. The biggest trip of his life! And he came home. The minute he came home, the calf began eatin'. No kiddin'! And it was funny. The first place he went when he got home was out to the stall. I think Uncle Jack and my dad drove to Portland to the airport to pick him up, you know. That was a long trip then. And so while we're all down at Grandma and Granddad's place waitin' for Granddad to come home, somebody has to be out lookin' at the poor calf."

Mom does an impression of bending over a calf, looking worried, stroking it, and saying, "Now, now. Don't you worry. Your daddy'll be here soon." Mom leans back, making sure we're still listening intently, and continues. "So here comes Granddad Frederick and my dad and Uncle Jack and of course Granddad was exhausted. I don't know how long a trip that could've been. So we all followed him out to the stall to see what the calf would do, and wouldn't you know, the calf started eatin' the minute it saw my granddad!"

Terri and I are both caught up in the story, amazed at the outcome. "They must've really had some kind of bond," I say.

"That's right! It was so amazin'. Granddad loved his animals. He used to enjoy drivin' into town with his two dogs sittin' on his lap and their heads hangin' out the windows. He would buy each of the dogs an ice cream cone and one for himself and then start drivin' home. The police stopped him several times, but they only gave him a warnin' and never gave him a ticket. He was kind of like the town character.

"I remember I used to get off the bus after school about three nights a week and run out to the barn, where Granddad would be milkin' his two cows. I loved to hear his stories because he had a really good sense of humor. I used to wonder how he came to have such a big family. One time, I asked him why he'd had so many children—there were eight in total, you know. He said, 'I didn't want that many children, but, well, your Grandma was pretty willin'.' 'Whadaya mean willin'?' I asked. He looked at me with a glint in his eye and said, 'I think it's time for you to go home.'

"In retrospect, I think Granddad always . . . as soon as he was settled somewhere, he wanted to move. I think my granddad moved so often because he thought he had to. He had to find a better life. Because he kept havin' babies! I'm gettin' away from the cows here for a minute. They can wait. Hold their milk. After Grandma had the twins—they had no birth control in those days—"

"Oh yeah, and a good Catholic family, at that," I say.

"Well, no. Grandma and Granddad were Lutheran, and that's kind of like Catholic. But after all those children, Grandma finally said to him, 'You're not gettin' next to me any closer than a ten-foot pole. I'm tired of pushin' babies out!'"

All three of us break into a fit of laughter. When I catch my breath, I say, "Laying down the rules."

Mom continues her Grandma Frederick impersonation. "'And if you wanna move again, you just go on. I'm settled and I'm not goin' anywhere.' That's when they had that house in White Salmon."

I can't resist following up the impersonation. "Tie that thing into a knot!"

Mom and Terri laugh.

"And they never had any more babies." Mom takes some time to catch her breath. "To get back to the cows. He taught me how to milk. One time, he said, 'Hey, you're doin' pretty good. You're gettin' some milk out of that cow. How'd you like to milk for me on Saturday mornings?' I said, 'No, thank you.' That cow had a bad tail and she'd whack you with it. I don't think she liked me."

"Animals are strange that way," I say. "Like that calf and that cow. You'd think they're not like humans. They don't have those kinds of feelings, but they do."

"They do. And even hens do. I've told you about havin' to gather eggs for Grandma after work. Two or three of them hated me. I'd reach under them to fetch the eggs. They'd peck at me and I'd say, 'You just stop that!' And they'd go, 'I can peck you if I want to.'

"Grandma sold a lot of those eggs. They were the best eggs in the whole world. I'll never forget this one experience connected with her eggs. About once a week when I stopped by Grandma's house after school, she'd have me deliver about a dozen of her fresh, brown eggs to a neighbor man who lived alone. My job was to deliver the eggs, get the egg bucket and the money for the eggs, and then go home and give Grandma her egg money. One time when I knocked at the neighbor man's door, he opened the door and said, 'Come right in.' I waited for him to go get the egg money, but when he came back, his pants were down and he exposed himself to me!"

Mom drops her jaw in mock surprise.

"I was so frightened that I dropped the dozen eggs—which broke, of course—ran out the door, and ran home as fast as I could. Grandma asked me where the money was and I told her what'd happened. She grabbed a large broom, took me by the hand, and we hurried back to the neighbor's house. I thought Grandma was angry at me for not bringin' home her money, but when the neighbor man opened his door, Grandma started callin' him bad names like a cheatin', nasty SOB and hit him over and over with the broom.

"She said to him, 'You get the goddamned money for me now and know I'll never sell you another egg for as long as you live!'

He got the money, gave it to Grandma, and we headed home, me in tears and Grandma still swearin' about the man. I was relieved that Grandma wasn't angry at me, but shocked that she knew all these bad words."

"You must've loved your grandparents tremendously," I say.

"Yes, I did. They were so fun to be around. There was never a dull moment in that house. I'm sure I told you about the time he sneezed and lost his teeth."

"Yes, you have, but I'd like to hear it again."

"Well, he was workin' for Uncle Jack. They'd dump the logs in the White Salmon River where it went into the Columbia River. And then Uncle Jack would tie them to a raft and then they'd tow them with a tugboat down to Portland."

"Like in that movie that Ken Kesey wrote the original novel for—*Sometimes a Great Notion*—and Henry Fonda and Paul Newman were in that. It was a great story," I say.

"Right. And that's exactly what Uncle Jack and Granddad did. They'd tie the logs together to make a raft and then Uncle Jack would take the tugboat down. I didn't know that Granddad had dentures. I wasn't there of course, but Uncle Jack told the story and Granddad had had kind of a bad cold and Uncle Jack told him 'Don't work today' and Granddad said, 'I'm goin' to work. We've got to get these rafts ready.'

"So there they were out on the water walkin' on the logs and suddenly Granddad sneezed and his teeth came out—"

I break into a convulsion of laughter, which makes Mom start giggling. It takes a minute or so to catch our breath.

"And his teeth came out and went into the river and he says, 'Oh my God. There goes my teeth!' And he dove in after them. Well, then Uncle Jack couldn't find him. Anyway, he lost his teeth. They went clear to the bottom and he never did retrieve them.

Finally, he came up and he goes like this." Mom bends over and pretends to have a hard time catching her breath. "And Uncle Jack was petrified. Well, somehow Uncle Jack got him out of the water. He was soakin' wet in his clothes and those cork boots."

"Oh, you couldn't swim in those," I say. "They'd be like weights."

"So anyway, he got up. Maybe he grabbed a log and just worked his way up. I don't know. So he said, 'Jack, you take me right straight home.' And he went to his room and he wouldn't come out. He said, 'You get ahold of Dr. Kloster the dentist and tell him I want a new set of teeth today.' Uncle Jack said, 'Well, he has to take a mold—' Granddad cut him off and said, 'I don't care. If he has any spare ones, bring 'em out.'

"I don't know what happened, but he did get a new set of teeth. Uncle Jack said, 'You don't tell a dentist you want teeth today.' Granddad said, 'I'm not leavin' this room without my teeth.' That was another story that made all the rounds in the family."

"With different variations on it, too, I imagine. It'd probably be great to get together and hear a completely different version from one of your relatives."

"That's exactly what would happen, Bob. It was, oh, we used to laugh, you know. My dad would get a box of oranges or maybe a turkey for Christmas when he was workin' at the mill. Wow! Oranges! We couldn't afford to buy any. They were at a real premium in those days. To this day, the smell of oranges reminds me of my dad sayin' to my brother and me, 'Don't touch those oranges until we count 'em. We have to share 'em with the rest of the family.' So we laid them all out on the bed."

"You were going to portion them out?" I ask.

"Yeah. For each member of the family. Some for Grandma and Granddad. Some for Aunt Louise and Uncle Jack. Some for Jake and Stella. And all the cousins, of course. My brother and I would usually end up with an orange apiece, or perhaps we'd have to share one. I don't think oranges have tasted that good since."

"Tough times."

"But fun times," Mom says. "It was just great. Now, Doris and Dorothy were the twins and were the youngest ones in Granddad's family. They were in high school with your dad's brother Uncle Dick Norris. And they were datin'. Outside my Grandma's bedroom window was a huge cotton tree that you could climb up into and if it was kind of sheddin' cotton, you could hide there and watch what was goin' on down on the porch with Aunt Doris and Aunt Dorothy and their boyfriends."

"Oh. What did you see?"

Mom gets a mischievous look on her face and says, "Lots!"

We laugh. I say, "C'mon, let's hear some details."

"I didn't know what . . . you know. I couldn't see too well, but Dorothy was pretty, well, adventurous."

"Did you see her boobies flop out?"

"Not only that, but her boyfriend's thing flopped out, too!"

"Oh boy, you saw the whole act?"

Mom gets wide-eyed and says, "Yeah!"

"That must've been shocking when you were . . . how old, maybe eight or something?"

Mom pretends to be shocked. "Wow, what are they doin'? Takin' off their clothes? My God, it's cold outside! So I'd ask Aunt Dorothy the next day, 'What were you doin' with your clothes off?' 'Whadaya mean? I didn't have my clothes off.' 'But I saw you and I saw John take his clothes off, too.'"

I act as if I'm Aunt Dorothy and look sternly at Mom. "Don't you dare tell Grandma."

"Yeah. Exactly. Granddad slept on the other side of the house and Grandma slept upstairs after the twins were born. So I'd often stay overnight at their place on Saturday night so I could climb out and get into the cotton tree. It was amazin' what you saw. But, you know, it was a fun time to grow up. We didn't have very much, but we had each other."

"I think you had everything that a lot of other people didn't have. That's for sure."

"I'm findin' that out, Bob, even today."

Mom reaches over and pats my hand. "You know, honey, when I look back, I think, 'You know, we had very few material things.' When Aunt Doris and Uncle Wes had a telephone and I was just startin' to date—I was maybe a junior in high school—we didn't have a phone. But Aunt Doris said, 'Well, you can give out our telephone number and you can be on the phone between five o'clock and 5:15, no more if you want your boyfriend to call you.'"

I laugh and say, "They really controlled you in those days, didn't they?"

"Of course. I'd go over there at five o'clock and some nights the phone would ring and some nights it wouldn't. But if we were in the middle of a conversation and it was 5:15, my uncle would come and without sayin' anything, just click, the call's over. And so I got to the point where I said, 'OK. You can call me between five and 5:15, but make a list of what you wanna talk to me about.' 'Why?' 'Because my uncle will cut us off.' 'After only fifteen minutes?' 'That's what he told me. That's what we have to do.'

"So here we are. Very romantic. 'What's on your list?' 'Can you go to the movies with me Saturday night?' My turn to talk. 'Do you have enough gas to drive from your place out here? Or do I have to ride the bike and meet you at the movie theater?'"

"You were like a lawyer even then," I say.

Mom laughs, then continues playing both roles. "'Well, I don't have enough gas this time.' 'Well, how much money do you have? Do you have enough money so we can have a coke after the movie?' 'Let me check.' 'Don't check. We don't have time!' No kiddin'. That's the way it went, Bob."

"It must've given a real intensity to the relationship."

"Oh, it did. This one kid called me and said, 'Would you like to go to the movie Saturday night?' That was all there was to do. 'Well, yes. Do you have any money for gas?' 'No, but I'll pick you up on my bicycle.' 'Oh. OK. That means I'll have to wear pants, not a dress.' 'That's right.' So he'd pick me up on the bike and I'd ride on the handlebars into town, which was about a mile. And that way we'd save money for a coke."

Mom looks worn out, so I suggest going to bed and continuing the stories the next day. She agrees and gets up slowly. I stand up, too. She gives me a big hug and a peck on the cheek. She looks me in the eyes for a moment, then says, "I'm so glad you're home. We've missed you so much. Good night, sweetie."

The next evening after dinner, we're at it again. Terri is out running errands, so there are just the two of us. This time, we start talking about music and how important it was in the Murphy household.

"You know, music has always been such an integral part of my life for as long as I can remember," Mom says. "I don't know if you remember, but your Grandpa Pat played the clarinet in a First World War band and toured Europe while he was in the service. He was always disappointed he didn't get to go to England and then to Ireland. Grandma Murph had a beautiful singing voice and whistled. Granddad Frederick would sometimes walk up through the woods to our house and chord on the piano—you know, he never had any lessons—and sing old time songs from his youth. These were such fun to listen to.

"Dad loved his music, but he was quite strict about learnin' the right way. I had to take classical lessons first and I remember Dad insisted I use a metronome when I was first learnin' to read music and then practicin' on the piano. When I was in high school, I wanted to take popular music lessons, but Dad insisted I also continue with the classical music lessons. I'm so glad I did, and music has been a big part of my life ever since I can remember. In a couple of the recitals I played in as a young girl, my dad and I played a duet, me on the piano and he on the clarinet."

"So what was it like when you were growing up and your parents were putting boundaries on what you could do or where you could go and the town you were living in was putting down laws and boundaries, and you were kind of a rebel yourself?" I ask.

"I was, Bob. They just finally said, 'You know right from wrong and if you don't do the right thing, you're gonna pay for it.' But you're right. There were rules, and my dad said this to me, 'You don't seem to be able to follow my rules.' And I said, 'They're such stupid rules!'"

I shake my head in wonder. I feel a strange sense of pride in Mom's teenage rebelliousness. "Can you think of any specific examples like when you were a kid and your teacher or your parents told you to do something you didn't want to do?"

"I can remember when I was eight years old, I was in Catholic school. And I remember I'd like to get out and run and do this and that. I was always scuffin' my shoes. It sounds like such a small thing. We were supposed to shine our shoes before we went to class and I thought I was a thousand miles away from home. It was really only like about thirty miles. They had the nuns come down from Goldendale. I went to Catholic school for two years. I remember that. Or maybe one year and summer school. I was always late to class, but I got good grades. Well, maybe I didn't pull my socks up as far as they should be. My shoes were always scuffed because I loved to get out and climb trees and do all that, so I was always gettin' in trouble for scuffed shoes. Finally, my dad had to come up. They would call him. We didn't have a telephone, so the school had to go through the telephone company and call Aunt Doris and Uncle Wes and they had to go over and say, 'Kay's teacher called and would like you to call them.'

"It was a mess, too, all over just a pair of scuffed shoes." Mom gives a disgusted look. "I don't know why this sticks in my mind, but I think one reason it does is my teacher was whackin' my hand with a ruler, and I said somethin' to her once, 'Don't you hit my shoes,' because we had maybe one pair of shoes a year. So my dad came up there—I remember this—and I thought I was in trouble with the teacher and I was gonna flunk this grade and have to go back to that stupid school again. I hated that school."

Mom brushes some lint off her sleeve. "And my dad came up there and we didn't have a lot of gas and he comes in this Model A. Putt, putt, putt, putt. And I'm thinkin', 'Oh, I think that's someone from my family.' And it was my dad. He was a real quiet, gentle person, but on that day he came in and said, 'I want to talk to the Mother Superior.' And the nun said, 'Well, can I help you?' He said, 'No!' And of course being a nosey kid, I was watchin' secretly. He gave the nun a lecture about 'Are you here to teach the kids or get after them for not polishin' their shoes? That's ridiculous!'

"I thought, 'My God, that's my father!' because he was usually so quiet and would tell me, 'Now you always do what the nuns tell you.' In the end, I didn't go back to that school. He let me get out and go to public school."

Mom sits back in her chair for a moment. I can feel the pride and love she had for her father. She leans forward again, takes a sip of coffee, puts the cup back down, smiles at me, and continues.

"You know, lookin' back all through my years, I think the main reason I went to church was for my father because it seemed he was such a staunch Catholic. He just said, 'This is the way it is in this home. You will go to Confession on Saturday. You will go to Communion on Sunday. And the rest of the week you can make your own plans.' And he was so quiet about tellin' me this. And then, when I went to Confession, I was thirteen years old. And White Salmon was such a safe place to grow up in then. I wanted to go out and play with the kids. I mean we'd have a ball game until dark out in somebody's field and then we'd all go home, but here I had to go to Confession. So I went in the confessional and said to the priest, 'I haven't sinned. I haven't sworn. I haven't lied. I haven't stolen. There's no reason for me to be here, so I just won't waste your time.'

"The priest said, 'What? Nothing to confess?' and gave me a bunch of prayers to recite to redeem myself and ask forgiveness for my 'lie,' which I didn't do, of course. After that, I went out and played with all the kids and then I walked home. Dad had already found out about the story. The priest had told him I'd lied to him in the confessional. And I said, 'Do you mean that priest came out and told you what I told him in the confessional?' I'd been taught that anything you said in a confessional was confidential. So Dad stood up for me. He said, 'OK. You don't really believe in this. I tried to teach you what I know, how I was taught.' And so he let me not have to go to church. He told me, 'You're right. You're old enough now to know right from wrong and you have seen the wrong thing that the priest, who's just a human bein', did.'

"I thought, 'Ohhh, I think both my dad and me are goin' to hell!' But that was so ingrained in me."

"So all during those years he was telling you I guess of how badly he wanted to visit Ireland before he died and never was able to?" I ask.

"Yes. I think it was because of his name and his heritage from his dad, not maybe so much the religion but the fact that he kind of knew about the history of Ireland and the potato famine and how bad that was and he knew that his ancestors emigrated from Ireland for that reason. I think my dad probably was like I was, Bob. He really didn't believe everything in the Catholic religion. I felt they were absolutely controllin' my life and I told my dad this. I said, 'That's not fair!' And he said, 'Yes, you're right.'

"I don't know for sure, but I think maybe that's the way he felt growin' up because when he was a boy, it was even stricter than when I was growing up. And then he gave me the opportunity—"

"And women didn't even have the right to vote until the nineteen twenties," I say.

"That's right. But he really gave me—and my brother, too—the opportunity to make our own choice. And he'd say to me, 'You have to carry good grades in school. Education is so important.' And he was the only one of his brothers who went to college. He knew what a struggle it was to get through school. They had nothin'! But he always felt he just wanted to get back and kind of see where he came from, but he knew he'd never be able to.

"Maybe my dad wasn't such a true, staunch Catholic, but he didn't know anything else. I think at heart he was quite a philosopher at times. He used to say to me many times, 'Sis, when you think you're goin' through what you perceive at the time to be a very difficult situation, don't waste time and energy askin' "Why?" or "Why me?" or complainin'. Life is simply helpin' you build character and you'll need a lot of character and stamina if you're to survive, and if you can survive and learn to be kind to others and learn to laugh, then and only then will you have a good and fulfillin' life.' He really had a strong impact on my life. He gave me a deep appreciation for everything we had and where we lived. Granddad Frederick, too. Granddad often used to say to me, 'Sis, don't ever forget this beautiful area where you were privileged to live durin' your growin' up years.'"

I reflect for a minute on this aspect of Mom's life that I didn't know before. I'm curious to know more, so I ask, "How about Grandma Murph? She didn't strike me as the type to be very religious."

"She wasn't and the only reason she allowed us to be raised as Catholics is of course she loved my dad, but she told me later, 'I don't believe in the Catholic religion. I'm not gonna become a Catholic. That doesn't mean that you can't raise your children as Catholics if you want to.' And that was one of the requirements to be married in a Catholic church. To Grandma Murph, it was more important to marry than to argue.

"I used to ask her a lot of questions. And one of the first things she said to my dad, 'Now, I'm gonna start a family. If you think we're gonna use any birth control, forget it.' Can't you see her doin' that? Then she says to Dad, 'Do you wanna go to bed with me or not?' I said, 'Mom! You said that to Dad?' 'Yeah, he went to bed with me.' So she was very open. She wasn't mean about somethin' if she didn't believe in it. And my dad would go to church. She'd sometimes go with him but not always.

"I remember one time she said to him, 'I don't understand all that gibberish. I'm not gonna go. You go ahead and go.' And my dad said, 'OK.' They had an unusual understanding, which was good. So here we are. We were raised. We're still alive. And I've felt all my life I was so blessed to come from the family I did. But, you know, it took me a long time to appreciate what they tried to teach me. I was such a little renegade. Would you like to hear just one more country-girl story?"

"Sure. I'll listen to any story you want to tell."

Mom chuckles. "This one's about the summer in my junior year. Did you know that on that hill above the mill where my dad worked and where they cut those logs to send down the flume to the log pond nine miles away, I spent four weeks in a kind of shack at the top of the hill to report smoke? All by myself!"

"Like a lookout?" I ask.

"A lookout, yeah. And they'd bring my dinners up to me on a mule."

"Did you sleep overnight in that place?"

"Yes. I think it was called Little Baldy Peak Lookout. I was there for about four weeks straight. And I did it because they paid me good!"

"That must've been a bit unusual back then because I imagine only young men would be able to do that," I say.

"I had my dad's neighbor put in a good word for me. And if anything happened and I got sick, they gave me a walkie-talkie type phone I could use to call."

"So you'd have to report in to headquarters once or twice a day?"

"Yeah, by a kind of radio. It had a keyboard. I can't remember exactly. I think it was a kind of typewriter to send out some kind of message. I'd hear it ring, then I'd say my name and give it my number. I'd have to say, 'This is what happened at six in the morning. This is what happened at six in the evening,' Like that. There were a couple of nights when I didn't sleep real well because I'm not the bravest person in the world."

"There must've been quite a few animals up there."

"A lot. And we were to report about those, too."

"Did you see any deer or bear?"

"I saw quite a few deer and some smaller ones like a coyote or that size. I didn't go outside very much."

"Did you see any fires?"

"I think I saw four that looked like smoke. Two of them turned out to be fires. They were surprised that my parents would let a girl do that work, but when I told my parents about the job, I said, 'I'm gonna make a lot of money and Christmas is coming.' My dad said, 'That doesn't make sense.' It took me a while to figure out what he meant. But I made over two hundred dollars!"

"Wow! That was a lot of money back then."

Mom looks pleased with herself. "That's right. It was. But I suppose they were a little desperate. Two boys were gonna do it from high school, but they joined the Army instead. So the school had an announcement. If anybody is interested, go see the principal. They were lookin' for a fill-in because they didn't have anybody on the date they had to start the fire season. And I remember one of the questions they asked me at the interview was 'Are you afraid of the dark?' I said, 'Yes, I am, but I won't go outside when it's dark.' 'Well,' they said. 'We'll consider that. We don't usually hire a woman to do this kind of work.' And I thought, 'Wow! They think I'm a woman!'"

We have a good chuckle, then I say, "If you were a junior in high school, that means it was probably around 1942, right in the middle of the war, so I don't imagine there were many young men around."

"That was in 1942 because I graduated in '43. I really wasn't old enough to do it. If it'd been you or your sister, I'd probably have said you were too young."

"I think you had some great times in high school."

"Oh yes. High school was a great time for me. What a rich, young thing I thought I was. Not only that lookout job, but I also had three part-time jobs. I ushered at the local movie theater one night a week and on Sundays; I did some bookkeepin' for a local feed store two afternoons a week—my desk was a piece of plywood on top of some bales of hay; and I worked in the fruit orchards on weekends when fruit was in season. Oh my, I thought I was so rich. And I even had my own bank account!"

Mom pretends to count money with her fingers, grins at me, then goes on. "My two favorite subjects in high school were cheerleadin' and bein' a drum majorette. One year, our little high school band was invited to march in the Rose Festival Parade in Portland. I was one of three drum majorettes and were we ever excited. I even used some of my hard-earned money to buy a pair of white boots to wear with my short outfit. Of course, my dad thought it was way too short, but we three girls were so excited and we were gonna get to stay overnight in Portland and after the parade were invited to one of the high school dances. We thought we were in heaven— but alas! After marchin' for five miles with the band, we all three had big blisters on our feet and our chaperone wouldn't let us go to the dance. The three of us thought that life had absolutely come to an end! It was still a thrillin' experience for us country bumpkins. I usually remember that when Rose Festival time comes around and I have to laugh at how inno- cent and naive we were."

"After you graduated from high school in 1943, there were still basically two more years of war, then that's when you went to secretarial school, right?" I ask.

"I went to a Portland business school. My folks couldn't afford to pay for college."

"Probably everything was geared toward the war. There probably weren't too many young men around."

"No, there weren't," Mom says. "But I thought, 'OK. I get to go to Portland. I think I'll find another girl who's goin' to Portland and we'll get an apartment together.' And they had what they called the U.S.O., the United Service Organization, for the soldiers and sailors and you'd go down and dance with them. My dad said, 'Don't think you're gonna get your own place to live and just have a big time. You're gonna go to school and you're gonna stay with your aunt and uncle, who have the same ground rules we have at home.' I thought, 'How did he know what I was thinkin'?' And my aunt and uncle were very strict. Then I went back to White Salmon before I interviewed for jobs."

"So that was a two-year school?"

"Yes. That would've been '45."

"Did you get good grades?"

"Yes. Because my uncle checked them. I couldn't escape!"

"So what kind of classes did you take?"

"I had typin', shorthand, bookkeepin', balancin' checkbooks, reconcilin' bank statements. I hated bookkeepin'."

"But you've put those skills to use throughout your life."

"I have. Yeah, I really have. Then I went back to White Salmon and I worked. I stayed with my folks and then they had a reunion or, no, a homecoming basketball game in the gym and your dad and Uncle Dick came. Your dad had his uniform on, his Army uniform on, really handsome. And I had my little short cheerleadin' costume on and boy I jumped around when I saw these two guys up in the audience because all there was up there was older mothers and fathers and grandmas and grandpas. Whoaaa!"

Mom throws her arms out to the side and pretends to wave some pompoms around.

"So your dad came down and said, 'You may not remember me.' I said, 'Yes, I remember you.' He was six years older than me. He said, 'Would you like to go out and have a coke?' I said, 'Yes, but I can't.' 'Why can't you?' 'Well, because my aunt and uncle brought me to the game and I have to go home with them.' I don't know where I got that. Maybe my dad used to say, 'You go with somebody, you go home with them. You don't go someplace with somebody and leave them and pick up on somebody else. No! That's not right.' So your dad said, 'Well, would you like to go to a movie?' And I thought, 'Hmmm' because I think I got my usherin' job back, which meant I got to see the movies for free, so I said, 'Well, what movie are you talkin' about?'"

I start laughing and say, "There you were, negotiating again."

"Well, whatever movie it was, I said, 'Well, I guess.' I wasn't really that enthused about goin' to a movie. I thought, 'I'd like go to a dance somewhere.' So anyway we went to a movie, and I don't know—your dad had to go back to the service for somethin'. He said he'd be gone about a couple months. Then I heard all these rumors that he'd supposedly been goin' out with Janet, Janet Harrison, and she wrote him a Dear John letter when he was overseas. So everyone was sayin', you know, cluck, cluck, cluck, cluck, 'How come you're goin' out with Bill Norris? Boy, he belongs to the elite family here. And Janet Harrison? What happened with that?' I'd say, 'Well, Janet Harrison got married to somebody else.' And they'd say, 'Oh!' and look all shocked. So the first date that we went on when your dad came back from wherever he had to go was dinner at Nana's and Granddad Hi's."

I bust out laughing at the image Mom has just created. Nana and Granddad Hi were Dad's parents. They were English and stuffy and damn proud of who they were and the status they carried in the community. They had a sawmill in Trout Lake during the Depression years and paid their workers in Norris Money, which was comprised of scrip and tokens redeemable at a hundred cents on the dollar in the general store that they also owned. Mom was from an Irish working-class family and was something of a brash tomboy. It must've been a bit like a commoner being invited to the royal family's house for dinner. Nana, especially, would expect Mom to have perfect manners and act like a proper lady. And if not, well, something would have to be done about smoothing those rough edges. In my head, I see a classic case of "stiff" versus "loose."

"Wow!" I exclaim. "That's jumping straight from the fryin' pan into the fire!"

Mom's laughing, too. "Right. You don't even go from the fryin' pan. You just jump right in there. And we sat and listened to Fibber McGee and Molly on the radio."

"What was that?"

"Fibber McGee and Molly was like Jack Benny and his wife. On the radio."

"I think that's something that no modern family can even imagine," I say, getting up to go to the fridge to grab a beer. "You know, how families would just gather around a radio in a front room and spend the whole night listening to radio programs. They had all those dramas like 'The Shadow.'"

"Right," Mom says. "And I thought, 'Oh my. I've jumped from cheerleadin' and jumpin' around to a proper finishin' school.' And the next thing I knew, we were married and on our way to California."

3

California Here I Come

WILLIAM "Bill" George Norris was born on January 22, 1920, in The Dalles, Oregon and attended grade school in White Salmon, Washington. He graduated from Columbia Union High School in White Salmon in 1938. He earned letters as the quarterback of the football team, the point guard for a state championship basketball team, and as a member of the baseball and track teams. After high school, he went to Washington State University for one semester, but in 1940 he and his older brother, Dick, built a sawmill at Bingen, Washington and with their father, Don, formed the firm of Norris Brothers.

In 1944, Dad enlisted in the 367th Fighter Group of the 9th Air Force of the European Theater. He spent time in both London and Paris. He flew a P-38 Lightning and eventually was made a flight leader and a captain. He performed numerous strafing and dive-bombing missions, engaged in multiple dogfights, and flew important escort missions, including one providing air cover for Winston Churchill and President Franklin D. Roosevelt as they crossed the English Channel on June 14th, 1944. He flew with the invasion of Normandy.

Dick was allowed to stay behind to help run the sawmill because it was considered by the government to be connected with the war effort.

After Dad returned from the war as a decorated hero with seventy-one combat missions, the Norris family sold the sawmill and moved to Arcata, California in 1946. They joined forces with the Van de Vanters, another lumber family from White Salmon, and created the Van De Nor Lumber Company.

Arcata in the late 1940s was a small lumber town lifting itself from the lean years of the Depression, World War II, and its relative isolation from the rest of the nation. In 1947, it saw incredible growth as the post-war economic recovery sent the town's population to three thousand, almost double what it had been in 1940. The year 1947 also saw building permits issued in Arcata reach an all-time high. The largest single project, for forty thousand dollars, was by the Van De Nor Lumber Company for construction of a new sawmill and remanufacturing plant. Van De Nor was one of about twenty-five independent sawmills with teepee burners scattered about the town. Dad's family was making its mark in a new territory.

A fire leveled the sawmill in 1948. The Norris family bought out the Van de Vanter share of the business and retained the name. The same year, Mom and Dad adopted Dick. I was born in 1951.

Dad's brother, father, and mother moved into a new house in Eureka. Dad and Mom lived in a two-bedroom house on the south edge of Arcata on G Street, which ran through town and was a part of the Redwood Highway. This is where Mom started her new life. It would be far from what she'd known before.

So now it's the third day of the King City mind movie running through my head. I know a little about the time shortly after Mom and Dad got married, but I want to hear more about those first few years of my own life. Mom has been on a good roll the past two nights. Again, it's evening and we're sitting at the dining table reminiscing.

"So tell me about those early days in Arcata. I have only a few vague memories, but it seems like a lot of stuff happened," I say.

"I was so young and so homesick when your dad and I moved to California. Up until the time I got married, I didn't realize what an overly protected life I was leadin'. There were so many family members always right there and quite a lovin' family at that.

"So yes, it was quite difficult for the first few years of married life. We didn't even have our own checkin' account, so I had to go to the lumber office and ask for money for everything I needed to buy. Not an easy task for an independent young woman to do. We didn't even have our own car, but had to use a Van De Nor car when needed. And yet Uncle Dick could have a new car every couple of years. That really got my goat. One day, in backin' out of our driveway, how could I possibly have not seen Uncle Dick's new car? Yet when I got out of the old company car, I couldn't even see a scratch on it. Amazin'!" Mom has an impish grin on her face.

"What a fussy young woman I was, so immature and so naive! Rather pitiful, really. There was another time when we were gettin' ready to go to a party somewhere and—wow—we could afford to take a couple of bottles of scotch, which was not inexpensive, even in those days! Your Uncle Dick told me—not asked, but told me—to hold a sack containin' one of the bottles. Gettin' out of the car, I accidentally dropped the bottle on the driveway and broke it. My only comment was 'Ooops!' Uncle Dick's reaction was a very mean look in my direction. To this day, I deny that it was anything other than an accident!"

Terri says, "Sure, Mom. Sure."

Mom looks at me innocently, shrugs, and throws her hands up.

"We adopted Dick after I had a miscarriage. Then I had another miscarriage before I finally was able to conceive you. And you and I both survived that situation." A smile crosses Mom's face. "I remember that day—wait a minute—what am I sayin'? I was *out* like a light and when I woke up they were puttin' this funny-lookin' little thing in my arms and I told the nurse to take you back and bring me the right baby. You were a very long little rascal with lots of hair and so small. But guess what? The nurse insisted she gave me the right baby and I'm glad someone else couldn't lay claim to you. You truly have been a joy in my life."

Mom reaches over and pats my arm.

"Do you remember January eleventh was Granddad Frederick's birthday? When I was pregnant with you, he called me—somethin' that he rarely ever did—and said, 'Sis, try and have the baby on January eleventh!' Since they performed a caesarean to bring you into this crazy world, I told the doctor the operation *had* to be performed on January eleventh. You were born on the day that a great man, Granddad Frederick, was born. It was a good day!

"Thinkin' back to the year you were born, I just now had a funny, funny story come to mind. I'm sure I've told you about it, but I think it's worth repeatin'. You were born at seven months— you didn't want to wait the full nine months, I guess—and when I went home from the hospital, you had to stay for a week or so. Then we brought you home and I had to go back to the hospital and when I came home the second time, you had a nasty cold and had to go back to the hospital. It was like playin' musical chairs.

"Well, Grandma Murph came down from White Salmon to be with us for a while and of course Nana wanted to be part of the *party*! The two grandmas were both tryin' to be the first in line to change your diapers when needed, which was probably done many more times than was necessary! Nana said, 'It's my turn, Murph!' She put on the gloves, but before she could find the baby powder, you couldn't wait any longer. The urge hit you and, what can I say?" Mom points her right finger at me like it's a toy penis. "Your aim was perfect. You hit poor Nana right in the face!"

Terri and I break up laughing. Mom grins with a look of satisfaction, as if she's relaying a story about poetic justice.

"Grandma Murph burst out with that wonderful laugh of hers. Dick wanted to know why we didn't just take you to the bathroom like he had to do. I was laughin' so hard because my mom was laughin'. Nana didn't think it was very funny and Dick kept sayin', 'Just take him to the bathroom.' Nana looked flustered for a moment, then went into the bathroom for quite a long time. When she returned to the nursery, she said to all of us, 'Please excuse me. I'm sorry, but I must go home and get cleaned up now.' That was just one of the many fun experiences we had in our house. Life was never quiet for sure."

I chuckle and say, "I can hardly remember anything about when we lived in Arcata. Most of my early memories start in Jacoby Creek. Those few years there were great, kind of our golden years as a family, don't you think?"

Mom clears her throat and thinks for a minute, as if searching for the right order of events for her Jacoby Creek memories. Something seems to come to her. "Yes, so not long afterward in 1956 it was off to Jacoby Creek to build a new house. They were good years. I have so many comical memories of you as a little boy in both Arcata and Jacoby Creek, but especially from those years in Jacoby Creek. You were a little rascal. I was probably your best audience. There was one time you wanted to take a shower with your Dad. You started to slip on the shower floor and grabbed ahold of the closest thing you could reach to keep from fallin'."

I fall back in my chair in mock surprise. "Oh no, not Dad's penis?"

Mom pretends to make a mark with a pencil on a piece of paper, as if to chalk one up for me. "You guessed it. I'm sure you must've pulled very hard because your dad let loose with a lot of painful yells. I thought it was hysterical! Back then, you just seemed to have a knack for bein' in the wrong place or makin' a wrong turn. Maybe the worst time was when you backed into the electric heater on the wall in the bathroom after you took a bath and burned your little bottom badly."

I grimace. "Yeah, now that was something I'll never forget."

Mom shakes her head in amusement. "I had to have you lay across my lap in order to put burn medication on the burn and then cover it with sterile gauze. You said to me once, 'Don't you *dare* tell anyone about this and don't you *dare* laugh!' This was probably after Nana and Uncle Dick stopped by and wanted to see *the big burn.* You would glare at them or anyone else who wanted to see the burn and announce *no way* and off you'd go to your room. We had to go into a room all by ourselves to go through this procedure of changin' the dressin'. It wasn't funny of course, but you were sure comical. I did have to smile when you couldn't see my face!

"Then there was the time you ran into a basketball pole at the grade school. When you came out of that with two black eyes, you told me if I told others about your eyes and the goose egg right smack in the center of your forehead or even took a picture of your black eyes, you'd get rid of me and get another mom who could keep her mouth shut!"

"I remember that," I say. "I was racing some other kid on the outside basketball court at recess and looked back to see how far ahead of him I was. When I looked forward again, there was the pole and *bam* I was on the ground seeing stars. I'd start bawling if someone even looked at me crossways. I guess I was something of a mama's boy, wasn't I?"

Mom tilts her head sideways a couple of times. "Well, I might have doted on you kids too much, too. Even though I was tryin' to raise you to be independent, it was hard to let you go anywhere on your own and not turn into a worrywart. I think you kids were kind of the same, too. That makes me think of when Dick first went to Scout Camp when he was in Cub Scouts and didn't even stay the first night. His counselor called me to tell me Dick was complainin' of a stomachache and thought I'd better come and get him. Turned out the stomachache was from bein' homesick! But I brought him home.

"A couple of years later, you went to Scout Camp, too, and the counselor called me." Mom acts like she's the counselor, holds an imaginary phone next to her left ear, and lowers her voice. "'Bob has a stomachache and you should come and get him.' Again, homesickness. A few years went by and Terri wanted to go to Brownie Camp. The first night: 'You'd better come and get Terri. She has a stomachache.' Homesick again!"

The three of us share a good chuckle. For a moment, we think back to those Jacoby Creek days. Then, wanting to hear more, I say, "What was that one story I haven't heard for a long time? Oh yeah, about the time you found Uncle Jerry. I think we were living in the Arcata house down on G Street. He'd disappeared for a long time and then someone found him down in San Francisco on Skid Row?"

Mom thinks for a few seconds, then remembers. "Oh. That

was Uncle Jim, one of my dad's brothers. He came out from North Dakota on the train. Somehow my dad and he had heard from someone about Uncle Jerry, Dad's youngest brother who hadn't been heard from in years. You were born but not walkin' yet and we were in Arcata because Dad and Uncle Jim finally got this trail or somethin' on Uncle Jerry and they got down there to San Francisco and Uncle Jerry wasn't there. Then they found out from somebody that he was at Fort Bragg livin' in a lumber camp."

"That was a long trip from San Francisco in those days," I say.

"Yeah. And so my dad and Uncle Jim found him. I don't know whether he'd been drinkin', but he wasn't drinkin' then—he was, well, like a bum. So they brought him up to Arcata, took him out, got some clothes for him, and got him in the shower. I remember thinkin', 'I know I'm a young mother and I should know what they're doin', but why do they have to get there in the shower with him?' We had a little funky shower set up over a tub. Anyway, Uncle Jerry just fell in love with you, Bob."

"So how old was he at the time? Probably in his twenties?"

"When he left?"

"No, in 1951 or so."

Mom puts her fist on her head, trying to recall Uncle Jerry's image. "He must've been . . . he was older than that because he'd left North Dakota to go to San Francisco for a job. There was nothin' in North Dakota at that time. And nobody'd heard from him, like with my brother. Anyway, you were just a baby. Dick was, what, two years older? So Uncle Jerry would come up on the bus. He was so tickled about you boys. Now he knew the DiMaggio brothers. He'd hold you on his lap and tell you all these baseball stories."

"Hmm. I don't remember any of that."

46

"Well, you were so little. So we asked him if he'd like to go to White Salmon for Christmas. It was our turn to go up there for Christmas. Of course, you know, I was pathetically homesick ever since we left Washington. So, we got up there and of course the story had already made the rounds in White Salmon about Uncle Jerry. I remember Uncle Jim died shortly after that and my dad said, 'He'd always wondered where Uncle Jerry was and he found him.'

"I don't remember all the little between things, what happened between here and here. My cousin Spud back in North Dakota and I were talkin' about it one time. He doesn't remember too much, either. You come from a very unique family on both sides here, Bob!"

We stop to laugh a bit.

A memory about Uncle Jerry from the time I spent in Seattle comes back to me, but an image of him from my childhood eludes me. I get serious for a moment and say, "You know, from that time until the time I saw him in Seattle in the late 1970s, a lot had passed. I wonder what he did in all those intervening years. Didn't he come back every once in a while, every four or five years and spend a week or so? I remember him in Jacoby Creek, I think. Maybe it was him. Or maybe that was your brother Jack. One of them brought Dick and me some of those airplanes made out of really thin wood, balsa wood or something. You'd stick the wings through the body piece and throw them. We had a lot of fun with that. That's one memory I have."

"I think that probably was my brother because he came out to Jacoby Creek after my dad died. Mom came down for a while. And somehow I think my brother had gamblin' problems because we woke up one mornin' and Mom's car was gone. This was in Jacoby Creek. We waited and waited and my brother was gone.

47

We couldn't find him and he was workin' in San Francisco, I think. I could be wrong about that. I filed a missin' car report and the police found him.

"We were havin' dinner at Jacoby Creek with Nana and Uncle Dick and your dad, of course. Here comes the police car. It's in the driveway with the lights shinin' and another policeman was drivin' my mom's car. Uncle Jack—my brother—was sober, but he looked like he'd been dragged through the gutters. I think he was gamblin'. And, oh, I'm sure that poor Nana thought, 'Oh my goodness. Oh dear. Not again!'"

I can't hold back. I pretend to be Nana reacting to the scene. "Oh dear, here we go again—one Murphy relative after another in the drunk tank!"

"She probably did think that. So anyway then Jack went down to Willits. They had a home for the mentally—"

"Your brother?" I ask suddenly.

"Yeah, he checked himself into that. And then he was gonna come home."

"Not the place in Napa?" I ask. "This one was in Willits?"

"This was in Willits. It was like somethin' in *One Flew Over the Cuckoo's Nest*. So he checked himself in for thirty days. I guess you could do that—I don't know. Then they called us and told us that he was gettin' ready to be released. But he didn't have any transportation. Could somebody, one of us, come down and get him? And your dad was very good—I'm sure there were many times he must've thought, 'Oh boy.' I mean, poor guy if you think about it. He was pulled two different ways: the Norrises on one side and the Fredericks and Murphys on the other.

"Anyway, he said, 'I think I better go down with you and then we're gonna go bring him back and have him stay at Jacoby

Creek.' Because my mom was there. Well, we get down to Willits to the—I forget what they called that—um, sanitarium. He was gone! So we asked the people there, 'What happened?'"

"This was on the day of his release?" Terri asks.

"Yes!"

"Wow!" I say. "Uncle Jack at the sanitarium, the mental institute, like in *One Flew Over the Cuckoo's Nest*. This is the first time I've heard this story."

"Lookin' back, I'm sure he had a gamblin' problem. But to get back to the sanitarium—"

"So you arrived at the sanitarium on the day he was supposed to be released and he'd already taken off even though he had no car?" The story has me a little confused. I want to clarify how things stand.

"What they did was give him a release to go to a place where you get checked in. It was a block or two away from the sanitarium itself. So as we're lookin' for him in the sanitarium, they said that they gave him a pass to go to this portion of this sanitarium. It was a separate little buildin'. And then the patients go there and wait in a nice livin' room and sit down and have a cup of coffee, somethin' like that. So we go there and here's your dad with me. Poor guy. I'm sure he's thinkin', 'Oh boy. My goodness.'

"So we get there and they say, 'Well, he's got to be here somewhere, but we don't know where he is.' He's not at the office to get him out, where they . . . what would you call it? A release thing he goes through? I don't know. So, I said, 'Well, we have to find him.' They weren't sure where to look. I said, 'Maybe he went back to the sanitarium.'"

Mom stops for a moment to look at Terri and me. We're so interested in finding out what has happened to Uncle Jack that both of us are leaning forward in rapt attention, our mouths slightly open. "The reason I'm tellin' this," Mom says, "is it was really scary. So they unlock a door and we go in. And then they close that door and lock it behind us. I remember countin' three doors we had to go through. We looked in his little cell—he wasn't really locked up. Everything was gone. Everything."

Mom stops again. I scratch my head and say, "I'm thinking just maybe he knew that you guys were coming to pick him up and didn't want to face you. Just skipped town. So you got to his cell and he wasn't there." I motion for Mom to continue.

"It was stripped clean. I remember one of the attendants said, 'He even took the towels!'"

Not expecting that punch line, intentional or not, I burst out laughing, which makes Mom and Terri start giggling, too. We have to hold our sides. Finally, Mom recovers, then goes on.

"Ohh, that was a very frightenin' experience for me. It was for my mom, too. When we got back to Jacoby Creek, I think my good friend Bernice came out and stayed with her because my mom stayed down from White Salmon for an extra week or two. So then we found out later that he'd forged my mother's name on her checkin' account and her checkin' account was wiped out!"

"Oh my God." I shake my head in bewilderment. "Stealing from your own mom, for Christ's sake."

"That's really sad," Terri says and shakes her head, too. "Very sad story."

"How long was it after that that you saw him again? Like another blank for many years?" I ask.

Mom sighs. "Yeah, another blank. And not for too long, Bob, because, um, my mom, who'd lost my dad and then later her second husband Grandpa Dude, was at loose ends. She didn't know what to do. And I was tryin' to encourage her to come down to live in our area. She didn't have to live with us, but we'd help her. And the thing was when Grandpa Dude died, he'd arranged if he died first, she'd get a small monthly income from the estate. It would pay for any hospital bills because she had no medical insurance. It would pay for any hospital bills and funeral expenses, plus any transportation for family members if she was in the hospital, and it really worked. Grandpa Dude had two brothers, one was a doctor and I don't know what the other one was. Apparently, that Falk family had a lot of money, but the minute my mom died that stopped, of course.

"So somehow—and I don't recall how, but my brother took off from the sanitarium—we get a call from Golden, Colorado. And there's my brother back there workin' in a Mexican restaurant. So my mom decided to go back there and live for a while. And so that was OK for a while. I flew back to see my mom when she was ill and in the hospital. And then Stella, Aunt Stella, met me there once. That's when Aunt Stella lost her wig."

"Lost her wig?" I'm not sure what Mom is talking about.

"You haven't heard that story?" Mom says.

"No, but I'm sure it's a good one."

"I'll tell you in a minute, but let me finish this one.

Anyway, there was a period of time there we didn't know where Jack was. So he was workin' in the Mexican restaurant and I flew back two or three times from Fortuna to see my mom near the end of her life. And Grandpa Dude's estate paid for that."

"Oh really? I'll be darned," I say.

"As you know, you can't put a body on a plane or train to transport it without a family member or an adult or, you know, a live person accompanyin' it. So when I was back before my mother died, her doctor said, 'She's not going to make it. You really need to make arrangements. Where do you want her buried? You need to make all the train reservations.' So here I was at the funeral parlor, she wasn't even dead yet, pickin' out her casket. Oh, it was a nightmare.

"So I left all her things in her apartment. You always have that false hope. I didn't want her to get better and go to her apartment and see it was gone. So I paid the rent for another month or two and bought a key for her. She had a little storage closet in the basement of the apartment, so I bought a lock for that and talked to the manager there. Then I came home and, sure enough, I wasn't home long and my mom had died, but all these arrangements had been made. As I said, you can't put a person in a casket on the train without somebody accompanyin' it. So my brother and Mom's body got on the train. I bought tickets ahead of time. But when the train got to Bingen, Uncle Jack went down with me and Kenny Gardner, who was a mortician there in White Salmon. We all met the train and got the casket off. The conductor was going to take off, but I said, 'Wait! Wait! Wait! My brother's on there somewhere.'"

Mom leans forward and, in a conspiratorial voice, says, "He was not on the train anywhere. We don't know where he got off. So that was the startin' point where he was missin' for thirty-five years."

4

The Wig and Other Stories

M OM settles back in her chair, takes a minute to get her thoughts together, then starts up again. "One time near the end of my mom's life, I called Aunt Stella. I said, 'You know, my mom isn't in very good shape and I'm goin' back this date to see her. Would you like to meet me there? We can have a few days together.' She said OK she would. She flew from Montana to Denver in kind of a little commercial plane, but not a very big plane. It was the kind where they opened the door and you went down the steps and you were on the runway, the tarmac there. So we went to the airport—my brother was there—to pick up Aunt Stella. And it was windy. And of course, as you know, Denver is a mile-high city and cold. It wasn't raining.

"So they open the door and Aunt Stella starts to step out and they have these hinges that you can catch something on. It caught her wig. And the wig went flying down the tarmac and off onto the runway. And Aunt Stella is on the top step of the stairs comin' down."

Mom takes a deep breath, pretends that she's Aunt Stella on the airplane steps, and yells out, "Kay! Get my hair! Get my hair! Run! Get my hair!" Mom's voice speeds up. "Stella's just screamin' at me. And some guy's runnin' out sayin' to me, 'You're not allowed out here.' I said to him, 'That's my aunt. I have to get her hair!'"

The three of us fall back in a fit of laughter. Mom continues, even more animated than before.

"So here's Aunt Stella shakin' her head. I'm runnin' down here. Here's the other guy comin'. My brother's runnin' after him. It must've looked like the Keystone Cops. Anyway, I got her wig!"

"In all the wind and everything?" I ask.

"In all the wind and everything. By this time, I not only have her wig, but also a bunch of brush and I don't know what else that got caught in the wig. So Aunt Stella comes down the airplane steps. I give her the wig. She grabs it from me and puts it on, but sideways!" Mom mimics putting on the wig in a huff. "Well, you can imagine what she looked like. So Jack is goin' out to get the car. Aunt Stella and I are headin' into the little terminal. And here comes this guy from the plane sayin', 'You forgot your baggage!' I don't think I'll ever forget that, ever. Aunt Stella yellin', 'Get my hair! Get my hair!' and wearin' that godawful wig sideways as if that was how it was supposed to go on. Oh, dear me."

"Great story, great story." I give Mom a round of applause. "You know, all I remember about Aunt Stella is I think probably when we visited Grandma Murph's and Grandpa Pat's place either in summertime or Christmas time. But I remember her as just having that really raspy voice and chain-smoking cigarettes and laughing hysterically, probably always with a drink in her hand. I think she and Grandma Murph used to just tell stories and howl at each other's stories."

Mom nods in agreement. "Over and over and over. And when

we'd go up to visit Grandma Murph and Grandpa Pat, I'd put you kids to bed and you'd hear all this laughin' and gigglin', so of course you don't want to stay in bed. So Grandma Murph would say, 'Now Kay, I know you're strict with these kids, but they have to be part of this, too, you know.' So she'd go in and get you and wrap you up in a little blanket. You'd sit there kind of half-asleep listenin' to these stories, laughin' right along with them. That's when you slept with Grandma Murph in Jacoby Creek. You'd put your arm around her at night in bed. Do you remember this?"

"More so in Jacoby Creek than in Willard."

"One night you said, 'Does Grandpa Pat ever hug you like this?' And Grandma said, 'Well, yes, when we sleep together. Of course he does.' And I remember you sayin', 'Hmm, that must've been quite a sight!' Oh dear."

"And about that time, she's probably howling again."

"Oh, she is. She is. She just laughed at everything. She was special. She could see the bright side in everything. I remember after Grandma Murph's surgery from bleeding ulcers many years ago when the doctors removed three-quarters of her stomach. They warned me when I went to see her a couple of days later that she'd probably be out of it for a few more days. I very quietly tip-toed into her room and found her sittin' up in bed. She asked me immediately before I could say a word, 'Well, did you bring my lipstick and comb? There're a lot of cute doctors around here!' She was such a character, and I was truly blessed to have her for a mother."

The conversation now shifts back to Uncle Jerry.

"You know, when I was living in Seattle back around the winter of '77, I met Uncle Jerry and his wife," I say. "He'd met her through Alcoholics Anonymous meetings. I guess he became a

55

famous speaker for the AA. They were in their seventies at least by then. He was a good storyteller and always had a grin on his face and always could make a joke out of the worst situations."

"And you know, when my dad and Uncle Jim found him and they brought him up from Fort Bragg or in that area, as they got out of the car, the three of them were laughin'. Here was this reunion, but lookin' back on those times, Bob, it had to've been—I don't want to say an eye opener—I don't think your Nana and Granddad Hi Norris had ever seen these things. Like the time in the garden with Aunt Stella out there in Jacoby Creek."

I look at Mom quizzically, not sure of what she's referring to.

"Your dad had built this garden clear at the end of the property. I don't know why. Probably Uncle Dick told him that was where it was to go."

"I remember that garden," I say. "It was out even beyond those briar bushes. It was a pretty big garden with strawberries and all kinds of things."

"Yes it was, and he didn't want the deer to get in there. So one time when Aunt Stella was stayin' with us, she decides she's gonna go out and weed the carrots or whatever. Well, first she had long pants on. They came off. She still had her panties on, but here's her long pants hanging on, what was it, chicken wire with a nail at the top of a post. Pretty soon she's gettin' too warm, so off comes the blouse and it goes up there. And pretty soon, whew . . . ." Mom wipes her brow as if to wipe some sweat off. "She's gettin' hot, so off comes her bra. Well, as you remember, Grandma Murph and Aunt Stella were pretty well-endowed and had a pretty good figure when they had a bra on. But when they took their bra off, whoops . . . ."

Mom makes a motion of her breasts flopping out and sagging

to the ground. I have to hold my sides while giggling. I say, "Two sandbags dropping."

"Yeah, two sandbags dropped right then! So here she's just out there. No bra, just her panties. And her shoes. And your dad brings along somebody from the mill or the lumberman's association."

"A Hollywood scriptwriter couldn't do better than this!" Terri says.

"Yeah. I don't know who this fella was. He was probably a bigwig who came up from San Francisco for somethin'. So your dad wanted to show him our house. And he's probably like 'Oh, you should see the back. Here's this wonderful treehouse. And here's our garden over here—'"

"With our live-in gardener," I say, mimicking a proud land-owner showing off his house.

"I'm not kiddin' you. We could hear Aunt Stella scream from the house. That far. What would you say? That was, about three-quarters of an acre. Maybe an acre. Anyway, we hear 'Oh my God!' She was on her knees diggin' and here's some of her clothes over here and some over there. I don't know what the outcome of that was, but oh, my mom and Aunt Stella talked about that and they could tell it fifty times and they'd still just be in hysterics."

Terri shares a memory of Aunt Stella. "That reminds me, Mom, of the time you said to Aunt Stella once, 'Well, what did you think when you saw that here it was Bill and this guy all dressed up in a suit?' And Aunt Stella said, 'I told them what in the H are you guys starin' at? My boobies was just floppin' around, so I reached for my "over the shoulder bolder holder" to cover them up!'"

That sets us off giggling again. After we stop, Mom says, "Oh my. I've told many people I don't think there was ever a mother who had any more fun than I did raisin' my kids. But poor Nana. She used to be so worried that I was gonna end up with three juvenile delinquents. And when she told me that, it was the first time I'd ever heard that expression."

The mention of Nana brings back to me the memory of formal Sunday dinners at Uncle Dick's house in Eureka.

"Well, you can imagine us kids when we had to go over there for those Sunday dinners all dressed up and everyone would be gathered around the fireplace with all those old paintings on the walls of that dark living room. Everybody had a highball in their hands. The grownups would be telling stories and the kids were just bored to death, you know, so we'd try to slip away and explore. It was like a museum. The lights were very dim. Everything was just fascinating. I mean, I remember even sneaking into Nana's bedroom and going through her drawers just to see what kind of underwear she was wearing! They had a long hallway with all kinds of expensive things hung here and there. Yeah, there was just a kind of an attractive gloom that pervaded the atmosphere. You just wanted to explore."

Mom sighs and says, "Yeah, those monthly dinners."

"She used to put in hours and hours in her kitchen preparing those feasts," I say.

"Of course she would. She was a good cook. And she wanted you and Dick to have a little white shirt and a tie. You boys would sit in the back seat of the car as we drove over to Eureka. I felt so sorry for you. But you were given orders to behave. You'd say, 'We know!' So when we'd get home, even if it was dark, I'd let you take your tie and your shirt off. And the first time that you did this on your own—and I didn't tell you you could do this—but both of you took all your clothes off. You went out and you ran around the picnic table. And I remember you yellin', 'We're free! We're free!'

"So then after that, I'd tell you to be really good at these monthly dinner parties and Nana was tryin' to teach you good manners. Anyway, as soon as we'd get home—oh your dad almost fainted when I did this—it was pretty dark and one of you said, 'Can we take our clothes off and run?' And I said, 'Well, of course. I'll join you.' 'Really?' you said. So I went clear down to my bra and panties and ran around outside with the two of you.

"Now it was dark, and we didn't have any outdoor lights that were shinin'. You boys were shoutin', 'We're free! We're free!' and I'm goin' 'I'm free! I'm free!' Oh dear. But that didn't hurt you at all."

"No, not at all."

"And it sort of made up, I hope, for havin' to wear a tie. It wasn't that you didn't love Nana and Granddad Hi, but she was sure I was raisin' a couple of little ruffians. I think it was just a matter of two different cultures. Nothing against theirs or ours at all. And yet it was quite interestin' when my mother would come visit us. Nana would always without fail come over and spend an afternoon—from Eureka to our little house on G Street."

"Maybe your family provided the only excitement in her life and she couldn't express it," I say.

Mom ponders that idea. "That could be. I've often wondered about that. And she liked my mother. She used to say to my mother, 'I don't know what we're gonna do with this girl of yours. She doesn't use the right fork.'"

Laughing, I say, "Grandma Murph must've been highly entertained by this kind of stuff. It's great that she had such a sense of humor. She could've gotten into a real battle."

"I know. So my mom would just say, 'Well, I don't know what to tell you, Dorothy. Do you want to go for a little walk?' I mean, she just handled it so well, but she was laughin' the whole time."

"Probably already making the story in her head to tell later to everybody else."

"Yeah, when she got back to White Salmon. I guess it was just two different cultures that really never did quite mesh. And that's hard to do, Bob. But we all survived. I remember when Granddad Hi died, my mother was in that same hospital on the same floor. I don't remember what Granddad Hi died from, but it might've been the effects from the hip surgery he had. That's when my mom had the kidney problem. When she was able to get up and around, she wanted a wheelchair and she just wheeled down and went into Granddad Hi's room and was visitin' with him and he was glad I guess to see her. He didn't tell her to get out.

"Anyway, the last time I saw Nana, she was very receptive to my approach. That was when Terri was in the hospital in Redding. She had to have her appendix out. She was over visitin' your dad and I flew over from Truckee to see her. I asked at the airport if I could use a car, but they didn't have any cars to rent and I didn't want to take a taxi because I had to get home before dark. So they loaned me a bicycle. You know, you're in your jeans and you're ridin' a bicycle, you really don't look very ladylike.

"So as I go down a hall to go to Terri's room, here comes Nana. And we meet like this." Mom uses the fingers on her two hands to pantomime two people walking toward each other. "And she goes over here, so I go over there, too. I went up to her and held out my hand. You know Nana. She's so polite, bless her heart. She kind of took my hand. I said, 'Nana, we're both here to see Terri. Would you meet me in the cafeteria? I'll just be a little bit and we'll have a coffee together.' She looks at me and says, 'Well, I don't know. It's gettin' pretty late.'

"But she was there when I went to the cafeteria later. And I guess that taught me it doesn't matter who makes the first move. Nana thanked me for the coffee. And I remember her last words to me were, 'We will look out for Terri for you.' Pretty nice of her. I'm sure she was raised by her English aunt to be very proper, but she could be a good sport.

"And you know, nothin' against the Norrises at all, they're a wonderful family, but that was a very difficult transition for me. I'm certainly not sayin' for just me, by any means, but our family was so kind of laid back, kind of loose. And then I married your dad and I felt the years that we were married—I knew first of all that he'd probably married me on the rebound. I know he thought a lot of me, but that was hard for him when Janet married another guy. And then I felt I really didn't live up to Nana's expectations of what her daughter-in-law should be."

Again, I can't resist teasing. "Wouldn't you say that was an impossibility?"

Mom grins back at me. "Now that I look back, absolutely. And there was nothin' against another person. But I think that in all of the time that I lived there, I thought, 'What am I doin' here? I really wasn't meant to be here in California.' But I didn't know why. It was probably I just didn't feel I measured up."

"And maybe at the same time there was a part of your *nomad blood* that thought, 'Hmmm, I wonder what's on the other side.'"

"There was. For a senior present when I graduated from high school, my dad said, 'What would you like for a graduation gift?' And I said, 'I know what I'd really like, but I know I can't have it. I'd love to take the car and drive across the U.S.' Well, you'd've thought I said I wanted to take a trip to the moon!"

61

"I can imagine so."

"And my dad said, 'What if you'd have car trouble?' 'Well, then I'd have it fixed.' I had this dream, not even thinkin' about all the what-ifs. I thought, 'Nothin' is gonna happen to me. I can just go and if somethin' happens to me, that's OK. It'd be just a detour.' And that was the one thing I always wanted to do and I always wanted to fly before I got married. Well, I was fortunate enough, I did eventually learn to fly. I didn't take a trip across to the eastern U.S., but I took it the other way, all the way to Japan. And I did start east and got to Ireland.

"As I've told you so many times, I admired and respected my dad so much. He was a very quiet, warm, givin', kind human bein' and he certainly not only talked but he also walked his deep Catholic belief. Much of my growin'-up years was spent bein' quite resentful of havin' to go to Confession and Communion. I didn't really believe a person here on earth had to go through another human like a priest in order to communicate with our Maker. I tried to do all the things that a good Catholic was sup- posed to do and yet after I grew up—even after I was married—I saw a lot of hypocrisy in the Catholic Church. So then when I had ninety percent of the responsibility of raisin' you three kids, I was at a loss as to the correct way to raise you. I felt all young people need some kind of a Christian upbringin' and teachin' Catholicism was the only way I knew.

"You know, Bob, it sure seems in this American society, we're raised and taught to try to please others and follow the rules set up—at home, then at church, then at school, then at college, then at a job, then you get married, and on and on. I can remember gettin' a lot of criticism because I would let you children tell me exactly what you were feelin' and thinkin', whether I agreed with it or not. I remember we used to have some very strong discussions. Your dad and Uncle Dick and Nana Norris and later even your stepdad Herb all thought I was too easy on you kids and would end up with nothin' but trouble. And what I was tryin' to accomplish was to build character, integrity, and help develop your own individuality and self-confidence—or whatever—so that you each would be able to face the cold, cruel world.

"Did you know at one time I asked your dad to quit his job with Van De Nor? I gave my word that I wouldn't contact my family for a year. I felt we needed to get away from family influence and interference and make it on our own. Bill and I didn't even have our own bank account for three years after we were married. I take the blame for a lot of this because I was not really mature and worldly enough to take a definite stand. I'm sure that we'd be together today if we'd done that, but isn't hindsight a wonderful thing? Of course, it doesn't ever solve anything and the 'could haves' and 'would haves' are really worthless. Well, anyway, time has passed and we've survived for some reason, right? Like you've said so many *many* times, Bob, all of our experiences have led us to where we are now."

"Yeah, that's what I believe," I say.

"My grandmother told me once that if there's a divorce in the family, it affects four generations. I thought, 'She doesn't know what she's talkin' about.' But it does. Four generations. My parents, your dad and I, you kids, and whatever children you would have. When your dad and I divorced, I thought for sure I was goin' to hell. I just knew it."

It's my turn to reach over and pat Mom's hand and give her some reassurance. "Nah," I say. "You're going to heaven, Mom. If anyone deserves it, you do. I have no doubt about that. So tell me about when you got divorced and then got married again and the Catholic Church let you know that you were no longer a member despite all your years of loyal service and playing the organ for every Sunday mass?"

"That's when Herb and I got married. I thought I really needed a father for my boys. First, I was a Catholic supposedly. I wasn't a good Catholic. And a divorce in the Catholic Church was a big no-no. And so Herb and I went to White Salmon and Uncle Jack and Aunt Louise were gonna stand up with us. We had it all arranged at a Catholic church in The Dalles. The priest said, 'Well, I'm sorry. I can't marry you.' And that Irish whatever comes to the surface. 'What do you mean?' I say. 'Well, you're a divorced woman,' he says. 'But I don't sin!' I say. And Uncle Jack and Aunt Louise are like this." Mom mimics two people with their jaws dropped looking back and forth between Mom and the priest.

"Like a tennis match," I say.

"And he wouldn't marry us. I remember this so clearly. He looked at me like 'She's crazy.' He probably thought I was. I said, 'I want your badge number.' 'Whadaya . . . my badge number?' he says. 'I'm gonna write to the bishop,' I say. And Uncle Jack's tryin' to get me out of there.

"So lookin' back on even after your dad and I separated, I went to church—this is in Arcata—and the priest refused to give me Communion. I was tryin' every way I could find to find some peace."

"Even after divorcing, they wouldn't give you Communion? In my mind, it seems like the Catholic law at the time was that if you divorced, the real sin in the church was getting married again," I say.

"This was in Arcata and I'd done so much work for that church, Bob. I went to play the organ for the choir for one month, and I stayed seven years. I used to take the altar cloth home once a month and wash it and take it back in. And I had two Sundays a month to have flowers there. Well, there weren't that many women that felt they had the time to help, and fortunately or unfortunately, I've always seen all this stuff that has to be done. Nobody else is doin' so. And of course the word got around that your dad and I had separated. I think we were both goin' through a really, really tough emotional time, so I felt that maybe if I'd go to church, I'd get some kind of support. Or maybe some kind of peace. So here's all these people one Sunday up at the Communion rail and the priest, Father O'Conner, looked at me and he just by-passed me."

"This was in front of everybody? He didn't tell you privately or anything like that?" I ask.

"No. Here I am and so he just went from here to here and I reached out and grabbed him."

I start giggling and can't stop for a minute. "That's great!"

"And he looked at me and I said, 'I want a Communion.' I guess he thought I was stickin' my tongue out at him. Well, maybe I was a little bit. So then after he served Communion, he goes back and I don't know what he gets, maybe the wine or somethin'. I don't think they served them together. I was so upset and I was on the edge of somethin', scared to death, very sad that your dad went out with another woman. And I'm not criticizin' him now, but I just think you don't do that. And so maybe we blew that clear out of proportion.

"But anyway, I got up from the Communion rail and walked right back in that room. And he said, 'You can't come in here.' 'Well, I'm here. I want to know why you wouldn't give me Communion.' 'Well, I'll tell you after church,' he said. 'No! I want to know now. I'm a good person. I'm a good mother. I don't swear. I don't steal. Blah, blah, blah.' 'Oh my,' he said. 'Sit down.'

"So we held up mass and he said, 'You cannot receive Communion.' And I said, 'You are one lousy priest. You're supposed to help me and I don't like you when you're like this.' Oh, I was just . . . but I was like I say, kind of on the edge, scared."

"You were within your rights, I think."

"I thought so. Lookin' back, can't you see the congregation watching this woman get up and leave and go back to where the priest was? Ohh!"

"I can see it," I say. "All of them just clucking away."

"There at the henhouse—cluck, cluck, cluck, cluck. It's a wonder you kids grew up to be halfway normal people."

"Ah, that's just society," I say. "I suppose we've all had some kind of innate sense of what is just and unjust."

"As a mother, you try to teach your kids what you know. And even though an underlyin' doubt was always in my mind."

"Mom, you always bargained, negotiated with us kids in the sense that I want you to try this and if it doesn't fit you, then you can quit. And of course we always went to the calendar and marked it down and quit! But that was a good way of doing things. Maybe that set the tone for us to negotiate our way through life. If this doesn't seem fair, we'll hang in there for a while and give it a fair shake, but after that, I'm outta here. You go ahead. I'm not gonna bother you. I'm just gonna head in another direction."

"And you were a pretty good little negotiator, too, Bob. Do you remember when you were attendin' Catechism classes at the Catholic church and had to serve mass with the priest? You were adamant about doin' it only once! That was the agreement between you and me. You could serve mass once and if you didn't like it or felt uncomfortable, that would be the end of that. Well, on the Sunday when you came out with the priest, you were wearin' your vestments and kneeled down at the altar. You faced away from the congregation and you had this *sign* between your feet. I still can't figure out how you did that. Anyway, the sign said, 'Mom, I told you this was a dumb idea!' The priest had no idea why, but the whole congregation was snickerin'. All I could do was throw up my hands. You won that round."

"But you always stood up for us and showed us you'd fight for us if you thought the world wasn't treating us fairly. You put on the boxing gloves a few times."

Later, after Mom goes to bed, Terri says to me, "I'm so glad you guys had the chance to talk these past few days. It was really good for her. I haven't seen her face light up like that in a long time."

We squeeze each other's hands.

5

My Own Jacoby Creek

THE stories I listened to at Mom's in King City in 2010 have become for me the main source of what my years in Arcata were like, but they're still Mom's version. The few images of my first five years I have that I can call my own are like puffs of smoke, born more from pictures seen or stories heard than from actual memory.

My memories become clearer after the family moved to Jacoby Creek, eight miles or so out of town. At the time, there weren't many people living out there, but the sounds, smells, and pictures of the next six years are embedded in my mind. As I aged and became further removed from that time, I tended to romanticize and even mythologize it. Influenced by such books as Thomas Wolfe's *Look Homeward Angel*, *The Web and the Rock*, and *You Can't Go Home Again*, I tried to recreate that idyllic world on paper in an effort to hang on to it. Here's what's still in my mind movie.

There I am on an early morning in the redwoods, fishing with Dad in the creek that flows near our property line. The sun is not yet over the ridge of high trees. The sound of the creek is enchanting. The chirping of robins and sparrows filters through the air and is swallowed by the forest. I feel a tug on my line and jerk my pole carefully. Dad is by my side, coaching me patiently and lauding my performance with a gentle word.

This singular image elicits the consummate joy that is my childhood. In this childhood, there is nothing more mysterious, wonderful, and ominous than the forest. Our entire family life is surrounded, infused, and dominated by the existence of the forest. The food, warmth, clothing, and shelter provided by Dad's toil originates from the forest. The redwoods are almost spiritual in their timelessness, their immense size and beauty.

I believe myself the luckiest boy alive. Dad is a man of the earth, a logger who cleared the timber of our land, built our house, and planted our garden with strawberries, carrots, beets, lettuce, and tomatoes. He is the man who built the treehouse that rests gloriously like a castle on a burned-out stump on the far side of the garden. Mom is a woman of country charm who lovingly cares for the garden, picks wild berries and makes thick, sweet pies, prepares the food Dad works hard to provide us with, keeps our home spotlessly clean, tells us stories that have us rolling with laughter, and gives us the endless warmth of her love.

There I am, a ten-year-old boy on an April day sprawled out among the dandelions sprouting through the unmowed grass of our backyard, which stretches for two acres before succumbing to the brooding forest. I scan the length of the yard. To my far left near the house is our baseball diamond, complete with make-shift backstop, pitcher's mound, and bases. It's a short distance to the left field fence. Beyond the fence stands our neighbor's dappled Appaloosa. The remote center field fence is marked by the beginning of the forest and a thicket of wild brambles. Right field is an open area, with Dad's toolshed marking the foul line. Behind the toolshed is a prominent landmark: a towering redwood tree.

At the entrance to the forest is a small, burned arch at the base of a dead tree that points to the sky like a charred finger. If you crawl through this burned section of timber, you enter another dimension: the dark forest with its soft, fern-covered floor. The forest is always dripping with moisture. It is somber, silent, old as time. Occasionally, you see the curious and wide-eyed deer that bound away to a safe distance upon hearing your approach and then stare at you. You see the squirrels that scamper up trees in lightning-quick movements, then stand upright on hind legs, sniffing the air, munching on some morsel of forest food they've scavenged. You see the sparrows and robins that flitter to and fro and chirp their warnings and admonitions in voices that are sharp and clear and echo throughout the forest. Whenever I enter the forest, I'm transported in time. I'm a dreamer, at various times The Great Explorer, The Great Pioneer, The Great Hunter, Davey Crockett, or Kit Carson. My brother, boyhood friends, and I wage spectacular battles in the forest, encounter fierce enemies—Indians, Nazis, wild savages—and always we emerge victorious.

There is the joy of country baseball, playing games of catch or flies-up with Dad, Dick, and my friends, of bouncing a rubber ball against the back steps of our house and imagining World Series games—bottom of the ninth, two out, me on the mound. There is the summer Little League, where four teams compete on the roughshod elementary school diamond, my team coached by Dad, who spends his evenings after work coaching us boys in infield practice, outfield practice, and game situations.

Baseball is an obsession and epitomizes the perfect joy of my childhood. This joy is in the oiling of a new baseball glove and breaking it in. It's in the sharp crack of bat meeting ball, the good-natured chattering and horseplay of my teammates, and the Saturday games where sometimes I play shortstop (my specialty is ranging to my right into the hole to snag a liner one-handed and fire a strike to first base, a step ahead of a slow-footed runner) and sometimes take the mound (the one game in particular when I pitch a no-hitter with my no-speed fastball and excellent control and Dad takes the team out for hamburgers and milk shakes to celebrate). It's in the feel of the earth, the dirt on my hands, my bat, and my game T-shirt with "Mavericks," the team name, written in bold letters on it. It's in the camaraderie with the other players, all of whom have solid baseball names like Eric Isaacson, Tim Flynn, Charles Gamble, Burt Nordstrom, and Tom Buck. It's in the shape of the field, the clumps in the outfield, the wooden backstop, the chalked foul lines that are never quite straight, the rickety wooden benches used for the stands, and the fields beyond the left field fence that seem like green oceans with scattered groups of sheep and cattle sailing on them.

There are the characters who live in Jacoby Creek: Old John, the hermit who lives in his one-room shack with its pot-bellied stove and grows the biggest and best vegetables around; Dude Falk, the retired rancher who has an acre of fruit trees and later on marries Grandma Murph, who comes from Willard, Washington to live with us after Grandpa Pat dies; the Okies who live in clapboard shacks at the end of Jacoby Creek Road, their yards covered with rusty frames of old cars with weeds sprouting out through the windows, their whiskey stills hidden somewhere in the forest, and their kids forever covered with fleabites; the Cook family, who run the largest sheep ranch in the county; and the McClean family, who live on the hill overlooking our house, that same hill, shaped like a large helmet, down which Dick, the three McClean girls, and I slide on cardboard boxes, hitting incredible speeds and sometimes crashing at the bottom.

There are all the golden places of mystery and discovery. Near the elementary school, there is the old Grange Hall, where Cub Scout and Boy Scout meetings are held, where the rear window is jarred loose and a friend and I can slip into the open space and explore the large kitchen, the storage closets, and the attic in which stacked scores of yellowing copies of *Boy's Life* are kept. We spend hours reading about the adventures of boy scouts who've saved lives and performed heroic deeds. We dream of duplicating those deeds to the delight and wonder of friends and relatives who'll spread the story to all corners of the world.

There is the treehouse on the six-foot deep, burned-out stump near the garden. The treehouse has a trap door on the floor. On summer nights, Dick and I often sleep in the treehouse and listen to the sounds of deer feeding on shrubbery at the base of the stump, the wind swaying the surrounding trees, and the ripple of the creek.

There is the rock quarry and cave—where bears are said to live—beyond the Okies' shacks. There are the forbidden, stagnant, insect-infested pools of green water near the quarry. Monsters are rumored to dwell beneath the surface of the pools, lying in wait to snatch an unsuspecting boy and drag him to the depths of the netherworld.

Eight miles away in Arcata, there is the Catholic church with its grim rows of benches, its pulpit, its dark closet for Confession. Every Sunday, Mom plays the organ for the church choir, while I play secretly with my plastic army men. On Saturdays, I have to attend catechism lessons. Much to their consternation, I always ask the nuns precocious questions:

"Why can't I see God?"

"How can God always have existed?"

"Why do I have to say ten Hail Mary prayers instead of just five to excuse myself to God? What difference does the number of prayers make? I mean, does God have some special book-keeper up there?"

"How can God see everything if he's got only two eyes?"

"Why is God always punishing people if he knows the plan of their lives anyway?"

"If God is so powerful, why did he make man evil?"

"Why is God always white?"

The nuns never give satisfactory answers. Invariably, they say, "Hush now. You just have to accept all this on faith."

"What's faith?"

I'm already becoming a royal pain in the ass, already beginning to question all forms of authority. Dad and Mom give me the nickname "Yeahbut" because every time I'm told to do something, I always respond with a "Yeah, but . . ." and protest that what I'm told to do is unreasonable.

There is Dad's sawmill out in the Arcata lowlands. I love to climb the huge log decks, explore the workers' lunchroom with its pinup pictures of naked women, play among the piles of sawdust, smell the pungency of freshly hewn timber, and listen to the roaring machinery that lifts, saws, carries, and stacks the logs and boards of Dad's world of toil and sweat. I love this world and its alliance of community. Nearly all the fathers of my friends work in the woods and sawmills as choker setters, fallers, sawyers, truck drivers hauling massive logs on dirt roads, planers, green chain pullers, all of them stained by the rich, masculine smell of the woods: sawdust, oil, and sweat.

This joyful world of mine is also in the November smoke that emanates from the fireplaces of Jacoby Creek, in the smell of freshly mown lawns, and in the April bees buzzing from flower to flower to gather their pollen. It's in the wild and terrifying winter rain that unleashes storms of unyielding power, in the winter flooding of the creek that changes the creek's course every year, in the clear and fresh green of the countryside after a spring storm, in the crackling of a winter fire, in the raw, damp smell of new firewood stacked in the woodshed, in the breakfast smell of bacon and fried trout, and in the sound of popcorn popping in the kitchen on Sunday nights. It's there in the salty mist of the Humboldt Bay fog that steals across the fields and forest on autumn mornings, in the spring smell of eucalyptus, in the summer clouds that hang in the sky like puffs of sea foam, and in the ochre-colored sunsets. It's in the darkness that prowls softly through the silence of the forest at night. It's in the earthy fragrance of the trees, the grass, and the flowers that surround me on this April day as I lie stretched out, head cupped in my hands, chewing on a blade of grass, and surveying the stretch and sweep of this very special world.

It's in the family library, in the books I love to read during the rainy Jacoby Creek winters—*Robinson Crusoe*, *The Adventures of Tom Sawyer*, *Grimm's Fairy Tales*, *Treasure Island*, *Gulliver's Travels*, and the entire collection of *Encyclopedia Britannica*; in the freedom of running through fields of waist-high grass with the family dog Trixie; in the family excursions to Stone Lagoon and Big Lagoon when we build great bonfires on the beach, cook hamburgers and hot dogs, and watch the infinite, swelling ocean on the other side of the spit that separates the lagoons from the ocean; in our first family trip to San Francisco on the old Highway 101 that takes ten hours to drive and watching my first major league baseball game at Seal Stadium—that same game when Warren Spahn pitches and Hank Aaron plays right field and I become a lifelong and loyal Braves fan; in the baseball games I play in my bedroom with a marble and a pencil, flipping the marble (the baseball) with the little finger of my left hand toward my right hand, which holds the pencil (the bat), and keeping score on sheets of paper, compiling averages, standings, statistics of all kinds for my imaginary players.

That world is also embodied in my grandparents. On Dad's side, there's Granddad Hi, who's a small man—five-foot, five inches— but seems much larger because of the way people always show their respect by tipping their caps in his presence and calling him Mister Norris. There are the monthly Sunday dinners at Granddad Hi, Nana, and Uncle Dick's home in Eureka's wealthy section, where there's a plethora of Victorian homes with large, well-kept gardens.

An air of formality hovers over those gatherings. We always have to wear our Sunday best and be on our best behavior. Often as many as ten to fifteen family members and guests are in attendance. Nana greets the guests at the front door, which has a doorbell with a deep, sonorous chime. Everyone shakes hands, takes off their coats, and Nana carries the coats off to her bedroom. The visitors enter the front room and sit on luxurious leather sofas and big armchairs before a blazing fire. Uncle Dick takes orders for "highballs" and the grownups settle into an hour or so of spirited conversations, while we kids roam the house to explore, play card games, read books, or sit stiffly with the adults and try to act grown up.

Granddad Hi's house is like a museum with a musty, formal

smell. The bedrooms at the end of the hall seem made for royalty with their brass beds, family photographs from another era, and chests of drawers with a smooth, lacquered finish and wooden smell. In every room, there are artifacts from all parts of the world to which Nana has traveled—music boxes from Switzerland, wooden carvings from Africa, chess sets from Spain, gems from Mexico, silk from Japan, and dolls dressed in native attire from many countries. There is the library filled with hundreds of worn titles, the ancient grandfather clock that strikes the hour with a haunting melody, the set of polished brass pokers and shovels placed before the fireplace, and the tapestries that depict hunting scenes and beasts of the forest and cover the walls of the front room.

After the highballs are finished, everyone gathers in the dining room around the long table set with the finest china. They feast on a rich banquet Nana has spent two full days preparing: succulent hams, turkeys, and roasts; mounds of mashed potatoes with rivers of butter running down the sides; steaming platters of corn, string beans, squash, carrots, and scalloped potatoes; and neatly covered plates of homemade rolls that never fail to elicit the praise of those present. Nana smiles humbly and urges everyone to "help yourself to as many as you want." For dessert, there's a variety of bulging, aromatic pies served with large globes of ice cream. When all have filled their bellies to bursting, out come cups of strong, hot coffee and, for the adults, another highball.

I see Granddad Hi seated at the end of the table in the position of honor, immaculately dressed, hair neatly trimmed, carving the meat, asking politely what each person wants to eat, joking and keeping up a running commentary on the events of the world, serving the vegetables in neat portions starting with the youngest child first, the plates rotating around the table until all but him have been served; then, after dinner, relaxing in his special chair before the television, smoking a cigarette from a cigarette holder, and telling us children stories. His stories always expound on family history and the resiliency, fortitude, and spirit of ancestors who overcame adversity and thrived. One story might be about Mayflower Mary, an ancestor who came over with the Pilgrims on the Mayflower and died giving birth to one of the first baby pilgrims in the New World. Another might be about Sir Henry Norreys, the sixteenth century nobleman who was Keeper of the King's Privy Purse and beheaded for allegedly committing adultery with Queen Anne Boleyn and treason against King Henry VIII.

The story that sticks in my mind the most is one about my great-grandfather.

"Let me tell you boys about your great-grandfather," Grand-dad Hi says, settling back in his chair, crossing one leg stiffly over the other, and clearing his throat. "Now there was a real American with spirit, pioneer spirit, the kind that's vanishing too quickly in this modern age. He was a self-educated man who came from a family of English immigrants, farmers who settled in the Oregon country after the Civil War. His mother taught him to read and write, add and subtract, and to live a good life according to the Bible. His father taught him how to hunt and fish, the value of honesty and prudence and hard work. His parents died when he was a young man, so he learned early on to fend for himself.

"Now he was a man who wasn't afraid to take a chance, and when the opportunity to run a gold mine down in Mexico at the age of twenty-two came his way, why, he naturally jumped at it. Mexico was a pretty wild country in those days and not the type of place for a man without guts and spirit. Your great-grandfather wasn't a big man, no bigger than myself, but he knew how to deal with all types, good and bad, and he was always fair, always rewarded those who were loyal and worked hard.

"Yes, he knew how to use his fists and he knew how to use a gun, and he had to use them both on occasion. But being a small man, he also knew the advantages of friends in the right places. Take, for example, his bodyguard. Now there were about a hundred men working for him at that gold mine and they were made up of mostly misfits, outlaws, and Indians, men who would turn on you in a minute if they caught you with your guard down. One of those Indians, the biggest and strongest of the bunch, was your great-grandfather's own personal bodyguard. And how, you may ask, did he manage to secure the loyalty of this wild man, this savage buck?"

Granddad Hi recrosses his legs and looks in the distance for a moment, as if to allow the question to ferment for a moment.

"Why the answer is quite simple," he says. "After picking out the biggest and bravest and most intelligent of those savages, he presented him with the best horse money could buy in those parts. It cost your great-grandfather a good half a month's salary to obtain that man's loyalty, but he knew that loyalty would probably save his life in due time, which it did. For anyone to own a horse in those parts, let alone a lowly Indian, was next to a man owning a Cadillac in these modern times. It was a mark of success and prestige that few men had. And you know from that day forward, that Indian never left your great-grandfather's side. He did all the cooking, cleaning, the making of camp, you name it, all because of that horse he'd gotten. He even worked as a kind of foreman over the other Indians.

"Now of course like all raw materials of this good earth, there's a limit to what you can take. And so it was with that gold mine. After about a year, they'd squeezed about every nugget they could out of it. There finally came the time when the company couldn't meet the monthly payroll. The rumor spread quickly among the band of misfits and there was talk of a lynching if they didn't get their money. Justice was swift and cruel in those days, and your great-grandfather knew that even his loyal Indian couldn't protect him from a hundred angry outlaws who wanted their whiskey and gambling money. The night before the scheduled payday when your great-grandfather found out for sure there would be no cash, he and that Indian quietly stole out of camp to head for the Texas border some three days away.

"Only the Lord knows what happened to that Indian after they reached the border, but I'll tell you one thing: If it wasn't for him, I wouldn't be sitting here so contentedly with my belly full enjoying the life I have now. And neither would you Norris boys or your father and uncle."

For a moment, Dick and I ponder the life of this man who braved the wilds of Mexico, wandered the earth, and survived to make the bountiful life we enjoy possible. I break the silence and ask, "What happened then, Granddad Hi? Where'd he go after that?"

Granddad Hi takes his time, as if trying to clearly picture his father as a young man, nods with a smile, and leans forward.

"Well, I don't know exactly how he made his way through the desert of Mexico up into Texas. Surely, he went through many hardships, but he was a clever man who'd learned well how to trap and hunt and find water. Somehow he made his way to Kansas City. Jobs were scarce back then and there were many people on the streets looking for work, but your great-grandfather was undaunted and within a few days landed a job as a clerk in a hardware store. After a year or two, he became the manager of the store and a couple years after that he bought the owner out.

"That was about the time he met my mother and married her and settled down. He spent most of the rest of his life quietly as a businessman who saw both good times and bad. At one time, he worked for a spell as a prison guard at the Stillwater Prison in Minnesota. It was there that he met Cole Younger, the infamous train robber and partner of Jesse James, and developed a friendship with him. We still have a letter that Mister Younger wrote to my father. Nana, why don't you get the letter out and show it to the boys?"

Nana retreats to her bedroom, sifts through her chest of drawers, and procures the letter, which is encased in glass. Everyone crowds around to look at the yellowed parchment with Cole Younger's signature fixed on it. We all emit exclamations of wonder as we scrutinize the proof of my great-grandfather's remarkable life. Dreams of adventure fill my mind when we return home to Jacoby Creek. I am only six or seven years old. It will be years before I'm capable of noting the racism contained in Granddad Hi's words.

On Mom's side of the family, there's Grandpa Pat. We sometimes spend Christmas with him and Grandma Murph in Willard, a small company town in Washington a few miles from White Salmon and built by the Broughton Lumber Company. This is where Grandpa Pat works.

The Broughton Lumber Company has two facilities. One is a mill up in the hills in Willard where logs are sawed into rough cut lumber and loaded into a flume that runs nine miles to a lower resaw-and-planing mill at a place called Hood on the Columbia River. There is a story about Granddad Frederick working there for a while and one time seeing a dead body come down the flume with some of the lumber and land in the pond where the flume ends. The Willard site also has small company houses for the workers, a cookhouse, and a general store. Grandpa Pat and Grandma Murph live in one of the company houses.

During those Christmas visits, there are treks into the woods to cut a young fir for the Christmas tree, the aroma of Grandma Murph's apple pies and oatmeal cookies (and licking the left-over cookie dough in the mixing bowl), the log flume that runs through the back of the property, the easy laughter and bright faces of all the Murphy family gathered together. One time, Grandpa Pat is sitting in his chair with a bottle of Olympia beer in his hand. Soon he finishes the beer and takes a nap, snoring loudly while Grandma Murph is in the kitchen. I'm captivated by the depth of sound coming from his large nose and want to find the source, so I get a flashlight, climb up on his lap, and use the flashlight to peer deep into the nostrils. Grandma Murph sees this, grabs her sides, and howls with laughter.

After Grandpa Pat dies, Grandma Murph comes to live with us in Jacoby Creek. I often sleep with her. She is a patient and enthusiastic audience for my inquisitiveness. At night as I lie next to her with my arm wrapped around her warm body, I pester her with questions about her body, her clothes, her smell, her life, her way of doing things. She answers each question with bubbles of laughter rising from her breast.

One night while watching her take a bath, I ask, "Grandma, what do you call those things on your chest?"

"Why those are my breasts, Bobby."

"What do you use them for?"

"Well, they're used for feeding babies milk and sometimes for loving. But child, you're too young to hear about that," she says, her breasts swaying with soft laughter.

"Can I still love someone even if I don't have any breasts?"

"Why of course you can."

"How come Mom's breasts are bigger than yours, Grandma Murph?"

"Well, she's much younger than I am. And besides mine haven't been used for many years!" Grandma Murph throws her head back and rocks with mirth. Bath water splashes against the sides of the tub.

"Grandma Murph?"

"Yes, dear. What is it now?"

"I think you better go to the gas station and get those things filled up with air."

Grandma Murph falls back in the tub, grabs her sides again, and lets loose with a piercing scream that pours forth from the depths of her belly.

"Ohhhhh! Ohhhhhh! Gooooooood Lord! Oh Bobby! Good Lord! You are a regular little stinker!"

Mom rushes from the kitchen to see what the uproar is about. When Grandma Murph catches her breath enough to explain what I just said, Mom, too, breaks into a fit of laughter.

The story makes the rounds with all of Mom's friends. That Christmas, Grandma Murph opens one of her presents and finds a bicycle pump with a pair of rubber breasts attached to it. When Mom and Grandma Murph start rolling again with laughter, Dad, Uncle Dick, Granddad Hi, and Nana all look on nonplussed and fail even to emit a grin.

Of all the things I love about Grandma Murph—her fruity smell, her laughter, her bright blue eyes, her soft grey hair, her water bottle she sleeps with, her cakes and pies and cookies that are way better than anyone else's—it's her stories I love the most. They're different from Granddad Hi's, which are generally serious with a motif of morality, greatness, victory over difficult odds, and the triumph of the American spirit, particularly that of the Norris family. The focus of his stories is usually on the strength, virility, and courage of the main hero, who is invariably my great-grandfather.

Grandma Murph's stories are funny. They poke fun at the weaknesses and idiosyncrasies of the members of her own family. She tells these stories with such color and generosity of spirit that it seems she's never suffered a moment in her life, that truly a life of poverty is the path to happiness, that warmth and laughter are to be found in the rags one is forced to wear day after day, in a diet of potatoes and cabbage, in freezing nights huddled four together in a bed in a midwestern farm winter, in their pilgrimage across the mountains, valleys, and plains of Montana, Idaho, and Oregon during the Great Depression.

In effect, Granddad Hi's stories make me feel afraid of life, afraid of not being able to survive in a dangerous world, of not being able to live up to the standards of what it is to be a man, respected and admired by the community in which he lives. On the other hand, Grandma Murph's stories make me feel warm and secure and give me hope and confidence to overcome the dark mysteries of existence with a light heart and a quirky sense of humor. Her constant giggle is infectious and invites you to join in the fun of living.

6

Brand New Life,
Brand New Me

A<small>LL</small> these things that I've outlined gave a warmth and sanctity to my Jacoby Creek childhood; they made me feel loved and secure. In that redwood world, I first began to understand things, form relationships and loyalties, and pile up sensations and feelings from which I'd soon, as Joseph Conrad wrote, "have to break and be thrown into an unrelated existence."

All was not well in Paradise. Despite all the characters among my relatives and friends, all the places and things that gave such hope, humor, love, confidence, and near perfection to my life, there were also the many imperfections—often hinted at in Grandma Murph's and Mom's stories but concealed beneath a veneer of humor—which, in my innocence and blindness, I did not and could not know.

I wouldn't learn the truth of Dad walking out on the family for many years to come. Neither Mom nor Dad ever blamed the other in their conversations with me. There had been no visible indication of any strife or trouble up to the divorce. It was true that Mom and Dad rarely showed each other affection in public, but they'd always given us children an abundance of warmth and tenderness. To me, their stoicism was natural, a manifestation of the logger's way of life. To show too much affection in this manly world, particularly in public, seemed indicative of an effeminate nature and was to be avoided. That's the way all my friends' families behaved. We boys didn't want to be seen as *sissies*.

Only after I'd grown up did I find out that Grandma Murph played a big hand in convincing Mom she should marry a Norris in order to improve the Murphy financial situation and status. Apparently, Grandpa Pat wasn't all that enthusiastic about the marriage. Even as he walked Mom down the aisle at her wedding, he whispered in her ear, "You don't have to do this if you don't want to." It's also possible that Dad's parents encouraged him to get married as an excuse to move out of White Salmon, where it was rumored creditors were hot on their tail for something related to that Norris scrip. One thing's for sure. Mom was never really accepted as an equal among Dad's family. Neither Nana nor Granddad Hi attended Mom and Dad's reception.

For that matter, in later years, Mom couldn't remember whether Dad actually proposed to her or not. He also never provided any alimony or child support. Uncle Dick offered to help Mom out financially, but the Irish in her wouldn't accept that humiliation, so she refused his help and instead mowed lawns, cleaned houses, and did others' laundry in order to feed us kids. I'm pretty sure, however, that Uncle Dick sometimes put some cash in an envelope and slipped it into the house whenever she was out.

As for the day we kids learned our family was splitting up, I have another film clip in my head. It may or may not be the way it really happened, but here's how it unrolls.

It's a spring day. We kids are outside in the backyard. There's no reason to suspect anything amiss as I see Mom and Dad come out of the house. They approach us—Dick's thirteen; I'm ten; and Terri's now three. I notice something different in Dad's gait. His usual proud bearing and brisk step are gone. His head is hung low and his strong arms hang limply at his sides. His lips are set in a hard line. A vacant expression covers his face. I've never seen him like this. He's always been so . . . invincible.

I look at Mom. Her eyes are red. Her lips are quivering, her face pale.

We kids are gathered together and told to sit down at the picnic table in the backyard. A cloud passes and blots out the sun. We sit quietly. Dad clears his throat, but has trouble saying anything. I look at Mom, but she avoids my gaze. Finally, Dad says, "There's something we want to talk to you kids about. We . . . uh . . . know you won't . . . uh . . . understand this at first, but . . . well . . . as you get older perhaps you can understand and . . . and . . . possibly forgive us."

Dick begins to fidget, as if he alone understands the portent of these first few words. Tears flood his eyes. He stammers, "Well . . . what . . . what is it, Dad? What're you tryin' to say?"

Dad looks hard at the ground for a moment, takes a deep breath, looks up, and says, "Your mother and I don't love each other anymore. We're going to get a divorce."

I don't remember much after that. There's one image of me in the forest pounding the earth with my fists. There's another of Dick trying to explain the meaning of "divorce" to Terri. The one thing etched in the film inside my head, however, is sitting next to Dad on the garage steps, those same steps against which I've bounced my rubber baseball and played a thousand imaginary World Series games, and watching him weep while repeating, "I'm sorry, Bobby. I'm so terribly sorry."

* * *

I was eleven when Mom and Dad divorced. Within a year, I was surrounded by a horde of strangers to whom I was required to refer as family. Both Mom and Dad remarried partners who'd also been married and divorced. Along with these new stepparents came two stepsisters with the stepmother and a stepsister and stepbrother with the stepfather. In years to come, a half-sister and a half-brother would be added to Dad's new family.

My stepfather, Herb Schlinkman, was a contractor who'd done a considerable amount of work for the Norris family, having built Granddad Hi's house in Eureka and portions of the Norris sawmill in Arcata. He was a tall, angular man of German descent with lean, hard muscles forged by his many years of labor. Many considered him the best carpenter in Humboldt County, and he took great pride in his work. He loved the outdoors, fishing, and hunting. His skin had the texture of leather. I remember him as a man who wore a perpetual grave expression and had a stubborn streak as thick and coarse as his skin.

My stepmother, Linda, was an attractive, large-breasted woman sixteen years younger than Dad. She was given to emotional outbursts and a proclivity to try out all the latest health and diet fads. She'd been working in a supermarket butcher section when Dad met her. The upper echelon of Humboldt society probably saw her as a commoner trying to upgrade her status by hooking on to a Norris, but to me she was simply a stranger I now had to think of as another mother.

Dick, Terri, and I stayed with Mom. When she and Herb married, we all moved to Fortuna, a small lumber town thirty miles south of Arcata. The house we moved into was built in the post-Victorian period and, with thirteen rooms, was one of the largest in Fortuna. Herb did a complete facelift on it, applying his most creative ideas and talents to remodeling practically every square foot. By the time he finished, he'd torn down walls to create open space, turned the attic into the master bedroom, built a modern kitchen half-surrounded by a serving bar, added dozens of shelves in all corners, put in an open deck leading to his giant workshop, built a roofed carport next to the workshop, fenced in a backyard with a compost pit, and made a garden area at the rear of a large expanse of lawn that took up nearly a quarter of a block. The place overshadowed the other houses of the neighborhood.

We moved into the house the summer before my sixth-grade year. It was the beginning of a time of confusion, bitterness, anger, and resentment. I felt as if I'd lost something precious and incalculable.

That first summer, I explored my new surroundings. There was the grammar school, two blocks away with its yellow concrete walls, asphalt basketball courts, and spacious field that contained three makeshift baseball diamonds and stretched out to some railroad tracks that called me to escape to faraway places; the large, modern high school on 12th Street with its many build-ings and gymnasium that seemed the center of Fortuna life, the parking area where numerous cars filled with laughing teenagers congregated, the football field surrounded by a cinder track and broad- and high-jump pits and metal stands that seated up to a thousand spectators; the wide, rock-filled field behind the stands that led to the poor section of town; Main Street with all its bustling shops—Bistrin's, Ben Franklin's 5 & 10, Daly's, Grunert's Sporting Goods, White Grocery, Patton Chevrolet, Rapin's Real Estate, and the Fortuna Beacon newspaper office; Rohner Park, which rested on the edge of a stretch of redwood forest and was complete with rodeo grounds, picnic tables, barbecue pits, basketball court, Little League diamond, and Babe Ruth League diamond; the hills beyond the park where the doctors, lawyers, and logging barons lived; the Fortuna Theater in the center of town; the bowling alley at the northern edge of town with Parlato's Restaurant, the most popular spot in Fortuna, flanking it; and the wide, salmon-filled Eel River, which swept past the outskirts of Fortuna and ran its course to the sea beyond the ranches, dairy farms, and lowlands of the little town of Ferndale.

I covered the length and breadth of Fortuna many times that first summer. Sometimes I walked; sometimes I rode my bicycle. I was always alone. I saw many boys and girls my own age, but they never beckoned me to join them. I didn't venture to speak to them, preferring to observe from a distance the life of this new town. I spent numerous hours at the high school tennis courts with my baseball glove and a tennis ball, bouncing the ball off a practice wall, playing World Series games in my head, pitching balls and strikes to an imaginary strike zone, ranging to my left and right to field hard ground balls, occasionally letting one get by for a base hit, the Braves always winning in the bottom of the ninth inning. I played the same game sometimes at the grammar school, occasionally taking time to watch a freight train rattle by on the tracks at the far end of the field.

I rode my bicycle to the river bar at the end of 12th Street to watch the fishermen, once or twice trying my own luck with a rod and line, but somehow the Eel River lacked the familiarity of Jacoby Creek and the early morning treks with Dad and Dick. Sometimes I walked to the bowling alley to watch the crash and thunder of balls meeting pins, listen to the laughter of men and women I didn't know, play the pinball machines near the pool tables, eat a hamburger and fries at the snack counter, and return home wondering if I'd always feel the same summer sadness that gripped me so thoroughly.

September came and with it my first day at school. Students flittered about, checking schedules and classrooms, fighting for desks next to best friends, gossiping loudly, showing off new school clothes, exchanging stories of summer adventures, laughing and teasing one another in a grand camaraderie of which I wasn't a part. There were three sixth-grade classes. I was in Mrs. Ivey's class. She was a middle-aged woman who'd taught for over twenty years at the school and was said to be the nicest sixth-grade teacher. I chose a seat in the back of the room near a window, where I could gaze out at the playground, wishing I was on one of the freight trains that passed.

One day near the end of the first week, I muttered a sarcastic remark about Mrs. Ivey. Although I was speaking more to myself than to anyone else, a dirty-eared, blond boy with muscular arms sitting in front of me heard the remark and snickered. It was the first display of acceptance I'd received since moving to Fortuna. I'd found a friend.

That was how my clowning began: a sarcastic remark followed by the joy and power I felt in making another person laugh. Much to the delight of the dirty-eared boy and a growing number of other classmates, I began imitating the way Mrs. Ivey lisped her s's and poked her chin with her right forefinger while reading us students a story, the way one student picked his nose or another ingratiatingly whined to the teachers for a favor, and the way some students smacked their lips while eating.

At this stage, my antics were relatively harmless. I was just another mischievous boy seeking attention. Soon, however, these antics regressed into telling stories that made the other kids laugh and ask for encores. The stories had one main theme:

the breakup of my family and the deficiencies of all the various members, old and new. As my popularity increased, I found new ways of embellishing the stories. I used four-letter words for emphasis and color and exaggeration for comical effect. I lost all inhibition and explored even the most sensitive of topics, including religion, sex, and bathroom behavior.

I became increasingly estranged from both families. After one year in Fortuna, Dick returned to Arcata to live with Dad and his new family. This left me, for all practical purposes, without a brother to grow up with. I was nearly eight years older than Terri, so there was a natural gulf between us. Also, I was now splitting time between the two families. During the school year, I stayed with Mom and Herb in Fortuna; in summer and on many weekends, I stayed with Dad and his family in the twelve-room Arcata house they'd moved into shortly after he remarried.

Of all the things I missed about the past, baseball was at the top. Since I was shuttling between Fortuna and Arcata, I couldn't attend the Babe Ruth League tryouts in either town. My dream of becoming a ballplayer was dead. To pass the time during the summers, I worked as a caddy at the Baywood Golf Course. I began playing golf, but it was no substitute for the intimacy and fraternity of the baseball diamond.

The first two years passed as in a dream. The world seemed devoid of meaning. There were the hunting and fishing outings with Herb, who was trying his best to teach me manly virtues, but I hated guns and had no enthusiasm to learn. I preferred my marble and pencil baseball games in the privacy of my room to the cold and wet and pain of becoming a man. There were the grade school friends who passed through my life like a procession of small soldiers, each marching to a beat of laughter encouraged by my morose humor. There were still the summer water-skiing trips, but now with brothers and sisters who were unreal to me. I'd spend hours alone hitting rocks with sticks of driftwood and carry on my imaginary baseball games. There were the long, rainy winter nights in my room reading baseball magazines and *The Sporting News*.

Time passed.

In my eighth-grade year, I met Shannon Kelly. I'd bought a table baseball game, StratoMatic, which advertised a statistical accuracy similar to the real major league players' performances if one played the games and managed the teams over an entire season. I'd started playing my first full season, the 1964 National League season, keeping all the pitching and hitting statistics, managing the teams, living in a dream world of baseball, neglecting my studies, keeping game-by-game accounts, and entertaining a desire to become a major league statistician. The games and statistics were my constant companions. Shannon and I were introduced one day at Rohner Park by a boy who knew we both had baseball table games. Shannon's was the APBA game. He was convinced it was superior to StratoMatic. I invited him to my home. We played a StratoMatic game between the San Francisco Giants and the Milwaukee Braves. Willie Mays, whom in real life I disliked because he was considered a better player than Hank Aaron, hit five home runs. I ordered the APBA game the next day.

I'd never met anyone like Shannon before. There was nothing he couldn't do well. He had all the confidence I lacked. He was a handsome boy who moved his five-foot, eight-inch frame with such ease, had such deep, green eyes, and carried such a confident satisfaction with himself, his abilities, and the world around him that it was impossible not to like him. His sarcastic humor coincided with my own. For the first time in a long time,

I'd found someone in whose presence I felt completely at ease, someone who could make me burst out in belly laughs, someone who reciprocated with a mirth that seemed to have no bounds. Best of all, Shannon, too, lived in a world of baseball dreams and fantasies.

In the beginning, our friendship centered around APBA. Shannon in effect became my surrogate brother and best friend. I soon visited his home for the first time. His father, who'd risen from childhood poverty to become owner of his own concrete company, was one of the wealthiest men in Fortuna. Their house was located on the outskirts of a residential area bordering Rohner Park. A fence line of high hedge faced the narrow road leading to the house. High shrubbery and a creek cutting through a small ravine next to the park provided natural boundary lines and protection against unwanted visitors on the other sides. The second story of the house consisted of Shannon's bedroom, his mother's immense wardrobe closet, and a spiraling cupola. The downstairs area was the most opulent I'd ever seen. The front room, in particular, was like a display room in interior decorating magazines. Rarely used except on special occasions, it was laden with antique furniture, paintings by his mother's brother, expensive vases filled with flowers that gave a spring fragrance to the house, and an immaculate, deep-blue carpet. The bathroom sinks had gold-plated taps. A garden of flowers and shrubbery, maintained by a professional gardener, surrounded the house on three sides.

The most identifiable fixture of Shannon's home, however, was not its opulence but his mother, Midge. Her beauty, grace, and soft Southern drawl suggested a lifetime of calm suffering, loving, and understanding.

"Hello, Norris," she said the first time we met. "I'm very glad to meet you."

Her first words to me were simple enough, but it was the way she said them, the way she looked at me with absolute candor, the way she seemed not to be speaking to me as an adolescent but as another human being that struck me. I knew at that moment she was someone with whom I could speak without fear of criticism or judgment.

I began spending more time at Shannon's home than my own. Shannon and I were inseparable. We spent hundreds of hours together playing APBA on our special "APBA tables." In my room, there was a wooden table with a Formica top, but Shannon's table was much better. It was a large, circular, glass table seemingly made for the express purpose of playing our beloved game. We'd polish the glass in a pregame ritual, as if we were groundskeepers preparing the infield for play, set up the game boards, select the starting lineups and pitchers, place the player cards in correct order, write down the necessary information in the scorebooks, pick out the special APBA dice (one was a little larger than the other to give a possible thirty-six number combinations that corresponded with numbers on the player cards, which in turn corresponded with more numbers on the game boards, which had all the possible game situations on them such as bases empty, runner on first, runners on first and second, second and third, bases loaded, as well as adjustments for strong-, medium-, or weak-fielding teams and differently-rated pitchers) and dice cup, sharpen our pencils, and place the current statistics at hand for vital information needed during the game to broadcast to our imaginary fans or for the managers (ourselves) to use for making decisions based on batting streaks, averages, pitchers' total innings pitched (the pitcher might've been tired from recent overwork), lefty-righty pitching and hitting percentages. You name it, we had it.

Once the preparations were made, we'd sit opposite each other. The games would begin, each of us announcing his own game, filling in the time between plays with commentary on the ballplayers, team standings, importance of the game to the pennant race, the weather, the pitcher's motions on the mound, the umpire's expression on a close play, the distance of a line drive to the outfield, the merits of a particularly difficult play, whatever came to our minds. The glass table was perfect for the rolling of the dice. They'd bounce on that table for an agonizingly long time in a clickity, metallic rattle that extended the drama of the moment before finally settling upon the fate of each player's turn at bat.

When announcing my games, I always struggled during the flash and click of the dice to think of something beyond my singular pattern of "Aaaand here comes the pitch. It's a ground ball to Wills at shortstop. He scoops it up and fires a strike to first. One down and the next batter is . . . ."

Shannon, on the other hand, was a master at instinctively spitting out euphonic baseball expressions and metaphors. In the capsuled moment of the dice, a continuous stream of baseball drama spilled from his mouth: "That was a close play at first. Alston doesn't like the call. Here he comes out of the dugout. He's walking to first base like he's walking to his brother's funeral. The fans are on their feet. Now here comes Durocher out of the other dugout. He's racing across the field. Both managers are screaming at Donatelli. Donatelli looks as if he's caught between bookends. Yeah, we've got a real donnybrook here today folks."

Shannon would twist his mouth to the side, let out a roar simulating the unified voice of the fans' disapproval, scoop up the dice with his thumb into the cup, which he held in the other four fingers of his right hand, and continue with the next play. At times, I became so absorbed in Shannon's game that I completely forgot about my own. I could almost smell the infield grass, feel the sunshine on my face, hear the cry of beer vendors and peanut vendors in the crowd, and see the nervous movements of the players between pitches and the cloud of dust rising from a runner's slide into second base.

We were thoroughly devoted to APBA and to each other. We developed a special APBA song and our own secret language so we could talk about the game in classes at school, at the hamburger shops, at the park, wherever we went, and not risk the ridicule of others who didn't understand our obsession. We had our own APBA attaché cases inside of which we fastidiously placed the game contents in designated spots: the team packets containing the player cards in the back flap; the schedules, batting average books (so we didn't always have to compute our statistics on paper or in our heads), pens, pencils, and rulers in the front pocket of the back flap; and the game boards, notebooks filled with all the players' statistics, scorebooks, dice, and dice cups on the bottom. We plastered team decals on the outside of the attaché cases to show the world we were not scholars but serious APBA enthusiasts.

We spent hours at a time on the telephone complaining to each other about the boredom of a Mets-Astros game (the two were weak expansion teams), comparing our leaders in all the statistical categories, describing in detail the excitement of a game in which two pitching aces like Sandy Koufax and Juan Marichal had hooked up in a 1-0 thriller, reporting on game-winning rallies and our favorite players and how they were performing, and trading new baseball expressions and gossip picked out of baseball magazines and *The Sporting News.*

Sports were everything to us. We often played basketball on the outdoor court at Rohner Park, taking on all challengers in games of two-on-two. In my freshman year at high school, I tried out for the junior varsity team and Shannon (a junior) tried out for the varsity team. We were both cut, but this inspired us to become better players. We put the same passion we had for APBA into our practice sessions at the park. Shannon was the purest shooter I'd seen. Often we shot a hundred free throws apiece. Shannon never failed to sink at least ninety. We played games of one-on-one, playing first right-handed then left-handed; played innumerable games of H-O-R-S-E, and practiced hook shots, jump shots, layups, set shots, dribbling, passing, all phases of the game until we were practically unbeatable against the others who played at the park. We developed an instinct for each other's moves both with and without the ball. I had long arms and legs, and was learning how to rebound and block shots. Shannon was developing an uncanny accuracy from twenty to thirty feet with a beautiful, high-arching shot that had perfect reverse spin and usually swished through the net (which we often bought with our own money) with a soft, whooshing sound.

When we weren't practicing basketball or playing APBA, we listened to radio broadcasts of baseball or basketball games. Shannon dreamed of becoming an announcer. He modeled his style after his hero Vin Scully, the Los Angeles Dodgers' announcer. We'd usually pick up the night games broadcast from Los Angeles on a radio in Shannon's upstairs room. To our ears, Scully was a magician with words. Through his voice, Dodger Stadium became our Land of Oz and the players legendary figures out of tales of folklore.

While listening to the broadcasts, we dreamed of a bright day in the future when we, too, would be favored enough to stroll along the Dodger Stadium infield, joking with the players, waving to the fans, and carrying our attaché cases to the announcing booth—Shannon the announcer, I the statistician.

In the winter, it was Chick Hearn, the Los Angeles Lakers basketball team's announcer, who thrilled us with his rapid-fire, emotional style that held us sweating with excitement over a tight, see-saw game decided at the buzzer by a jump shot from the corner.

I made the junior varsity team in my sophomore year. By midseason, I was one of the starting guards. We lost our first four games but came back to win the final eight games in a row to finish in a tie for first place. Shannon was cut from the varsity team again, but he attended all the games and cheered me on, giving me a confidence I'd lacked since my Jacoby Creek Little League days.

Only with Shannon and our world of dream, imagination, baseball, basketball, and APBA did I feel truly secure. Away from that world, I was still a sullen clown torn between two families, still shuttling back and forth between them. I saw very little of Dick, who now lived in his own world of cars, nice clothes, the *right* crowd, teenage social status, the coming of manhood. He had no use for my childish behavior. He showed an open contempt for Dad's new family, refusing to speak to the younger stepsisters (one of whom he once slapped at the dinner table), demanding Linda's strict attention to the washing and ironing of his clothes, almost coming to blows with her on more than one occasion, and taking advantage of Dad's relative wealth by asking for and receiving an expensive new car. I didn't understand him. He didn't understand me.

I took little interest in Terri and was ambivalent in the face of her pain and tears when she returned to Fortuna from weekend visits to the Arcata family, her underarms often black and blue with pinch marks and her mind poisoned with stories about how evil Mom was, how Terri had been adopted and would never inherit any of the Norris money, how she was a helpless child who'd never marry, and many other things she didn't fully comprehend but still had an intuitive feeling for—the darkness of her future as depicted by our stepmother.

I felt neither love nor hatred toward my Arcata stepsisters, Michelle and Alice. I was conscious only of a subtle competition for Dad's love and attention. Herb's son and daughter, Tommy and Sandra, had graduated from college and were already living on their own, so I rarely saw them.

I didn't know what to make of Linda. On some days, she worked her tail off keeping Dad's house clean, cooking for large numbers of family members and their friends, doing the laundry and ironing piles of shirts and pants. On other days, she lay in bed, complaining of various ailments, refusing to work, and demanding Dad's attention. I didn't know if these displays of ennui were real or fake, and I didn't care.

I couldn't get excited when a half-sister, Linda D., was born. I didn't feel anything when Dad and Linda lost another child to miscarriage and Linda fell into a depression that lasted for months. I didn't understand what Dad meant when he told me he'd had an operation to get *fixed* and would have to have another operation to get *unfixed* because his wife was "showing suicidal behavior." About a year later, my half-brother Billy was born. I just shrugged my shoulders and continued to play APBA.

It was the same with the Fortuna family. I took no interest in Herb's attempts to educate me in using tools, cleaning and using a gun, building a campfire, a house, a table, finding clams on the beach at low tide, erecting a tent, splitting firewood correctly, or changing spark plugs in a car. I was insensitive to Mom's efforts to keep the house clean, prepare nutritious meals, wash our clothes every day so we could always have fresh underwear, pants, socks, shirts, and even bed sheets. I was insensitive to the depression that came over her whenever she heard rumors from Arcata sources about how she'd failed as a mother, instigated the divorce, been kicked out of the Catholic Church, dropped a rung on the social ladder because of the difference in the bank accounts of the Norrises and Schlinkmans, or lost the love of her children. I think this last one hurt her the most and was the most poisonous one spread by none other than Linda. I was insensitive to Mom's love, her sacrifice, her warmth, her ability always to give without expecting anything in return.

The only person I cared about was Shannon. The time spent with either of my two families was merely an obligatory slice of life to pass in preparation for the next time with Shannon, a laying up of a fresh collection of exaggerated stories to tell of the inadequacies, depravities, and strangeness of the hodgepodge of relationships I had to endure, told always with the biting sarcasm of a young cynic to the delight of Shannon's own warped sense of humor. He was an appreciative audience to these tales, urging me into stretches of imagination, howling with laughter the more I stretched the truth.

In the summer after my freshman year, I began working for Dad at the Van De Nor redwood manufacturing plant, which was now in Eureka next to Humboldt Bay. Mondays through Fridays we followed the same routine: get up at seven o'clock, get washed and dressed, climb into Dad's '64 Ford pickup, stop at the Arcata donut shop to buy a dozen donuts, drive the eight miles to Eureka, and arrive at the big warehouse at the foot of F Street. The ripe smell of the plywood mill across the bay in Samoa hung in the air, mixing with the fresh smell of redwood boards that were run through the dry kiln and stacked in long rows to be loaded on railroad boxcars and sent to different parts of the world. The sound of industry was everywhere: the clatter of the green chain conveyors, the high screech of the planer and dry kiln, the shouts and bantering of the workers, the dull whine of forklifts, the grinding of the chipper that turned waste into chips to be sold to the plywood mill, and the heavy thud of the massive clippers that trimmed the boards into various lengths.

This was Dad's world. It was slightly different from the earlier days when the Norris family was just starting up its business and Dad spent most of his time getting his hands dirty with the other workers. Now he was working in the office with Uncle Dick and a cast of other characters. There was Ann, the secretary who'd worked for the family for twenty years and always showered me with compliments and attention. There was Dave, the tall, distinguished, sixty-year-old salesman who loved to tell jokes, had a quick smile, played an excellent game of golf, and always dressed immaculately. There was Bud, the bookkeeper who was all arms and legs and listened to all the San Francisco Giants games on the radio, becoming depressed when they lost. He had a voracious appetite and never hesitated to eat half of the donuts if the others weren't quick enough to take their share. I liked Bud best because we could talk at length about baseball and he treated me like a younger brother. There was always plenty of work for me to do: typing invoices; washing cars; helping Bud with the books; stamping and sealing scores of letters, bills, and invoices; filing paperwork; and running errands in the company truck.

During these summers of working for Dad and saving some money, I began taking trips to San Francisco with Shannon. Our minds had been filled for some time with a romantic vision of the City, a vision stimulated by the magic of radio and the voices of our favorite sports announcers. We often talked about the City as if it were a secret place imbued with mystery and adventure that called to us like a siren in the night. We were growing bored with the dull characters and slow pace of the small lumber towns of Humboldt County. We needed something new, a breath of fresh air to inject some life into the mundaneness of our existence.

We took our first trip by bus during my sophomore year to see a professional basketball game. San Francisco was an enormous playground pulsating with excitement. On every street corner lay a wealth of characters to see, drama to watch, comedy to laugh at, dialogue to listen to, movement to be swayed by, a treasure chest of sounds, smells, and sights to devour. We walked the swarming streets drunk with innocence and joy.

After our first visit, we were two addicts in need of larger doses. Over the next three years, every penny we earned working for our fathers went toward our trips. In the beginning, we took the Greyhound bus, but after Shannon's parents bought him a new sports car, we took our pilgrimages in it instead. We'd check into downtown hotels under false names, usually the names of obscure baseball players, hole up in a room for three to five days playing marathon sessions of APBA (going out only for baseball games at Candlestick Park or wandering the nighttime streets), then check out of the hotel without paying by dropping

our suitcases from the second floor to an alley and walking out
the entrance nonchalantly as if going out for coffee.

After the APBA sessions when we prowled the streets, our
breasts heaved with an unbearable joy to be a part of the pan-
orama that surrounded us. There were the sharp cries and
strident voices of the shoeshine men and newsstand vendors.
Our favorite was Smokey Joe, who sat on the corner of Powell
and Geary Streets, a dwarf of a man with an oversized head.
His eyes bulged out of their sockets; his short legs were bowed
like a miniature cowboy; a long, fat cigar protruded from his
thick lips as he said, "Dere ya go, dere ya go. Whadaya wan'?
Whadaya wan'? Dat'll be a quarter, young man. Dere ya go."

There were the street artists in colorful costumes who played
music, performed acrobatics and mime, and juggled bowling pins.
There were the throngs of shoppers streaming in and out of the
clothing stores, department stores, shoe shops, hat shops, all the
shops that lined the downtown area. There were the cable cars,
filled to bursting with tourists, clanging up and down the hilly
streets. There were all the women dressed in the latest fashions
who walked proudly and sensuously, their heads tossing about
and hips swaying. There were the gaudy prostitutes filing up
and down Eddy Street who called out to passersby, "How 'bout
a date, honey?" There were the Black pimps in pink, red, and
purple costumes who prowled softly through the shadows. There
were the hollow-eyed winos in tattered clothes who hung out
on Market Street.

There were the street corner food stands with their aroma of
hamburgers and grease, the coffee shops with a wide selection
of waffles and cakes, and the sleazy theaters on Market Street,
where we could see double features any time of the day. There
were the neon lights and billboards showing naked women

on the Broadway Strip, the ringing sounds of Chinatown, the grandeur of the spacious ballrooms, bars, and restaurants of the Fairmont and Hilton Hotels. There were the cheap and tottering rides of Playland before it was closed down. There was the Greyhound Bus Depot, where we played pinball machines and watched strange men who lurked in the shadows.

There was an abundance of characters everywhere we went. Humboldt County was dull and moribund in comparison. At the center of our vision of the City stood Candlestick Park, the home of professional baseball, the site for the contests that had stimulated our young hearts for years, the stage for all we deemed good in life. We always went to the stadium two hours before game time to watch batting and fielding practice. Everything about the place excited us: the cries of the vendors, the crack of bats meeting balls, the sounds of the scoreboard organist playing "Take Me Out to the Ball Game," the cheers and taunts of the crowd, the rhythmic dance of the players taking infield practice and whipping the ball around the horn, the pitchers running laps, the foul balls landing in the stands and the crowd scrambling for them, the public address announcer calling out the starting lineups, the days of warm sunshine and nights of fog rolling off the bay, the wind that swirled dust in mini-cyclones around the pitcher's mound and the base paths, the hot dogs and peanuts that always tasted better simply because we were at the ballpark, the starting pitchers warming up on the sidelines and occasionally chatting with the fans, the uniforms the players wore, the scorecards in which we kept notes of every nuance of the game, and the fans of every shape, size, and nationality.

Here were the players we'd read about, dreamed about, managed in our APBA games, the players whose exploits we'd listened to on the radio in Shannon's room: Willie Mays, Orlando

Cepeda, Juan Marichal, Gaylord Perry, Sandy Koufax, Tommy Davis (Shannon's favorite after he'd led the National League twice in batting and knocked in 153 runs in 1962), Willie Davis, Don Drysdale, Maury Wills, Hank Aaron, Jim Bunning, Willie Stargell, Roberto Clemente, and all the others of that glorious age of baseball. Here we witnessed the games that still burn in my memory: the time the Braves beat the Giants 17-3 and Tony Cloninger, the Braves' pitcher, clubbed two grand slam home runs (he also hit another that landed about three feet foul in the right field stands) and added an RBI single to drive in nine runs; the time Gaylord Perry pitched a one-hitter, allowing only a scratch single up the middle by the Chicago Cub second baseman Glenn Beckert in the seventh inning; the time Jim Bunning outdueled Juan Marichal by hitting a home run in the tenth inning to win the game 5-4; the many home runs and shoestring catches by Willie Mays; the line drive home runs and singles by Willie McCovey, who hit the ball harder than anyone we'd ever seen; and the pitching duels between Koufax and Marichal, Drysdale and Perry, when the Dodgers and Giants played out their intense rivalry.

Often after the games, we went to the hotels where the teams stayed in the hope of catching a glimpse of our heroes, snatching a few words of conversation, or collecting an autograph. One time, we followed two Dodger players, Wes Parker and Jeff Torborg, to a movie theater, sat behind them, and mimicked their every move. Another time, we met Bill Sudakis, a Dodger rookie, in the hotel elevator. He pinched my stomach and said, "Take care, kid." I turned ten shades of red. Another time, we knocked on the Pittsburgh Pirates' announcers' room door, hoping to meet Bob Prince, the famed announcer, but instead met his assistant Nellie King, who took us out to breakfast and invited us the next day into the stadium announcing booth so we could see how a game was actually broadcast. We once saw Vin Scully walking down the street and Shannon, in a state of great excitement, darted across the street yelling, "Vinnie! Vinnie! You're the greatest!"

Scully was visibly startled, but still kind enough to give Shannon an autograph.

There was never a dull moment during those trips to the City. If the crowds at the ballpark and in the streets were not enough to entertain us, we entertained ourselves by dancing in the streets, running zigzag courses like football halfbacks eluding tacklers through the throngs of people in the downtown area, playing slow-motion games of mime baseball or football in the aisles of the movie theaters, biting people's shoulders and scampering off like madmen, always spur-of-the-moment foolishness to make each other laugh. If I did something particularly original and insane that struck Shannon a certain way, he'd hit the ground as if shot by a bullet, curl up like a fetus in a struggle to catch his breath until seemingly ready to explode, and let go with a long, piercing scream, his arms and legs suddenly extended as if electrocuted. It was his famous scream laugh. I loved it.

San Francisco was for us the gateway to the outside world. Although we lived in a genuine paradise tucked away in the redwoods, impervious to the events of the 1960s—the Vietnam War, the Civil Rights movement, the political assassinations, the drugs and sexual revolutions of that generation—we were becoming dissatisfied. There was too much to life, the world was too big, for us to be contained forever behind the redwood curtain. Innocence wouldn't last forever. But while it did last, it was splendid. While the world remained a dream and we created our own diversions, life was one continuous joyride, a marathon APBA game played in a San Francisco hotel room.

I moved back to Arcata for my final two years of high school, mainly because I wanted to play basketball for Jerry Paul, an extraordinary coach. Shannon graduated and spent a year attending a vocational school for announcers in Los Angeles. I began hanging out with John Cady, whom I'd first met at a two-day summer golf tournament three years before. He'd been in my foursome the first day, forgotten his golf shoes, and had to play in a pair of slippery street shoes. He managed to shoot an 88 and ended up taking second place. We'd often seen each other at the Baywood Golf Course the next two summers. We'd always have a good laugh about his having to play in street shoes that day.

John was a small fellow, about five-foot-seven and a hundred and thirty pounds, but he possessed a determination to compete far superior to many larger athletes. He wrestled, played golf, and ran cross country. His father was the athletic director of Arcata High School, a muscular Indian who'd been a star athlete in his own time, an independent man who'd built his own house and could do just about anything with his hands—carpentry, plumbing, fence-building, fixing cars, growing a garden.

John was easy to make laugh and fun to be with. I began spending most of my free time with him at his home, just as I'd done with Shannon in Fortuna. Although he wasn't good enough at basketball to make the varsity team, he loved to play and often watched the basketball team's practices after school. In the fall, we ran cross country together. In spring and summer, we played golf. We both had our moments of glory. I played on two championship basketball teams and made the all-county team my senior year. John won the county golf tournament his junior year by playing the last four holes in one under par and sinking a difficult six-foot putt on the final hole to edge four other players by a single stroke.

When Shannon returned from a year in Los Angeles, I introduced him to John. Shannon often drove up to Arcata on the weekends. John had a key to the Arcata High School gymnasium, so the three of us often snuck in and shot baskets. Shannon and I introduced John to our APBA games. The only time I spent at home was to sleep and eat an occasional dinner.

My high school years were coming to an end, bringing the need to face the future. The immediate concern was the draft and the Vietnam War. The race riots that spread across the country in 1967 and made the news every night began to encroach upon our consciences, too, but in 1968, the outside world flooded our TV screens with news about the Tet Offensive in Vietnam, the assassinations of Martin Luther King and Robert Kennedy, the violent Democratic Convention in Chicago with Mayor Daly's police force beating up protesters. We could no longer avoid the reality of the country coming apart at the seams.

Soon I was catapulted into an entirely different and pivotal experience. It was as if the forces that enveloped the country so violently at the time combined with the ironies of individual fate to open a door to the rest of my life. That experience, like the earlier ones, lies fixed in my childhood and adolescent mind movie.

It's a Saturday near the end of January 1969, the day of the high school championship basketball game, the biggest day of my life, a day I've dreamed about many times. Arcata High School's basketball team is the smallest team in the league, but relying on an intense and swarming defense, we've somehow pulled off one upset after another until we're actually in a position to tie for the championship with a victory in our final game.

A few hours before the game, Shannon, another friend named Troy, and I go to the beach in the dune buggy Shannon's parents bought him. We're driving along the surf when Shannon makes a sharp turn and hits a sunken log. The dune buggy flips, catapulting me out of the passenger seat. I'm airborne, my feet above Troy's head, the dune buggy at a forty-five degree angle to the beach. The world below passes in slow motion. I land on my left side in the surf. Darkness covers my vision. Initially, there's no pain, no bodily sensation, only a gentle awareness that life is probably over and my spirit is leaving my body. A thought comes: "If this is death, it isn't so bad, so bad . . . ."

A silent, black roar fills my head. I'm face down in the surf. The next moment of consciousness is of being carried away from the surf by four men. There's still no bodily sensation, just a whirring sound in the back of my head and a view of the beach in front of me as I scan the limited border of my vision. I'm aware of bodies moving on both sides of me, but I can't see above their waists.

Spasmodic convulsions grip my body. A stream of water spews from my lungs. An icy chill spreads from head to feet. Panicked, gasping noises escape my mouth as I fight for breath, lungs and throat and head pierced with the pain of daggers ripping my flesh. Miraculously, one slow, tiny breath enters my lungs. A short, painful exhale follows. Then another and another, each time getting slightly deeper until finally a full breath comes. The men set me gently on the sand and cover me with a blanket. A moment later, when the sensation of my left hand gripping sand registers, I know something is wrong with my left arm. It's snapped in two. Faces peer down at me.

An ambulance finally arrives. We're taken to the hospital. Somebody has contacted Mom about the accident. She jumps in her car immediately, rushes to Shannon's house to pick up Midge, and races to the hospital in Eureka, passing the ambulance on the way and arriving first. Dad arrives a bit later. As I'm wheeled into the operating room, I hear him say to Mom, "Whose insurance is going to cover this, yours or mine?" Mom looks at him uncomprehendingly, rage crossing her face, and says, "How can you think of such a thing right now? This is your son we are talking about!"

Shannon suffers only a minor concussion. Troy is uninjured. Both of them are kept overnight for observation and released the next day. I undergo a four-hour operation. The basketball team wins the championship game without me. The next day, the players and some fans visit the hospital. They put the net they cut down during the victory celebration around my neck and give me the game ball.

I feel only a great sadness. All the well-wishers seem like phantoms who've come to taunt me with their joy and health. How can I explain to them what I feel? How can I articulate the mute bitterness that engulfs me, the inexplicable feeling of betrayal in having been deprived of the peaceful calm, the warm blackness, the physical nearness of death? How can I voice the revelation I experienced the moment I woke from the operation: to subsist in the real world is to be tied to a sad and evanescent dream?

It takes a few months for the arm to heal. After my release from the hospital, I spend the first two weeks in Fortuna, lying motionless in Herb's reclining chair, helpless as a trussed chicken, my body wracked with soreness and stiffness, plunged into a black melancholy.

When I'm able to move around a little, I return to school in Arcata. During those final months of my senior year, I'm consumed by depression. I finish the school year without looking at a book. There's no purpose in studying, working, planning for a future. When I'm named to the all-county basketball team, I shrug it off with a "so-what" attitude.

The thought of escaping Humboldt County becomes an obsession. If Shannon and I don't go to college, we'll be drafted and probably end up on the front lines in Vietnam. A viable alternative seems to be joining the Air Force or Navy. We pay a visit to the local Air Force recruiter, who offers us the world. We'll never have to carry a gun, never have to go to Vietnam, never have to sweat. We can play basketball all year round, travel to exciting places, meet beautiful women, enter a life of glory, triumph, wealth, sunshine, and fame. We buy it hook, line, and sinker. Just sign the dotted line here, boys.

We join the Air Force in September 1969.

7

The Road to Conscientious Objection

I KNOW I've made a mistake the day I arrive with a faceless swarm of other confused enlistees at Lackland Air Base outside San Antonio, Texas. Somehow I survive the grueling weeks of basic training—the incessant screaming of the drill instructors, the stripping of each soldier's individuality, the hours of close order drill, the training in the use of weapons, the early morning wake-ups, the physical conditioning in the desert heat, the barracks inspections, the scrubbing of toilets and floors on our hands and knees, the tasteless food in the chow halls, the loneliness, the classrooms where the soldiers are inculcated into obedience and conformity. I add fifteen pounds to my skinny frame and contract pyorrhea of the gums.

It's strange that something like pyorrhea would have such a strong influence on the course my life takes. If not for that bloody, pillow-stained condition, I might've passed through the Air Force experience like any other automaton on the American merry-go-round. I'm on the verge of being accepted into a special training program where volunteers are placed under simulated conditions that American astronauts experience in space. The volunteers are tested for stress, blood and body chemistry and mental changes, and many other things. The gist of the program is that, after six months of testing, the volunteers have their choice of what career field to enter, what locations they want for future assignments, and a chance for fast promotion. All this disappears when the problem with my gums is discovered. On my last day of basic training, I'm given my assignment: military policeman.

While the majority of airmen return home on leave and report to other bases for their technical training after basic training, the others chosen to be military police (the most despicable and lowest career field in the Air Force) and I have to remain at Lackland for ten more weeks of specialized training. The hand of irony has played a cruel trick. Country bumpkin that I am, I've joined the Air Force thinking I'll never have to carry a weapon, but now I'm to be trained in the art of combat and the use of deadly weapons. I know I can never kill another human being. It's always been and still is an abstraction. Besides, I lack the courage even to use my fists to defend myself. The very thought of violence makes me sick to my stomach.

I pass through the training without incident. But during those days of martial arts training; war games; kitchen labor called K.P.; stripping, cleaning, loading, firing, and handling of M-16 rifles, .38 pistols, hand grenades, bayonets, and knives; the classes on crowd dispersal, first aid, attack upon and retreat from an enemy, arrest and seizure, drugs, communism, terrorist activities, patriotism, military police history; and the propaganda the instructors use to inculcate the soldiers into submission and obedience, there grows within my heart an inchoate attitude of rebelliousness. It lies dormant, simmering below the surface, waiting silently for the right moment to emerge from its hiding.

For a while, however, the Air Force succeeds in brainwashing me. One image sticks in my head: a drill instructor during a training session in the use of a truncheon screaming at me in front of a gymnasium full of military police trainees. "Goddamn it, Norris! You dumb shit! You've got a left-handed stick! I told you to get a fucking right-handed stick. Now get your ass over to that pile and bring me a right-handed stick!"

"Yes sir," I bark, turning redder each time I return to him with another "left-handed stick." Finally, it dawns on me that all the sticks are the same. A wave of shame passes through me. For the rest of the military police training, the drill instructors call me Left-Handed Stick.

For my first assignment, I'm sent to Beale Air Base in the Yuba City-Marysville area near Sacramento, California. I'm put on the flight line as a security guard for B-52s, which look to me like gigantic prehistoric birds of prey. Thus begins my time of walking in circles on the flight line in the rain and heat, thinking, changing, growing, wondering what the purpose of my life is. I buy a Volkswagen bug and return to Arcata on rare days off, a drive of seven or eight hours from the Yuba City-Marysville wasteland. In doing this, I'm committing a military crime by going beyond the two-hundred-fifty-mile limit placed on leaves taken by members of Strategic Air Command bases, but I'm so lonely and frustrated I go anyway and am usually drunk for two days before driving like a maniac to get back to the base on time and not be AWOL from my next shift.

During this time, I'm thinking about Vietnam and having a gut feeling that the war is wrong. Although we're not allowed to take anything other than our guns and military equipment on the line, I smuggle a portable radio and earphones and listen to the lyrics of popular songs instead of just the melodies—songs by Bob Dylan, Crosby, Stills, and Nash, and all the others protesting the war. I'm also reading the underground newspapers that are finding their way on base and contain antiwar, anti-government stories about the My Lai atrocity, the shooting of Ralph Bunch at the Presidio, and the hysteria running rampant on American college campuses.

All the little irritating items of military brainwashing and propaganda gradually build up inside of me. Things I've taken for granted before now make me bristle. There's the time three of us guards are called before the squadron sergeant after roll call, and he reads us our rights and charges each of us with defecation on duty.

"What's defecation, Sarge?" I ask.

"It's taking a shit inside the marked line you are NOT supposed to enter, only guard, and you know that only the flight crew are allowed inside that line, and last night one of you smartasses took a FUCKING SHIT inside that line and right under the cockpit—that's what DEFECATION means!" the sergeant screams.

"You've got to be shittin' me," I say.

The sergeant doesn't think my remark is funny. There on the table as exhibit A for the prosecution is the big, black turd, hard as a rock, found the day before under the cockpit of the bomber I walked around for half my shift before changing to another place to guard. They're actually planning to court-martial one of the three of us who was stationed on that post during the night and use the turd as evidence.

It's the final straw in realizing that military life isn't for me. From that day on, I can't keep my mouth shut in pointing out the inconsistencies and lies whenever I spot them. I miss haircuts and am constantly reprimanded for my shoddy appearance during inspections. I lose days off and am forced to undergo crowd control practice in case we're called upon, like the National Guard, to break up a civilian demonstration. I know my sympathies would be with the demonstrators. I begin to think that if there really is an enemy, it's the military. If the situation ever really comes up, I'll cast aside my weapons and join the other side.

My order to fight in Southeast Asia comes through. I'm given thirty days leave before having to report first to a base in Texas for a month of intensive war training and later to a base in northern Thailand near the Cambodian border. This happens shortly after Nixon escalates the war into Cambodia, where B-52 bombers are now dropping tons of napalm. When I leave Beale Air Base for the start of my thirty-day leave, I know I'll never make it to Texas.

Two weeks later, I'm in a car accident. I'm unhurt, but it's like a sign from the heavens. Here's a chance to try to get out of the Air Force by faking a back and neck injury. The next day, I'm at the doctor's office complaining of pains from the accident, whiplash that can't be detected on the X-rays. I leave the office wearing a neck brace and armed with a letter from the doctor recommending I be let out of the service.

I hitchhike back to Beale Air Base, tell the clerks I've been in an accident, and am assigned to the transient barracks. I go to the base hospital every day, but the military doctors seem to know I'm just trying to shirk my duties. I keep insisting the whiplash is the real thing. The doctors give me a bottle of Darvon pills and send me back to the barracks.

This goes on for three weeks. It's as if no one else on base is aware that I'm back and not in Texas. I'm content to wait for something to happen, but nothing does. One day, I run into Terry

Yavitz, another security policeman I know from a distance. We've rarely spoken to each other before, but when he asks me what I'm doing on base, I'm overjoyed to be noticed by someone. He asks if I want to smoke some pot. Off we go for a drive in his VW van. There I am, stoned for the first time, loving the feeling as we park and watch the most beautiful sunset I've ever seen. I confess everything right there, half expecting him to turn me in to the legal department. Instead, he says that he's involved in the underground effort against the war and is one of the writers for an antiwar newspaper being printed secretly off base in Yuba City. The paper is called *Spaced Sentinel*.

In the next few days, I find myself a member of a group of five short-haired hippies stationed at Beale, each of the others in his last few months of military service, each radically opposed to the war, actively involved in writing for *Spaced Sentinel*, and spreading antiwar propaganda around the base. Two of the members are the base photographers and so also working for the base newspaper. As such, they have access to classified information and use this in some of the stories that appear in the off-base publication.

We meet every night in the photographers' barracks room to smoke pot, listen to music, talk about revolution, and discuss my case and what should be done about it. Their room is a veritable den of iniquity with its black lights, strobe lights, and posters of Jimmy Hendrix and Bob Dylan plastered on the walls, along with the black light posters that glow surrealistically in the dark when only the black light is on. Scattered about are all sorts of hip magazines, newspapers, and books I've never read before. Piled high next to the stereo are dozens of rock 'n' roll records. Next to the records is an assortment of pot-smoking paraphernalia. In this room, we form a kind of conspiracy. It's exciting to be a member of a bona fide *movement*, a very important member at that, being the first war resister they've known.

We spend hours discussing pacifism and Gandhi and Thoreau and Tolstoy, all people I've heard of but know little about. Soon it's apparent that I have to make a *statement* because it won't be long before the base clerks discover I haven't carried out my order. We decide I should go to the base legal department to find out what my rights are and what I need to do to file for conscientious objector status. Although I'm sure I don't qualify as a religious C.O. because I dropped out of the Catholic Church when I was twelve years old, my friends tell me a Supreme Court precedent-setting ruling in May established that conscientious objection to war can legally be recognized for moral and ethical grounds, too.

The first lawyer I talk to is a true military hard-ass who tells me I'm crazy and should go immediately to see my commanding officer. He points out all the negative aspects of what I'm considering. If I don't recant my current position, there's a strong likelihood of being court-martialed, pinned with a five-year sentence, a dishonorable discharge, and a life of shame and hardship. I leave the lawyer's office depressed and wondering what to do next. Shortly after, I meet another former security guard who everyone thinks is just another dude who can't cut it in the military. He tells me he's now off the flight line and happy to be doing menial chores and not carrying any weapons. I tell him my story. He knows another lawyer who once picked him up hitchhiking, talked to him like a human being, and treated him as an equal. He advises me to go see this other lawyer, Jerry Mahoney.

I do the next day. Jerry takes an immediate interest in my case. He's relaxed, confident, friendly, and encouraging. He tells me that he, too, is an antiwar man and spent eight years of school studying to become a lawyer. When he was drafted, he considered going to Canada, but decided he could work better within the system rather than throw away his career and eight years of schooling. He's very professional about finding out all the details of when I returned to the base, what I've been doing, what I've said to the clerks, the security police, and the other lawyer. He accepts my case and says it's the most important one he's ever had.

We set the wheels in motion for applying for conscientious objector status. We have meetings every day. He counsels me on how to answer the questions that will be asked at various interviews with officers and chaplains who will judge whether my application and beliefs are sincere. It's all serious stuff. I feel I'm in over my head intellectually, but Jerry gives me confidence. Most of these interviews go smoothly.

About a month after returning to the base, I'm summoned to appear in my commanding officer's office. Two other high-ranking officers are present as witnesses. Lieutenant Colonel Arnold is seething but controlled. At first his questions are polite, almost sympathetic, but as I continue to give vague answers in the manner Jerry has counseled me to do, Lieutenant Colonel Arnold becomes increasingly frustrated and begins to leer at me. For the first time in my life, I'm facing the hostility of a man who holds my fate in his hands.

Lieutenant Colonel Arnold's face turns red. In a fit of controlled rage, he stands over me and bellows, "Airman, if you don't straighten up and straighten up fast, I'm going to send you to prison for five years. I'll make an example of you to show what a coward and a communist look like and how they're treated in this man's Air Force. I insist you tell me everything. Why have you changed so suddenly? Who are the people that have influenced you? Where do they live? Are you part of some organization? Are you connected with this filthy communist paper spreading propaganda around this base? I demand some answers to these questions and I demand them now!"

I feel like the enemy I am, but I just sit there not saying anything, tears coming to my eyes. Lieutenant Colonel Arnold relaxes a bit, seemingly gaining pleasure from seeing my will weakening already. He decides to give me one more chance. I'm to go back to the barracks, get my thoughts and emotions in order, and return to his office the following morning, at which time I'll be given the final official order to go to Southeast Asia.

I go straight to Jerry's office, scared and confused. He reassures me everything will be all right and that the next day it's imperative I not say a direct no, but continue to give vague responses to the order I'll be given.

The next day, there are three more witnesses and a secretary to record every word spoken. When given the order, I reply, "I don't feel I'm mentally or physically capable of killing another human being."

Lieutenant Colonel Arnold says, "Boy, I'm gonna court-martial you. You're gonna regret this for the rest of your life. You're gonna wish you never laid eyes on me, you sniffly little coward."

I'm spared having to endure pretrial confinement. I have to work every day mowing lawns, emptying garbage cans, cleaning toilets, and other chores around the lieutenant colonel's office until the court martial some three or four weeks away. Jerry continues to work hard on my case. We meet several times a week to discuss strategy for the court martial.

One day, I receive a letter from Uncle Dick. As the spokesman for the Norris family, he apparently has taken it upon himself to express the family's disappointment. Nah, that's too light. I should say their renunciation because of the shame I've brought upon the family name, particularly after Dad brought such honor to the family as a decorated pilot during World War II.

Sept. 22, 1970

Dear Bob:

Your father has just informed me of your refusal to comply with an order from your commanding officer. I was shocked to hear this Bob and I certainly hope that you come to your senses before it is too late and try to make whatever amends possible to rectify this horrible mistake.

You must have been told that you will have to face a Court Martial and will be given a prison sentence which will brand you an ex-con and a coward for the rest of your life. You will not be able to vote or hold a public office, work for any government agency or for that matter, just who the hell is going to want to hire a person without integrity or personal pride? You may think that you have lived for a long time but believe me, you just haven't even started your life and I hate to see you throw it away. Because that is exactly what you will be doing if you follow the course you are on now.

If you go to your commanding officer now and try to correct your mistake, you may get off rather easily, but if you don't, you are going to regret this the rest of your life and this is not just an old square talking either. These are facts and I don't think you are so stupid that you can't understand them. God help you if you can't.

Your father, your mother and all of your friends, and I will do everything we can to help you if you change your mind, but if you don't, then I guess you just won't have much of anything or anyone.

Please give this a lot of thought Bob, because you have an awful lot to lose and nothing to gain by your actions.

Sincerely,
Your Uncle Dick

My attitude is that if the Norris family and society don't need me, I don't need them. I make a vow to carve out my own independent existence, no matter how desperate things might become.

The day of the court martial finally comes: October 6, 1970. The military courtroom is grey and solemn. The sun outside is shining brightly on the parched Sacramento Valley landscape where I've spent many days and nights walking around B-52 bombers before finally making my decision. Several faceless men in nondescript military dress take the stand, pointing their accusing fingers at me as I sit next to Jerry at the wooden table facing the military judge. The judge sits in calm repose, weighing the facts of the case as they are presented to him. Meaningless military words fill the courtroom.

". . . willful disobedience to a direct, lawful order . . ."

"The accused was handed his order at 1300 hours on 30 June 1970, but failed to report to . . ."

"And so, Your Honor, the full sentence of five years at hard labor is requested to make a lasting example to the . . ."

Shannon's parents have been allowed to come down from Fortuna and observe the court martial because Jerry has decided to use Midge as a character witness. I don't remember her exact words, but a tremendous feeling of appreciation comes over me as she speaks to the court. Then it's my turn to speak. The prosecuting attorney has no questions. I tell the judge I'll try my best to get along at the prison rehabilitation program that I'll be sent to, but I believe the Air Force will fail in attempting to rehabilitate me. My conscience will not allow me to participate in war in any form.

When finished, I rise from the stand. I feel dizzy. The courtroom recesses for the judge to come to a decision. An hour later, he emerges from a dingy room to call me before him. The verdict: not guilty of the original charge of willful disobedience to a direct lawful order, but guilty of a lesser charge of negligent disobedience to a lawful order. In essence, an entire day of deliberation has boiled down to the way I responded to Lieutenant Colonel Arnold's final order to go to Southeast Asia. I never said "no." It's a lesson in the power of language. That single sentence I repeated over and over has perhaps saved four and a half years of my life. At that moment, however, there is little consolation other than achieving a moral victory. I still have to spend six months of hard labor at the 3320th Retraining Group in Denver, Colorado.

A military policeman places handcuffs around my wrists and leads me to a patrol car waiting to take me to the base prison. Jerry and Midge Kelly follow me to the patrol car.

I force a smile and say, "It could've been worse."

Jerry shakes my hand. Midge says, "You were very brave on the stand. I was proud of you. Make sure you write to us."

I get into the patrol car. A cloud of dust rises behind the car as it lurches toward the prison. I crane my neck for a final look and see Jerry and Midge grow smaller through a brown haze until they're tiny specks in the distance.

8

Hard Time

T HE cell door slams behind me. I'm placed in solitary confinement for the first two days because I'm supposed to be separated from the other prisoners until I'm given a medical checkup to make sure I have no communicable diseases. All I can do is pace the floor of the eight-foot-long, four-foot-wide cell with its concrete walls, solitary bed with one blanket, and one barred window looking out on a desolate landscape.

After my checkup, I'm allowed to join the other prisoners in a separate ward that has two cells—each with six beds and six lockers—a recreation room with a bookshelf containing western and romance novels, a ping pong table, and a TV we can watch for two hours in the evenings. There are four other prisoners. Steve, a twenty-one-year-old from Los Angeles is in jail for thirty days for punching his commanding officer. Jerome, a twenty-year-old Black guy from Chicago who went AWOL for six months, is waiting for his own court martial. John, a Texan who was busted for drunk driving on base, is serving a twenty-day sentence. And Bob, a New Yorker who was also AWOL for a month, is waiting for his court martial.

The days pass slowly. The routine is to get up at six in the morning, clean the jail, go with an armed escort to breakfast at the chow hall, return to the jail to wait for our daily assignments of going to different spots around the base to scrub toilets, dig ditches, strip and wax and buff office floors, and other general cleaning duties. It's not such a bad existence. Sometimes I even run into a friend who turns me on to a few joints I can easily smuggle back into the jail because the guards don't frisk me when I return in the evenings. The nights are fairly relaxed. We go to the chow hall again with one of the armed guards, return to the jail for a couple hours of ping pong, then get locked up in our cells at nine o'clock, when the lights are turned off. On Sundays, we just lounge around the jail hoping we'll get a visitor.

One Sunday, David Yavitz brings me four tabs of mescaline. After he leaves, I give one to Hank, a huge Black Panther member who just entered the jail two days before. We eat the tabs and spend the rest of the day in the back of the jail watching the walls pulsate and change colors. He tells me he joined the Air Force to get trained in the use of sophisticated weapons so he can later train other Black Panthers in guerrilla warfare in preparation for the violent struggle that's coming between whites and Blacks across the nation.

At one point, tears stream down Hank's cheeks in a mescaline-induced display of emotion and he says, "You a good man, Bob, and I have a good feelin' 'bout you, but you see the day's gonna come when we Blacks gonna hafta blow all you mothafuckin' whites away cause it's the only way we'll ever achieve freedom from white rule."

Hank scares me with his talk about violent revolution. I try to steer the conversation toward nonviolent resistance and the importance of what Martin Luther King was trying to do. It seems

I've traveled light years from my APBA days and visions of the City. Hank discounts the effectiveness of civil disobedience, but seems to trust me. For a short time, I think we're friends. Every night during our two hours of free time, we smoke the pot that I've smuggled back in the jail. The other prisoners begin to join us in the back cell, where we can blow the smoke through the barred window, which has a lever to open the glass to allow in fresh air. One of us always stands guard in the front to make sure we aren't detected.

One night, the fire alarm goes off and all six of us prisoners are herded outside in what we're told is a fire drill. We have to stay outside for about fifteen minutes, then are led back inside. The first thing I notice is the film capsule we've stored the pot in is sitting on the window ledge in the back cell. I pick it up and hand it to Hank, who stashes it in a hole in the wall. A minute later, I notice blue ink all over my hands, so I go over to a wash basin to try to wash it off. Hank has ink on his hands, too.

The prison doors burst open. Five guards and the prison warden rush in, shouting orders. Everyone freezes. The guards separate Hank and me from the other prisoners. They spread-eagle Hank against the wall. He screams obscenities at them. One guard cracks Hank over the head with the butt of an M-16. Hank slumps to the floor and is dragged to one of the solitary confinement cells. I'm spread-eagled in the same way and told that if I open my mouth, I'll get my head bashed in, too. One of the guards finds the capsule of pot. I'm thrown into another solitary confinement cell next to Hank's and through the walls I can hear him singing, "Freedom. Freedom. Sometimes I feel like a motherless child . . . ." He keeps it up far into the night.

We're stuck in solitary for two days. The guards check on us almost every hour. Our meals are brought to us twice a day on trays that are placed on the floor just inside the cell door. We're also taken out of the cells twice a day for interrogation sessions, but neither of us says a word other than we want to see our lawyer. On the second day, Jerry Mahoney shows up at the jail. It takes him just a couple of minutes to figure out the guards bungled their bust because they didn't actually catch us with any pot in our possession. The blue ink we had on our hands was just circumstantial evidence.

Jerry goes over to the window ledge where the pot was found and sprinkled with some invisible fingerprinting powder. He runs a finger across the window ledge and gets the same blue ink on the finger. All Hank and I had to do was accidentally touch the window ledge to get the stuff on our hands. Jerry has blown a hole in their case against us, which could've added another year to our sentences. The story spreads throughout the base about the incompetent guards who busted their own prisoners inside their own jail and messed up the job so badly that they couldn't even prosecute.

I'm stuck in that solitary cell for the last two weeks of my stay at Beale's jail. One day, the guards take Hank away. I never find out what happened to him. I have no contact with anyone until the day comes for me to gather up my few belongings and be shipped by plane to Denver to complete my six-month sentence at the 332oth Retraining Group, where all the Air Force's nonviolent prisoners are sent in the hope of rehabilitating them, retraining them in a different career field, and sending them back into service to complete the time remaining on their four-year obligations.

I'm greeted at the Denver airport by an unarmed military policeman who drives me to Lowry Air Base. It's almost like basic training again, the way the prisoners are herded into open bay barracks, a hundred in each barracks, and given a strict daily regimen to follow: get up at four in the morning, have the beds made and living areas cleaned and be shaved, showered, and on the parade ground lined up in formation and ready at 4:15 to be marched a mile away to the chow hall for a breakfast of cold toast and runny eggs. We have to be done eating by 5:30 as that's when the regular soldiers on the base begin their breakfast. It's a madhouse to compete with a hundred prisoners haggling and pushing and shoving over the ten showers and ten sinks in the latrine. Someone's always getting knocked down and tension's always in the air, but no one can really fight because if he does, he'll get shipped out to Fort Leavenworth, Kansas for the remainder of his prison term. From what we all hear, you don't want to end up in Leavenworth with its brutal guards, hard labor, beatings, and time spent in The Hole.

When we return from the chow hall, another hour is spent cleaning the barracks. Then there's the morning inspection in which half of the prisoners have to remake their beds, redust every corner of their living spaces, and stand at attention for two hours waiting for the head guard to reinspect the premises. For the first two months, we go to rehabilitation classes for five hours a day. Basically, they're brainwashing classes. The military psychiatrists, chaplains, psychologists, doctors, and instructors all have one common theme: to show us prisoners that our way of thinking is wrong and bad and nonconformist and that the only way to become human beings again is to follow the path they're providing for us. In essence, that way is to pound repeatedly into our heads the fact that we've committed crimes against society and must change our thinking, our behavior, our very selves if we ever want to become worthy citizens again, reenter the military and eventually society and carry on with lives of dignity and worth despite the terrible stigma of shame we now have branded on our souls.

They tell us that they're offering us a second chance, something that only a country as great as the United States would do for its citizens, something only a humane and advanced democracy would think of doing. They tell us we're lucky to have this second chance. If we blow this chance, then God help us because, great as our country is, we'll never be able to live decent lives if we don't commit ourselves to rehabilitation.

That may be true for the other five hundred prisoners, but not for me, the lone prisoner of conscience. All the therapy classes, private psychiatric sessions, role plays, and discussions about morality, duty, obligation, and correct thinking only drive me deeper into myself. I can see right away that the first step toward rehabilitation is for the prisoner to admit he was wrong to have committed his crime. All around me, the prisoners are playing the game, showing their willingness to do what's expected of them. In their condescending, avuncular manner, the people in charge are pounding repeatedly in our heads what a mistake we've made in resisting authority and how we'll come around sooner or later to see the light. I continue to insist I haven't done anything wrong. I've merely refused to be sent to another country to kill people I have no quarrel with.

Still, it's not that I don't have any doubts about myself. These daily therapy sessions do put questions in my head. The psychiatrists are too skilled at twisting around my attempts to explain my thoughts and feelings. They're too skilled at showing me the contradictions of what I say, the lack of logic, the inconsistencies. They seize on my inarticulateness and turn it against me. Often, I want to fall on my knees and beg them to stop, to leave me alone. I quit talking to them, start giving them the silent treatment, but this only inspires them to mess further with my mind, to show me how *insane* I've become. Ever so gradually, I begin to believe them. They have me so tongue-tied and disoriented that I can't think straight. As each day passes, they're getting closer to breaking me down and getting me to admit they're right. They tell me I can be kept in the program indefinitely, even after completing my sentence. The threat seems real and scares me.

There are many hippies and counterculture types in Denver in 1970. Some of the prisoners who've passed through the rehabilitation course and returned to active duty can go into town during their off hours. Some of these hippie airmen come back on base with a stash to share with others. I've made friends with a few of them. Occasionally, we're able to sneak away for some tokes off a hash pipe.

One day, one of the prisoners turns me on to a hit of windowpane acid. I take it early in the afternoon, shortly before attending one of our psychiatric lectures and workshops. I start coming on in the middle of the class. It's excellent acid. I have no problems dealing with it. All the typical physical symptoms and sensations are there, but what I feel most distinctly is an absolute acceptance of everything. All is as it's supposed to be. All events of the past are as they're supposed to be. All events in the future will be as they're supposed to be. Each of the prisoners, the psychiatrists and guards, the mountains surrounding us, and the physical objects in the room and buildings has its own significance. It's my first experience of cosmic awareness and interconnectedness, my first experience of seeing and feeling the cosmic humor inherent in all things. Surrounded by about thirty other prisoners, I just sit there in my chair, a big Cheshire cat grin fixed on my face, completely absorbed in the experience, in the new thoughts and emotions, and in the awareness that everything is going to be OK.

Later on when we prisoners are marched in the snow to the chow hall about a half-mile away, I observe the most incredible sky and sunset I've ever witnessed. The cold wind penetrates my skin and stirs my thoughts and emotions. I feel at peace (almost as if I belong to the prison) and at one with everything and everyone. That night, well beyond the peak of the acid trip, I spend two hours engrossed in the sounds of a Grand Funk Railroad album playing repeatedly through the earphones of a fellow prisoner's stereo. From that moment forward, I resolve to resist peacefully and passively the military's attempts to rehabilitate me, while harboring no ill feelings toward them. I realize that, in the overall scheme of things, they too have their roles to play.

The idea of using the APBA game comes to me to further my cause. Why not? The authorities are already convinced of my insanity to have done something so absurd as to defy every young man's duty to fight in a far-off war to save democracy and crush the communist threat.

I've kept my APBA attaché case with me throughout my entire Air Force experience, occasionally bringing the game out to pass certain lonely hours back at Beale Air Base. It's in my prison locker with my other belongings. I start playing the game during the two hours of free time we prisoners have every night.

What a delight it is to spread the game boards and notebooks out on the little desk I'm allowed for writing letters, to take out the player cards of the 1967 National League season and the dice and dice cup and arrange everything neatly on the desk. I rattle the dice, scoop them back into the dice cup, mark down in the notebook each player's turn at bat, and announce the game in a low mumble. I replay the games in my head during the psychiatric sessions, answering the psychiatrists' questions with answers pertaining to end-of-the-month batting averages, team standings, and pitching leaders. The psychiatrists shake their heads and jot something down in their own notebooks.

Some of the other prisoners, most of them Black, start crowding around my desk in the evenings to relieve their own boredom and cheer for their favorite team. Some call me "that gone dude." Those same prisoners turn me on to a joint here, a pipe of hash there, and on three occasions a hit of acid.

The prison psychiatrists and authorities leave me alone. The therapy sessions end. I'm put to work every day doing the same clean-up details and cafeteria kitchen chores I had to do at the Beale Air Base prison. Once in a while, the guards get nitpicky like the time I have to do two hours of close order drill by myself on the parade ground because I was out of step marching to breakfast that morning, but it isn't bad considering how I'm back at my desk that night, APBA dice rattling in my hand, the same group of bored prisoners hanging out watching the game and good-naturedly ribbing me. One night, the prison warden comes to see me and asks a lot of questions. I explain to him that I'm not going to change my mind about rehabilitation. I don't care if I get a bad discharge. I just want out of the military. It's a waste of time for the Air Force to keep me beyond the end of my prison term. The warden nods in agreement.

On the day my prison time is up, I'm given back my duffel bag with all my belongings: two changes of clothes, an extra jacket, and nine hundred dollars. I'm also given my *undesirable* discharge papers. I have to sign a paper, acknowledging that if I ever set foot on a military base again, I'll be prosecuted. A security police car escorts me to the Denver airport. Snow is on the ground. The Rocky Mountains rise up in the distance. The driver lets me off at the airport. There are no handshakes, no words exchanged, just the driver's silent nod. I'm now an ex-con cast once again upon the face of the earth to wander and make my way the best I can.

9

Nomad Daze I

A ND so a new chapter of life started—my return to society, my "nomad daze." Looking back on it now, I can see it was a time that was no less important than what preceded it, but in a strange way more remote emotionally to me. Over the next twelve years, I'd dive head-first into the counterculture and be almost constantly on the move, jumping from job to job, developing no lasting relationships, and having no direction in life. The one constant was Mom's complete and unconditional love and support.

I'd changed a lot by the time I got out of the slammer. I was a confused young man, but determined to prove I could survive the scorn of society and family. I wanted to believe that Dad and Uncle Dick hadn't meant everything written in their renunciation letter, but pride wouldn't allow me to take the first step toward any kind of reconciliation.

I first stopped in Truckee to see Mom and Herb. They'd moved there two years before when Herb got a foreman job on a big construction project. Mom was overjoyed to see me. Herb, not so much. I returned to Fortuna and moved into a large, four-bedroom house at the end of 12th Street with Shannon and two other roommates. He'd managed to get out of the Air Force in the same manner as Uncle Dick had evaded service in World War II. Shannon was the oldest son of a family whose business was considered important to national security. He was now working for his father at their concrete plant on the Eel River.

Within a week, I found a job at the Louisiana Pacific plywood mill in Samoa. The job interview was a rude awakening to the realities of getting along in the real world. I had to write on the application form that I'd been in the military and kicked out with an undesirable discharge. The administrative head who did the hiring and firing was a guy called "Fat Manny" who'd played football at Humboldt State University. He asked me detailed questions about what happened and shook his head in disappointment at my answers. Fat Manny got his start at Van De Nor Lumber Company, so when he hired me, I figured he must've felt an obligation to Dad and Uncle Dick. I became a green chain puller and started out at the minimum hourly wage.

I had to hitchhike twenty miles every morning to catch the Eureka ferry that took the workers across the bay to the plywood mill. I usually caught a ride out of Fortuna with loggers on their way to work. The mornings were wet and cold. The other millhands at the ferry dock shuffled about, trying to keep warm as they waited for the ferry. The sun rose as we crossed the bay. The screams of sea gulls filled the air, mixing with the hum of the ferry's motor. The ferry would arrive shortly before the 7 a.m. sirens called the millhands to their stations.

The work was boring and repetitive: pulling large sheets of wet plywood as they came rolling down a long conveyor belt and stacking them on wooden carts that were hauled away by forklifts to the dry kiln, where the sheets were dried, stacked, and eventually pressed together into different sizes and lengths of plywood. It was harder labor than any I'd done in prison, but getting a salary and paying my own rent helped bring back some purpose and direction to my life.

June came and I still hadn't gone to visit Dad. I made a down payment on a used sports car. Not having to hitchhike any longer was a relief, but I was tired most of the time. The thought of having to spend the rest of my life on the green chain was depressing, but there seemed no alternative. As if on cue, I had another accident.

One night a few months after starting the new job, I was working a midnight overtime shift feeding strips of dried plywood into a machine that sprayed the sides with glue, compressed them, and cut them into wide sheets to be used as middle sections between two outside sheets of clean, high-grade plywood. I was feeding the individual strips into the compressor. One of the barbs sticking up from the links of chain rolling into the compressor caught the rubber glove I was wearing on my right hand. It pulled my arm into the compressor. With my left hand, I tried to reach the button that shut the compressor down, but the button was too far away. The chains were grinding into my flesh. I gave a desperate pull against the grinding action of the chains. My arm was suddenly freed, but a long gash along the forearm was stripped down to the bone. Another worker called for the foreman, who wrapped the arm the best he could and called an ambulance.

Dad was at the hospital when the ambulance arrived. Someone from the plywood mill called him about the accident. It was the first time I'd seen him since returning from prison. Luckily, a neurosurgeon was on duty. He unwrapped the bandages. Dad turned his head away. Tears formed at the corners of his eyes. In that moment, I felt an unspoken intimacy with him. The surgeon examined the arm carefully and barked some orders to a nurse. I was taken into surgery.

When I awoke the next morning, there was a cast on my arm. My fingers protruded from the end. Dad was seated in a chair next to the hospital bed, dark rims under his eyes.

"How are you feeling?" he asked.

"Tired."

I lifted my right arm with my left. I tried to move the fingers and found I could. I looked at Dad. He was smiling. "They had you in the operating room for about six hours. The doctor said it was a difficult operation, but you pulled through like a champ," he said.

"Will I be able to play basketball again?"

"The doctor said if you work hard at rehabilitating the arm when the cast comes off, it should be normal in about four months."

"Dad?"

"Yes?"

"Thanks for coming."

Several visitors came to see me. Mom flew over from Truckee to be with me for two days. The Kellys came in every day. In a gesture of reconciliation, Dad paid off the money I still owed on my car. The plywood mill paid all the hospital and physical therapy bills, as well as six months of compensation. For two months after my release from the hospital, I spent two hours every day at a physical therapy center. To speed up the rehabilitation process, I also spent hours at a time bouncing, lifting, shooting, and throwing a basketball against a wall and catching it with the injured arm. In the beginning, the pain was excruciating. The arm throbbed so much at night I couldn't sleep. Gradually, the pain subsided, and flexibility returned. Within four months, it had recovered its full strength.

Shannon and I moved into a small house in Eureka. In the fall, I signed up for some general education courses at Redwoods Junior College and began training for the basketball season. Tryouts for the team were to be held in October. Although I was only two years older than the other students, I felt poles apart from them. It was as if my experiences in the military and prison had aged me. The others seemed like children with their bright enthusiasm and optimism, their social cliques and parties. Most of them were fresh out of high school and, like myself two years earlier, had never been beyond the boundaries of Humboldt County.

I abandoned myself to basketball. At the practices, I was like a madman racing up and down the court during the different conditioning, dribbling, defense, jumping, and shooting drills. Offensively, I was inconsistent. My passes often hit the other players in the head, bounced a step beyond their reach, or soared too high for them to catch. My shots were poorly selected and sometimes forced. Only my defense showed any consistency. I made the team as a second-string guard.

The team had a mediocre season. I had a few good games, but I didn't feel a part of things. I was too different from the others. Study seemed superfluous. I had no academic interests. The classes were easy enough to pass with minimal effort. After two semesters, I dropped out of school to go back to work at the plywood mill. I was twenty-one with no education, a bad military record, and no prospects. The future seemed bleak.

Two months later, Herb passed through Humboldt County to take care of the final business of selling the Fortuna home. He called me and we went out to dinner. He was now the foreman of a construction project on the north side of Lake Tahoe. He offered me a chance to go to work for him as a laborer and get into a union. He explained this might be the last chance I'd have to make something of myself. I believed he had more concern about Mom's anxieties about my future than any altruistic intentions, but his offer provided a chance to escape the vacuum I'd fallen into. I said sure, thanks, appreciate it. Two weeks later, I moved to Lake Tahoe and rented a one-room cabin about twenty minutes from the work site.

My workdays consisted of carrying tools and boards for the carpenters, digging drainage ditches, nailing off roofs, sweeping up sawdust, and hauling garbage to a nearby dump. I spent most of my time alone, thinking about where my life was headed. I grew a beard and my hair reached down to my shoulders. Near the beginning of winter, Herb and I had an argument. He told me to cut my hair and shave my beard or he'd fire me. I flipped him the bird and quit.

I returned to Arcata, moved in with a hippie friend, and spent the winter getting high, living on my savings, and playing in an amateur basketball league. I was going through more changes I didn't understand. I felt a fundamental sense of not belonging, of no longer being an American. Something burned in my heart, calling me to make a move to thrust me out of my lethargy into confronting the outside world again.

One day while browsing through a bookstore, I found a book titled *Europe on Five Dollars a Day*. The book explained how it was possible to experience the world on a small amount of money and a lot of faith in one's fellow man. All a person needed was a passport, a backpack, and an adventurous spirit. The idea hit me like a hammer.

I set about making preparations. I still had about a thousand dollars in savings. I went to a travel agent and bought a round-trip ticket for a flight out of New York to Europe for two hundred dollars. The return ticket was good for a year. I applied for and got a passport. For another hundred dollars, I bought a three-month pass that was good for all the rail lines in western Europe. I was ready to hit the road. Three weeks later, the amateur basketball season ended. The next morning, I was out on the highway, thumb out, waiting for my first ride. With me were my life belongings contained in a small, leather backpack: three changes of clothes, a down-filled sleeping bag, a nylon poncho, five hundred dollars, and a leather bota bag for carrying liquid.

Three quick rides carried me beyond the redwood country to Highway 20, which cut across California to Lake Tahoe. An old rancher in a cattle truck picked me up and took me as far as Sacramento. I waited three hours before a Mexican in a beat-up Chevrolet pulled over. The Mexican chattered nonstop as we caught up with his friend, who was hauling a forklift on a flatbed truck to Reno. We plodded behind the truck at fifteen miles per hour. The sky was clear with many stars. We inched our way up the mountains. A full moon illuminated the snow blanketing the Sierra pines. Early in the morning, we arrived in Reno and parked the car to get a couple hours of sleep. Just after dawn, I caught another ride that took me into the desert. The driver let me out when he turned off the main highway.

The Nevada desert stretched out in all directions, a mixture of auburn wasteland, rolling tumbleweeds, and splotches of unmelted snow. In the far distance were the Rockies, their snow-topped peaks barely discernible on the horizon. They looked like a jagged spine. A VW van with a woman and two children on their way to Denver, Colorado stopped.

For the rest of the day, we continued through the Nevada

wasteland. By nightfall, we were partway into the Utah Salt Flats. We pulled to the side of the road on the outskirts of Salt Lake City to sleep.

Morning was a peaceful calm—grey clouds breaking up with traces of sunlight shimmering through them. We proceeded through the Wasatch Mountains, the road slick with snow and ice, across the Continental Divide, and on to the plateaus of Wyoming. A carpet of snow covered the land. The road seemed to continue forever. Occasionally, a jackrabbit bounded across the road. Here and there a distant elk lifted its head to scan our movement. At Cheyenne, the woman and her two children turned south. The ride had covered two days and three states.

Sticking to hitchhiking as my main mode of travel but once in a while riding a bus when I was stuck too long in one place, I passed across the Great Plains of Nebraska, out of the snow now and through farming towns with red-brick buildings and dirty, main-street sidewalks, where old folks sat languorously on benches watching the movement of the world. I stopped in Omaha and spent two days reading in a public library and walking the streets. I slept in a cheap room one night and the bus depot the next to save a few dollars.

On and on now, another six hundred miles to Peoria, Illinois. A rainy night. A three-dollar motel room with plaster walls and a rattling steam heater. A saggy mattress. A six-pack of cheap beer. A newspaper with stories about returning prisoners of war and Watergate. Morning and a bus ticket to Gary, Indiana, where I took a Skid Row room for one night. Across the expanse of Indiana, where squares of long, furrowed fields, ready for seed, stretched in all directions. Another ride to Cleveland.

Thoughts of the Kent State shootings filled my head as I

passed through Ohio into Pennsylvania and on toward Buffalo, New York. I spent one night sleeping in a wooded field off the shore of Lake Erie. Early the next morning, I walked along the beach, then stopped to watch the whitecaps form. The lake was an immense ocean that disappeared beyond the horizon. Grey clouds covered the sky. The sun struggled to break through. I continued another three miles through pollution, dilapidated ghetto buildings, broken glass, and abandoned cars to downtown Buffalo. I found the bus station and bought a ticket to New York City.

At last, there I was: bounding through the door of the Port Authority Bus Terminal. My first impression of New York was an endless forest of skyscrapers that made the redwoods pale in comparison. I stood transfixed, overwhelmed by the sound of car horns and construction machinery, by the smell of exhaust fumes and Armenian bakeries. I walked the sidewalks, mouth agape and mind empty. I found the William Sloane House YMCA on 34th Street and took a room.

For the next week, I explored the sights: Greenwich Village, Yankee Stadium, the Empire State Building, the United Nations, Rockefeller Center, Madison Square Garden. I watched double features in afternoon movie theaters for a dollar, then ate at ethnic delicatessens. A cast of characters filled this world—midget paraplegics, hipster pimps, hollow-eyed beggars, decrepit winos, Central Park artists, and sophisticated men and women in their business attire.

Finally, I was on Icelandic Air Lines Flight 181 on my way to Luxembourg. I was leaving behind the country of my birth, the country I no longer felt a part of, venturing forth with no itinerary, just the hand of fate to guide me. It was as if some divine source was dragging me toward an unknown destination.

It was blind obedience to a gut feeling, not unlike my refusal to fight in the Vietnam War.

The flight took fourteen hours, stopping once in Iceland to refuel. At last, the plane touched down in Luxembourg. I was on foreign soil for the first time in my life. After passing through customs, I walked around the fortress city. The medieval architecture and narrow, cobble streets were pleasing to my eyes, as was the green, wooded landscape that surrounded the city.

I was anxious, however, to be moving, to begin the adventure, so I boarded a train to Brussels, Belgium. I found a compartment to myself where I could be alone and think. In Brussels, I took a midnight train bound for Paris. The night was long with scattered periods of sleep. Early in the morning, the train arrived at the Gare du Nord. A heavy mist covered the city. I searched for three hours before finding a cheap room on the Left Bank. Fatigued from jet lag and walking, I passed out on my bed and slept for nearly eighteen hours.

For the next two days, I walked the streets of Paris and watched the frenzied movement of tourists and natives alike. High cirrus streamlined an azure sky. Flowers were blooming. The trees in the parks dressed themselves in green. The fragrance of spring was everywhere. Lovers walked arm in arm. Children bounded to and fro, ignoring their parents' admonitions. I was surrounded by activity and scores of people. For some reason, Paris intimidated me. I wasn't comfortable and felt the need to retreat from all the confusion to a quiet place where I could reflect on why I was in Europe, what I should do, and where I should go. I headed to Switzerland, to the Alps, where I could camp out and set my mind at ease.

I journeyed first to the foot of the Matterhorn. I spent three days there in solitude. On the third day, as I sat staring at the mountain, loneliness fell upon me. I hiked down the mountain road to the village of Visp and boarded a train to Florence, Italy.

I wandered through the city, barely conscious of the history surrounding me. I passed through the Uffizi and was attracted to Botticelli's paintings. At the Michelangelo Academy, I found in the *David* a moment of poignant thought, of tender expression, of profound emotion preserved for eternity. What men these Botticellis, these Da Vincis, these Dantes! What purpose of mind they'd possessed. Perhaps art was the road to salvation. Perhaps art could liberate the soul from the pain of living.

I left Florence and spent two days on the trains, getting off only to buy bread and wine. One night, I stopped in Naples and slept in an abandoned construction site. I awoke several times to the sound of rats scurrying around me. I boarded a southbound train early the next morning. The compartments were crowded, so I slept on the floor of the narrow corridors. I rode the train ferry that crossed the strait between the mainland and Sicily. There were only a few peasants on the train from Messina. About half the distance across the northern coast of Sicily, the train stopped at the fishing village of Cefalu. On an impulse, I got off.

The sun was high in a cloudless sky. It was very warm. The village lay at the base of a large headland. The buildings were all old. The smell of fish and sea filled the air. Long lines of laundry on rooftops flapped in the breeze. Copper-skinned children ran laughing and shouting through the narrow, meandering streets. Many small skiffs were moored in the harbor, where weather-beaten men patiently mended their nets. A castle rested on a hill overlooking the village. Nearby was an old cathedral.

I walked along the long stretch of beach outside the village for about a mile until I found a comfortable, isolated spot to camp. The white sand shimmered under the hot sun. I washed my clothes and hung them to dry on a tree. For most of the next two days, I lay on the beach and watched the fishermen in dinghies gather in their nets. It was a peaceful time and the States seemed far away.

On the third day, I packed my things and walked back into the village. I boarded the first train back to Messina, settled in an empty compartment, not knowing where to go next, and contemplated my future as the countryside flashed by the window.

I headed up the western coast of Italy. In Paola, I boarded a train inland to the mountains. The train chugged up a steep incline until the ocean was far below. The sun was a dazzling brilliance on the water as the train rounded the final bend to wind its course toward the heel of the boot of Italy. The country was green and fresh with many beech and pine trees. In the village of Cosenza, I waited a few hours before catching another train.

The next evening, I was in Brindisi, a southern Italian port town, boarding a ferry to the Greek island of Corfu off the coast of Albania. The following morning, the ferry approached the island. The sun was just above the calm sea. The town of Corfu was bleached in the morning light. Low mountains rose jaggedly in the distance. Once on land, I exchanged some money, then set out to explore the streets of the town before hopping a bus into the countryside.

I joined a group of travelers at a camping site a few miles north of the town. It was a peaceful place across the road from a stretch of white beach. There was plenty of shade provided by a grove of olive trees. Most of the other campers were young people: Germans, Scandinavians, Canadians, French, Dutch.

The days on the island were tranquil days of lounging around and lying nude on a ledge of rock by the sea. The outside world ceased to exist. In the evenings, small groups gathered at a nearby cantina for suppers of *souflaki,* cucumber salad, and potatoes cooked in olive oil. Everyone drank *ouzo,* the potent Greek wine. The local patrons, warm and friendly people who'd lived their entire lives on the island, danced to the music of a jukebox. There was much laughter, handshaking, and toasting of drinks.

Afterward, the travelers returned to the camping site to gather around a fire, pass bottles of *ouzo,* and watch the stars. The conversation was animated. It covered many topics in many languages—voyages to other lands, politics, music, art, literature, philosophy. I'd never seen such a gathering. Poets, musicians, painters, political dissidents, refugees, everyone was involved in something important and meaningful. Their lives seemed fulfilled and exciting. I was in the midst of a kind of international underground group with its own grapevine of information, its own lifestyle that enabled all to travel in an inexpensive manner to many countries exchanging cultures, knowledge, and love. I envied the zest and capacity for life these people had. More than that, I envied their ability to speak several languages. I could barely manage in my own.

When it came my turn to speak, I told of my experiences as a conscientious objector and my life in military prison. I was baffled by the response of the others. There was an admiration for what I'd done, for the courage of my convictions. The others listened respectfully and offered encouragement and advice. They flooded me with names and addresses in many countries, offers to stay should I happen to visit. They gave me books to read. I bathed luxuriously in this much-needed encouragement.

A woman entered my life. Her name was Kreta, a lovely Norwegian with soft, blue eyes, a radiant smile, and long, flowing blond hair. She was an artist who'd just come from Spain. Her lust for life was infectious. Her uninhibited approach to life made a great impression on me. The image she created of the world as she'd experienced it was rich with romance, vibrant with life, alluring in its potential for adventure. She excited me most when she talked about Spain.

"You must visit Spain by all means if you are traveling in Europe. Your education will not be complete without the experience. It's so different from, yet so representative of, Europe. If you want to understand life, then you must see Spain," she said.

"Spain is the true melting pot of culture, not your America with its machines of destruction and your people so much like spoiled children. And Spain's artists! Her Picassos, her Dalis, her Goyas, her Velazquezes, her one and only El Greco, who was really a Cretan but found refuge and a source of inspiration among the Spanish people. You, too, may find inspiration there to explore the confusion in your heart. You have an artistic soul. I sense that. Perhaps there's a writer or painter in you somewhere. You have to go to Spain."

I spent the next week with Kreta, swimming and laughing, sunbathing and drinking, sometimes smoking pot, learning about the world of art. It was a time of broadening my perspective, of dreaming and thinking and reading, but soon the wanderlust was upon me again.

On the morning I left Corfu, the sky was filled with grey clouds, strands of dawn-light sifting down through them. Far away on the water, a freighter moved along peacefully. Seated on the edge of the road next to the beach, a Greek boy watched the freighter's steady movement. I kissed Kreta goodbye, hoisted my backpack, hitched a ride into town, and bought a bus ticket to Athens.

I spent three more months bumming around Europe. From Athens, I hitchhiked through the pastoral Yugoslavian countryside;

the Alpine meadows, forests, and mountain peaks of Austria; and the deep green of southern France before heading to Spain.

I traveled about Spain for three weeks on rickety trains. From the windows, I could see everything with a casual air: dusty red plains, dark mountains in the distance, olive trees in high hills, slow-moving rivers, long stretches of empty space, and ancient villages.

I rented a room for a week in Seville. From there, it was on to Madrid to see the Prado Museum. I spent an entire day there studying the paintings of El Greco, Velazquez, and Goya. Bosch's *Garden of Earthly Delights* held me in complete awe. I felt a kinship with Bosch's madness, with his distorted perception of the world, his hallucinogenic portrayal of life and its absurdity. In my ignorance of the world of art, I'd never dreamed the insanity of man could be portrayed with such power of sinister projection. I resolved that if I could ever learn to express myself in some medium, the picture of man I eventually portrayed would contain parallels to the grotesque perception of Bosch.

My money was nearly spent. I boarded a train to Paris, where I confirmed my reservations on a Luxembourg Airlines plane back to New York. I hitchhiked to Luxembourg and spent my last night sleeping in a wooded field an hour from the airport. A day later, my plane descended upon the runway of John F. Kennedy Airport. The European experiences and revelations and the entire dream-ambience of that portion of my life were gone. It was as if I'd awakened from a long, undisturbed sleep to find myself grappling with reality again.

After passing through customs, I took a bus from the airport to downtown Manhattan. It was the middle of summer, hot and muggy, and sweat poured off me. The harsh sounds of jackhammers, hydraulic equipment, and car horns blasted my ears. The smells of soot, garbage, and pollution burned my nose. I bought another bus ticket to New Jersey to escape the congestion. It was near sundown when I got off the bus. I found a place to camp on the outskirts of some town. Early the next morning, I packed and ate a breakfast of oranges and cheese. I checked my wallet. I had twenty-two dollars left. Then I walked to an onramp leading to Highway 80, the great road west.

Two rides took me into Pennsylvania, where I hit the jackpot. A Navy man being transferred from the East Coast to the West Coast swooped me off the long stretch of highway. We breezed through the thick green of Pennsylvania. Then it was on into Ohio. Halfway across the state, we stopped for a night's rest. With an early start the next morning, we plowed straight through Ohio and Indiana into Illinois and Iowa, then across the Mississippi River westward to Nebraska, through dusty corn and wheat fields, then into the plains of Wyoming as far as Cheyenne. It was a long day, the summer sun spilling waves of heat on the road. A steady haze lay constantly before us until nightfall. We pulled over by a truck stop to sleep.

In the morning, it was out of Wyoming into the Wasatch Mountains of Utah. In Salt Lake City, we parted company, the Navy man heading south and I west. A Mormon student gave me a ride fifty miles into the desert before his car developed a radiator leak and the engine overheated. The driver disappeared to the other side of the road to hitch back to Salt Lake City. I began to walk. Soon I was in the middle of a straight stretch where I could be seen from a long way off. I set my backpack down and waited.

A white sea of salt surrounded me. The road ran straight as far as I could see until it narrowed into a cloud of heat rising into the distance. The afternoon sun beat down on my shoulders.

A strong wind sent tumbleweeds rolling at great speeds. Particles of sand lashed at my body. I stood for what seemed an eternity with only an occasional freight truck rumbling by. Finally, a family in a pickup truck stopped and gave me a ride as far as Wendover on the Utah-Nevada state line. Shortly after sunset, a station wagon on its way to San Francisco stopped. I slept in the back, waking to the sight of the Oakland Bay Bridge.

By late afternoon, three more rides took me to Arcata. I was back where I'd started. I believed I'd set a hitchhiking record: from the East Coast to the West Coast in four days. I had only about fifteen dollars left, but knew I'd find a job soon and make it through the initial tough month or so it would take to get my feet back on the ground.

The journey had given me an answer to what I'd been seeking since my court martial. The single sentence I uttered in response to my order to fight in the Vietnam War had saved four and a half years of my life and instilled in me an inchoate awareness of the power of language. The experiences in Europe had now reinforced that awareness and stimulated a need to express myself. I now had a purpose. I'd try to become a writer. I'd learn the craft. Through the writing, I'd rid myself of the confusion and derangement that clung to me so tightly.

I found a job as a janitor in an elementary school in Orick, a town of eight hundred people on the California coast about fifty miles north of Arcata. I rented a small room near the school and started training to be a writer. I was practically illiterate. I had no idea of the fundamentals of grammar or what comprised good literature.

I had to work only five hours a day, five days a week. I often took strolls along the isolated stretch of beach south of Orick, along the riverbank of the Mad River, and on the logging roads that led into the redwood forest that skirted the town's eastern flank. I spent most of my free time, however, reading all the books I could, copying down sentences and descriptions that appealed to me, and recording in a notebook my recently completed journey. Near the beginning of December, when the winter rains started, I quit the job, returned to Arcata, and went back to school.

I found another job at a small redwood lath mill in Arcata. In March, I entered the journalism department at Humboldt State University. My boss at the lath mill agreed to let me work part-time in the mornings to accommodate my schedule of afternoon classes. I also began playing amateur basketball with Shannon again.

The next two years were like a return to innocence. All that existed was study and basketball. There was even a partial return to normalcy in my family relationship. Dad was retired and occupied with building a new house. He'd converted to the Seventh Day Adventist faith and with it came a greater acceptance of my refusal to fight in Southeast Asia. He even offered to give some financial help for my schooling.

I bypassed all the required general education courses to concentrate on writing and literature classes. Two of my classes required the students to do actual fieldwork and turn in stories to the local newspaper every week. When five of my stories were accepted and printed with my own by-line, I felt that particular joy every writer craves: seeing his name in print.

After nearly two years of study, it was time to get serious about writing fiction. Once again, I had to break away from Humboldt County and find my way in the world. I'd gotten as much as I could out of my studies at the university. I packed my belongings—a few changes of clothes and two boxes of books—into my car and moved to Los Angeles. I found a small apartment and a job working as an assembly-line bookkeeper in the main southern California office of Bekins Moving and Storage.

In the evenings and on weekends, I spent hours at the typewriter, working on short stories that became increasingly longer as I looked ahead to being able to write a novel. I was like a marathon runner in training, starting out with short sprints and working gradually into longer and longer endurance runs. Sometimes I worked on character sketches, sometimes on place descriptions. At other times, I practiced stylistic devices such as stream-of-consciousness narrative, alliterative writing, understatement in the Hemingway tradition, or metaphorical comparisons.

The truth was I had no style of my own. I was in a stage of imitating every writer I fell in love with, only to abandon him or her shortly and copy the style of the next writer who struck my fancy. Of all the writers I was frantically trying to study, Henry Miller appealed to me the most. Miller's intoxication with language, his free spirit, his exaltation of life as seen from the gutter, his unbounded ego, his faith and sense of humor and love of the cranks and artists who inhabited his world all stirred in me deep emotions concerning the life I'd chosen to pursue. Miller instilled in me a belief in the divine guidance of the artist. He made me want to be a writer, to plunge into the depths of human experience.

Nearly a year passed. I made preparations for returning to Europe. Still under the influence of Miller, I decided it would be impossible to write in the U.S. I believed if I was to experience the true artist's life, I had to live and work where the artist and his work were appreciated and encouraged. The U.S. seemed the antithesis of that ideal. I'd return to Paris to recapture the past, in particular the events of that journey I'd taken four years earlier in search of an identity and a direction in life. I believed I was ready to begin a novel. On January 11, 1977, I boarded a plane to Paris, not knowing what the future held, but filled with confidence and a faith that there was meaning in everything I'd experienced, in everything that would come.

10

Nomad Daze II

I FOUND a cheap room at the Hotel des Mines on the Boulevard Saint-Michel. It was a small cubicle with a bed, a sink, a writing desk, a closet where I placed my duffel bag containing the few necessities I'd brought with me, and a window that looked out on a brick building next door and a drainage pipe decorated with pigeon shit.

I accomplished little the first week except the daily entries I made in a journal. I passed much of the time reflecting on my past while walking the gloomy Parisian streets.

The walking prepared me for the writing. As I paced briskly up and down the major boulevards and narrow, winding streets, along the Seine, past the thousands of nondescript faces, by the centuries of man's architectural achievements, the outline of the novel took shape. Everything came back in a vivid recapturing of the past: the months I spent in the Air Force prison; the journey across the U.S. and Europe when I made one discovery after another hitching around, riding trains, and sleeping in the streets; the long nights of study after returning to the States and poring over ideas and literary works and language unintelligible to me in the beginning but which gradually took on a semblance of meaning through my perseverance and many attempts of putting down on paper all the experiences that fate had provided me with. It was all interrelated—each suffering, adventure, chance encounter, action, result—and I saw it all taking shape as something more than transient thoughts as I walked and walked that first week.

At first, the going was slow and tedious, but each day brought progress. I set up a disciplined program of writing four hours, reading four hours, walking the streets, returning to the room for a couple more hours of writing, then retiring to bed to think of the day before falling asleep. The cubicle in which I lived and worked became as familiar as any place in which I'd lived. I thought of it as my little haven of refuge for the insane.

I found myself visiting all the places Hemingway had written about in A Movable Feast. The Closerie des Lilas was now a high-priced cafe for tourists. There were no famous writers or artists to be seen. The statue of Marshall Ney was still there, but gone were the war veterans who wore medals on their chests and sipped their aperitifs at the Closerie. The sawmill beneath the flat at 113 Rue Notre Dame des Champs, where Hemingway and Hadley had lived, was gone and the flat itself condemned and boarded up. The Shakespeare and Company bookstore was still on the Rue de l'Odeon. Much of the old atmosphere still prevailed, but there was a newer commercial side to the store.

My wandering took me to all parts of Paris. There were the many nights exploring the Left Bank with nothing else to do but watch the street people—the old women sprawled over vents on side streets to keep warm, the musicians strumming their guitars, a hat partially filled with coins at their feet, the slow-moving, red-cheeked gendarmes patrolling their beats, the gaudy prostitutes.

There were the leisurely daytime strolls. I loved the smell of the creperies, where thin pancakes were dispensed to street customers by old women hovering over circular griddles on cold, grey days. I loved window-shopping, peering at the individual shops of each street—boot shops, glove shops, perfume shops, bookshops, clothing shops—each with its own unique display. I often lounged in the brasseries, the bars where people stood and drank. Outside each bar were crowded tables that faced the streets. Seated at one of these tables, I could engage in more people-watching. There were the ubiquitous food markets and fish marts with their neatly arranged rows of fresh fish stacked on ice. There was the smell of the sea at dusk when the fish marts were given a fresh douching, the water flowing to the streets, men in long rubber aprons with buckets in their hands laughing and bickering with one another.

There were the day noises of construction: jackhammers, hydraulic equipment, shovels clashing with rock, trucks grumbling and changing gears in a high-pitched whine. Often my strolls took me to the Seine, glittering with barges and boats. I watched it flow in a timeless march past architectural wonders. The Louvre: I went there as often as possible to study the grim, mystical atmosphere of Rembrandt, the still lifes of Chardin, the sensuality of Reubin, and all my favorites of the Impressionists. The Notre Dame Cathedral: its peak pointed to heaven in impressive supplication. The Eiffel Tower: it loomed over the grey, winter landscape like a stairway to the gods.

I loved the parks with their pondering sculptures, bundled women, children playing soccer, lovers in intimate embrace, drifters tossing breadcrumbs to pigeons, bare trees in death slumber awaiting their spring birth. I often ran through the Luxembourg Gardens, my favorite of the parks. The running was best when my writing was slow and wearisome and I was troubled. I was free of everything except the rhythm of arms and legs pumping, heart beating, images and abstract thoughts racing through my mind. And always, at the end of those invigorating and therapeutic walks when the world appeared with much clarity, there was the return to my cubicle, my drab little haven, my place of rest, of work.

One day after I'd been in Paris for about two months, I returned to my cheap hotel room to find two men at the front desk trying desperately to communicate a message in English to the clerk, who spoke only French. I'd picked up a little French by then and was able to give a crude interpretation to the clerk. The two men were very happy and invited me to have a cup of tea with them at a cafe across the street.

Hassan was an Iranian businessman. Ataullah was an Afghan motel owner. Both were in Paris on business trying to sell carpets. They were disgusted with Paris because the people seemed cold and indifferent to them. I was the first person who'd helped them. They were so impressed with my friendliness that they invited me to return with them to their countries. Hassan said that life in Iran was not expensive, and it was easy to find an English teaching job. My money was dwindling rapidly and the chance for adventure in a country I knew little about appealed to me. I accepted the invitation.

Hassan and Ataullah first had to visit a friend in Germany. Two weeks later, I took a train to Basel, Switzerland, where I rented a room and phoned Hassan. The next night, he met me at the German-Swiss border. From there, we went to a tavern in Lörrach to have a drink and meet Thomas Knorr.

Thomas was a small, thin man in his early thirties. He had curly, blond hair, a handsome smile, and amiable, blue eyes. He'd first met Hassan eight years before in Iran when he smuggled everything from guns to hashish to make a living. In recent years, he'd turned to a more legitimate and profitable trade. Through Hassan, he began buying rare and valuable carpets and selling them to collectors in Germany. He was proficient in Farsi and Pashto and now spent six months of every year traveling into the deserts of Iran and Afghanistan to live and trade with nomad tribes. He was the proprietor of a veritable house-museum and an expert on the art and history of the Near East.

After several beers, we went to Thomas's house in the hills above Lörrach. His wife and two children were in bed, but Ataul-lah was still awake and greeted me warmly. Thomas showed me around the two-story, brick-and-stone farmhouse. Inside were dozens of handwoven carpets of every conceivable size, shape, color, and pattern. They were everywhere, abounding on the floors, in large, wooden chests, and on the walls of every room. There were also many other types of artwork scattered here and there: china, pins, bracelets, jewelry, boxes, paintings, stoneware, sculptures of bronze and stone, everything ranging in age from centuries in the past to the present.

Thomas led us outside to his barn. A yurt was assembled inside the barn. It was circular with a fence of thin, pointed reeds that surrounded the base. The basic support was an interwoven framework of branches of a thick, strong wood curved at the top to form half arches. Overlaid on the foundation was a covering of animal hides that formed the walls and ceiling. Inside the yurt, a circle of stones was placed in the center of the dirt floor. This was the fireplace. There was an open spot in the center of the ceiling for smoke to escape.

Hassan was tired and returned to the house to go to bed. Thomas lit a kerosene lamp. He, Ataullah, and I sat down on some carpets and smoked a pipe of hashish.

"Hassan says you are a writer," Thomas said. "What kind of book are you writing?"

I explained how I was trying to use my experiences as a conscientious objector to the Vietnam War as the basis for a novel about a drifting, alienated generation in search of itself.

"I hope you can be comfortable while you are here. You may use the yurt as your room and workplace for as long as you like. Ataullah also sleeps here, but he is quiet and won't bother you."

Ataullah nodded and smiled.

"You're very kind," I said.

"Think nothing of it. Many people in many places have helped me. I was a stranger to all of them, yet they gave freely of themselves. I'm in a position now to help others, so I do. It's the way of the nomad. Please think of my place as yours while you're here. Good night."

The days at Thomas's passed quickly. There was a continual stream of vagabonds, poets, musicians, drug smugglers, and art connoisseurs from all parts of the world passing through. It seemed his house was a stopping point where they could share a meal, a story, a drink, and a pipe of hashish. Thomas and his wife Undine—a stocky woman with a gentle face—were kept busy from sunup to sundown. They treated all their guests as if they were members of a large, international family.

Of all the people who passed through the doors, Ataullah remained the one who attracted my attention most. We often went for long walks together in the afternoons. Ataullah spoke longingly and proudly of his home. He didn't like the fast pace of the Western world, the way people "all are like machines." He spoke of the vast stretches of desert and of the remarkable way the desert could change and how a man could think and feel a closeness with the Almighty Allah in such an environment. There was no need for the machines of the West, no need for the crazy, reckless traffic, the airplanes and modern skyscrapers and computers and insurance and a mad obsession for money. He longed for the simplicity and leisureliness of Afghanistan, where people had time for one another, where there was a pride in their virility, strength, and tradition.

One day while walking along a path in the hills behind the house, Ataullah said, "I like this path. There are no cars on it and I think of Afghanistan, my other life. It is much different here, Bob-*jan*. You must come to visit me. There are no cars or machines. We are a close family and do not need these things. The children laugh and play. The men and women are happy. The people here in Europe are all for themselves and their machines. In Afghanistan, we need only the family to be happy.

"You must always be who you are, Bob-*jan*. I miss my home very much. That is why I smoke the hashish more in Germany than at home. So I can dream. But I am not afraid. I wear my own clothes here. I know the people laugh, but I am not afraid of them."

There was something about Ataullah's honesty and sincere need for open communication and companionship that I admired. He was not a large man, but he was solid with strong, massive hands. His hair was cut short and cropped down on his head. His beard was thick and black, his lips full and expressive. There was a light darkness to his skin, almost a sallowness, but he seemed a healthy man. He complained occasionally of a sharp pain in his stomach, which he attributed to the different food he was eating. His eyes were dark brown, squinted between flat eyelids. His gaze was probing.

That evening, Thomas offered to share a pipe with two local German friends, Ataullah, and me. Hassan had gone into Lörrach to one of the bars. We went outside to the barn and entered the yurt. Ataullah built a fire. We sat around the fire, smoked a bit, and passed around a bottle of wine. Thomas brought out a cassette player and put on a rock 'n' roll tape.

I sat quietly, legs crossed, and watched the actions of the others. Thomas was intently rewiring one of the speakers. The two Germans, one somewhat laconic and meditative, the other giggly and drunk, were engaged in a private conversation. Ataullah stood up and began dancing at one side of the yurt in a rhythmic expression of the hands and face.

The drunken German appeared to make fun of Ataullah. There was a mockery in his laughter. Ataullah completed his dance and sat quietly before the fire. He took a drink from the bottle, a scowl slowly forming on his face. The drunken German reached for the bottle. Ataullah kept a firm grip on the bottle and looked the German hard in the eyes.

"You do not take the bottle. You do not order. You say please first." Ataullah's voice was both threatening and restrained.

There was a moment of tension in which Ataullah and the German stared at each other, both gripping the bottle. The moment passed. The German relaxed his grip and politely asked Ataullah to pass him the bottle.

After the two Germans went home, Ataullah turned to me and said, "Bob-*jan*, I know what that man is. I know his life. My inside eyes can see his inside eyes. He is nothing inside. But I am a guest here and cannot tell him the truth of what I know."

Thomas put on a tape of Afghan music. Ataullah explained

everything in Afghan music was symbolic of a spiritual quest. The sound of birds could be heard mixing with the strange wailing of a human voice, the pounding of bongo-type drums in metaphysical rhythm, and the sad strumming of a *dambura*.

Ataullah began dancing again, his eyes closed, his hands moving in circular and outward gyrations, his body spinning in a whirlwind like an ice skater in a graceful twirl, his head jerking back and forth, appearing to slide from shoulder to shoulder. The music was pleasing, the fire hypnotizing, the ambience mystical. I applauded the performance. Ataullah was pleased.

"When the Afghan dances, he is trying to release the inside man to the outside." Ataullah pointed to the sky and showed the circular movements of his hands. "When a man has reached his best, he can do this. It is very nice, yes?"

Satisfied with the evening, Ataullah went to bed. I stayed up a little longer with Thomas, enjoying the quiet, the fire, the companionship.

"It's very nice here in the yurt, don't you think? But in the winter it takes a lot of wood to keep warm. I'm too lazy to cut so much. You can stay here as long as you want in the yurt if you want to cut the wood. It would be nice for you, Bob. You could have a typewriter here to work. It would be very peaceful."

"That's very kind of you to offer. But I think I'll continue to Iran with Hassan. One of these days, when you have some free time, I'd like to speak with you about that part of the world. I'm afraid I know nothing about it."

"Yes. When the time is right. When the time is right, I will tell you what I know and what you need to know. But not tonight. Soon. I promise you."

Over the next few days, I came to know Thomas much better. Although he was but five-foot-seven and a hundred twenty-five pounds, he seemed a much larger man. Everyone around him, including the vagabonds who continually passed through his home, looked up to him for guidance and entertainment. He carried himself with what was, to me, a spaced-out self-assurance. At times, his eyes bulged out of their sockets; they were always scanning, perceiving. He looked people directly in the eye. His countenance—whether in thought, action, or speech—showed a continual activity of the brain. His forehead was lined with small wrinkles, not from age but from perpetual pondering.

His body was one of the most flexible I'd ever seen. He was more comfortable sitting on his haunches, feet flat on the ground, chin rested on his knees, than in an upright chair. When on the floor playing *Karumbo*—an Afghan game of skill that resembled a combination of billiards and marbles and was played on a board with chips to be flicked by the player's fingers into corner pockets—his legs were flat on the floor, his feet pointed outward at right angles, and his head perched forward to see things as closely as possible. In this position, he looked like a simian on all fours.

One evening, Thomas invited me upstairs to smoke a pipe, play some *Karumbo*, and visit. Our conversation turned to various philosophies of life. I felt a bit like an inexperienced student listening to the pleasant lecturing of a wise, old savant. An outpouring of words flowed from Thomas's mouth. His speech was a gentle expression without pause. I had the feeling there was so much inside Thomas, such an abundance of knowledge and energy, that it was to my detriment to interrupt him. I listened intently. He spoke of smuggling experiences and adventures in distant lands, his life in California with the people surrounding the Jefferson Airplane rock band, his years of study of the languages and art of the Near East, his trips to the remotest regions of Pakistan, Afghanistan, and Iran in search of rare carpets. He spoke of his dreams of international brotherhood, freedom, adventure, and his need to stay in touch with people who'd not lost their dreams.

A few nights later after everyone had gone to bed, Thomas and I took some psilocybin. We put on our coats and went for a walk. The night was cold but invigorating. We walked to the highest point of the hill behind his house. We could see all of Basel on one side and Lörrach on the other. The lights glimmered below in a U-shape as if we were on an island surrounded by a sea of stars. Nearby were black silhouettes of bare trees. Snow was on the ground. Thomas looked wistfully into the distance.

"Bob, this may be one of the most beautiful places in the world. This spot is right at the southern tip of the Black Forest and is unique. From here you can see three countries. I love this place. But it's so hard to live here much of the time. There are many games to play. People are coming and going all the time, people wanting to smoke a pipe, straight customers looking at carpets, people staying as if I'm running a motel. Everyone wants something. It's very difficult to handle constantly."

"I've noticed," I said. "You're on the go constantly from morning to late at night. It must put a strain on you. It seems to me eventually you're going to collapse. I can't believe your wife puts up with cooking for all these people. And your kids probably would like to spend more time with you."

"Yes, it does get to them and to me, but it's important to experience it. There's so much that keeps me here. Especially my mother and father. But I'd also like to live in a community where there's brotherhood and people helping each other. Here there's too much suspicion and narrow thinking. Most of the people here are trapped by their environment. I need to break free from it all. I think often of the things I've done in the past, the adventures, and sometimes I believe I was closer to being free in those days. It's possible, I think, to find such a place. Did I tell you about my six friends who have a farm in New Zealand? I helped them make all the connections and contacts. They made one run, sold their dope somewhere in New York for an incredible price, and now they're completely free with their lives.

"This is my dream: to have a group of people who are together and could set up a kind of world community, say, with one group in California, another in Canada or Spain or South America, and maybe one here in the Black Forest. In this way, every couple of years everyone could trade environments and not fall into the same pattern of life. It would be healthy for all involved. Everyone would be continually learning new cultures and ideas. But this is all very idealistic and would take a lot of money with people who were intellectually and spiritually committed, a kind of international utopia for artists and free thinkers where they would not be hampered by politics and wars."

A heaviness came over Thomas. He sighed, a cloud of breath passing from his mouth into the night air. He seemed for a moment very much alone.

"But these are all just thoughts," he said. "Too fleeting, too fast. Ah, Bob, Asia will change you."

We returned to the yurt, built a fire, and as shadows danced against the animal-hide walls, I listened until the early hours of the morning to what Thomas knew about the history, religion, and politics of Iran and Afghanistan.

Hassan bought a new BMW car, which he said he'd later sell in Iran to cover the cost of the journey. Ataullah would take a train after Hassan and I departed.

We spent a day passing through the Swiss Alps. In the

beginning, Hassan's driving frightened me. He flew along the mountain roads as if in a grand prix road race, taking chances passing other cars at high speeds on blind corners. He laughed at my fear and told tall tales of his adventures as a driver in the Iranian military.

We arrived in Milan, Italy and took a room. The next day, the journey continued east through a thick fog to Trieste. We entered Yugoslavia. I took notes on the passing scenery: distant blue hills, scattered farms, stone-and-brick houses, peasants pacing the sides of the road with hoes slung over their shoulders.

We continued into the night toward Bulgaria, the BMW rushing past Soviet military trucks on a winding, rocky road. We arrived at the Yugoslav-Bulgarian border early in the morning. A Bulgarian military guard detained us for two hours before granting our visas at dawn.

We entered Sofia. Military transport trucks moved slowly along cobble streets. There were no smiles on the faces of the men and women shoveling dirt on the sides of the road, nor on the faces of the ubiquitous police. We headed into the country, passing over dirt roads and cobble roads and through peasant villages and industrial towns. Everywhere we passed, we saw old peasant women with slouched backs, bundled in woolen scarves, socks, and sweaters, packing hoes over their shoulders, pacing slowly in groups of three and four to the fields.

We arrived in Istanbul, Turkey, where I got a visa for entry into Iran. We spent a day exploring the activity of the streets, visiting mosques with high-reaching minarets, and haggling with vendors and merchants of all types. The streets were full of older American cars, horse carts, all kinds of carts competing for limited, dirty space.

We headed east toward Ankara. The road from Istanbul to

Izmit was a solid stream of trucks and buses carrying great amounts of supplies and goods to Iran—gas, food, construction equipment, pipes and girders, tires, wood, people, even other cars and trucks. On this road, Hassan proved his ability as the self-proclaimed best driver in the East. He swerved to the left and right to pass trucks in front of us, paved new lanes in the dust, narrowly missed oncoming traffic, squeezed between huge trucks where there seemed no space, and passed to the extreme left of trucks passing other trucks. He weaved and honked, braked and shifted gears furiously, and screamed at the other drivers.

Finally, we arrived in Ankara and spent the night. From Ankara to the Turkish-Iranian border was roughly fifteen hundred kilometers. Hassan told me that the next section of road was the most dangerous part. Kurdish bandits were said to be in the mountains and would stop cars traveling alone. It was best to drive during the day and in groups of three or four cars.

We left Ankara on a sunny morning. Ahead were sun-baked hills with stone-and-mud houses scattered throughout. In the distance lay looming, white mountains. We climbed higher into the hills. Strong winds howled. We passed sparse, wind-sculpted brush, thin patches of snow, and an occasional mountain village where the soil was worked by hand.

We headed into the high eastern mountains, the road rising to summits where wind flurries were a blinding white, then dipping to lower elevations where boulders of slush and white mud crashed against the sides and frame of the car. At one point, we passed a mountain village of about twenty-five rock huts covered with snow. I wondered how these mountain people could survive the winters.

It took two more days to reach the Iranian border. In that time, we once encountered Kurdish bandits on horseback, passed a wreck involving a bus and a truck near Erzurum, and saw several trucks forced off the side of the road. A blizzard forced us to stop for several hours before we could start moving again. We covered ourselves with our sleeping bags and waited for the storm to subside. When we were able to start again, the road became worse, filled with large potholes. Trucks approaching from the opposite side splattered the BMW with slush and thick, brown mud. One truck sprayed us with small stones and the windshield cracked.

Finally, we dropped out of the last elevation to the lower ground. We were out of the snow. The road was muddy, but getting better. We passed two more villages of mud hovels where wild dogs roamed the streets. When we reached the border, hundreds of cars and trucks were backed up. We waited an entire day before being allowed into Iran.

Three days later, we were in Hassan's home in the holy city of Mashad. Hassan was welcomed home as if he were a conquering hero returning from distant lands. His mother, father, three brothers, and two sisters treated me with much warmth and hospitality. In the beginning, there was much for me to become accustomed to: the squat toilets, sitting cross-legged on the floor for long periods of time, the sound of the Farsi language, not being able to see the faces of the women, who had to wear the *chador* in the presence of a non-Muslim.

There was much visiting to be done. Hassan had many cousins, aunts, uncles, nephews, and nieces, all of whom lived in various parts of Mashad. He often took me to visit friends in the bazaar. From there, we went for walks around the Holy Shrine of Imam Reza and the site where the tomb of the prophet was laid.

The time came when I could no longer stay with Hassan's family. Hassan introduced me to some carpet sellers in the bazaar.

I could obtain a small commission for luring foreign tourists to their shops. This job was known as "street hawking." Another street hawk by the name of Ali offered to share his room with me.

Ali had come to Mashad as a boy after living his first few years in a family of shepherd nomads. He'd picked up portions of five languages from making his living on the streets. His room was located on the bottom floor of a two-story, brick-and-mortar structure near the bazaar.

I began spending my days with Ali walking the streets near the holy shrine and the bazaar. Ali was known in all the shops. He was the quintessential guide. He knew where to get the best prices, both on the black market and in the shops, as well as find the best and cheapest hotels, entertainment spots, jewelry, carpets, and transportation.

Mashad was a clean city undergoing great changes. Old buildings were being torn down and replaced by modern buildings on nearly every street. There was activity everywhere. Women in *chador* strolled by languorously; swarthy men in turbans lined the streets; peddlers pushing carts of fresh fruit and nuts hawked their goods; children laughed and played; cars and horse-drawn carts paced to and fro; and men squatting on their haunches spread out their knives, bracelets, tools, pipes, samovars, and rings of precious stones before them for tourists to see. Sounds from the various bread shops, grain shops, copperware shops, and carpet shops filled the air. I walked about in a daze.

In the evenings, Ali's friends often stopped by the room. They spoke of falling in love with European women they'd met on the streets. They implored me to write love letters in English for them. There seemed an unspoken paranoia about them. When they spoke about their dreams, they did so in a low whisper. Many expressed a desire to marry a European woman. It was the only way they could obtain a passport to leave the country. They had a strong fear of the obligatory military service and the punishment given those who refused to serve. When I pressed them for specific reasons, they said it was forbidden to discuss politics or religion with a foreigner.

Meeting Ali's friends, hearing their stories, and seeing the fear they felt about resisting the government's authority made me reflect deeply about my own antiwar and prison experiences. I'd sought to escape the country of my birth and find another life abroad. I could empathize with these young Iranians and their paranoia and dreams of escape. I wanted to explain to them how I'd found solace, therapy, and a means of venting some of the insanity of my thoughts through the medium of writing, but the realization that I was powerless to do so hit me hard.

The days dragged by. An inexplicable emptiness came upon me. The excitement of being in a different and strange land was replaced by boredom and restlessness. I thought obsessively about death. The idea of walking the streets became repulsive. For days, I spoke to no one but Ali, who left early in the mornings and returned late at night. In the gloom of the room, I felt like a prisoner in a cell. The folly of my past filled my thoughts. Nightmares full of death visions plagued me.

One morning, while bathing my face in cold water, I looked at my reflection in the mirror and saw a stranger staring back. I knew then I had to move on again.

A few days later, I went to the Afghan consulate and got a thirty-day visa. I called Hassan to thank him for all his help and his family's kindness. I said goodbye to Ali. The next morning, I boarded a bus to Herat.

I crossed the Iranian-Afghan border and proceeded to Herat. It was a city of low, brown huts clustered tightly together and enclosed by mud walls and towers. The first thing I noticed when crossing into Afghanistan was the conspicuous absence of Western influence. It was like stepping into the pages of the Old Testament. Time had changed nothing. The people of Herat in the narrow bazaar streets had a distinct peace and dignity. They moved about their work as if it did not matter, as if it could be done either the next day or the day after. The coppersmiths, the cobblers, the saddle makers, all the various shopkeepers worked as they had for centuries. There were some shopkeepers who, in the intense heat of the afternoon, dozed in their stalls.

I saw few beggars. The men were proud of bearing and distinguished in appearance. They met every man's eyes on the level with a straightforward glance. Their faces carried an expression that showed no fear. Their bodies were strong and supple. The few women I saw in public were shrouded in full-length *burqa* with embroidered masks.

I spent two days in Herat and left the following morning on a bus. The sunrise cast varied tints from golden brown to violet on the low, distant mountains. The bus entered the open desert. I was the lone foreigner on a bus loaded with Afghan men. A sea of bobbing turbans atop dark, proud faces filled the bus. Across the glaring distance, there was nothing but an empty stretch of desert.

We came to Kandahar, Afghanistan's leading commercial center. The people had a freer air about them than those in the villages the bus had passed. The city had much less the atmosphere of a remote fortress than Herat. We stopped for tea in a cafe that was full of smoke and rich, masculine smells.

The bus continued toward Kabul, stopping three times during the day for the Afghans to roll out their prayer carpets and, facing Mecca, pray. At Ghazni, we saw a sunset that bathed the eastern mountains in fiery red and deep violet.

Two hours later, the bus arrived in Kabul. Two of the Afghan passengers helped me get a taxi to Ataullah's motel. Ataullah was surprised and pleased to see me. He introduced me to his partner and brothers, then showed me to a room. He brought some tea and we visited for an hour.

The city of Kabul was located in a large plain surrounded by high hills rising into the Hindu Kush mountains. The whole of the city seemed a mass of mud huts, although the newer part bore signs of modernization: apartment buildings, a hospital, and a university. There were many wide streets lined on either side with poplar and mulberry trees. There were also many gloomy, narrow lanes.

I spent most of my time relaxing, reading, and walking the streets around the central bazaar area. In most places, the streets were full of primitive wooden structures on which were laid mats of hemp. There were rows and rows of stalls where the traders squatted cross-legged. Those who couldn't afford to buy a stall sat on the street corners and sold their goods. It was always crowded. Donkeys laden with wood, brick, and straw often passed through all the activity. Occasionally, camel caravans passed slowly.

Ataullah's motel was a run-down place with a kitchen and about twenty rooms filled with tattered carpets and beds of rope called *charpoy*. The people who frequented the motel were mostly of the younger, vagabonding set, Europeans who'd come east to the lure of cheap living and an easy access to drugs. They were reminiscent of the drifting bohemians I'd met on my journey through Europe four years earlier. Those people had instilled in me an excitement with their talk of literature, philosophy, and revolution. The people I was now surrounded by, although much the same in appearance, were a more decadent type. They talked only of drugs. They smoked hashish all day, stared into space, and didn't try to interact with the local Afghans.

One night, I was in the kitchen talking with Ataullah's brothers, who were trying to teach me some Pashto. An Australian man stormed into the kitchen complaining about a lack of sugar served with his tea. Ataullah's brothers argued he'd been served plenty. The man was high on heroin. The air grew more oppressive with every word he spoke.

"Give me more sugar," he demanded.

Sensing a violent confrontation, I intervened. "It seems to me a petty thing to argue over."

The man took notice of me for the first time. "You've got to put these people in their place or they'll walk all over you. You should know that as a white man."

"I just got here a few days ago. I don't know about the local customs, but I think you're being a bit demanding."

He regarded me for a moment, then took two steps toward me. "Well, if that's the case, welcome to Afghanistan, mate." From his back pocket flashed a switchblade knife, the blade suddenly open and about an inch from my throat. Ataullah's brothers formed a quick circle around us. I noticed a scar on the man's neck. There was a moment of terrific suspense. Then the man's jaundiced eyes closed heavily. He laughed a loud, insane laugh and withdrew the knife. He left the kitchen in hysterics, bumping into walls and furniture on the way out.

Ataullah was busy much of the time. Although occasionally I helped his partner write business letters in English—for which I was given free room and board—I spent most of my time alone, avoiding any contact with the other Westerners. There was, however, one man of interest staying at the motel. He was a German named Rolf who lived in a VW bus on one of the parking spaces. He was different from the other travelers. He wasn't sluggish and dull, but enthusiastic and energetic. He made his living hauling travelers in his VW bus to and from Europe. He was about forty, spoke five languages, painted abstract landscapes and portraits, and was well-versed in literature and philosophy.

I usually visited Rolf in the evenings. We'd prepare a dinner of rice with raisins and lamb meat, then retire to the top of the bus to smoke some hashish, watch the stars, and discuss life. One night, I told him about my journey from Paris to Afghanistan and the various adventures I'd had.

"So what have all these experiences taught you? You seem to me to be more of an observer of men than an active participant in their affairs," Rolf said.

"I suppose you're right about that," I said. "The one political stand I made landed me in jail and I've spent a good portion of my life since then trying to rationalize what I did. This journey I've taken has carried me halfway around the world in search of something I can't put a name on. I know I don't care much for capitalism. I have an attraction for some form of socialism, but I can't commit myself to what I don't understand. Idealistically, it seems the best answer to man's inability to live together peacefully, but socialism, too, has a history of violence and upheaval. It's all pretty hard to figure out. What do you think?"

Rolf considered my question for a moment, scratched his head, then said, "Socialism, communism, Marxism, all these 'isms' have no soul. They're connected only in terms of class struggle and a fight for equality in the production and consumption of material goods. In that sense, they're not so different from capitalism. What about the spiritual struggle? Islamic Marxism? It's a joke! It's just another form of cultural imperialism that would force people to conform to a standardized way of thinking and behaving.

"Democracy, individual freedom, human rights? Also a bunch of rubbish that can never be inflicted upon impoverished nations and peoples. What do uneducated peoples know about such things? They think only about where the next meal comes from. It doesn't matter what form of government they live under. It seems to me, there's only one reality and that's mankind's inability to organize itself. I think we have to accept man's weaknesses, his greed, his stupidity. And love him for it all. No one can possibly know what the answers to life are until after we die. It's like the preacher said, 'All is vanity and a striving after wind.'

"You can't save the world alone or through any ideology or 'ism.' That's the only truth I know. Oh sure, you can chase after a spiritual path. Become a Christian, Muslim, Hindu, or Buddhist if you must. But you won't find any answers there, either. I've tried. The world's religions are just a bunch of exclusivist groups, too. Stick with science, knowledge, the art of survival. Study languages, communicate, make life interesting for yourself, that's what I try to do. Here, go on, have another hit off the pipe. Concentrate on the moment, look at the stars, appreciate what is here and now. If you're meant to find any answers, they'll come to you in due time."

We continued to smoke and watch the stars. I thought about what Rolf had said. It made sense to me. It was much better to be carefree and let things take their own course rather than get too muddled up in some false ideology. But still I wanted clear answers to my questions. I wanted my life to mean something. I wanted to put a stop to the confusion that raged in my brain.

I wanted to understand the forces that had driven me to this part of the earth.

Rolf cleared his throat and said, "You know, you remind me a bit of myself when I was your age. I wanted to experience everything, to find all the answers. Like you, I couldn't be contained within the walls of my own country and culture. I rambled about and learned to speak the languages of some other countries. I asked different people all the same questions and found no answers. I lost my own identity and found myself, too, as a man with no country.

"But how glorious to have the entire world as your home. Most people don't know this. They don't have the spirit to reject the boundaries that bind them. It's up to the individual to take that first step, to cut those ties. So what holds people back? Perhaps love? Love of convention and family ties? As far as I can see, all of love is just a wishful image. The actual occurrence never lives up to the image. In moments of suffering, knowing we are loved does little to help or comfort us. When we lie at death's door, our family and lovers can do nothing for us but cry. So what's the answer? Do we end by hating the things and people we once loved? Do we end up loving the things that brought us misery and sadness?"

Rolf took a deep breath and sighed. He stroked his chin, then continued. "No doubt you think I'm rambling, but surely you'll have these questions and many others in your own mind as you continue east. What you've experienced thus far is nothing compared to what waits for you in India. You'll see the very worst of human misery and despair. Not only despair, but also self-pity. The adage of the constant work of one's life being the making of one's death will never have been so evident. You must experience India if you're to have any fathomable idea of what I'm saying."

I stared at Rolf. Something about the certainty of his words frightened me, as if he possessed a vision of my future. I wanted to ask a question, but nothing formed in my mouth. He laughed.

"There's no need to fear India," Rolf said. "As an artist, you must experience it. India will wrap itself around you in ways you cannot imagine. If you feel fear, that's natural. Fear is in everything a man does. Ah, but why go into it any further? You'll see. You'll see."

The time came to continue east. My visa would soon expire. Ataullah and I embraced with a genuine fondness, knowing we'd never see each other again, but glad we'd been able to share a portion of our lives together.

I took a bus into Pakistan as far as Rawalpindi, where I bought a train ticket. The ride through the dusty Indus Valley was long, hot, and uncomfortable. There were many stops where soldiers either boarded or got off the train.

I spent the night in a cheap motel in Rawalpindi and the next day took a crowded train to Lahore. In the brilliant sunshine, the train swept past rice fields and stagnant pools full of white lotuses and standing herons, past people slapping pie-shaped, cow-dung patties onto the sides of mud huts to dry, past men with bullocks and submerged plows preparing rice fields for planting. In the different train stations were fruit vendors and their carts and janitors in white uniforms sweeping the platforms with palm fronds. Each town had its shantytown by the railroad tracks, smaller towns of grass huts, cardboard shelters, pup tents, hovels of paper and twigs and cloth. Everyone in these shantytowns was in motion.

The train arrived in Lahore. Processions of rickshaws, pony

carts, hawkers, and veiled women filled the narrow lanes. The larger streets were congested with swarms of jostling people. Recently, there had been an uprising against the Bhutto regime for allegedly rigging the elections. There was now a curfew with the military patrolling the streets at night. Late that night, as I went to sleep in another cheap motel room, I heard muffled sounds of gunfire coming from the streets.

I crossed the border into India the next day. There was a long wait at the border as the customs officials took their time examining each passenger's baggage. The train arrived in Amritsar in the early evening. There was no train to Delhi until the next morning. I slept that night on a bench in the station waiting room.

The next day, I arrived at the station in the old section of Delhi. A seething swarm of people surrounded the passengers as they got off the train. Everywhere skinny, brown rickshaw drivers and hawkers of cheap goods clamored for attention. I was swooped up by one driver. He took my duffel bag, hooked it on his bicycle rickshaw, and pedaled me to a section in a bazaar area where I could find a cheap room.

We rode past entire communities living on the streets. Women in tattered rags with cracked feet and rings in their noses stood cooking pots of vegetables over smoky fires. Children ran here and there. The narrow, winding streets and wide bazaars were littered with debris and thick with intimate odors. Cripples walked the streets alongside half-naked natives. Thousands of people with rickets, leprosy, skin diseases, and bloated bellies lined the filthy streets. Vehicles of many types competed for limited space.

I found a room in an old, ramshackle motel. A single window overlooked a narrow street in the bazaar. The heat in the room was suffocating. It was impossible to sleep soundly.

For the next week, I walked the streets. Everywhere I saw poverty, hunger, disease, violence, and misery. I walked through the refuge quarter of the city. I went there every day to stare at the chained-off society. Its air of unreality lured me. The people lived in houses built of tin and boxes.

The older people appeared almost glad of their misery. They were scattered about in different poses of contorted collapse. There were people with catalepsy, with tuberculosis, with syphilis, with different kinds of worms, with eye diseases, with many saddening things. Some lay prostrate on the chained-off streets, their faces gaunt and colorless. When they closed their eyes, they looked dead.

Garbage lined the streets. More than once I saw, resting in the piles of garbage, a dead baby whose skin was parched and cracked. I bought a bottle of wine from a black market dealer, got drunk, and passed out on the streets.

I was struck by the stoicism with which these people bore their maladies. I felt humble and meek, filled with a despair that wouldn't go away. As I returned each night from these visits to the refuge quarter, I inevitably stopped at the same stall in the bazaar. Exhausted from destroyed emotions and the heat, I bought fruit or liquid refreshment. The shopkeeper was an old, wrinkled man who'd seen many generations of suffering and still held his head high, composed like a Buddha. His impassive repose was like a display of great dignity.

I was overwhelmed by the abstracted silence of this man. One night, in a moment of extreme self-pity, I seized the old man's hand and wrung it with all the force of my gratitude. The shopkeeper simply smiled and passed his hand gently over my head.

Dysentery overtook me. I lay for two days in a sweating fever on the *charpoy*, the sole piece of furniture in the room. I became like the prostrate death-forms of the streets. I was so weak I couldn't lift my body. Finally, the fever broke. In my weakened condition, it was all I could do to drag myself into the streets to the shopkeeper's stall. The old man gave me tea, fruit, and yogurt in silence. My strength gradually returned.

Over the next few days, I went to a park with some trees that provided shade to sit under. I'd stare at the sky for long periods of time, lost in thought. What had I learned from this journey? What had I gained? A deeper awareness of the suffering of mankind? I knew only that my own tribulations were nothing compared to those of the swarms of people I'd seen in Delhi.

A new desolation crept into my soul, a heavy, aching loneliness. I felt weak and hollow. I'd lost all feeling of empathy. I could no longer feel even pity. There was no room for pity, not where all required it. I sighed heavily, got up, and trudged back to my room. It was time to move on, to go forward, to leave the baggage of Asia behind, to find a new life. With my final three hundred dollars, I bought a plane ticket to Los Angeles.

11

Back in the U.S.A.

W HEN I arrived back in the United States, I was a physical and emotional mess. The reverse culture shock I experienced was probably not dissimilar to that of the Vietnam vets who'd fought in the jungles of Southeast Asia and returned to an America indifferent to the revelatory changes they'd undergone. I felt estranged, as if I'd undergone a secret experience and discovered things I could never fully share with my fellow countrymen. There were times in the ensuing months when I felt as if I'd died and found myself reborn in an altogether alien country. Where once there might have been a semblance of political, philosophical, and religious ideas and convictions to hold on to for guidance, there were now giant question marks attached to everything I thought, everything I saw, everything I experienced.

Thank God for Mom! As always, she provided the proverbial shelter from the storm. After landing at the Los Angeles airport, I used the last of my money, a quarter, to make a phone call to a friend I made while living in Glendale. I hitched a ride from the airport to his house. He loaned me twenty-five dollars for a bus ticket to Mom and Herb's place in Truckee, where I knew I could stay long enough to figure out my next move. There was also a check for seven hundred fifty dollars from selling my car before leaving for Europe.

The two months I spent with Mom and Herb was a much-needed time of recuperation. Both Mom and Herb were working. Terri was married and living near Sacramento. I had most of each day to myself to write and think about the future. I worked on my manuscript. My routine was to work on the book from 10 a.m. to 3 p.m., go out for a four-mile run, greet Mom as she returned home, and visit with her until late in the evening. Herb was friendly enough, but I knew he didn't want me freeloading for very long.

During this time, the relationship with Mom changed from a mother-son relationship to one of best friends. Our conversations took on a secret, conspiratorial tone. We confessed things that we'd never told anyone else. I told Mom about getting busted for pot in the Beale Air Base jail, about the time I took acid in the Denver jail, about the heroin addict in Afghanistan who put the knife to my throat, about the letter of renunciation from Uncle Dick, and about how India had wiped away any thoughts of the possibility of a benevolent Creator.

Mom told me about her agonizing days of waiting to hear from me, knowing I was going through emotional challenges in trying to figure out where my life was leading me. She showed me the world map she placed pins on every time she got an aerogram or postcard from me so she could keep track of my progress and where I was in the world. She told me about the time she finagled her way on to Beale Air Base shortly after my court martial, stormed into Lieutenant Colonel Arnold's office demanding to see me, and was escorted off the base by the security police because she insulted him when he wouldn't let her. The security police told her she could be shot if she tried to get on the base again.

During these evening gabfests, I began to appreciate what an extraordinary mother I had and what she'd accomplished in her life. Up until this time, the only thing that really mattered in my life was what happened to me. Me. Me. Me. What a self-centered ass I'd been all these years, without ever realizing it. I supposed Rolf was right in what he'd predicted about feeling self-pity when I experienced India. And perhaps through that self-pity, a certain empathy for others was born.

For the first time, Mom explained to me about how difficult it had been for her to get a private pilot's license, the resistance she encountered by many men, and the pride she felt in having never given up and, through determination and persistence, being hired by the Truckee Airport to fly fire patrol for the Forestry Service for two summers, then becoming chairperson of the Reno chapter of Ninety-Nines, the women pilots' organization whose first president was Amelia Earhart.

Mom's passion for flying began in high school when a barn-storming group came through White Salmon. She and a friend had saved some money and used it for a flight with a real pilot. She knew if she ever got a chance, she'd try to get a pilot's license. That chance came in Fortuna. She began taking ground school classes in the mid-1960s. She was the only woman in the class. Mom's eyes would light up when she talked about those days.

"I had to go through a long course of ground school first and spent many, many hours very early in the mornings studyin' about the whats, whys, and hows of that seemingly intangible thing—to learn to fly. But I was motivated by one man in the same class who thought women shouldn't become pilots. I used to tease him a lot and I bet him twenty dollars I'd get a better score on the final test. Well, your mother won that bet and he actually paid up. Later, we became quite friendly.

"After that, when I was in flight school, I used to think, 'What am I doin' here? This is so far above what I'm capable of learnin'. I must be a bit crazy!' But finally, I realized because I studied so hard and so much, the outcome would give me many wonderful experiences.

"My instructor at flight school was Paul LaPrelle. We called him Papa Bear. He was a real taskmaster. When he told me I was ready to solo, I disagreed with him. I didn't think I was ready. He said to me very sarcastically, 'Well, would you let me know when you are ready?' And I did. And instead of makin' three take-offs and landings, which was the basic requirement, I made about seventeen and was in the air for probably over an hour. Maybe that's why he asked me to fly to Wichita, Kansas with him one time. We went through the Cessna airplane factory, and I got to fly a small plane by myself back to Fortuna."

Mom puffed out her chest and smiled.

"Shortly after we moved to Truckee, I worked at the Truckee Tahoe Airport. This was before I went to work for George Pifer at the Truckee Justice Court. I flew quite a bit durin' that time. I was fortunate enough to fly a fire patrol for the Division of Forestry a few days a week for two summers. The area was buildin' three new ski resorts, so several airports in the area had pilots fly fire patrol lookin' for smoke from trash fires and reportin' them. I was gonna be flyin' a different, slightly larger plane than what I was used to, so I had to go up for check rides before they turned me loose to complete my mission.

"One day the instructor said to me, 'Kay, do you know anything about Basque sheepherders?' I had no idea what he was talkin' about. He told me this group of sheepherders from Spain would take their little herds of sheep up into the meadows below the Sierra Mountains so they could graze on the plush meadows. There was a small landin' strip in one of these areas not too far from the airport, so he and I rented a Forestry plane for the afternoon, flew northeast of Truckee, and landed out in one of these meadows, hopin' one or two of these Basque sheepherders would come through.

"Wow! It was a lucky day, for shortly after landin', we spotted three men herdin' their sheep through this meadow. They didn't speak English and we sure didn't speak their Basque language, but we offered to share our picnic lunch, which I'd prepared for us to take. We also had a container of lemonade, although these men had their bota bags of wine with them. By usin' a lot of sign language and body language, we spent a fantastic afternoon gettin' to visit with these Basque men. They were very clean and so well-mannered, plus very friendly and were chattin' and chattin'—not a word did we understand! But we laughed a lot. They helped finish our sandwiches, showed me how to pet the sheep, and shook our hands and bowed several times as they prepared to get on their way.

"It's always so amazin' to me how easy it is to have these experiences and how over the years they all become interconnected somehow and offer us such an incredible opportunity to learn more about people in other parts of this world. I've been so lucky in this respect and I sure envy you, Bob, and all the travelin' experiences you've had."

Mom then confessed that sometimes she thought perhaps she was never meant to be a mother and that some of the heartaches in her children's lives were the result of her naivety and inexperience. All she wanted for us, she said, was to be happy and content in whatever life had to offer.

She looked me straight in the eye and said, "I know when I had you three children, my main purpose in life was to raise you to be free spirits, independent, adventuresome, self-confident, and perhaps most of all to be very self-sufficient if and when you would lose either me or your dad. I received a lot of unsolicited advice tellin' me I was either too strict or not strict enough with you three. I didn't want to be either. I just wanted to be your mom and hopefully, as the years passed, to be your trusted friend. I guess all my life I've actually been a dreamer and a bit of a rebel. I can see that you inherited that part from me."

I patted Mom's hands. "You are my trusted friend, Mom—the best I ever had."

"Thank you," Mom said. "You know, I was just thinkin' today of the years you kids were growin' up and all those times I was told that I was bein' overprotective and spoilin' each of you. Actually, I think I was rather strict with each of you, but I am now and always have been very proud of all three of you. Don't ever forget that. I'm so proud to be your mom.

"That reminds me of a dinner here in Truckee we had with George and Helen Pifer, the Bonars, and the Haskells. Anyway, we were discussin' the Vietnam War and I made the remark that I'd support and pay for my boys to go to Canada rather than go to Vietnam. Herb and George both became irate and told me I was crazy. I said to George, 'This is my house. If you don't like what I said, go home.'"

Mom pointed her right index finger at the George in her mind. "And he did! Helen stayed for dessert. Herb stormed upstairs to the bedroom." Mom shakes her head in disgust. "That was so typical of him. The rest of us had a great time for the rest of the evening. Once again, I didn't control my Irish sassiness. Maybe it's one of the reasons I've survived this long."

Mom chuckled to herself. "That George is a stinker. I think I've probably quit workin' for him at least a half a dozen times and he's fired me several times, too. Once, I walked out durin' a court proceedin' and just went home. He called a recess and came up to the house to get me to go back to work. I told him to leave me alone, but he wouldn't, so I called the sheriff's department and told them I had a trespasser on my property. They came but wouldn't do anything because it was the judge I wanted to get off my front porch. That was the joke around Truckee for quite a while. It's a wonder we've remained friends. I get so aggravated at George, but I have to admire him, too. He's really a fair man and always takes the time to hear the defendant's point of view durin' a trial."

Mom always had a way of getting in the last word or move to make her point, but she never did it in a mean or spiteful way. Shortly before I left Truckee, Herb was complaining to her about my eating all his Wheat Thins crackers. He made some comment about "your son is going to eat us out of house and home with all his freeloading." Mom didn't say a word. Instead, she went to the store, bought about fifty boxes of Wheat Thins, and distributed them in all of Herb's clothing drawers, toolboxes, and workshop benches so that no matter where he went, there'd be a box of Wheat Thins staring at him. She also ate early so he'd have to eat dinner alone. She didn't talk to him for about a month. In the end, he apologized to her.

One night, Shannon phoned me. He was thinking of taking a trip to Seattle to meet some friends and play basketball. There was a league for players six-foot and under. He'd made friends with one of the players the year before and was invited to play on a team if he was ever in the Seattle area. I told him I was ready to go. The following week, Shannon drove his pickup truck to Truckee. We loaded my belongings in the back and were off to Seattle.

We spent a month in Seattle staying with Shannon's friends, playing basketball every evening, sometimes looking for jobs during the days. Our savings dwindled quickly. Shannon returned to Fortuna to go back to work for his father. I stayed on in Seattle after finding a job as a mailman for a firm of corporate lawyers. A week later, my basketball season ended when I was disqualified from playing in the league because I measured a half inch over six feet.

I passed the weekdays of that winter collecting and distributing the mail of a hundred and fifty lawyers and secretaries on the top three floors of the First National Bank building. I spent the evenings and weekends either pacing the wet Seattle streets or locked up in my room drinking cheap beer and smoking pot. I began an affair with one of the secretaries, who had a love and knowledge of literature far greater than anyone I'd met in a long time.

Amanda was a thirty-five-year-old divorcee with two children. Her house was about a fifteen-minute walk from my place. I was enamored of Joseph Conrad and Hermann Hesse. Many of our conversations were about their books. She introduced me to Raymond Mungo's *Famous Long Ago* and *Return to Sender.* The first book was about his experiences with the Liberation News Service, which had been an antiwar underground news service he cofounded, and the latter about his wanderings in Japan and India. Amanda had taken a creative writing class from him at Montana Books, a Seattle bookstore he co-owned. She thought since our life experiences were similar, he might be able to help me with my writing. One day, she took me to the bookstore to introduce us, but he was out of town.

Amanda also loved to hear my stories about the Boylston Avenue area, a place alive with decadent characters. Sex and drugs were traded openly after the sun went down. The people who occupied the streets looked like refugees from a war—worn-out prostitutes, prostrate winos, older homosexuals, teenage gangs, glassy-eyed addicts. I sometimes heard screams and the sounds of blows in the rooms around me at night. Amanda's warmth and kindness were a salve for the dark pessimism that often crept into my thoughts. She encouraged me to keep writing, to examine the soul-purging I'd undergone in India.

Winter passed. The urge to move on consumed me. I'd saved about a thousand dollars and was tired of the tedium of my job. Shortly before I left Seattle, Mom sent me a letter with Uncle Jerry's address. She'd just found out he was living in Seattle and thought it'd be nice to look him up, which I did one weekend.

I bid my goodbyes to Amanda, took a hit of orange sunshine LSD that one of the younger lawyers gave me, and spent a nineteen-hour bus ride to Fortuna hallucinating and immersed in introspective wanderings.

At first, I tried to involve myself in sports and old friendships, but a growing misanthropy gnawed at my insides. I pissed away most of my savings in the local bars, brooding in a corner, occasionally launching a soliloquy against the world, which would be greeted with jeers and shouts of "pipe down over there ya fuckin' idiot!" I was becoming the town drunk. Sometimes I stayed at Shannon's place; sometimes I flopped on the couch of any friend I hadn't yet insulted and who still saw some humor in my waywardness.

When sober, I hung out at Shannon's dad's concrete plant,

rode with Shannon in the cab of his mixer on deliveries, or shot baskets with him at Rohner Park. The Kellys landed a contract with the state to pour the concrete for a bridge south of Garberville. The job would take over a year to complete. They planned to set up another portable concrete plant on a river bar near the job site. I tagged along with Shannon one afternoon to see where they were setting it up. Afterward, we stopped for a beer at the Village Green, a small resort restaurant two miles south of Garberville and just off Highway 101.

I'd bought a rattletrap VW recently and was down to my last fifty dollars. I asked the owner, Dick Leary, if he needed any help in the kitchen. He told me to come in the following day to start cooking lunches. Shannon and I left the restaurant and found a small apartment about two miles away on the Old Redwood Highway.

Dick was a plump, alcoholic Irishman in his sixties who'd been a communist in his youth. He and his wife, Pat, loved literature. Dick took me under his wing and taught me everything he knew about cooking. In the evenings after shutting down the restaurant, he'd bring out a bottle of scotch and regale me with tales of his adventures. My favorite was about the time he and Pat lived in the Carmel Highlands, ran a general store, and drank in the evenings at the Nepenthe restaurant with the artist colony that resided nearby. Henry Miller often frequented Dick and Pat's store, trading manuscripts for food when times were bad. Dick introduced me to a new world of literature to consume: writers such as Malcolm Lowry, Frederic Prokosch, and Mikhail Sholokhov.

That summer, a new lover entered my life. Aundrea Harnish had just graduated from high school and was working as the salad girl at the Village Green when I began cooking. Her long blond hair, slim athletic body, shy smile, and virginal radiance wrenched from me a deep longing. We went for long walks in the redwoods, swam in secret places along the Eel River that only she and her friends knew about, took drives in my VW, and went on dinner dates whenever I'd saved a few extra dollars. She dreamed of becoming a dancer and confessed a strong desire to escape from the dreariness of small-town life. Our relationship was doomed from the start, but I was blind and mesmerized by her beauty.

The chief obstacle was a jealous and paranoid father. He was one of the many marijuana farmers transforming the local economy. Twice he entered the restaurant, high on cocaine, slandered me to my face, and stormed outside screaming hysterical threats should I ever set foot on his property. At harvest time, he spread throughout the local bars a rumor of me being a narcotics agent.

In September, Aundrea went away to college in San Luis Obispo. Her father's threats subsided. With the approach of the long, rainy winter, business at the Village Green slowed to a standstill. My working hours dropped to five hours a day. Shannon moved back to Fortuna until work on the bridge would start up again in the spring. Winter passed with a terrible meaninglessness.

Aundrea returned to visit her family for a three-day weekend near the end of winter. She came to the apartment on that Sunday morning. I'd already drunk four beers by the time she arrived. We spent a desultory day driving to Eureka. The day ended with my passing out on the apartment bed while making love. A week later, I got a Dear John letter.

Shannon returned in the spring. My hours at the restaurant increased, but the realization came that I'd once again have to hit the road if I was to make anything of my life. I was twenty-eight years old, living a hand-to-mouth existence, and feeling as if my youth had abandoned me. Then came the letter from Raymond Mungo.

Shortly after moving to Garberville, I'd written Raymond a fan letter in which I'd outlined my difficulty in putting down on paper what I'd experienced in Asia. I'd also included a synopsis of my novel about my conscientious objector days. Raymond had left Seattle and was now living in Carmel. He invited me to visit anytime I wanted.

At the end of the summer season, I quit my job. I had enough money saved to last a few months. Dick and Pat wrote a reference letter and wished me luck. On a warm October day, I headed to Carmel. Raymond was staying at Cynthia Williams' place in the Carmel Highlands overlooking Point Lobos and the Pacific Ocean. I'd be allowed to stay until I found a place of my own. Cynthia was a landowner and the matriarch of a local family with connections to many artists, musicians, writers, activists, and bohemians.

I spent that first week with Raymond smoking some sinsemilla weed I'd brought from Humboldt County, watching the 1979 World Series between the Pirates and Orioles, exchanging life stories, and discussing books and writing. He was a small man with a large appetite for adventure and ironic humor. He loved baseball. The World Series heroics of Willie Stargell, the Pirates' aging first baseman and stalwart of my APBA days, enthralled us both. We hung on the edge of his every at bat, and guzzled copious amounts of beer in celebration of his many hits.

One time during that week, we visited the artist Ephraim Doner, who lived just up the road from Cynthia's. Although we arrived unannounced, Ephraim greeted us warmly. He was in his mid-seventies. His white hair and beard were disheveled, his clothes tattered, and his smile wide and warm. He served us wine, asked about my travels, told stories about his friendship with Henry Miller, and talked about his younger days wandering along the Dalmatian Coast and painting portraits for meals in bars and restaurants. He challenged me to a game of ping-pong on his table outside and beat me handily.

After the World Series ended, Raymond put in a good word for me, and Cynthia kindly rented me a three-room shack with a wood stove in Pacific Grove for a hundred and twenty dollars a month. Three days after moving into the shack, I found a job as a salad man at Andre's, a French restaurant in Carmel. The owners liked my work. When one of the line cooks quit, they broke me in on the lunch sauté line. That's when I met Mike Feig.

Mike was the head day chef at Andre's. He was three years younger than I, had joined the Air Force after high school, and spent most of his four-year tour in Europe. He stayed in Spain for another year after his discharge, wandering from place to place, living among the peasants and picking fruit to stay alive. After returning to the States and attending a culinary school on the G.I. Bill, he moved to the West Coast. He was half German and half Wampanoag Indian. He stood about five-foot-nine and had a dark, handsome face and long, muscular arms. In high school and in the Air Force, he was a running back on football teams and a strong-armed catcher on baseball teams. He was also a former boxer who made it as far as the Massachusetts Golden Gloves championship fight in the hundred-forty-five-pound division before falling victim to a series of vicious punches in the third round. That knockout ended his boxing career.

Working with Mike, I learned Andre's day menu in about a week. The pressure of the job was tremendous. The two of us were responsible for all the preparation and cooking of up to three hundred gourmet lunches a day. Every day, we raced around the kitchen like two mad dancers in a frantically choreographed ballet, knives flashing, sauces simmering, stockpots boiling in the early morning before the rest of the restaurant crew came in two hours before serving time.

From 11 a.m. to 3 p.m., we churned out fifteen to twenty plates at a time with fish or meat constantly on the broiler, vegetables in the sauté pans, potatoes in the deep fryer, eggs in the poaching pots, all the while pans flying across the narrow line and landing in the bucket placed at the end of the line for the pot and pan washer to pick up. Our work resembled an artistic performance—orchestrating the movement of the waitresses, waiters, prep cooks, dishwashers, and bus boys alike; coordinating the color, taste, harmony, and balance of each dish; and carrying on great debates above the tumult of the kitchen.

It was exhausting work. At the end of each shift, we went for fiercely competitive, five-mile runs. The course was a hilly one that ran along the coast and through the wind-sculpted pines that guarded the path alongside the Links at Spanish Bay golf course. The loser had to buy that evening's beer.

When Mike was kicked out of his apartment and faced with returning to his hometown in Massachusetts because he couldn't find a place that would allow him to keep his pet dog, he moved into my Pacific Grove shack. He taught me everything he knew, all the shortcuts and nuances of food preparation and running a kitchen. Every day, we had to make, in addition to the regular menu, a chef's special of the day, an omelette of the day, a quiche of the day, and a fish of the day. He was a master at taking the scraps left from the previous night by the head chef and creating culinary works of art. One day it was a Swedish special, another a German, another a Lebanese, another a Japanese.

During the day shifts at the restaurant and evenings at home,

Mike took great pains to instruct me in all the details. "Now ya gotta remember yer basic sauces," he'd say, "yer basic muthuh sauces—brown, bechamel, tomato, velouté, and hollandaise—if ya wanna become a French chef" or "When ya boil eggs, ya gotta wait till the water's boilin' before ya put the eggs in; then ya gotta boil 'em for exactly nine minutes, take 'em off the burner, and put 'em in ice water to stop the cookin' process if ya wanna have the yolks perfectly centered and have the perfect color and texture" or "When yer cuttin' carrots, ya gotta first cut off a little section so's to have a flat area to place on the cuttin' board. That way the little bugger doesn't slip on ya and ya don't slice yer finger off" or "When you're mixin' the clarified butter into the yolks of the hollandaise, ya gotta make sure both are the same temperature and ya gotta start by jus' pourin' a few drops in and gradually increase the amount; otherwise, your sauce is gonna break on ya" or any of a hundred other tips.

We worked double shifts two days a week. On the day shifts, there was a frantic rush to combine quantity and quality, but in the evenings, there was a more relaxed pace. The evening dishes he produced drew high praise. His sauces complemented the entrees and vegetables in color and taste with precision; his garnishes and desserts were sculpted with fine detail and aesthetic appeal. He was the star of the show. The daytime waitresses loved his easy manner and gentlemanly compliments; the nighttime waiters respected him as their tips were in large part dependent upon his skills; and the kitchen staff worked hard for him because of his fairness and good-natured banter.

Not every day, however, went smoothly. There were also the times the work was too overwhelming, the orders coming in droves, a mistake on one meal upsetting the rhythm and flow, Mike taking the blame on himself as if he'd let everyone down, even if it had been a mistake written on the order ticket. One time in the middle of a lunchtime rush, he had eggs stick in a pan three times in a row. The pans hadn't been sufficiently tempered, so it was impossible to flip the eggs, this while other pans were on burners, meat on the main broiler, potatoes in the deep fryer, plates in the top broiler, and new order tickets piling up at an impossible rate. In a fit of rage, Mike threw the hot egg pan across the kitchen. It narrowly missed Ray the dishwasher's head before smashing against the wall. Ray showed up for work the next day wearing a football helmet.

One time on a day off, Mike and I took some magic mushrooms and drove to the top of a peak overlooking Monterey Bay. Mike spoke about his full-blooded Indian grandmother, who was ninety years old and had the wisdom of the ages etched on her rugged face. He spoke about how he loved and respected her, about how confused he was about love and life. He spoke of his child who was in Washington State, something he'd never confessed to anyone before, and of the disappointment he felt in not having lived up to his obligations. He spoke of the loneliness of always following an incomprehensible instinct in rambling aimlessly and not being sure if he'd ever find a permanent home.

By the time winter passed, we were ragged and worn out. The long hours at work and the excesses of alcohol we consumed were taking a toll. We talked sometimes about moving on. He'd fallen in love with the daughter-in-law of the restaurant owners, but the clandestine relationship was becoming a burden. She kept promising her divorce would be finalized soon, but Mike was impatient and wondered if, in the wake of having failed as a father with one child, he could take on the responsibility of helping raise his girlfriend's two children. My own love life was a disaster, too.

One night in a drunken state when the two of us were crying the blues, we tacked a map of the U.S. on a wall in the kitchen, took out a dart, and vowed we'd move to wherever the dart landed. I threw the dart. It landed in the heart of New Orleans. The next morning, Mike recanted, but I'd made up my mind. Two weeks later, I quit the job, cashed my final paycheck, had a mechanic give my VW a tune-up, packed my belongings, left the shack to Mike, said goodbye to Raymond and Cynthia, and headed toward New Orleans.

I took Interstate 80 as far as Cheyanne, Wyoming, where I headed south on Interstate 25. I planned to pass through Denver and continue to League City, Texas, where I knew my brother Dick was living. I called Mom shortly before leaving California to tell her of my plans. She gave me Dick's address and suggested I stop to see him. I hadn't seen him in nine years.

On the fourth day after leaving California, I knocked on Dick's apartment door. He opened the door and stared at me through glazed, hungover eyes. He'd changed considerably. His hairline was receding. He was soft in the arms and belly. With a tired gesture, he motioned for me to come in. I sat down on the sofa in the front room while he made coffee. We spoke about our lives as children romping through the redwood forests and about various old friends and the directions their lives had taken. We agreed I should spend some time.

Over the next few days, I noticed in Dick a distinct weariness of spirit. Our attempts at extended conversation contained few meaningful words. He spoke mainly about his accomplishments. He'd become obsessed with making a success of himself. Material things carried a great weight with him. After years of working nighttime bartending jobs to pay his way through ground and flight schools, flying as many hours and garnering as much experience as he could, he finally landed a pilot job for a Houston corporation at a good salary. It was difficult to pinpoint the vacant aura that surrounded him. I guessed it had something to do with his own particular brand of loneliness, his own search for identity.

He bragged about the girlfriends in different cities to which he'd flown corporate executives, the conquests of barmaids, models, and sophisticated women. He reminisced about his high school athletic exploits, the high-powered cars he'd driven, the expensive restaurants in which he'd dined, and the celebrities he'd transported and drunk with during his various flying jobs. These stories reeked of vicariousness and illusion, yet I too trumpeted a fictional version of my own past, coloring my stories with exaggerated details of the glittering, fast-paced sin of the cities I'd seen and the women I'd loved around the globe. It was a mournful testament to the actual confusion and sadness of our lives that we couldn't go beyond the fiction of dream lives to confess to each other the crises we'd undergone and the humility gained.

That's not to say that our reunion was a disaster. Quite the contrary. It was as if we had an unspoken agreement not to do any emotional or intellectual probing of the separations that had marked our lives, of who we were and what we hoped for. We did have many good times: going to baseball games at the Astrodome, spending afternoons getting drunk and playing golf, sharing recipes and cooking gourmet dinners at the apartment with his current girlfriend and other pilot buddies. We did our best to cherish the moments we had. We were still brothers.

12

Oil Rig Work and
Other Adventures

I GOT a job for a catering company that provided kitchen and cleaning services for the oil rigs. A helicopter shuttled me from Galveston to a drilling rig a hundred miles out in the Gulf of Mexico. I was put to work mopping floors, scrubbing pots and pans, setting tables, and cleaning the walk-in cooler and freezer. The Leo Clark was one of the oldest drilling tender barges in the Gulf. The rust, filth, grease, and grime were overwhelming. The men who worked on the barge included ex-cons, Vietnam veterans, rednecks from Texas, Cajun coonasses from Louisiana, and a couple of college kids working for the summer. Everyone worked twelve-hour shifts.

There was a rebellion the first week among the catering company workers. The steward poked a finger while peeling shrimp, suffered a case of blood poisoning, and had to be taken ashore. The night cook, who was next in line in the kitchen hierarchy, became the head steward. Bill was a portly Black man in his late thirties from Philadelphia. He shared a bunk with me. Two of the galley hands refused to work for "a goddamned nigger."

Dissension spread quickly to the regular rig workers—the roustabouts and other laborers. One time, I heard a low murmur of "nigger lover" when I passed by one of the galley hands.

My friendship with Bill was brief. I'd brought a small stash of pot with me. In the few days I knew him, we often snuck to the back of the barge in the evenings to smoke a joint and watch the sunsets and the sea. Bill told stories of his vagabonding throughout the U.S., of how he'd cooked on ships in many ports, of the narrow escapes he'd had, especially in the South. He told me he had to be constantly on guard because the few Southern Blacks who worked the rigs were "white on the inside and just token members of the work crews." Bill thought it was just a matter of time before he'd be gone again. In the mornings when our work shifts were completed, he'd usually go to his bunk and read the Bible.

The chief engineer filed a negative report on Bill to the catering company. Two days later, a new catering crew was brought out. Everyone but me was replaced. I was promoted to Bill's former position of night cook. Before he left, he showed me all the shortcuts of his work routine. My duties now included preparing midnight suppers and morning breakfasts, as well as all the pastries, desserts, and breads for the crew of sixty men.

One of the new galley hands was a Vietnam veteran who confided in me his many and varied tales of horror in the jungle during the war. He'd been a tunnel rat and still had recurring nightmares. One night, he dreamed a Viet Cong was coming at him with a bayonet. He lashed out with his right foot and woke up screaming, blood spurting from where he'd gashed it on one of the loose springs on the upper bunk.

Another galley hand was flown out. He rarely spoke in anything but ingratiating tones, as if his whole life had been one of obsequious cowering to figures of authority. During breaks, he'd sit in a corner staring at the walls. He was another of the many laborers picked off the streets of Galveston—drifters and alcoholics who took the minimum wage they were paid, worked the two weeks offshore to dry out, got some food in their bellies, stuffed a few dollars in their pockets, and were never seen again.

Hurricane Allen came near the end of my third two-week stint. It was the second largest hurricane of the century. At its peak, it filled the entire Gulf and had sustained winds of up to two hundred miles per hour. All the rigs in the Gulf were evacuated two days ahead the storm, an enormous process involving thousands of men. Hundreds of trips by helicopter were necessary as the choppers held a maximum of only thirteen men. Before our helicopter arrived, winds were blowing up to sixty to seventy miles per hour. Sudden booming gusts rattled the Leo Clark in a vicious patter of sprays. The sea rocked the barge like a cork. With each sweeping blow, water gushed through the galley garbage hatch. The galley hands and I labored furiously to fasten everything securely and mop back the flow of water on the floor. Finally, the helicopter arrived, and we were taken ashore.

The Galveston and Houston areas were evacuated. Dick's company decided to fly its three Lear jets to Oklahoma City until the hurricane blew itself out. Dick's jet was the last to leave. He waited until the last possible minute so I could fly in the jet with him and escape the storm. I rode in the co-pilot's seat and got bombed on scotch. Two days later, I read in the paper that one helicopter had crashed during the rig evacuations. The pilot and twelve rig workers were all killed. I quit my job and headed east.

I spent two days looking for a job and a room in New Orleans. I had a strange and ominous foreboding about the place, so I continued east until I arrived in West Palm Beach, Florida. It, too, had a dark atmosphere. The gulf separating the very rich and the very poor was obvious. This was during the aftermath of the 1980 riots that swept Miami when three white policemen were acquitted on a murder charge, contending they'd beaten and killed a Black man for no reason. Cuban and Haitian refugees were a big problem. There was tension everywhere.

I found a room for forty-five dollars a week in a run-down motel in the Cuban section of town and met Tommy Edwards, a blonde, powerfully built young man from South Carolina. He had a room in the same motel and was working as a heavy equipment operator at a job site on the outskirts of town. We became roommates and moved into a two-room bungalow after I found a job as a day cook at a Hilton Hotel.

In the languid evenings of early autumn, exhausted from our days of labor, we swapped life stories while swilling bottles of beer. Tommy told me about his youth, about growing up in a small South Carolina town, about how his mama raised five kids after his daddy left home never to be seen again. He remembered months of eating nothing but tomato sandwiches on dry bread. There was one memory of his daddy's liquor still and the bottles hidden in different corners of the shack they lived in. One day, his daddy beat his mama and Tommy pissed in one of the bottles. Later, his daddy drank from the bottle, puked, grabbed Tommy, and beat him until his ears bled.

Tommy joined the Army, but his memories of that time weren't clear. He said he was chosen for Special Forces training near the end of the Vietnam War. At the end of the training, he was one of a few who were picked to experience simulated prisoner of war conditions. He was given a drug being tested by the Army for interrogation purposes. About a week later, just coming off guard duty and still armed with his M-16, he was thrust mentally into another world. He was inside the enemy's camp. The barracks building across the road was the Viet Cong's headquarters. He sprayed the side of the barracks with three bursts from his M-16. Someone clubbed him from behind. That was all he remembered.

He said he spent four months in a psychiatric ward. The Army discharged him after he signed some papers. He didn't remember what he signed, but it had something to do with returning twice a year for electric shock treatments and receiving seventy thousand dollars. He quit going to the military hospital after three years of treatments. The pain was too much. He felt he was losing his mind.

He remembered only bits and pieces of the next three years. He didn't know what happened to the money. When he first returned home, he went into the wooded swamps outside his hometown and lived in seclusion for six months with his two dogs. That's all he remembered. He said he now moved every four or five months because the government was after him. He couldn't write or telephone his mama. The government had her phone tapped and checked her mail. He said if they ever caught up with him, there'd be hell to pay. And more shock treatments. His speech was already impaired. He said they'd have to kill him before he let them drag him back to that hospital.

Gary Minch, a friend of Tommy who also worked as a heavy equipment operator at the same job site, moved into the bungalow in December. He was a short, muscular, embittered Vietnam vet who was wounded in the war, returned to his home in New Jersey, married his high school sweetheart, had two daughters, started his own trucking business, found his grip on life gradually slipping away, and now hated the America he returned to. He began selling drugs, got busted, and lost his business and family while he went to jail for a year. He drifted from job to job down the eastern seaboard until finally coming to Florida.

The three of us shared an inability to cope in an indifferent America. Confessions of our brushes with death filled our evenings. We bought five-dollar bags of pot in the Black ghetto of West Palm Beach, piling into the rusted-out Ford van I bought for five hundred dollars after my VW died, me at the wheel, Tommy on the passenger side to do the bargaining, and Gary in the back with a baseball bat in case there was trouble. The beer we drank and the pot we smoked loosened our tongues and strengthened our memories. Gary and I were the voluble ones. Gary spoke with bitter, morbid pride of the times he'd killed, the patrols in the jungle he survived, the smell, taste, and sound of the horrors of war, the fights in prison, the drugs taken, the cold burn of the shrapnel still embedded in his back, the nightmares that haunted his sleep. I countered with my own vital Asian and road tales.

Gary and I began to ignore Tommy, who often sat at a distance during our discussions, brooding and giving off a look of incomprehensibility, as if he was listening to a foreign language. Sometimes he turned on the TV and stared vacantly at it, waiting for commercial breaks when he could mock the announcers and the products they were selling. One night, he turned away from the TV, stared intently at Gary, and said, "You're not as tough as you think you are."

They began wrestling on the sofa. Suddenly, Tommy's eyes rolled back. He fell to the floor, muscles cramping, mouth frothing, face quivering, and screaming, "No more! Please, no more!"

I jumped out of my chair, shouted to Gary, "He's having a flashback!" and vigorously massaged Tommy's back and neck.

Gary slapped Tommy's face, pressed Tommy's body against

his own, and shouted, "You're with us, Tommy! You're OK! We love you, man! It's not real! You're with us!"

Tommy finally relaxed. He was breathing hard, his face pale. Tears were in his eyes. Three days later when I returned from work, Tommy was gone.

Winter passed. Neither Gary nor I were making much money. We were fed up with our jobs and with Florida. We decided to head back toward Texas and try to find jobs on the oil rigs. In April, we loaded our belongings into my van and headed across the Everglades, up the Florida panhandle, passed through Alabama into Mississippi, then on to Louisiana. All along the Gulf Coast, we looked for jobs, but Gary couldn't pass the physical exams because of the shrapnel in his back. Our money was nearly gone, only fifty dollars left between us.

We pitched camp outside of Houma, Louisiana. We smoked a joint. Gary wanted to explore the forest. We entered the forest. Gary was once again a point man on patrol in Vietnam. He painted his face with mud, got down on his belly, and crawled through the thick, black brush. He was more alive than at any time since we'd met. This game went on for an intolerably long time. He came upon a snake and killed it with his hands. He made animal sounds and shouted hysterically, "We killed the Cong! We killed the Cong!"

The next day, I hooked on with a catering company in Houma. There was a one-week job on a platform being converted from a drilling to an oil-production rig. We drove back to Venice on the tip of the peninsula that stretched below New Orleans into the Gulf. I filled the van with gas, parked it, handed over our last twenty dollars to Gary, and told him to hitchhike to Dick's place. We agreed to meet there in about ten days. Then I hopped a boat for the four-hour ride on a stormy sea to the rig.

On the second day, with live natural gas in the air, there was an electrical fire. The fire alarm was sounded. All the workers ran in a panic to the life raft stations. Luckily, there was an extinguisher next to where the fire had broken out. A quick-thinking engineer grabbed it and doused the fire before it had a chance to spread. If another two or three minutes had passed, the whole rig might've blown up.

When the job finished, I drove back into Houma, cashed my paycheck, and continued to Dick's place in League City. I arrived at 4:30 in the morning. Gary answered the door. "I knew you'd make it!" he said. "I knew that was the sound of the ol' van. I knew you'd be coming today. That's what I told them!"

Dick got out of bed. His new girlfriend, Dottie, a petite, swarthy woman in her mid-forties, rolled out of bed, too. We went to the front room to have some coffee and exchange stories from the past several months.

Later that day, Dick called me aside to talk about Gary. Gary had arrived four days previous and done nothing but lie around, waiting for my arrival to decide his next move. Dick didn't like the idea of having someone around who had no money and no initiative to look for a job. Gary was just too strange for him. He didn't like the way Gary looked at Dottie. He was afraid to leave her alone with Gary in the apartment. The attempted assassination of Ronald Reagan had happened two days before. Gary's comments about how he'd kill John Hinckley in a minute if he had the chance scared Dick. Dick was to start a new job flying a company plane to different parts of Texas and Mexico soon. He wanted Gary out of the apartment as soon as possible.

The next morning, I rousted Gary out of bed and we drove to Galveston. By mid-afternoon, after checking several job possibilities, we found Gary a job as a galley hand aboard a tug that would be out to sea for two months at a time servicing oil barges all along the Gulf Coast. He was to ship out of Port Arthur on the Texas-Louisiana border the following evening. I gave him an old backpack to stuff a few sets of clothes in and drove him to Port Arthur. We parted with a handshake. I promised to ship his other things to him when he got settled.

Three days later, I was assigned to a three-week stint on the Gulf Commander, a drilling rig out of Port O'Connor, Texas. The crew of fifty-five men was as rough as any I'd seen. The work was demanding. Three galley hands quit in my first two days. The catering company had difficulty finding more help to send out. The regular crew—the riggers, roughnecks, roustabouts, welders, toolpushers, rig foremen—complained incessantly about the uncleanliness of their working conditions and the blandness of the food. After the galley hands quit, there were only two of us, the head steward and me, to cater to their needs. Then the head steward hopped a boat to shore. I was left alone to prepare four meals a day to fifty-five men with voracious appetites. The head toolpusher could provide only one roustabout per twelve-hour shift to help wash pots, pans, and dishes. At one point, I worked forty-eight straight hours before another cook was sent out. He'd been offshore on another rig for four weeks with only two days off and was on the verge of collapse himself. I got four hours of sleep before going back for another twelve-hour shift.

At the end of the three weeks, I was in a state of near neurasthenia. On the day I left the Gulf Commander, however, the crew members made a point of shaking my hand and needling me as if I was one of their own. Their banter was full of friendly innuendo. During that three-week stint, three rig workers were hospitalized. One had his right hand crushed under a pipe. Another sustained spinal injuries when he fell off the personnel basket—a rope basket at the end of a long cable on which supplies and crew members were lifted from a supply boat by an enormous crane on top of the rig—and landed on the supply boat deck during a crew change in stormy weather. The third received a concussion when smacked in the head by a flying cable that snapped while heavy equipment was being lifted.

There was in the crew members' banter a form of appreciation of the work I'd done and of my not abandoning them as the other catering service hands had. From that day forward, I had a great respect for those hardened individuals who faced the sea, their work, and life with an uncompromising tenaciousness.

The next few months flew by. I was hired by a different catering company that assigned me as a steward for two oil production rigs. I rotated between Corpus Christi and Galveston, working two-week stints on each rig with a week off in between. The pay was better and the number of men I had to cook for was reduced to ten engineers and one galley hand on each rig.

There were many wonders of nature in the Gulf. The colors of the sea and sky changed hourly. On some days, the sea and sky blended together in a satin blue and changed progressively to sapphire and indigo. At sunset, the coast became a purple line and the few clouds rust-colored as the crimson sun sank slowly below the horizon. On some days, the clouds were leaden, the sky black, and the sunsets became a long line of vermillion between the sea and sky. At night, a massive depth of black often hung over the rigs and strong winds swept at us from out of a vast obscurity. One time on the Samedan A, the rig out of Corpus Christi, in the wake of a violent storm, a double rainbow formed—one rainbow making a complete circle within the other rainbow whose meeting points rested upon the surface of the sea just fifty feet off the side of the rig.

The men on the Samedan A were a great bunch. In the evenings, their work finished and supper eaten, they often went down to the lower base of the rig platform and fished for mud sharks, red snapper, mackerel, and many other fish of odd shapes and sizes. Sometimes after supper, a couple of us would go to the top of the rig, a hundred and fifty feet in the air, smoke pot, and watch the shifting moods and colors of the sea.

One of my favorite guys was the captain of the Sea One, the crew change boat that stayed out for weeks at a time. There were five oil-producing rigs surrounding the main rig the engineers lived on. The Sea One provided transport from rig to rig. The captain was in his late fifties. He had an Indonesian wife who worked as his deckhand. On two occasions, I was allowed to board the boat while the engineers checked the instruments on the other rigs. The captain and I shared a joint and settled into tales of exploits around the world.

He'd been many places, working tugboat and barge jobs from Alaska to South America. He'd lived for a year with the natives in the jungles of Brazil. He'd also had successful businesses in different parts of the American mainland, but in the end couldn't cope with the insanity of American life. It was too fast for him. He said he had little faith in politics and business. Both led ultimately to war and destruction. He was a rich man but had no use for money for anything beyond the food and clothing he required. He loved the sea, the perfection of nature. He said he thought he was selling himself out by working for the oil companies and that age was the reason a man became more conservative. He planned to go back to South America in two years to retire to a simple life.

After my last stint on the Samedan A as we rode the Sea One back to shore, he clasped my hand and said, "I get good vibrations from you, Bob. Good luck to you. You have the right attitude for one so young. I know life will treat you well. The suffering you've witnessed and experienced has left a positive mark on you. Good journey to you wherever you go."

In late August, Dick and Dottie got married. Mom, who was now separated from Herb and working as a legal secretary in Portland, Oregon, flew down for the wedding and a weekend of partying. It was the first time that Mom, Dick, and I had been together in over twelve years. When Dick and Dottie exchanged their vows, Mom shed tears of happiness. I promised to meet her in a month in Portland. I'd saved about four thousand dollars and was ready to begin serious work on a novel. I left League City two days later.

I drove my old Ford van through the desert waste of Texas, New Mexico, and Arizona to Los Angeles, where I stayed with Mike Feig for a few days. He'd finally married his girlfriend from Andre's in Carmel, quit the job there, and found work in a popular Hollywood French restaurant.

From Los Angeles, I headed up the West Coast to Humboldt County to see Shannon and also to spend time with Dad and his family. A full month after leaving Texas, the van limped into Portland on its last legs. The four months I spent with Mom were a nourishing time. I was proud of the way she'd forged an independent life, of her unyielding desire to improve herself, of the years she spent attending night school to become a qualified legal secretary. Her enthusiasm for life was infectious. I played competitive basketball again in a local city league, finished writing a novel, and recuperated from the exhaustion of working on the oil rigs. Quite often I had dinner prepared when Mom got home from work. We shared stories of what we'd seen and done over the previous few years.

As my money began to run out, I thought about going to Alaska to work in the northern oil fields, but I found out my old high school buddy John Cady was cooking in an oil camp outside of Evanston, Wyoming. We exchanged a few letters. He was on good terms with the boss of the catering company and managed to land me a job. I took a bus from Portland in mid-January 1982, stopped in Fortuna for a three-day visit, hopped another bus headed east, and arrived in the bleak, snow-covered emptiness of Wyoming with ten dollars remaining in my pocket. I began washing pots and pans for five dollars an hour the next day.

The camp was about twenty miles outside of Evanston. There were close to a thousand workers living in the prison-like compound. John had been at the camp for a few months and was one of the head cooks. Over the next few months, we renewed our friendship and passed the time working long hours, playing golf at the Evanston course on our few days off, drinking copious amounts of beer, playing poker with the other kitchen hands— many of whom were Czechoslovakian refugees—and watching Atlanta Braves baseball games on cable TV. I worked my way up to the head baker job and saved a lot of money.

I'd continued to correspond with Raymond Mungo since leaving California two years earlier. He too had been on the move a lot. In July, I received a letter from him detailing how he and his boyfriend Robear managed to rent a house in Maui from a fellow writer who'd lived on the island, was headed to Boston to take a newspaper job, and needed someone to take over his place. Raymond wrote that I could have a room and stay as long as I wished. The lure of the easy pace of life and the potent marijuana was too strong to resist. At the end of August, I quit my job, took a bus to Salt Lake City, and bought a plane ticket to Maui.

The few months I spent on Maui were wonderful. There were the lazy afternoons of swimming in the ocean and driving in the high hills of Haleakala, the volcanic crater that rose above the island. There were the spectacular views from up high of the sparkling Pacific and the thick foliage of the lower valleys. There was the colorful array of flowers speckling the gardens of the residential areas, the bright beaches, the towering palms, the Maui Mountains on the opposite side of the isthmus that divided the island, the perpetual clouds that capped the mountains, the seaside village of Wailuku resting in the foothills, the vast stretches of sugar cane bristling in the winds, the slow movement of stocky, brown natives going about their daily business, the windsurfers riding the waves on the west side of the island, and the constant coming and going of tourists on the dry east side.

I grew fat and lazy. For all my good intentions, I completed only a few pages of hack work. My money once again began to run out. There was the possibility of going back to work in a tourist restaurant, but I was tired of the cooking trade. A change was called for. I felt a need to be jolted into a different reality. Raymond was called back to the mainland to promote a new book. There was no need for me to stay on the island. Besides, I couldn't afford to rent the house by myself.

Raymond suggested I go to Japan. He'd been there before on two previous occasions and had fond memories. Two of his books were translated into Japanese and sold well. He told me of the possibility of teaching English as a foreign language. Many foreigners who passed through Japan earned an income that way. The idea was appealing. Raymond gave me the name and address of a friend who lived near Kobe and would let me stay until I got set up.

For a long time, I'd dreamed of living, working, and studying in a foreign country. On my journeys abroad, I'd respected and envied those who spoke more than one language. I'd vowed one day to learn to speak a foreign language myself. Now it seemed there might be a chance.

We found a young couple to take over renting the house. On a January day, two weeks after Raymond and Robear returned to the mainland, I was on a plane to Osaka. I had only about a hundred dollars remaining, but there'd be some income tax money returned to me in the spring. I'd been in tighter situations before. I was confident I'd ultimately survive.

Mom in high school, 1942

Dad's high school graduation, 1938

Dad (right) with Army Air Force pilots, 1943

Mom and Dad's wedding, 1946

Mom, Dad, Dick (right), and me (left), 1952

Grandma Murph and me, 1955

Grandpa Pat (Mom's dad), 1954

Mom the skating instructor, 1960

226

Mom, 1967

Me in the 4th Grade, 1961

Arcata High School basketball, 1969

Friends Tim Crowley and Shannon Kelly, 1970

Mom and Granddad Frederick, 1979 (four months before he died, one day after his 99th birthday)

Bob the head baker and assistant at a Wyoming oil camp, 1982

BOOK TWO

BOOK TWO

13

Itami City I

A WEEK after landing in the Osaka-Kobe area, I found a job through the classified ads in an English newspaper. I began teaching at an English conversation school called Umeda Center Language Academy, UCLA for short, in Nishinomiya, on the Hankyu Railway line halfway between Osaka and Kobe. On my first day, I met Maureen, a Canadian teacher who invited me to stay with her and her friend Yuko Makishima in Itami City until I could find a place of my own. Yuko found a cheap apartment near her place a few days later and talked the landlord into renting it to me.

The apartment was one of three on the second story of a two-story building. Each had a six-mat room, a three-mat room with a closet, a narrow kitchen space, and a small squat toilet. The only furniture—a futon, a small electric heater, and a *kotatsu*, a low wooden table with a portable heater attached beneath it— was provided by Yuko's parents. There was no bath, so I went to a nearby *sento* public bath. The landlord and his wife lived on the first floor.

How I came to love that *sento*! At first, I was a bit self-conscious,

but gradually became more relaxed. The master and other customers, mostly older, treated me kindly. I'd take off my shoes
at the entrance, greet and pay the master, and enter the men's
locker room, where I'd strip, put my clothes in a locker, and
enter the steam-filled bathing room. In the middle of the room
was a long trough of water. Along the walls were taps where
bathers soaped and rinsed themselves. At the far end was a large
tub in which bathers soaked contentedly. A forested mountain
overlooking a calm lake was painted on the tiled wall behind
the tub. I'd squat on a miniature stool next to the trough, rinse
myself with a plastic bucket, put soap on a towel for scrubbing,
scrub my body, rinse again, then immerse myself in the large tub.

After moving into my apartment, I fell into a routine—get up
about nine o'clock, study some Japanese, write for about an hour,
read, do some stretches, go to work, return in the evenings to
Maureen and Yuko's for dinner, go home, write for another hour,
and go to bed. Everything about my new life was stimulating.
Even the most commonplace things and events gave me a thrill
of discovery: the squat toilet and the pine sprig designs on the
sliding doors in my apartment; the old hat factory—where most
of the *sento* bathers worked—on the way to the Hankyu Railway
Itami Station; the train ride to work and the salaried commuters
who looked like characters out of the 1950s with their dark suits,
sleek hair styles, and white socks; the mom-and-pop shops in my
neighborhood with their friendly shopkeepers who smiled and
waved when I passed by; the ubiquitous billboards with their
kanji lettering; the rapid-fire sound of the Japanese language;
the bows people performed in their greetings, conversations,
and partings.

I read Japanese novels in English translation and filled notebooks with daily observations of the world around me. I was

overwhelmed by the kindness of everyone I came into contact with. The Japanese staff at the UCLA school loaned me books on teaching methodology and gave advice on how to deal with the students. Maureen and Yuko cooked dinner for me every night and gave me tips on where to shop, wash my clothes, and find used goods for my apartment. The Ogawa family that ran the *sento* taught me simple expressions. Shoppers at the local markets came to my rescue when I was confused about prices. I felt there might be a future for me in Japan.

By the end of March, the days were becoming warmer. I began jogging four or five times a week around Koya Park, which was only five minutes from my apartment. In the afternoons when I had no classes, I'd lace up my running shoes, head out the apartment door, and go down the stairs. I'd turn left at the narrow road leading to Route 171, pass the police station and Itami City Hall, cross Route 171, run up the incline leading to the park—a refuge for ducks, swans, and other birds that spent every winter on its man-made pond—and enter the two-and-a-half-kilometer path that circled the park.

I'd get into a rhythm, legs and arms pumping, heart beating, images and abstract thoughts racing through my mind. Japanese phrases I'd learned recently flashed in my mind as I headed through the stretch of cherry trees. On the right and across the street was a row of high-rise apartment buildings with long lines of brightly colored laundry often flapping in the breeze. Beyond the apartment buildings were three baseball diamonds. Sometimes softball games were in progress. On the third field, fathers and sons played catch.

Inside the park and lining the edges of the pond, dozens of birdwatchers with their cameras gathered. Occasionally, a group of school children in uniforms squealed in delight, waved, and shouted encouragement as I passed by them. On the back stretch, I'd run past a hospital, where construction workers in the parking lot sometimes stopped to watch. Finally, I'd run through a back entrance to the park and up a slight incline where families were eating *bento* lunches. I'd complete two more laps and return to my apartment.

At the end of these invigorating and therapeutic runs, I liked to drink a beer and sit down to think and write in my journal.

My tourist visa would soon expire. Although the UCLA school offered to give me sponsorship for a year if I signed a contract, I turned their offer down. The six-day week was a bit demanding. I wanted to have more time to devote to study and writing. I thought it better to extend the tourist visa for another three months, continue working at UCLA until April, when I'd finish paying off the key money for my apartment, and try to find sponsorship from another school where my hours might be reduced.

Although I didn't really consider myself a teacher in the professional sense, I liked teaching. I felt more a student. In my first few weeks on the job, I was finding out how little I really knew about my own language. I reexamined the fundamentals of language structure, becoming conscious of the words I chose to express myself to be as clear as possible to the students, who came from all ages and walks of life.

During the lessons, the conversations, particularly with the higher-level students, covered a wide range of topics. I believed I could learn as much about Japan in my little teaching booth as I could traveling the entire country. I didn't know how long the job would last as I was working illegally on a tourist visa, but for the time being my salary of two hundred twenty thousand yen a month for teaching eight hours a day, six days a week allowed me to pay my bills and put a little in my pocket. I could extend my travel visa for another three months in April. Beyond that, I trusted in faith and good luck.

One day, I was walking to the UCLA school from the Nishinomiya train station when I bumped into another American whom I recognized from some pictures I'd seen at the school. Ron McCrum was a rotund man in his early fifties and had a broad smile. He'd quit UCLA two weeks before I started working there. He'd set up his own school in Mukonoso. I had a half hour before my first class started. We agreed to have a cup of coffee together. Ron said he had too many students to handle by himself and wanted to hire a couple of teachers. He invited me to go out to discuss the possibility of working for him.

We met again a few nights later at a *yakitori* grilled chicken shop near the Mukonoso station. Over beer and chicken, Ron talked about his school and how he'd started with two students and now had thirty-five, about his life as a photographer in the States, and about meeting his Japanese wife when she was a homestay student on an exchange program that he'd been involved with in Seattle. He talked about the changes Japan had undergone from the time he was a serviceman stationed in Japan in the 1950s to the last few years after he returned to settle permanently. He warned me about the need to stay clear of schools like UCLA that exploited both teachers and students. He talked about the importance of the conversation teacher creating a relaxed atmosphere in which the students could do the majority of the speaking. He exuded confidence and enthusiasm and gave me many tips on teaching and surviving in Japan.

I took an immediate liking to Ron. I liked the way he joked and bantered with the cooks and other customers at the *yakitori* shop. I decided that night to work for him as soon as I could. The next day, I gave my notice to UCLA.

I began working for Ron the first week of May. Ron had rented another three-room apartment in the same apartment building he and his wife Mayumi were living in and converted two of the rooms into classrooms. The third room was the office and waiting room. Noriko, one of Ron's former students, had signed on to be the secretary. Each of the classrooms had a whiteboard, a table, and enough chairs for seven students and a teacher. The office had a desk and chair for Noriko, two sofas, a copy machine, a word processor, and a bookshelf with textbooks, books on teaching theory and methodology, and some dictionaries. Another teacher worked the morning and afternoon shift; I worked the evening shift; and Ron took some of the private students in his own apartment.

The change from UCLA to Ron's school, which he called RIS for Ron's International School, was what I needed. I'd paid off my apartment key money and could make do with a reduced salary. Ron started me out at a hundred fifty thousand yen a month for teaching three classes a day Monday through Friday. Each of the hour-and-a-half classes had from three to six students. The atmosphere was relaxed. I had the freedom to experiment with various teaching techniques. Ron sometimes sat in on my classes and afterward discussed with me ways to improve my teaching. He and Mayumi often invited me to their apartment for dinner and a few beers. Our friendship developed quickly.

I started taking Japanese lessons. I saw an ad in a local English newspaper, called the teacher—a woman named Imanishi who spoke English well—met her in a coffee shop in Umeda, and continued meeting her at the same coffee shop twice a week in the morning before going to work. Ron agreed to let us use his school for our lessons. He put Imanishi's name on the books as a salaried Japanese teacher and began paying for my lessons.

Imanishi was stiff and nervous in our first lesson. She'd just graduated from a six-month training course in teaching Japanese to foreigners. I was her first student. She gradually began to relax and grow confident. Soon we were often joking with each other. Whenever I made a particularly glaring mistake in pronunciation or grammar, we'd have a good laugh.

Imanishi prepared extensively for our lessons. She brought in pictures, maps, graphs, charts, props, anything she could think of to make a point clear and help me remember a new expression or pattern. She always related the material to my personal life. She taught me baseball expressions, literary expressions, vocabulary to explain where I came from, what my life history was, where I'd traveled, what I'd seen, and what I wanted to order in restaurants. She drilled me in correct pronunciation and the time length of Japanese vowels. She insisted I use standard Japanese rather than the Kansai dialect, although she took the time to point out the differences in intonation, verb endings, reduced speech, and male and female patterns. She always listened patiently with interest to my tales of misadventure with the language. She counseled perseverance and effort when I told her of my frustration about not making fast enough progress and not understanding what people were saying. She consoled me by explaining how she'd studied English for over eight years and still had trouble understanding a conversation between two native speakers.

Studying Japanese induced me to see more clearly the difficulties of my own Japanese students studying English. I often wondered why so many Japanese students were reticent in the classroom. Now I began to understand the obstacles involved in constructing a simple sentence in a language totally unrelated to one's own. There was no concept of singular and plural in Japanese; the subject was often omitted; the verb came at the end of the sentence. In addition, the Japanese had a way of responding three or four times to a speaker's single sentence. If this response—called *aizuchi*—wasn't given, the speaker seemed to have difficulty continuing. A native speaker of English responded to entire thoughts or opinions. If a student couldn't think in the second language, and had to grope through a tension-ridden thought process of internal translation—clause by clause and sentence by sentence—from one language to another, it was no wonder so many classes were filled with silence and confusion. I empathized with those students. I resolved to make myself a better teacher, a teacher as committed as Imanishi.

In the evenings after I'd come home from work and taken a bath, I'd sometimes go for a walk. I enjoyed the narrow, labyrinthine streets of the neighborhood. The architecture of the homes was different from anything I'd ever seen—the slated roofs, the ubiquitous gardens of trimmed shrubbery, each garden with its stone shrine and walls of stone or concrete, the narrow, wooden gates that looked as if they were made for dwarves.

Aside from Ron, my other new friends included Mr. Inatsugi, whose nickname was Ian, Shigeya Kitamura, and Yuko. Ian had been one of my students at UCLA and switched to RIS when I started teaching there. He was a bureaucrat who worked for the Hyogo prefectural government and also lived in Itami. His hobby was talking to people overseas on his ham radio set. His English was good, and he was one of the most polite men I'd ever met. In the past two months, he'd invited me for dinner at his home twice. His wife prepared a feast on both occasions and his two little girls sat shyly at a distance listening to their father and me converse in English. Ian also visited my apartment once and brought a used television as a present. He offered to be the guarantor for my next visa application. He gave me a lot of encouragement in studying Japanese and adjusting to life in Japan.

My best friend was Shigeya. One night, shortly after coming home from work, I found Shigeya's business card in my mail slot. On the back of the card, he'd written a greeting in English and offered his services if I wanted to open a bank account. He worked for one of the local banks. His job was riding a motorbike around Itami every day collecting deposits from businesses and individuals while also trying to meet a monthly quota for soliciting new accounts. Two days later, I met him near the *sento*. We visited for a few minutes and agreed to have a beer sometime.

A few nights later, Shigeya showed up at my apartment with beer and snacks. He'd just gotten off work. We stayed up until three in the morning drinking and exchanging life stories. His dream was to become a professional painter. He hadn't used English since graduating from university two years before, but he was adept at articulating abstract ideas. He'd belonged to a translation club in university. He loved John Lennon and could recite the lyrics to many of Lennon's songs.

Shigeya stayed at my place regularly. The dormitory he lived in was an hour-and-a-half commute from Itami and he often missed the last train when working overtime at the bank. I offered my apartment as a kind of atelier for him. Shortly afterward, he brought some canvases, paints, and brushes, and spent two days working feverishly in the three-mat room while I studied Japanese in the six-mat room. When he finished the painting—a colorful, surrealistic depiction of a forest seen from a distance— we surveyed it from different angles, commented critically, and sat down to more beer and life confessions.

Shigeya was interested in my travels, experiences, and writing. He wanted to help me adapt to life in Japan. Our conversations were a mixture of Japanese and English. Our dictionaries became dog-eared. I saw a lot of my earlier self in Shigeya, in his passion for life and art.

Two months after I first met her, Maureen returned to Canada to pursue a nursing degree. Yuko and I began going out frequently. Before long, we were sleeping together. We carried on a tempestuous and passionate relationship for a year and a half, but too much alcohol, confusion, and misunderstanding led to its demise. For any readers interested in the sordid details, I refer them to *Toraware*, the novel I wrote based on the whole affair. There are still a few copies circulating somewhere in the world.

On one weekend in June, I flew to Korea, applied for a six-month study visa at the Japanese consulate there, and luckily the application was approved. Ron's idea about putting Imanishi's name on the school's books as a Japanese teacher and my name as a student worked. When the visa expired, I could apply within Japan for an extension of the same type of visa.

Of all the people I encountered in my first few years in Japan, the Sasa Softball Club had the biggest influence on me. They became my Japanese family during my first four years in Japan. In effect, they raised me from my first baby utterances of Japanese until the time I could stand on my own two feet. They accepted me as one of their own and allowed me to participate in their family dramas, rituals, and celebrations. Through them, I made my deepest connection with Japan and came to feel as if, finally, after fifteen years of wandering and searching, I'd found a place to call home.

Indeed, baseball itself was my textbook for years. Every night for at least those first four years, I religiously watched the one-hour evening baseball news program at eleven o'clock, furiously copying down new vocabulary, question forms, grammatical patterns, and idiomatic expressions in my notebook. I memorized all the professional Japanese players' names and their *kanji* characters. Always the next day, I tried to use the new vocabulary in baseball conversations with my buddies and their friends. Most Japanese men loved baseball, so it was easy to engage in baseball conversation anyone I met and in so doing activate the new knowledge I'd gained and get a lot of listening practice and repetition in the process.

Soon I was able to extend my conversational ability beyond the topic of baseball. By using different verbs and nouns and fitting them into the many sentence and grammatical patterns I was learning, I could make the switch easily enough. Eventually, I was able to converse on a number of topics, and Kamejima's liquor shop, where the players hung out, became my main classroom. I spent countless hours there practicing Japanese conversation.

Like so many other fateful experiences in my life, the day I met the Sasa Softball Club still plays out in my mind like a movie. There I am that July day arriving back at my apartment after having jogged at Koya Park. The rice field across the street glimmers in the afternoon sun. Sweat is pouring off me. I'm thirsty, so I grab a few coins off the *kotatsu* and head to the liquor shop on the narrow street that runs past the *sento*. I stop in front of the shop, put the coins in a beer vending machine, and push the button for a five-hundred-milliliter can.

A burst of laughter comes from inside the liquor shop. I peer around the vending machine. Seven men—all in their thirties and forties and dressed in softball uniforms—are seated on empty beer crates, drinking, joking, and obviously taking an interest in me. I recognize one of them as a regular customer at the *sento*.

Suddenly, all of them get up, come outside, and surround me. I can't understand much of what they're saying.

One of the men, whose name is Uchihashi, thrusts a softball and a glove into my hands. I stare back, unsure of what to do. Uchihashi makes some exaggerated motions of throwing and catching a ball.

"*Kyatchi booru yaroo. An'ta to bokura.*"

The others laugh heartily. I put on the glove and toss the ball to Uchihashi. We begin to play catch. Uchihashi moves back a few paces until he's about twenty meters away. I cut loose with some strong throws and hear exclamations of approval from the onlookers. A smile spreads across my face. I haven't played any ball since my Little League days, but the simplicity of the ritual that was such a big part of my childhood hasn't lost any of its thrill. Uchihashi throws me some ground balls, which I field smoothly and fire back as if to nip a speedy runner by half a step. Now there are fly balls to catch. I settle under them, catch the ball one-handed, and fire strikes back to Uchihashi, who applies the tag to an imaginary, sliding runner trying to score. One of the other players signals the runner out or safe.

The players motion me inside. They pour me a beer. Everyone drinks, jokes, claps one another's back, and carries on a lively conversation with much gesturing and single-word exchanges.

"*Namae?*"

"Robert."

"*Kuni?*"

"America."

"*Shigoto?*"

"English teacher."

"*Kanojo?*"

"No, no girlfriend."

"*Toshi?*"

"I'm 32."

"*Yakyuu ga suki?*"

"Yes, I like baseball."

From the scraps of conversation I can understand, I find out the team is comprised of local players who've played together for twelve years. In their younger days, they captured several local fast-pitch softball championships. They're now playing at a lower level of competition but are still near the top of their league. Although most of the teams in the local leagues are made up of members from a single company, the members of the Sasa Softball Club work at a variety of jobs. Some work at Itami City Hall, some at the fire station, some at the nearby hat factory, and the others seem to have their own businesses. The team sponsor is Kamejima's liquor shop. It seems no foreigner has ever played in the league, but they need a first baseman. Uchihashi, who works at Itami City Hall, is sure he can pull the necessary strings with the town officials to allow me into the league. They played their final summer league game today, but there'll be a practice game the next Sunday. The new league will start in the fall.

The party lasts into the night. I'm given a team uniform and an autographed softball. Everyone shakes my hand firmly when I finally depart. A pleasant buzz hums through my head as I stumble home.

The following Sunday, I get up early, too excited to have slept well. I drink a cup of coffee, put on my uniform, and begin applying some oil to the glove I bought the day after meeting the team. It's starting to loosen up and take shape from the numerous coats of oil I've applied and from the three-hour practice I took part in with the team the day before.

I feel good about finally making a connection with the people in my neighborhood. I've been too isolated my first few months to try to make many friends, unable to express myself beyond a few basic pleasantries. Until I met the Sasa Softball Club members, it seems most of the Japanese I've met are always waiting for me to take the first step toward a relationship.

I hear a car horn. It's Ikemoto, the forty-one-year-old, power-hitting left fielder who works as a fireman. Ikemoto was the first to greet me at the team practice. He took me under his wing and made sure I understood where to be and what to do during the practice. Afterward, we went out to a *yakitori* shop for some beer and grilled chicken. His manner and speech are gentle and full of cheer and encouragement.

Most of the other players are already warming up when we arrive at the park. Everyone greets me with smiles and shouts. I warm up with Uchihashi on the sidelines before taking some batting practice. Players' wives and children and assorted spectators gather on the sidelines and spread out box lunches and thermoses of tea.

Sasa Softball Club takes the field. I'm positioned at first base and toss grounders to the infielders. It feels wonderful to hear the chatter of the players and fans, to watch the pitcher take his warm-up throws, to feel the summer sun on the back of my neck, the pop of the ball meeting my glove, the dust on my hands, and the competitive jitters churning once again in my stomach.

The umpires signal for the game to start. Our pitcher goes into his motion and fires a fastball. The home plate umpire pivots to his right, shoots out his right arm, and bellows, "*Sutoraiku!*" On the next pitch, the batter bounces a slow roller to the shortstop, who scoops it up and side-arms a perfect throw to me at first base. I throw the ball to the catcher, Uchihashi, as I've been told to do on an out at first base, and revel in the satisfaction of a well-executed play. The next two batters fly out to Ikemoto in left field.

I bat seventh in the order. The game is still scoreless when I come up to bat in the bottom of the second inning with one out and a man on first base. I enter the batter's box and tap the head of the bat on the rubber plate. I take the first three pitches, then step out of the batter's box and ask the umpire for the count.

"*Tsuu wan,*" the umpire says, showing me one finger with his left hand and two fingers with his right hand.

It seems strange to me. If the count's two balls and one strike, the umpire should've indicated two fingers with his left hand and one finger with his right hand. Everything seems reversed in Japan.

The pitcher delivers the next pitch on the inside corner. I swing and miss. The catcher throws the ball to the third baseman. The ball continues around the infield. I step out of the batter's box again, bend over to grab some dirt, wipe my hands on my uniform, adjust my cap, and step back in the box. The first baseman tosses the ball to the pitcher, who turns around to face the plate. A look of astonishment crosses his face when he sees me still in the batter's box. A suspended moment of confusion ensues. The catcher and umpire look toward the Sasa Softball Club bench, gesturing frantically.

Ikemoto jogs toward the plate, grabs my arm, and gently pulls me to the sidelines.

"What're you doing? I've got one more strike," I say.

"*Robaato-san. Auto datta.*"

"What do you mean out? The umpire told me two balls and one strike. That was only the second strike."

"*Chigau, hantai. Tsuu sutoraiku wan booru datta yo.*"

I realize my mistake. Strikes are given in the count before balls, not the other way around as in American baseball. I suddenly feel deeply embarrassed. I turn to the umpire and players in the field, shout, "*Gomen nasai!*" and bow deeply. The umpire laughs, tips his cap, and signals for the next batter.

After three innings, the score is tied 1-1. Ikemoto has blasted a long home run to right field for our lone run. In the top of the fourth, the other team puts its first two runners on base with a single and a walk. I've seen enough Japanese baseball on TV to know the next batter will bunt. I move ahead three paces and keep my weight forward on my toes, ready to charge the ball if it comes my way. The batter lays down a hard bunt that bounces into my glove. I whirl and unleash a powerful throw to cut down the lead runner at third. The instant the ball leaves my hand, I know it's into orbit. I watch in disbelief as the ball sails above our third baseman's outstretched glove, continues in a straight line before falling to the ground some five meters beyond, and finally comes to a halt in a distant ditch. By the time Ikemoto retrieves the ball, all three runners have rounded the bases and stand at home plate, waving at me and shouting, "*Gaijin-san ookini!*"

My face flushes. The whole world is staring at me. Uchihashi is having a heated discussion with the home plate umpire, who eventually signals the batter back to second base and the runner ahead of him back to third base. The rule is only one extra base on an overthrow. The score is now 2-1.

The next batter attempts a suicide squeeze bunt toward first base. I again charge the plate and catch the ball on one bounce. The runner on third is streaking toward home. My momentum propels me forward. There's no time for a throw. I dive toward the plate, my gloved hand outstretched, and tag the sliding runner.

"*Auto!*" the umpire cries.

A loud cheer erupts from the Sasa Softball Club bench. I jump up, making sure the other runner won't try to score. I toss the ball back to the pitcher, dust myself off, and return to my position. The next batter lofts a fly ball to center field. The runner on third scores easily. The next batter strikes out.

The score remains 3-1 throughout the fifth and sixth innings. I lead off the bottom of the seventh inning with a line drive single to left field but am left stranded as the next three batters fly out. We lose the game. Several of the other team's players come up to me to shake my hand and say, "*Naisu geemu.*"

The Sasa Softball Club players gather together at Kamejima's liquor shop. They discuss the game amid more joking and laughter. Kamejima, who has retired from playing but still attends the games, pours me a beer.

"*Yoku ganbatta. Naisu battingu, Robaato-san.*"

"I played terribly. It was my fault we lost the game. I'm really sorry. I'll do better next time."

Kamejima, Ikemoto, Uchihashi, and the others won't accept my apology. They keep talking about my base hit and play at home plate on the suicide squeeze attempt. They tell me not to worry about the throw. It was just a practice game and there'll be much time for more practice before the league starts again in the fall. I feel among friends, a regular team member. There's much I want to tell them about my life, much I want to learn about them, but my Japanese is still too limited. I have to renew my study efforts.

Later, Ikemoto and I go to the *sento*. The hot water dissolves all my stiffness and the tension of the day. Ikemoto talks to the other bathers about the game. They shoot approving glances my way. As we leave, Ikemoto pats me on the shoulder.

"*Otsukare-sama. Kondo mo ganbaroo.*"

Back at my apartment, I fold my uniform and place it in the closet. I put my glove on top of the uniform, pause for a moment, put the glove back on my left hand, pound the pocket a few times with my right fist, then replace it on the uniform. I can't wait for the next game.

On a Saturday night in late July, the team had an informal party at a wealthy patron's home in the hills above Itami City. With its magnificent woodwork, spacious, matted rooms, and large, neatly manicured garden, it was the most beautiful home I'd been in in Japan. In the main room, five tables—complete with bundles of *sukiyaki* pans and ingredients, plates of *sashimi*, and lots of beer—had been set. The team members and other guests changed into *yukata* and I was introduced around. We then went into the main room, where an introductory speech was given by the patron. After the speech, the beer and food flowed. I made the rounds from table to table. There was much laughing and toasting of drinks. After dinner, there were more speeches. I stumbled through my own speech in drunken and broken Japanese. At the end of the evening, I was chosen to lead the team in a *banzai* yell and accidentally knocked over several beer bottles with my outstretched arms. No one seemed to mind. Everyone laughed uproariously. Later, I returned with Kamejima to his liquor shop for more drinks and food.

I spent a lot of time at Kamejima's liquor shop. Kamejima was a small man with a sharp wit that kept everyone in stitches. Although he'd retired from playing, he was still the team organizer and decision-maker who had the final word in all the plans and activities of the team. His shop was small—only a few customers could stand and drink together at the same time—but it was usually filled with regular customers. I liked its friendly atmosphere.

Kamejima introduced me to many customers and friends. I was, in many cases, the first foreigner they'd met face to face. I was often besieged with questions about the United States, my family, my life, my impressions of Japan, the differences between Japan and the outside world, and why I'd come to Japan. My Japanese was too limited to explain much, but this didn't seem to matter. I was Kamejima's friend and that was enough. He took it upon himself to be the person responsible for my well-being. He had the ability to intuit what I wanted to communicate. He acted as interpreter, despite knowing no more than a few words of English, to the barrage of questions that were invariably invoked by my presence at the shop. Sometimes Kamejima even took me on delivery runs around the city and introduced me to shops where I'd be treated well. His wife and two children also seemed to adopt me as one of their own.

One day, Tsutomu and Shinichiro, two team members, showed up at my apartment with a used washing machine in the back of Kamejima's little truck. They hauled the washing machine up the flight of steps, hooked it up on the balcony, and showed me how to run it. When I asked how I could repay them, Tsutomu said, "My neighbor was going to throw it out anyway. Besides, you can save money by not going to the coin laundry."

As July moved into August, I kept myself busy with writing and studying. The August heat was suffocating. Sometimes when seated in the nude at my *kotatsu* and an electric fan cooling my sweaty body, I'd break away from *hiragana* and *katakana* lettering practice to smoke a cigarette and stare out my back window at the wide, pellucid sky. An occasional plane floated across this canvas. I'd watch the shadows grow in the glare of the sun on the colored tiled roofs, listen to the sound of carpenters hammering and sawing at a far-off apartment building, and think of all the experiences I'd accumulated in my life.

August passed into September. The insistent scream of cicadas faded, then disappeared. The days were still warm, but the nights grew increasingly cooler. By the end of September, the rice fields had turned yellow-green. The colors of autumn were sharp and vivid. There were several quick evening showers that left the streets and tiled roofs of houses glittering in the fading light. A violent typhoon swept through the Japanese archipelago and many areas were flooded. In mid-October the rice fields were harvested. In the early evening dusk, the long poles on which the rice plants were hung to dry looked like rows of straw soldiers standing at attention.

Near the end of September, a strong typhoon drenched the area. The streets in the neighborhood flooded over. The rain and wind continued for two days. I was forced to stay in my apartment and listen to what sounded like the end of the world. The following days were magnificent, with a stillness and clarity that contrasted sharply with the violence of the storm.

I was still jogging four or five times a week and felt in good shape. Ron's school was growing at a fast pace and another teacher had been hired. Overall, things were going well. The only thing that plagued me was not knowing how long I'd be able to stay in Japan, or whether I wanted to settle into the life of a permanent expatriate.

I was busy throughout November. I went to the immigration department in Osaka to apply for formal permission to work while on a study visa. I hated having to rationalize my existence to a faceless bureaucracy. There was always too much paperwork to fill out. If only one frivolous form was forgotten or filled out improperly, the applicant was made to feel like a boy who's been caught lying or cheating. I especially hated having to sweat through the period of waiting for an answer. A week later, I felt immensely relieved when I received a letter of permission from the immigration department to work no more than twenty-five hours a week.

Winter was on its way. I found a kerosene heater in the garbage pile down the street where people dumped their used goods once a month. Much of the furniture that now furnished my apartment had been taken from the garbage pile: the lights, carpet, two-burner gas stove, bookstand, and electric fan. It seemed people just threw out their old goods when they bought or received new ones. In most cases, these goods were cleaned and still in working condition before being set out. As the days became colder, I sometimes slept until noon, preferring to stay beneath the warm covers of my futon. In the evenings after work, I'd light my kerosene heater, sit at the *kotatsu*, and study Japanese.

In January, I was given another six-month extension of my visa. The *hatake* garden outside my kitchen window lay dormant, its furrowed rows piled with fresh dirt. Of all the things that surrounded my little corner of the world, the garden and rice field next to it reflected the changes in season. The sounds of Itami filtered in through the window—a motor scooter buzzing along a side street, a dog barking, children laughing.

I thought I could spend many more years in Japan. I'd made considerable strides in my study. There was a discernible improvement in my life with the passing of each day. I could now speak enough Japanese to make most of my wants understood. My comprehension was also improving. I could see the vague possibility of becoming reasonably fluent if I spent another few years here. The thought of returning to a life in the States was no more than an abstraction.

One evening in early February, I met Tsutomu at the *sento*. He was in an unusually depressed mood. I asked what the matter was. He said that another team member, Matsumoto, had committed suicide the night before. There'd been no note left behind, but apparently Matsumoto owed a lot of money to loan sharks. His wife and daughter found him that morning in his car with a rubber hose running from the exhaust pipe through a small crack in the driver's window. There'd be a team wake for him in two weeks.

That night as I lay in my futon, I thought about the last time I'd seen Matsumoto. Near the end of January, the softball team had a meeting and party that lasted well into the night. I'd drunk too much. The last thing I remembered about the night was drinking in a bar with two of the older members of the team, men in their fifties who rarely played anymore but still attended the team parties. One of them was Matsumoto. I remembered him as a good-natured man who delighted in playing practical jokes. Every time I met him, he made it a point to sit next to me and pour me drink after drink. I'd always felt comfortable in Matsumoto's presence, despite understanding little of his strong Osaka dialect.

Near the middle of March, Sasa Softball Club had its first game of the year. After the game, the team members, still in their uniforms, gathered at Matsumoto's house. At first, everyone took turns kneeling in front of the family altar with Matsumoto's picture on it, ringing a bell to call forth Matsumoto's spirit, and saying a silent prayer. Then Matsumoto's widow and daughter began serving food and drinks. The mood became festive. Everyone got drunk. There was much singing and laughter. Kamejima and Matsumoto's widow capped the evening by reading some farewell messages in front of the altar.

14

Itami City II

M OM and her friend Judy came to visit at the end of March. It was her first time to travel abroad. Ron, Mayumi, several of the RIS students, and Yuko joined me in welcoming them at the airport. It was wonderful to see the joy on Mom's face as she and Judy were presented with bouquets of flowers and several small gifts. After many bows, hugs, kisses, giggles, and smiles, I returned with Mom and Judy to my apartment. It was crowded, but they were thrilled to be in a foreign country and to have already been greeted by so many friendly people. Extra futons had been loaned to me. Mom and Judy slept soundly.

Those three weeks passed quickly. The depth of the friendships I'd been fortunate in making revealed itself in a manner I couldn't have foreseen. Mom and Judy were treated like royalty by nearly everyone I knew. I hadn't asked a single favor of anyone, yet all who knew me went out of their way to make Mom and Judy's Japanese experience one they would never forget.

Yuko took them to the *sento* and showed how to take a Japanese bath. Some of the older women customers surrounded Mom, insisted on scrubbing her back for her, and while laughing uproariously, pointed first at Mom's large breasts and then at their own smaller breasts. Yuko translated for them, and all had a lot of fun. The next day, the owner of the coffee shop above the *sento* treated them to lunches. Ron, Mayumi, and some students gave two parties in their honor at Ron's apartment. Mayumi took them on a three-day tour of Kyoto. Ian drove us around Itami, and his wife prepared an elaborate lunch for a cherry-blossom-viewing picnic at one of the parks near Kobe. Two of the RIS students spent an entire day with them, driving to Mt. Rokko, treating them to lunch in one of Kobe's finest restaurants, and guiding them around many of Kobe's shrines and temples. Shigeya and another artist friend drove us to Nara for a day of cultural exploration and to view the Giant Buddha statue. They also gave Mom and Judy paintings they'd just completed. Yuko took time to take them shopping. She also gave a party one night at her apartment. Shigeya and several of the Sasa Softball Club members attended. As usual, there was much drinking and laughter. People in the neighborhood dropped by to say hello, offer their services in any way they could, and give gifts of fruit and vegetables. Mom and Judy joined in several of the classes I was teaching. Imanishi even gave Mom a free Japanese lesson.

There were few quiet moments during those three weeks. Mom and Judy were thoroughly exhausted by the time they had to return to the States. I was pleased to see Mom enjoy herself so much. She'd been as vibrant as a schoolgirl. She'd relished each moment, each new discovery, each new friendship, as if a significant source of life sustenance could be drawn from it. I sensed deeply the love and pride she held for me. I'd done little for her through the years, so I was doubly appreciative of the extraordinary kindness everyone showed. I wondered if I'd ever be able to repay my Japanese friends for the joy they'd given so freely.

Many people went to the airport to say goodbye. Tears were shed and hugs given. Mom vowed to start studying Japanese and return in the next year or two.

A few weeks after Mom returned to Portland, there was a phone call for me at the school. Mom was calling to let me know that Midge Kelly had died of cancer. Later, at a noodle shop with Ron, I tried to remember exactly what Mom said. All I could remember was that Midge died on May 16. The mama-san brought us a beer and two glasses. Ron poured my glass full, then filled his own. I emptied half the glass in two swallows. He filled the glass again.

I drank in silence while Ron talked about death. A few years before, his first wife lost five family members in the same year. She lost her grip on life after that, he said. She became bitter and misanthropic. They divorced. He sighed and said that seemed so long ago. He had no reason to return to the States.

The States were far away for me, too. But the phone call brought back the past with a sudden clarity. The distance made me feel helpless and guilty. Why hadn't I gone to see Midge the last time I was in Fortuna before heading off to work with John Cady in Wyoming? Didn't I have a premonition then that it'd be the last time I ever returned to Humboldt County? I sat in the bars for three days in a drunken and drugged stupor, as if frozen in time, unable to pay the proper visit to Midge, one of the most influential people in my life. Instead, I quietly slipped out of town on a bus to Wyoming.

I thought of my court martial. Midge was a character witness for me and faced up to all the military authorities on my behalf. She was powerful and beautiful that day. I thought of all the love and support she gave me through the years. Remorse took a grip on me.

"We'd better get back to the school," Ron said.

Three empty beer bottles were lined up on the counter.

"You go ahead," I said. "I'll be along in a few minutes."

Ron rose, paid the bill, and left the shop. I ordered another beer. I still had fifteen minutes before my first class. I was glad Ron didn't mind my drinking. He seemed to understand my need to be alone.

As I finished the last of the beer, I realized Ron was another in a line of father figures in my life. Through the years of my wandering, there'd been a few. Perhaps it was my silence, my refusal to judge others' lives, my ability to listen, that attracted these men to me, men who literally or figuratively lost their sons and saw in me a chance to pass on the scraps of experience and knowledge they'd acquired, pass on in effect what they'd failed to pass on to their own sons, as if to atone for their failures and leave a lasting mark on the world. I always readily accepted what they gave me. I'd accepted little of what Dad tried to give me. The irony was that Dad's silence, the very thing that stood between us many years before, comprised his legacy to me. Above all, this legacy of silence turned out to be my ticket to survival. My foolish pride had prevented me for too many years from understanding Dad's wisdom.

It was time to return to the school. The students would be waiting for me. I walked the narrow street leading back to the school. Two women on bicycles passed me by. I nodded a greeting, recognizing them as mothers of children studying at the school. The humid day, coupled with the beer, made me feel dizzy, lethargic. I thought how nice it would be to forget about all responsibility. I felt on the verge of a long binge.

By the time the last class was over, I'd sobered up. Everyone had gone home. I locked up the school, went downstairs to where my bicycle was parked, and started to ride home. I was thirsty again. I looked forward to the bottle of *sake* I had at home. I took my usual route through some back streets and past the Mukunoso rice fields, which were now flooded for the planting of the rice crops. A warm stillness was in the air. I passed a lumber yard. The freshly stacked lumber gave off a strong smell that reminded me of the time I worked in the sawmills after returning to Humboldt County from my time in prison.

I passed a stretch of shops and the bullet train overpass. A train sped along, sending blue electric sparks into the night. I headed along a straight stretch. On the left were some onion fields that ran into a series of rice fields. The first summer frogs were croaking. A solitary man, hands in his pockets, looked longingly out across the flooded fields. Moonlight flickered on the water.

I pedaled up the last uphill section of the road. This part of the ride always took my breath away. I was sweating when I reached the traffic light at the peak, where the road ran into a T-junction. There was no traffic, so I crossed against the red light and turned into the dark side streets of my neighborhood. The fields gave off a coarse, sweet odor. I arrived at the apartment, parked my bicycle under the shed with the other tenants' bicycles, and climbed the single flight of stairs.

I was home. The word stuck in my mind as I unlocked the door. Had I finally found a place to call home after nearly fifteen years of rambling? It seemed suddenly inconceivable to me, yet I'd lived in this same apartment for nearly a year and a half, longer than any other place I could remember living in since graduating from high school. I filled a glass with ice taken from the small freezer section of my portable fridge, grabbed the bottle of *sake* off the kitchen floor, sat down at the *kotatsu* in the six-mat room, and poured myself a drink. The first swallow burned my throat. A warm flash passed through me. I gritted my teeth and took another drink. I fell into a revery. Countless scenes, some real and some imagined, took possession of my thoughts.

There was a knock at the door. It was Shigeya. He'd missed the last train. He smelled of whiskey. His suit was rumpled. He wore his characteristic smile.

"Sorry for bothering you. Too much drinking," he said.

"Come on in. There's a pillow and some blankets in the closet. Have another drink?" I raised the bottle to show him.

"No, thank you. Too much drinking with Fukuyama-san."

Shigeya's face was red, eyes droopy. He stripped to his underwear and passed out on the floor of the three-mat room with his glasses still on. I took off his glasses and put them in the closet. I returned to the six-mat room to continue drinking alone. I left the sliding panel doors between the rooms open and watched him sleep. Against the wall was the canvas he was currently working on. It was a big canvas, about three feet by five feet. He liked working with big canvases. This one had changed many times in the last two weeks. It started out as a distant city seen from inside a dark forest. Now it was a jungle and ocean scene with an island in the distance. He'd started with dark colors, then switched to light greens, oranges, and reds. He had an abundance of energy when he painted.

I became quite drunk, plunging willingly into a dark loneliness. I slept a fitful sleep filled with strange dreams.

The rainy season accentuated my gloom. An almost haunting stillness pervaded the days: grey skies, the melancholy blue of hydrangea blooming, the rice field across the street green and still, reflecting the dark outline of the surrounding houses. I looked out my window one day to see three children with a long net lazily fishing for frogs in the rice field. No sound escaped their lips. Two birds fluttered across the landscape, emitting weak warbles. Black smoke rose from the smokestack of the *sento*. I felt utterly isolated, faced with a growing depression that dragged at my limbs.

One night, I went out with Kamejima and Tsutomu to a bar. I drank too much and at one point, feeling rather cocky with my improved Japanese, responded loudly and cynically to what I thought was a stupid question by another customer asking if I was really an American: "Am I American? Am I American? I don't know. What do you think? I think I'm German. No, wait. I think I'm Chinese. Are you Japanese?"

All conversation in the bar stopped. Everyone stared at me. Kamejima grabbed me, paid the bill, and drove me home. Feeling guilty about my behavior, I went to his shop the next afternoon to apologize. There were no other customers, so we sat on some beer crates and drank a cold beer. Kamejima told me that the bar owner's parents were killed by Americans during the war and that I should be more sensitive about others' feelings.

Remorse enveloped me. I felt compelled to talk about my frustrations in dealing with some Japanese. I was tired of all the same questions constantly being put to me as if I were the sole representative of the outside world and what it thought about Japan. I was also suspicious of all the kindness I was receiving, the way people were always paying for me and wanting to take me places. I wondered if there weren't ulterior motives behind these acts and if I'd be expected to pay everything back somewhere down the road. I had a paranoid feeling that I was being used.

Kamejima thought for a while, then said, "You think too much. Don't worry about it."

At the end of June, I received another six-month extension on my visa. From the middle of July, the days became hotter. I'd look out my kitchen window and sometimes see the wind blow over the rice field, sending off rippling waves of light. I quit the lessons with Imanishi and began studying Japanese at home. I bought a new textbook and tapes and spent an hour or two every day repeating after the tapes or taking dictation. Green persimmons sprouted on my neighbor's tree. Cicadas screamed out their summer song. The rice field turned lime green. I started jogging again, which helped clear my head. Slowly, my funk withdrew to a less dominant place.

Autumn came. Leaves changed color. The rice field was harvested. The sound of insects lingered, then disappeared. The nights grew colder.

Basketball and books got me through that winter. I went to a gym in a suburb of Osaka on Sundays. Although I'd been a guard through the years I played in the States, I now became a forward-center as I was taller than most of the Japanese players. A team made up mostly of players in their thirties asked me to play for them. We played a slowdown game and relied on good defense and rebounding to be competitive. All the other teams were comprised of college kids and men in their twenties who loved to run and gun. There were several tournaments and league games during the winter. I hadn't played competitively for a few years and had slowed down considerably, but I still had a decent shooting touch and could block out under the hoop and get a lot of rebounds without having to jump.

At the end of December, I received my final six-month extension of the study visa. I'd have to apply for a work visa in June in order to continue living in Japan. I had a series of dreams that seemed to underscore my dilemma. In the dreams, I belonged to neither Japan nor the U.S. Characters from both the past and present inhabited these dreams. The language used was a mixture of Japanese and English. In some dreams, I returned to the States as a criminal, shunned by both family and friends. In other dreams, I was in Japan as a bystander observing kidnappings or murders. The criminals often told me to go away. I'd head off in a fog and become lost.

February brought its false spring—periods of three days of cold weather, followed by four days of warm. Throughout March and April, it rained constantly. The cherry blossoms bloomed briefly, then fell victim to the wind and rain.

When June came, I put together a teaching visa application package—financial reports from RIS, the school's letter of recommendation, my contract, letters from my guarantor Ian, my university transcripts with about a year and a half of credits, and my own letter explaining why I wanted to continue living in Japan—to be submitted to the immigration authorities. Two weeks later, I received a letter stating I'd been given a six-month teaching visa.

August brought with it old horrors of death-imagery. The nation was absorbed in the fortieth anniversary of the victims of the atomic bombs dropped on Hiroshima and Nagasaki. On August 12, a Japan Airlines jumbo jet crashed into a mountainside west of Tokyo, killing five hundred twenty people and becoming the worst disaster in airline history. Miraculously, four people survived, but the mood of the nation was dark and somber. The *Obon* holiday, usually a colorful and festive time of year, was morose and dispirited. Everywhere I went, I saw downcast faces.

I saw little of anyone outside work. The Sasa Softball Club members wouldn't gather again until the autumn league started.

Shigeya had been dating a new girlfriend steadily for the last few months and rarely spent weekends at my place anymore.

The August nights were debilitating. The screams of wild cats fighting kept me awake and restless. The heat drove me out into the dark streets, among bats dive-bombing around the few dim streetlamps on the way to Koya Park. One night, I returned home late and found a bat banging against the walls inside the six-mat room. I slammed the sliding door shut, rolled up a newspaper, waited a minute until the noise died down, and peeked inside the room. The bat had found a spot on one wall to clutch with its talons and was hanging upside down. I tip-toed into the room and swatted it with my best home-run swing. It dropped to the floor, stunned. I quickly picked it up by one wing and tossed it out the open window. I slammed the window shut and slumped to the floor.

I contemplated my future. I'd reached the point where a fundamental decision had to be made: Did I want to return to the States, where the only work I could find would probably be as a cook? Or did I want to commit to a life in Japan? If I committed to living in Japan, I'd have to make some serious efforts toward a career. Teaching at RIS was becoming the equivalent of working at a language sweatshop. I had no academic qualifications to rise above the position I was in now. The school was increasingly geared toward business growth. The familial atmosphere that existed in the beginning had lately turned into something resembling a factory assembly line, with students and teachers rushed in and out of the partitioned classrooms like so many goods. RIS was now a carbon copy of UCLA. We weren't educating the students anymore. We were merely feeding off a business phenomenon that saw a greater perceived need for English on the public's part than there was a supply of qualified institutions. I did enjoy teaching English, but I'd reached my peak in salary and position unless I made a move to improve myself professionally. I was burned out. I had to get out of the country to gain strength and a different perspective. I'd saved some money and could afford a round-trip plane ticket to the States. Ron agreed to give me some time off in October.

One day late in September, Ron called a teachers' meeting and had me give a presentation on a new teaching technique using some props and indirect correction of students' mistakes. I didn't prepare adequately and lacked confidence during the presentation. It was as if I were outside my body observing the ridiculousness of it all—me stuttering and stammering; the blank, uncomprehending faces of the other teachers; my own thoughts drifting and disconnected. Later, I overheard one of the other teachers make a joke about my inarticulateness and inability to speak convincingly to a group of native speakers of English.

I was determined to find a correspondence course, graduate, and move on to a new job. I hoped the trip back to the States would ease my mind and provide a direction out of my waywardness. I'd hit bottom many times in the past, but always with a reserve of strength hidden in the resilience of youth. The question in my mind now was whether there was any of that resilience left. I was, at thirty-four, feeling old and broken.

I withdrew some money from the bank, paid off two months of rent to the landlord, got a reentry permit from immigration, bought a round-trip ticket to San Francisco on Korean Airlines, and left Japan on October 4.

Raymond and Robear picked me up at the San Francisco airport with a cold beer and a joint. They were settled comfortably now in a house in Pacific Grove that they were renting from

Cynthia Williams. We spent two days partying together before I hopped a Greyhound bus to Humboldt County. I spent two weeks visiting with Dad and his family. Everyone was healthy and getting along well with their lives. I talked to Dick and Dottie on the phone. They were both working and now had a dog. I headed to Fortuna to see Shannon and John Cady, who'd moved in with Shannon and was working as the head cook for Parlato's Restaurant.

The Kelly house was quiet with Midge gone. Shannon's dad spent his days at the concrete plant and kept to himself in the evenings, reading magazines and watching television. Shannon, John, and I played basketball, drank beer, smoked pot, and talked about the old days. John and I played golf twice. He could still shoot close to par. One day, I visited Herb, who'd moved back to Fortuna after the divorce with Mom. He seemed happy to see me. We went out to dinner. He said he was keeping busy fishing, working side jobs, and dating a new woman friend. There was no trace of bitterness in him. He had only good things to say about Mom. He didn't tell me he had cancer of the lungs. Within a year, he was dead.

I took a bus to Portland to spend some time with Mom. I slept in late every day, went for runs in the afternoon, and prepared dinners for when she returned from work. In the evenings, we stayed up late visiting and reminiscing about her trip to Japan. We made plans for her to take another trip the next year.

One weekend, we drove up the Columbia River to White Salmon to visit her Uncle Jack and Aunt Louise Frederick. We spent Saturday afternoon at the local graveyard, where Grandma Murph and Grandpa Pat were buried. We placed flowers on the graves. Mom told stories of growing up in White Salmon. I gained strength from her optimism, humor, and love. When the time came to return to Japan, I was ready to make a renewed effort in my Japanese study and to pursue a degree in Teaching of English as a Second Language. It was time to get serious.

I arrived back in Japan near the end of November. Ron had kept my job open for me. I immediately set out to find a school that offered correspondence courses. I found an American university, Newport University, that had a branch in Tokyo and offered credit toward a degree if one could document enough life experience. At the end of the year, I was given another six-month visa. In January, I submitted a portfolio to Newport University and was accepted into its correspondence program for a bachelor's degree.

One night in January, I was out drinking with Iwado, a businessman in his forties who was one of the longtime students at RIS and had been a member of one of the more interesting classes. The class was the last one on Saturday afternoons. In the past, all the members often gathered for a party at Ron's apartment or some restaurant. The original class members were four young, good-looking women and Iwado. The four women eventually went their separate ways with four new members taking their place. Iwado and I talked about what had become of the original four. He mentioned that one of them, Shizuyo, was working for a Danish company and that she'd recently done some translation work for him on the side. I said I'd like to see her sometime. He gave me her phone number.

Shizuyo had been one of the most interesting and intelligent students I'd taught. Her English was excellent. She'd always impressed me with her uninhibited participation in class, her philosophical attitude toward life, her inquisitiveness, and her keen sense of humor. Her class was a joy to teach. I'd not seen her as anything more than a highly motivated and articulate student, but talking with Iwado made me think that she might be just the type of person I'd like to spend some time with.

I called Shizuyo that night. We agreed to meet for a drink that weekend. She lived in Nishinomiya, about a half hour from Itami by train. We decided to meet at a *yakitori* shop near her apartment. It was the most enjoyable date I'd had in ages. We began seeing each other on weekends. During the week, I often called her at night from a pay phone near my apartment. She had such a zest for life, an interest in language, a zany sense of humor, and an openness and honesty of expression that it seemed our friendship bloomed overnight.

Before long, I was spending Saturday nights at her place. Within a few weeks, I'd practically moved in. We were like two twins separated at birth who'd waited a lifetime to find each other again. Our conversations lasted deep into the night, confessing every detail of our life histories, our love affairs, adventures, childhoods, friends, successes, failures, hopes, and dreams. These conversations always started out seriously, then took multiple twists and turns, a single thought or word digressing into a flurry of related and unrelated stories until, panting and out of breath, we realized the original point we wanted to make was now lost and irretrievable and our only recourse was to summarize the whole evening with a final drink, a fart, and an explosion of laughter that left our sides aching. Shizuyo brought a sense of balance back to my life.

As spring approached, I felt the need for a change. I'd now spent nearly three years working at RIS. I'd learned as much about teaching from Ron as I could. I needed exposure to a different atmosphere, different teaching methods, and different students. I needed to widen my experiences in Japan. I set my sights on teaching at a junior college or university after I got my degree. I found a vocational language school in Ashiya that had an opening for a part-time teacher. Seido Language Institute had an organized curriculum, published its own materials, had connections with several private schools, and had a good reputation. They hired me to teach some classes twice a week beginning in April.

Not long after, Shizuyo heard through a friend about an employment agency called Career Max that was looking for a native speaker of English to work two days a week as a proofreader and copywriter for a large chemical company in Kobe called Bando. I went to Career Max for an interview and passed. They agreed to sponsor me for a work visa when my current visa expired at the end of June. That job also started in April. I consulted with Ron and he allowed me to teach just one company class and a private lesson at a client's home for RIS until my visa ran out.

Shizuyo and I were practically living together. She called me Bobu-chan and I called her Shi-chan. I kept my apartment in Itami, but spent much of my free time at her Nishinomiya apartment as it was closer to Seido. I was still playing softball and basketball on weekends and jogging around Koya Park three times a week. Shigeya was still using my Itami apartment as his atelier.

On May 6, Mom and Aunt Louise arrived for a three-week visit, which turned out even more interesting and fun than the 1984 visit. They were perfect travel companions. They could make an adventure out of the most mundane of activities.

I had to work much of the time, but was able to take them along both to observe and to participate in some of the lessons, especially with the evening adult students at Seido Language Institute and the engineers at the company class I taught on

Saturdays in Osaka. RIS students who'd met Mom on her previous trip took her to various activities and sights. Ian, Shigeya, Sasa Softball Club members, and many others in the neighborhood showered Mom and Aunt Louise with many hours of conversation, friendship, and entertainment. I'd improved in Japanese enough to do a much better job at interpreting when we were together. Most of all, Mom's openness and sense of adventure allowed her to experience a Japan that few tourists ever can. She fell in love with everyone. Everyone fell in love with her. I was so proud of her. She was proud of me, too.

After Mom and Aunt Louise left, I made good progress in my studies. Nearly every night, Shi-chan and I sat opposite each other at her table and immersed ourselves in books, tapes, and written reports. She was disciplined and hard-working. Her goal was to become a simultaneous interpreter. She was attending interpreting classes two nights a week. We were both student and teacher to each other. In addition to my correspondence course, I was continuing to study Japanese. Her explanations of difficult vocabulary, idioms, and grammar were very helpful. She always remembered to weave into our conversations, which were half in Japanese and half in English, expressions I had difficulty with, in order to reinforce them in my memory.

She often told stories about her family. Her father was from the small fishing village of Yuasa in Wakayama Prefecture. His had been an arranged marriage. He'd spent part of his youth in Korea. During the 1930s and World War II, many Japanese families had migrated to Korea, Taiwan, and Manchuria. After the war, he returned to Yuasa and worked a variety of jobs: fishmonger, clerk, security guard, and supervisor of prisoners making work gloves at a state prison for women. Shi-chan's mother ran a small stationery shop and bookstore out of their home.

Shi-chan said her father was a dreamer-philosopher with grand ambitions and little common sense, a stubborn, loquacious man who loved to expound on his theories of history, science, philosophy, and politics to anyone with a sympathetic ear. He loved to drink. When Shi-chan was a child, he often came home stinking of *sake* and covered with mud and blood from a fight with someone who either hadn't agreed with his theories or simply got tired of listening to him. He was an inventor with a hundred ideas but no wherewithal to carry them through.

One of his schemes came near the end of the 1960s. He wanted to become an international businessman. The most practical idea seemed to be taking advantage of his Korean contacts. He set up a business importing fish from Korea. Things went smoothly until the oil shock of 1970 and the normalization of bilateral relations between China and Japan combined to destroy his business. As Japan no longer recognized Taiwan, trade between the two countries deteriorated. All the big Japanese trading companies in Taiwan moved their operations to Korea. Small companies like Shi-chan's father's couldn't compete. By the time he decided to give up, he was burdened with a ten-million-yen debt.

Shi-chan said it nearly destroyed the family. She remembered a depressing home atmosphere throughout her junior high and high school days. Her brother and father fought. Her mother and father fought. She and her brother fought. In the midst of all this family feuding, however, her mother remained a rock of stability. She worked all day in their stationery shop and bookstore. She took on side jobs knitting. She worked as a runner for the local pachinko parlor, returning goods exchanged for cash at a pawn shop every night back to the pachinko parlor, where they would again be given to customers as prizes. She delivered magazines and newspapers to the train station. For the next fifteen years, she never missed a day of work. Mainly due to her efforts, the family, with Shi-chan's father again working salaried jobs and Shi-chan and her brother working part-time jobs after school, managed to pay off the debt.

After graduating from high school, Shi-chan moved to Kobe to attend Kobe Women's University. For the next four years, she supported herself by working as a receptionist in an English conversation school, a hostess in a bar, a coffee shop waitress, and an assortment of other jobs before finally graduating with a degree in English. She paid her own way in attending a three-month homestay program in Britain and another one-month homestay in California. She took on part-time jobs tutoring junior high school students in their homes and teaching adults in another English conversation school. She never stopped studying. She passed Japan's top-rated English proficiency exam while attending RIS and used her new qualification to get a job at a Danish-run company in Kobe that manufactured pumps. She was working directly for the company president as a combination translator-interpreter and person in charge of inventory control.

We were completely relaxed with each other. We'd both been independent for so long there was no need to worry about playing a particular role in the relationship. We were both accustomed to entertaining ourselves, keeping ourselves occupied. Often for long stretches in her apartment, we both were quietly absorbed in reading, taking notes, or writing, but when the mood hit us for conversation, we gave totally to each other. We never argued. I'd never felt so relaxed with a woman. Shi-chan once said, "I feel totally naked mentally with you."

A year passed. I turned thirty-six. I was still hesitant about marriage. Shi-chan found a new job as an assistant teacher of Japanese in Arizona for a year at Thunderbird School of Global

Management. The job would start in September. She gave me an ultimatum: either we got married or the relationship was over. I realized I'd never find a better life partner. On March 21, 1987, Shi-chan's thirty-first birthday, I asked her to marry me. We got married on May 8, 1987.

About the same time, I finished my bachelor's degree. I saw an ad in a language magazine for a full-time teacher's job at a vocational school in Fukuoka called KAINS, applied for the job, and was hired at a salary of three hundred thousand yen a month. The job would also begin in September.

Shi-chan and I had little money. We couldn't afford an elaborate wedding ceremony and neither could her family. Our wedding consisted of going to Itami City Hall and registering the marriage there.

When I announced to the softball team that I was going to get married and move to Kyushu to start a new job, they went out of their way to hold a wedding party for us. At least seventy-five people showed up. The team rented a local hall, charged everyone two thousand five hundred yen, hung American and Japanese flags on the wall, and had everyone get up and give a speech. Shi-chan's family came all the way from Yuasa to attend. At the end of the party, there was much handshaking, hugging, and crying.

Looking back on those first few years in Japan, I can't count the times Sasa Softball Club members helped me out. I had little or no money most of the time and I continually pleaded with them to show some restraint with their kindness. They always laughed at my protestations, poured me another beer, and told me, "Don't worry about it. In the future, you can help somebody else who needs it." I hope I've been able to heed that advice. I'm forever grateful to them for everything they did, for their friendships and generosity, and especially for the wonderful memories they gave Mom, Aunt Louise, and Shi-chan.

15

Fukuoka

Soon after getting married, Shi-chan and I took a honeymoon to the West Coast. We visited all my old friends and family members. Then we went our separate ways for a year: she to teach Japanese at Thunderbird American Graduate School of International Management in Glendale, Arizona and I to teach English in Fukuoka. I now had a three-year marriage visa.

The job at KAINS turned out to be a dead-end street. The owner was a minor league *yakuza* type who exploited both students and teachers. He could control most of the teachers because he was sponsoring their visas. He had them working a lot more hours than the original agreements. They had to comply or else he would stop the sponsorship. They couldn't find another job without a letter of release from him to the immigration authorities. With a marriage visa, I wasn't so easy to manipulate.

In the beginning, I was sent out to various companies to teach their employees in the evenings in addition to having to teach the students at the school during the day. The time spent working at KAINS, however, wasn't wasted. I put in a kind of apprenticeship at that school. In teaching large classes of varied levels of students five hours a day, I could try out many of the teaching methods I was studying about in doing my master's degree papers. There were many failures in my experimentation, but over time I ironed out the wrinkles. I kept the things that worked and eventually developed my own style of teaching. I became confident in what I was doing and felt I could teach any age, level, and size of class and do a good job. I knew that eventually patience, perseverance, good luck, and timing would pay off in finding a better job.

The companies I was dispatched to liked my work. After the six-month contracts that the companies had with KAINS ran out, I negotiated my own contracts with them on the sly. After a year and a half at KAINS, I quit the school and started working independently. Japan's economy was booming. Many companies had big budgets for their training programs, which included English study for engineers who were being sent abroad to work. One of my contracts was with Kyushu Matsushita Electric Company. They had about a thousand workers at their various Kyushu factories to train. I eventually became the head teacher in their program, as well as spending one day a week in the head office as the coordinator between the foreign teachers and the office management. The Kyushu Matsushita job didn't pay much, but it proved valuable when I applied for and got a permanent resident visa in 1990. It was also invaluable for completing my master's degree. My master's thesis was about using oral proficiency interviews as the central component of the Kyushu Matsushita English training program.

During that first year in Fukuoka and shortly before Shi-chan returned from Arizona, I attended some monthly workshops of the Fukuoka branch of the Japan Association of Language Teachers. I met a professor from Fukuoka Women's Junior College at one of those workshops. We got on well and he told me there was an opening for a part-time teacher and I should apply. I had to go through an interview that was mainly in Japanese, but I got the job.

After Shi-chan returned, we moved into a bigger apartment near Ohori Park. She found work for a local businessmen's group organizing an international homestay event. Children from over forty countries and territories in the Asia-Pacific region were to visit the city for the event, which was called the Asian-Pacific Children's Convention in Fukuoka. It was held to coincide with the Yokatopia Expo, an event commemorating the one hundredth anniversary of Fukuoka's incorporation as a city. The purpose was to promote exchange among children of different linguistic and cultural backgrounds. Shi-chan did translation, interpretation, organizing, and various kinds of legwork. She was indispensable to the success of the event.

That job catapulted her into a job teaching at the Inter Group's new interpretation school in Fukuoka. Through the next few years, she taught interpreting classes, acted as the coordinator between teachers and management, and did actual interpretation at a variety of international events and meetings. The stress was tremendous.

In addition to working all the time, we both kept up our studies. I was getting closer to completing my master's degree and Shi-chan wanted to pass Japan's highest interpreters' exam.

In 1992, I finished my master's degree. In total, it had taken seven years to finish both the bachelor's and master's degrees. At the same time, an opening for a full-time foreign teacher came up at the junior college. I applied. There were about fifty others who applied for the job. Most of them had much better resumes than I did, but in Japan, connections were as important as qualifications. In my three years as a part-timer at the junior college, I'd helped some of the full-time Japanese teachers in the English department with the papers they were writing in English. I did a lot of proofreading for free and some of their papers got published. I often went drinking with them. Two of them were baseball and literature fans, so we had much in common. The students seemed to enjoy my classes. The candidates were whittled down to two people: me and a woman who'd graduated from a famous university. The deciding factor was an interview conducted in Japanese. My interview went off without a hitch. I made some jokes that had the interviewers laughing. I proved that they didn't need to provide any special treatment or interpretation in order for me to do the job competently. My competitor panicked during the interview and didn't speak Japanese well. I was hired. At forty-one, I had my first full-time job, complete with insurance, bonuses, research funds, housing allowance, and a few other benefits. I joined the teachers' union and began paying into a retirement fund.

In Japan, there's a relationship system between older and younger members of almost all schools, companies, and groups of any kind. The relationship of *senpai* and *kohai* is a fundamental element in Japan's seniority-based social structure. Relationships are mainly determined by age. The older and more experienced *senpai* are responsible for mentoring the younger *kohai*, while the *kohai* are obligated to listen to and follow the *senpai*. In my years of living in Japan, I've been fortunate to make many good friends. The best *senpai* I ever had was Ichikawa-*sensei*.

We first met during my three years as a part-time lecturer at the junior college from 1989 to 1991. We hit it off immediately. Our relationship centered on three Bs: books, baseball, and beer.

Ichikawa was a short, skinny man with thick glasses and a

quick smile. He was absent-minded and continually losing and forgetting things. He walked with short, hurried strides as if always in a rush to get to an important destination. He always wore a key chain on his belt. You could hear the keys jingling in a strange, hectic rhythm when he was walking in the hallways to his next class. When he spoke, he had a difficult time voicing the first few words. He'd take his glasses off and while cleaning them knit his brow and gasp a long *anoooo* as he slowly organized his thoughts. His listeners had to wait an agonizingly long time, but once the initial words came out, the small trickle soon became a slow stream, then eventually a steady flow with various detours that caused the listener to wonder sometimes where Ichikawa was going. As often as not, he abruptly ended his discourse with a non sequitur punch line and a booming laugh. He'd then look around with a curious gaze, as if amazed at his own thought process. Everyone loved him.

The books part of the relationship involved mainly American literature. Ichikawa's specialty was Jewish-American literature, particularly the works of Bernard Malamud. In the beginning of those years, he asked me to proofread an English paper he was writing. After that, we went out drinking a few times. The conversation usually turned to baseball, our own life stories, and the turbulent events of the 1960s. When I told him I'd been a conscientious objector to the Vietnam War from within the military, refused my orders to fight, was court-martialed, and spent time in a military prison, he smiled broadly and said, "That's one of the greatest things I've ever heard. That must've taken a lot of courage. I respect you for that."

Our friendship deepened in 1991 when the opening for a full-time foreign lecturer in the English department became apparent. Ichikawa encouraged me to apply for the job. He did a lot of behind-the-scenes lobbying for me as the best teacher for the job. The night before the Japanese interview, I went out drinking with Ichikawa. He coached me on what kind of questions would be asked. Thanks to him, my dream of teaching at a Japanese college became a reality.

From the very beginning of my career as a full-time college teacher, Ichikawa took me under his wing. I was now his *kohai* and in a sense he was responsible for me. Now that we were full-time colleagues, we had a lot more time to spend together. He advised me to build up my resume to increase the chances for promotion in the future. He was a member of some academic associations called *gakkai*. He wanted me to join them and start writing papers and giving presentations. He introduced me to such Japanese writers as Kaiko Takeshi and Oda Makoto, both of whom had some of their works translated into English. He also encouraged my writing of novels.

Those first two years—1992 and 1993—were boom years. The eighteen-year-old population was at its peak and the junior college had to turn away half of its applicants. The school was swimming in money. The average class size was around sixty-five students. Ichikawa and I were still in good shape. Although I was forty-one and could no longer run because of arthritic ankles, I still had a lot of energy and stamina. Ichikawa was forty-five, but he was still playing in a fast-pitch softball league in Kyoto, where he returned on weekends to spend time with his wife and children. He'd taught at Kyoto University of Foreign Studies for fifteen years after graduating from the same school but returned to Kyushu to live with and take care of his mother, who'd been living alone in her house in Kurume. We both could still drink prodigious amounts, which we did frequently, and somehow manage to get through the next day's work.

Ichikawa had a deep concern for social issues and the down-trodden in life. His research included not only the Jewish-American experience, but also that of all American immigrants and minorities. Our conversations over the next few years covered a wide range of topics: the Civil Rights Movement, the Transcendentalist writers, the Industrial Revolution and the waves of European immigrants to the U.S., the internment of Japanese-Americans during World War II, the Beatniks, Howard Zinn's writing and the history of resistance in the U.S., the slavery issue, the counterculture of the 1960s and 1970s, American baseball history and the importance of the life of Jackie Robinson, John Steinbeck's novels and the Great Depression, and many other things.

My favorite Ichikawa stories were the ones about his involvement in the anti-Vietnam War movement when he was a university student, as well as his later experiences in the U.S. In 1968, he joined a group of about a hundred students from Kyoto heading to Sasebo Port near Nagasaki to demonstrate against the port call of the American nuclear aircraft carrier U.S.S. Enterprise.

"I did many activities in my university days at Kyoto University of Foreign Studies," Ichikawa said one night at a bar after classes. "I joined the Blue Helmets. There were many student groups in those days. They wore helmets to show what group they were in. The Blue Helmets were part of the *Shaseido* group. We were socialists. We were crazy and intense. We were against the communists, against the capitalists, against the Vietnam War, and against nuclear weapons.

"When the American nuclear-powered Enterprise warship came to Sasebo in January 1968, people and students from everywhere in Japan went there to protest. I left Kyoto with many other students. We got off the train at Hakata Station and spent the night there. The next morning, we went to Sasebo. When we got off the train, there were people and police fighting everywhere. We were there just a few minutes and my friend got a big head injury. I had to take care of him, so I took him to the hospital. Then I went back to the demonstration. Another friend got arrested.

"Later on, my university found out we were in Sasebo. They threatened to kick me out of school, but in the end they didn't. Oda Makoto and people from his *Beheiren* antiwar group were in Sasebo, too. I got a big influence from his first book about traveling in America and India with no money. It's called *Nandemo Mite Yaro*. He helped four American soldiers run away from their ship and go to Sweden. He's been a famous man since then, but like an enemy to the Japanese government."

I asked him about his experiences in the United States.

"The first time I went to New York, I stayed in the YMCA. Every night, I could hear fights outside in the street and ambulances. I made some American friends at that YMCA. One man was a former Army man who fought in Vietnam. He had many tattoos on his arms. I went drinking with him every night at a bar. He told me many stories about Vietnam and how he hated his government for sending so many Americans to die for nothing.

"Another friend was a Black man in Harlem. I saw some people in a park there playing softball. I asked if I could join them. He said, 'Sure, come on.' He took me to his apartment later and I had dinner with his family. He was very poor, but a great guy. He said some day he wanted to come to Japan."

After that night, Ichikawa often asked me to explain in detail how I came to be a conscientious objector within the military, my struggle to find my identity, my adventures traveling across the U.S. and abroad, and how I came to be a writer. He thought my life story would be ideal as a textbook for Japanese students. He encouraged me to write the story in easy English.

I joined two academic associations that he was a member of— the Japan Association of Comparative Culture and the Malamud Society of Japan. Ichikawa quit the junior college job in 1994 to take a job as a professor at Kurume University. He continued to teach part-time once a week at the junior college. Although no longer full-time colleagues, we continued to go to conferences and have remained great buddies through the years.

From 1989 to 1993, Mom visited Japan three times. I could see that life was taking its toll on her both physically and mentally. She was a single woman in her late sixties still working full-time, dealing with the body slowly breaking down, frustrated with the American government and society at large, reflecting on her life, and questioning some of the decisions she'd made and things she'd done.

At one point, she entertained the thought of leaving the U.S. and trying her hand at teaching English in Japan, but the idea never made it past the planning stage. Mom did, however, turn into a lifelong student of Japanese. The combination of taking Japanese evening classes at Portland State University, spending time with Japanese students through a sponsorship program she participated in, and her visits to Japan and interacting with local people all helped her improve steadily. In one letter, Mom wrote:

Despite my frustrations in not making fast enough progress, every little thing that I finally learn just makes me want to learn more and more. You know me, just a cockeyed optimist who always thinks life truly is a bowl of cherries even though there are a lot of pits.

All of Mom's hard work and study, as well as her openness and enthusiasm, seemed to come to fruition during her 1993 visit with another friend. I was in my second year as a full-time teacher at the junior college, so it was especially gratifying to see her pride in me and in knowing that for both of us late bloomers, our years of stubbornly grinding away and not giving up had produced fairly good results.

Shi-chan and I moved to an apartment in the town of Chikushino so I could be closer to the junior college, which was in Dazaifu, an historical area that was the former governmental center of Kyushu, had many temples, a famous shrine, and a national museum. It was a great place for Mom and her friend to explore and practice speaking while Shi-chan and I were working. I took them up to the junior college, which was on a hill overlooking Dazaifu, and had them participate in some classes. The other teachers, the students, and the staff were very kind to them.

After Mom returned to Portland, she wrote about what this trip meant to her.

> This was such a special trip, perhaps because I discovered I'd retained a bit more Japanese than I thought I had. And, more importantly, when I would converse with some of the local people, they seemed to understand what I was saying. This was so great for me as I was going through a very discouraging period in my studying. I'm going to sign up again for a basic class because I feel now I will get a lot out of it.
>
> I think so many times during the day about my visit with the two of you. It was really a treat and I thank you both so much for the trip. I'm convinced that I

must have been a Japanese in my former life as I am
so interested in the language, culture, and people. I'll
probably turn into a lifetime student!

During the six years I worked full-time at the junior college, I
was a bit of a trailblazer. Previously, foreign teachers hadn't been
allowed to serve on committees (there was a perception that the
Japanese language was too difficult and that foreigners couldn't
handle any responsibilities beyond the classroom) and had to
teach one or two more classes than the Japanese teachers. The
contract was for two years with supposedly only one extension.
The Japanese teachers usually got automatic tenure when they
started. I thought this was unfair and wanted to be treated the
same as the Japanese teachers. I was active in the department
meetings and able to convince the others that I could do just as
good a job on the committees as they could. In my second year,
they put me on two committees. The school didn't collapse, so in
my third year, they started using foreign teachers on more committees and reduced the number of classes foreign teachers were
responsible for to the same number as the Japanese. They even
had me chaperone students participating in overseas homestay-
study programs during two summer vacations. The first time,
I took a group of twenty-four students to San Francisco in 1993
with a Japanese professor. In 1995, I took a group of eighteen
students by myself to London. After my initial contract expired,
I was given a new contract. I'd basically become indispensable,
a part of the furniture.

Maybe it was the discipline of having written many papers
for my degrees, maybe Ichikawa's encouragement, or maybe
having some job security, but I had a burst of energy and cre-
ativity. I rewrote the same novel I'd been working on for years

and found an independent Japanese publisher that wanted to publish it. *Looking for the Summer* was published by Touka Shobo in 1996. Ichikawa helped me put together a novella based on my conscientious objector and travel experiences. He introduced it to his publisher in Osaka. Osaka Kyoiku Tosho published *The Many Roads to Japan* as a textbook with Japanese notes in 1997. Touka Shobo published my second novel *Toraware* in 1998. In addition, I published eleven academic papers and gave four presentations at academic conferences. In just six years, I'd put together a decent resume.

The eighteen-year-old population began to plummet in the mid-1990s, so the school decided to build a four-year university on the same campus in order to snare the students and their parents' money for four years instead of just two. Eight of the fifty junior college teachers were chosen to move over to the university with another forty teachers recruited from around the country. I was one of the eight. After six years at the junior college, I was promoted to associate professor and became a university teacher.

16

Earthquakes and Cancer

O N the morning of January 17, 1995, Shi-chan received a
call around 7:30 from her mother. A large earthquake had
jarred the family house in Yuasa. The TV on top of their kitchen
cabinet had toppled and crashed on the table. Some glass cases
in the second-story clothing shop had fallen over and glass had
scattered all over. No one was hurt, but it was the worst quake
they'd felt in a long time. The quake was supposedly centered in
Kobe and the family was watching the news on the upstairs TV.

Shi-chan switched on our TV and woke me. At first, there
were only pictures from a helicopter trying to assess the damage.
The city had not yet come to life. Reports were broadcast telling
commuters in Kobe and Nishinomiya to stay home as some of the
main lines were closed. Most of the Osaka subway lines, train
lines, and highways were still open. Commuters there were told
to stay tuned. There was a section of the Hanshin Expressway
that had collapsed, but there had been only a few cars on it.

The aerial views showed a few plumes of smoke rising here and
there, but the overall mood was not one of panic. It was more of
a wait-and-see attitude that conveyed a sense that the damage

was limited. There were a few confirmed reports of deaths and injuries piling up, but the numbers were not staggering. As the day progressed, however, it became evident that this was no ordinary earthquake. The TV stations began sending out more helicopters and the images were horrifying.

Trains had flipped on their sides; many sections of track had snapped in two or torn loose; cars had been catapulted off the toppled sections of elevated expressway; commercial buildings in downtown Sannomiya suffered pancake collapses; water and gas mains ruptured; and entire neighborhoods were engulfed in flames. The number of dead, missing, and injured rose dramatically. It was a day off for me. Shi-chan and I sat riveted to the TV. My stomach turned over when I saw that the Hankyu Itami Station had collapsed. We made dozens of calls to our many friends in Itami City, Kobe, and Osaka, but couldn't get through.

I finally tore myself away from the TV about one in the morning. I was tired and had to work the next day. I woke at five to the sound of Shi-chan's sobs. She'd stayed up all night, watching the inferno engulf Nagata-ku, the area in Kobe where she'd lived for four years as a university student and two more years after graduating. Some of her old friends were still living there and may have been trapped in the blazes and rubble. She pointed to the screen and cried out, "That's where I used to live! I know people who live there! That's where I used to live!" All I could do was embrace her.

Over the next few days, our shock turned first to frustration, then to anger. Why had the government not responded more quickly? Why had the National Guard not been called out in the first hours? Why had the government initially refused help from outside the country? Why had the Japanese people been lulled into a false sense of security?

Later in the week, the news reports showed a few signs of reborn hope. Blankets, portable toilets, clothes, food, water, and medicine from all over the nation poured into the evacuation camps. Interviews in the streets showed a stoicism, determination, and emotional strength that was unbelievable to me. Among the many ruins and smoldering ashes, makeshift shops cropped up here and there to dispense hot meals for little or no money. There was little looting. Even the infamous Yamaguchi *yakuza* group pitched in, directing traffic and passing out food and blankets, first to the elderly, the sick, and the pregnant, then to the healthy and the young.

The phone lines gradually opened up. Over the next few days, we contacted all of our friends. Some had evacuated; some were staying in school grounds set up as temporary shelters; some were still in their homes but without gas and water. All were uninjured. I was impressed by everyone's strength and sense of humor in coping with having to start from scratch in putting the pieces of their lives back together. In the end, well over six thousand people were killed, forty thousand more injured, and hundreds of thousands made homeless.

Just two months later on March 20, Aum Shinrikyo cult members punctured bags filled with sarin nerve gas and left them on some Tokyo subway lines. Victims were left choking and vomiting. Fourteen people died and more than five thousand people were injured, some of them blinded and paralyzed. For days, the TV news stations replayed images of rescue workers and Self-Defense Force soldiers wearing hazmat suits and gas masks and descending into the subway entrances to help the injured. A dark mood fell upon the nation.

In the States, Mom was preparing to retire. She'd found a nice man, Thor, who seemed a good partner for her. They started living together the year before and it was working out well. She wrote that she "hadn't felt this good in many years, both emotionally and physically." They thought about retiring in Costa Rica, but a trip there to check things out threw a monkey wrench on that idea. Too much crime, too expensive, and too crowded. They decided instead to move to a retirement community in Newport Beach, California that had excellent facilities and activities.

Not long after, Terri's health went downhill. In addition to knee problems that had plagued her since a serious water-skiing accident in adolescence that required surgery, she was suffering from symptoms of an ailment doctors wouldn't be able to diagnose correctly for a few years to come—multiple sclerosis. The various treatment and drugs they'd try always had severe side effects.

As Mom had always done, she put her priorities on family matters and us kids over everything else. She moved out of the Newport Beach apartment and back to Portland to live with and take care of Terri, who'd be in a wheelchair for the next year. Soon she was back working full-time with a different law firm and living with Terri in an apartment in Beaverton. Thor stayed behind in Newport Beach.

Just as things were settling down, Mom learned in early 1997 that her beloved Uncle Jack had cancer and was fading quickly. To make matters worse, after a disappearance of nearly thirty years, her brother Jack began phoning and harassing her. He was usually drunk and accused her of many horrible things. Mom could not understand his anger and attitude. Not long afterward, he died, leaving Mom feeling confused, frustrated, and full of guilt.

All this was happening while the four-year university was

being constructed on the junior college campus. Most of the paperwork had been submitted to the Ministry of Education for approval and possible funding. Administrative staff and teachers associated with the new university were being sent out to high schools throughout Kyushu and Okinawa to pitch the university to high school counselors and presidents. This was a new challenge for me—going on the road to be a salesman and explain in polite Japanese why going to our new university would be better than going to a more established school. It's hard to say whether I actually recruited any students or instead convinced the high school counselors that sending any of their students our way would be a big mistake.

Those last few months before Fukuoka International University officially opened were a stressful and insanely busy time. Both the administrative staff and the eight teachers being promoted, in essence, had to work overtime for two schools. There were all the end-of-the-school-year activities for the junior college that included final exams, entrance exams for incoming students, preparations for graduation for the second-year students, the endless meetings associated with these things, and committee responsibilities to wind down the year. There were also many meetings every week concerning preparations and carrying out a variety of entrance exams for the university. People were running themselves into the ground and ready to snap.

Shi-chan, too, was driving herself mercilessly. Since returning from her year in Arizona, she'd spent the last ten years putting together a resume that any Japanese woman would've been hard-pressed to exceed. After two years of doing much of the correspondence with the forty countries and territories that participated in the Asian Pacific Children's Convention in Fukuoka, interpreting and coordinating the ceremonies in that week-long event, and translating all its booklets, pamphlets, and letters, she moved on to an even more exhausting schedule at the Inter Group's newly established Fukuoka branch interpreting school. As there were few qualified people who could be found in Kyushu, the company relied on her not only to teach classes and act as coordinator handling teaching materials for instructors and students, but also piled on her shoulders the majority of interpreting requests that came to the school.

One week she'd have to interpret for a Malaysian political group, the next for a California avocado grower, and the next a Canadian lumber company. Each time was for something completely different without enough time to prepare, to learn the new specialized vocabulary, and to meet with the scheduled speaker. Sometimes it would be a simultaneous interpretation job, sometimes a consecutive interpretation job. From 1992 to 1997, she amassed more than fifty of these assignments and established a reputation as one of the most reliable and competent interpreters in Kyushu. This put her at odds with a few of the other members of the Fukuoka Interpreters Association. They probably were jealous of her accomplishments. She was burned out, feeling as if she was developing ulcers, and ready for a change. She quit the job and started freelancing in October.

The United Nations Habitat Program planned to set up a regional office in Fukuoka in August 1997 and put out an ad for the position of secretary for the manager. Shi-chan applied for the job, beat out many others and made the cut to the final two applicants, but didn't do well on the test of using Microsoft software. After moving out of our apartment and into an old two-story house where we had some office space, we'd bought a Mac computer. Shi-chan had worked a bit on PCs with Microsoft, but she was more accustomed to the Mac. She lost out on the job.

Her stomach pains got worse, so she went to an internist, who did an endoscopy exam, found an ulcer, and took a biopsy. A few days later on January 17, 1998, the third anniversary of the Kobe earthquake, the lab report came back: cancer. We were devastated. Within two weeks, she was in the hospital preparing for surgery to cut out three-fourths of her stomach.

The day of her surgery has a permanent place in my mind movie.

I get up early on the morning of January 30. My arthritic ankles and sprained knee take longer than usual to function. I take a painful, teeth-grinding bicycle ride in the cold to the hospital and arrive at Shi-chan's room at ten o'clock to see her laughing and joking, already the cheerleader for all the patients on the cancer ward. The nurses come in later to prepare her for surgery. They stick a tube down her nose, give her a shot, wash the polish off her toenails, dress her in a green smock and night cap, and put her on a gurney. Outside in the hallway, several patients are lined up to cheer her on. The nurses wheel her out of the room and into the hallway. Shi-chan waves at everyone and says, "I'll be back soon" in Japanese.

A lump forms in my throat and tears well in my eyes as we take the elevator to the second floor. There's barely time to lean down and kiss her before the nurses wheel her into the operating room. The two hours in the waiting room drag on for an eternity. The surgeon finally appears and calls me into a side room, where he outlines on a whiteboard the details of the surgery and explains that everything has gone according to plan except for one detail: the tumor was slightly larger than anticipated, so he cut out a larger section than planned, including the pylorus. He says he stitched the remaining stomach portion to the duodenum.

He shows me the removed section of Shi-chan's stomach. It's in a Tupperware container filled with ice. The mass of pink matter looks like a flattened squid with its tentacles cut off. I can see the cancer itself looking like a pale bruise on the pinkish slime. It has little white strands spreading outward. The surgeon is handling the stuff with wooden chopsticks. I feel I'm going to be sick, but at that moment, Shi-chan is wheeled out of the operating room, barely conscious, her eyes glazed over. She makes a weak attempt to flash the "V" sign before being wheeled into the intensive care room. I'm allowed a few minutes at her bedside. I touch her arm and say, "Can you feel me?" A barely audible "yes" escapes her mouth as she smiles weakly, then says, "I'm cold."

In the following days, I did my best to keep her family in Yuasa up to date on how Shi-chan was doing. Her recovery was going well. She could stand and walk a little bit on the second day after the operation. She was still in a lot of pain and had to take an extra dose of painkiller. By the third day, I could help her take some short walks around the hospital. She'd bonded with the other three patients in her room and their families. She told me, "Don't use the word 'cancer' when you talk to them. It's still taboo, especially with those who have cancer."

About a week after the surgery, Shi-chan ate her first semi-solid food for lunch. The nurses told her she had to chew thirty times for each bite. Afterward, she felt very heavy. The next day, the stitches from the operation were removed. The scar was clean and looked like a large exclamation point running from her belly button, the dot, to just below her breasts. She also took her first bath.

On the following night, we took our first walk without an IV-drip pole. Still having to bend over slightly, she put her arm in mine. We walked around her ward, then took the elevator down to the darkened first floor. We sat down on some benches. She got down on her knees and tried to fart, saying "I can't push it. I don't have that feeling. It has to come naturally." We did two more laps. At the end of the first lap, she stopped suddenly and cut loose with one of the longest, squishiest farts I'd ever heard. It sounded like a goat braying. A satisfied look crossed her face as she said, "Oh, that felt good. I've been waiting forever for that to happen."

Her first bowel movement came two days later. The next day, she had some white diarrhea, probably from the laxative she was taking. She said she was starting to regain some of the feeling of being able to use her bowel muscles. She was getting anxious to be released from the hospital.

Shi-chan came home on February 16. In the final meeting with her surgeon, we found out that when they took the biopsy during the initial endoscopy, they found the cancer at the same location of the ulcer. Thanks to that, the cancer was found early. It was a fast-spreading type, so if it hadn't been detected early, she might have died within a few months. The surgeon said Shi-chan would be at sixty percent full health for the first two to three months, and eighty percent for the following two or three months.

Over the next several days, Shi-chan's good friend Ide came over and did all the cooking, shopping, cleaning, and taking care of Shi-chan while I was working. Shi-chan was having difficulty learning the patience of chewing thoroughly. She was so hungry that she'd wolf a meal down, often eating too much at a time instead of stretching out a full meal into two lighter ones. She'd then suffer acid reflux for up to an hour. In the evenings, we took walks along some of the back streets of our neighborhood.

One night about two weeks after she returned home, Shi-chan broke down. She heard me tell a friend on the phone that I couldn't go out drinking because I had to take care of my wife.

"You're using me," she said curtly. "Don't use me as an excuse for not doing what you don't want to do." She glared at me for a moment, then said, "I saw Nomiyama-san at the supermarket today. How much does she know about me?"

"The whole story," I said.

Shi-chan went on a rant that included such things as "I think Fukuoka gave me cancer"; "My past is coming back to haunt me"; "I was more comfortable in the hospital"; "I have to get out of Kyushu"; "I run away when I see people I know in the supermarket"; "I can't stand going out in the day"; and "I hate these people." Tears streamed down her cheeks. She stormed out the door and went for a long walk.

I'd committed the cultural crime of telling too many people about her cancer. I'd blabbed to most of my colleagues, my friends at the sports club where I swam, my drinking partners, and our neighbors. Nomiyama was one of our neighbors from the apartment we lived in prior to moving into our house. I supposed that was typically American of me to think that because I knew these people cared about Shi-chan, they'd want to know. I hadn't considered the situation from Shi-chan's Japanese viewpoint. I remembered when I was eighteen years old and recovering from the dune buggy accident and surgery on my left arm. It took me a long time to snap out of the depression I fell into. All I could really do for Shi-chan was try to be patient and listen to her.

For the next few days, Shi-chan gave only curt responses to my attempts to talk. There were no smiles. She seemed to be just going through the motions in getting through each day. She decided to go back to Wakayama Prefecture for a cousin's wedding in the middle of March. We both needed some time away from each other. She left on March 14. Two days later, I heard from Mom that her Uncle Jack passed away.

It was a busy time for me. Touka Shobo finished up the final review printing of *Toraware*. Since it was now between semesters at the school, I had time to help write some letters in English to send, along with a review copy, to potential reviewers, to other writers for possible blurbs for the covers, and to distributors. I wanted to share with Shi-chan the realization of the different dreams I'd had for a long time about getting published, being promoted to a university, and having a stable income for some time to come, but it was difficult for her to respond.

Things were winding down at the junior college. There were still some English department and faculty meetings to attend and the graduation ceremony was coming at the end of March, but all my final paperwork was turned in. The English department had a farewell party for me. They were all like family members. We'd shared many great times over the past six years. We guzzled a lot of beer that night, made many toasts, took many pictures, and shared many laughs. It wasn't, however, like anyone was moving away. We'd still be working on the same small campus, so there would be plenty of chances to continue seeing one another and going out occasionally.

On the other hand, things were really gearing up at the university. The new buildings were completed, and I moved all my things into a new personal office. There was a nice view of Dazaifu below and the surrounding mountains. The cherry blossoms on both sides of the road leading up the hill to the campus were nearing full bloom. There were many new teachers to meet and visit with. Everyone was anxious to start the new school year and meet the first group of students.

Shi-chan returned on March 25. She looked healthy but tired. She did smile at me when I hugged her and said, "Welcome home." Two nights later, we had a serious talk. "I want to go back to the Kansai, where I can speak my own language," she said.

"I'm sorry, Shi-chan, but there's no way I can leave here," I said. "I don't have the energy or strength to start from the bottom again. I could be in a wheelchair in a few years. Besides, I've worked too hard for too many years to get to where I'm at now with this new job. I'd be a fool to quit."

She looked down at the floor for a moment, then looked me in the eye. "I know I'm being selfish. I'm sorry." Tears came again. She went into the front room to sleep under the *kotatsu*. For the next few days, she didn't leave the house and spent most of the time resting at the *kotatsu* and watching TV.

We had a couple more discussions. She made a list of options for herself under two headings—one for continuing to live in the Fukuoka area and one for leaving the Fukuoka area. She felt that Fukuoka hadn't been good for her. All the bad things started when she began working for Inter Group and eventually burned herself out trying to please everyone and not being able to say no to all the responsibilities heaped on her shoulders. She'd tried her best, but Fukuoka had drained her. She didn't want to go through life thinking she would've been happy someplace else.

Ide had also told her that she spoke in her normal tone of voice when she seemed to feel comfortable but switched to a higher pitch when she seemed to want someone to like her. Shi-chan said she hadn't been aware of this. She said, "When I was single, I was a fighter. I was myself. I used my own voice. But now I'm your wife. I use a higher voice when I talk to people. I'm not myself. I have to return to myself."

I gave Shi-chan a back massage. Her whole body was stiff. She understood that I couldn't move again, that I was in Fukuoka for the long haul. I told her I thought she'd have to be in top shape physically and mentally if she was serious about starting over in a new place with no job, no friends, and no support network, especially in a bad economy. I suggested she had the option of traveling around Japan, writing a journal, or painting different landscapes. Art was as good of a therapy as anything.

Basically, I told her she should take her time, get strong first, make some contacts, and think this thing through before making a decision. In the meantime, do things for herself—stretch, play the piano or *shamisen*, go out in the garden sometimes, do some yoga and meditation. She could make our house her home base if she wanted to. Time would reveal what the next course of her life should be. I'd always be there to support her.

"You're too good to me. I really love you," she said.

The next day, she hugged me while I was doing the dishes. That night, she crawled back into bed with me. She started going for walks again, going to dance lessons with Ide, and doing chores around the house. Her energy, sense of humor, and strength improved.

The first month at FIU was an exciting and exhausting time. Even before classes started, there was much work to be done: orientation activities for the students, who came mainly from all areas of Kyushu; homeroom activities and schedules to be explained; faculty and committee meetings to attend; and an overnight trip to a hot springs resort with all the inherent preparations for sleeping arrangements, activities for teachers and students to get to know one another, and preparing meals and transportation for close to four hundred people.

The first month of a new semester was always a madhouse, but this was something different. The students seemed more motivated than usual. It was gratifying to see the kids work hard and earnestly. All my classes proceeded smoothly, but in trying to build an environment in which the kids would continue to stay motivated, I used up most of my energy. It took longer than usual to get into teaching shape.

These kids were first-year pioneers. If they felt they'd made the right choice in coming to FIU, they'd be indispensable for future recruiting. There were endless faculty and committee meetings, both formal and informal, for the organization and planning of the formation of the student council, different clubs based on the students' wants and needs, sports teams and facilities needed, yearly events with a focus on the school festival and its activities, international events and homestay programs, events for interacting with the local community and other universities, and many other things. From early on, teachers were intent on having an "open door" policy in which students could come visit their teachers almost any time without needing an appointment.

When the Golden Week holiday arrived after that hectic first month, we were all ready for a break. Mom paid us a week-long visit during the holiday. Our oldest niece Keiko, who was now sixteen and eager about her English study, came up from Yuasa at the same time.

Mom's visit, more than anything else, helped snap Shi-chan out of her funk. It rained during most of that week, but that allowed Mom to spend a lot of time with both Shi-chan and Keiko. They played many tunes on the piano and helped one another to send e-mail and check the internet on our computer. Mom told Shi-chan about her own depressions following miscarriages, a cancer operation for taking out her uterus, and losing her parents. Mom later reported to me that when Shi-chan confided in her that she was thinking of leaving Fukuoka, Mom said, "If you want to, you can come stay with me as long as you want. Terri and I will take care of you."

"But wouldn't you hate me if I separated from Bob?" Shi-chan asked.

"No, honey. You're my friend. Friends help each other." Mom said they cried together and hugged.

Most of our time was spent relaxing at home. Mom told us family stories and helped with the cooking. She and Keiko hit it off. Keiko's English had improved a lot and she wasn't shy about trying to use it. On the one day it didn't rain, I took everyone up to the school to see the new buildings and offices.

There was a noticeable change in Shi-chan after Mom's visit. She was more energetic, filled with humor and hugs. She began playing the piano again, reading about walking and yoga, occasionally hitting some golf balls at a driving range, laughing at things on TV, and regularly changing flowers in the different rooms.

The next few months flew by. Life was good. Especially gratifying were the things connected with the publishing world. Touka Shobo sponsored a promotional event by renting a large hall, printing up large posters, and arranging a book-signing after I gave an hour-long speech in Japanese about my books. About a hundred and fifty people attended and we sold forty copies of *Toraware*. Two of Japan's major English newspapers, as well as an English magazine in Kobe, gave the novel positive reviews. I finished putting together a simple homepage that had excerpts from each of the three books and copies of the academic papers I'd published. I received some e-mails from a few teachers who read the papers, put into practice some of my teaching ideas, and found them useful.

Shi-chan's recovery continued in a positive vein. Her physical strength returned and she began going for daily treks on the trails at the nearby Tenpai mountain. She often took pictures on these treks. When she felt strong enough in the fall, she took a camping trip to the island of Yakushima by herself and spent three days hiking its trails. She came back rejuvenated, as if she'd undergone a transformational spiritual experience. After that trip, she recruited some students and began teaching English to adult students on Friday evenings and Saturday afternoons on the second floor of our house. It was good to see her enthusiastic about life and work again.

17

A Time of Calamities

As FIU started its second year in April 1999, we were in a good groove. I now had a simple homepage to promote my books and papers. Shi-chan's school at home had about twenty students. She was actively practicing both the piano and *shamisen*, going for treks in the Tenpai mountain trails, and had an interpreting class for second-year students at FIU. Her regular medical checkups showed she was healing well.

The term Y2K started to appear in the news. People around the world were fearful that a computer bug would prevent online clocks from rolling over from 1999 to 2000 and instead turn them back to 1900, which would cause banks, electrical grids, nuclear power stations, and just about anything driven by a computer to fail. There were reports of people stocking up on food, water, batteries, generators, and other survival goods.

I'd told Shi-chan many times about my journeys to Europe and around the world in 1973 and 1977 and how they'd changed my life. I'd always wondered what happened to many of the characters I met, especially Thomas Knorr, the German I met in Lörrach with Hasan and Ataullah before that fateful journey to Iran, Afghanistan, and India. I felt a sudden strong desire to see him and thank him for helping me back then. I also wanted to introduce Shi-chan to Amsterdam, Florence, and other places that had played a role in setting me on the many roads that eventually led to her. For once, I'd have no serious responsibilities during summer vacation, so this might be the last chance to take such a trip, especially if the Y2K worries proved to be true. Shi-chan enthusiastically agreed.

In July, both Shi-chan and I had health checkups. All her numbers came back perfect. We were happy about that, but going to the hospital made her a bit sad because she met two other people who'd been in the hospital at the same time she had her surgery. They both were back for further operations because their cancer had returned. Another patient died a few months earlier. We were lucky Shi-chan's cancer was discovered early. The others had it in later stages of development.

In my case, my beer guzzling finally caught up with me. My liver numbers were astronomical the last two years, so I decided to have a detailed checkup. The doctor found I had a fatty liver and told me the next step if I continued drinking at the same pace would be acute alcoholic hepatitis, followed by the big C. I cut back on the booze.

Amsterdam was as wonderful as I remembered it. We checked out the "coffee shops" and I smoked some great weed. We did a lot of walking the streets like I used to do. The ankles held up well. We sometimes went to a huge park where a variety of street musicians performed—a reggae band; an old Dutch couple playing a flute, bongo, and guitar; a Mongolian group playing string instruments and doing throat singing. One day, we went to a cheese market in a suburb of Amsterdam, a weekly event where thousands of kilograms of cheese were stacked up and checked for quality and bargaining took place between whole-sale buyers and sellers. When we went to the Van Gogh and Rembrandt museums, Shi-chan got shivers up and down her spine. The Red Light District fascinated us with its myriad of characters. The streets were packed with tourists. We enjoyed hearing a multitude of tongues.

I called Undine Knorr and was shocked to learn Thomas had died. We missed seeing him by about three days. We went to Basel, Switzerland, saw more museums, took a bus tour of the city, then crossed the German-Swiss border into Lörrach, where we spent a day with Undine and her two children, now twenty-seven and twenty-three. We reminisced about that time twenty-two years before when I'd stayed at their place before heading east. Apparently, Thomas had spent about seven years in prison for trying to smuggle hashish and hit the alcohol and drugs hard after he got out. Undine said he lost all the idealism from his youth.

It seemed Undine needed to talk about the "good days." She drove us to the hill where they used to live and took us to the high point where you could see Switzerland, France, and Germany all from the same spot. We ate dinner together and promised to stay in touch. I gave copies of my books to her as a present in memory of Thomas, who during all these years had remained in my own memory as a guiding angel who helped set me on a path that changed my life. Undine and Thomas had many adventures in those days. She told us some stories about Afghanistan, India, and the hardship of life on the road.

After an emotional farewell, it was on to Florence, Italy. Shi-chan couldn't stop exclaiming, "Ohhhh, ohhhh, wow, ohhhh!" when she saw the massive Duomo. We went to several museums, climbed a high hill from which we could see the expanse of the entire city, saw Michelangelo's *David*, and gorged ourselves in some local restaurants. We spent our final two days in Rome. The trip was like a second honeymoon.

One night while we were in Florence, my ankles were sore from all the walking. I propped myself on our bed and Shi-chan massaged my left ankle. We were both still feeling sad about Thomas's death. A serious look came to her face. She said, "We were fated to come together. I really believe that. I think we were both traveling many different paths, and those paths were fated from the beginning to come together. I know I say this all the time, but don't you think so?"

"Yes, it sure seems that way. I've believed for a long time that someone or something has been guiding me throughout my life. And it seems that for a long time Thomas was somehow connected to that belief."

Shi-chan finished rubbing the left ankle, shifted on the bed, and started on the right ankle. She was quiet for a moment, then said, "I'm glad I got cancer."

"How's that?"

"If I hadn't gotten cancer when I did, I'd probably be dead now. I believe that. The doctors told me that my cancer was the fast-spreading type and I know that if I'd gotten that secretarial job for the United Nations Habitat in Fukuoka, I'd have ignored the pain in my stomach and kept working and it would've been too late by the time I finally went to a doctor. Do you remember all that?"

"Oh yes, I remember everything."

"Do you remember what a bitch I was all the time? I really was a bitch when I was interpreting. I hated all those people in the Fukuoka Inter Group and in that interpreting association. They were always trying to put me down." A frown marked her face.

"I remember the pressures you were under all the time, the way your company kept giving you all the most difficult jobs," I said. "And the way every job was for a totally unrelated group or company—every time something different without enough time to prepare, to learn the new specialized vocabulary."

"And I started getting pains in my stomach and for a while stomach medicine would relieve the pain temporarily, but it got to be too much and finally I went to the internist. I had to swallow that stomach camera and they found an ulcer, but just to make sure he took a biopsy and a week later the lab report came back with a diagnosis of cancer. The ulcer and the cancer were in the exact same spot. Isn't that amazing?" Shi-chan rubbed her stomach with both hands for a few seconds.

"It sure is. We were incredibly lucky," I said. "If it hadn't been for the pain of the ulcer, you'd never have found the cancer."

Shi-chan smiled and said, "Honey-chan, you're the only one who understands me."

"I try my best." I smiled back at her.

"Do you understand why I'm glad I got cancer?"

"I think so."

"Cancer gave me a new life. God was telling me to stop my old life. God was telling me that I was killing myself. Cancer is now my great teacher. Just think. If I hadn't got cancer, I wouldn't know about hiking in the mountains. I wouldn't know about taking pictures of nature in the mountains. I wouldn't know the enjoyment of playing the piano and the *shamisen*. I wouldn't know the joy of teaching English. I wouldn't be learning about Van Gogh and Rembrandt and Michelangelo and the Renaissance. I just feel so alive now."

The return to Japan jolted us back to reality. My test results came back from the lab: positive for hepatitis C. I had no idea of the exact route, but I figured the odds were that I contracted it back when I was twenty and in that plywood mill accident that ripped my right forearm to the bone. The surgeon gave me a blood transfusion. Screening of blood didn't really start until the outbreak of AIDS in the 1980s, so anyone who had a blood transfusion before 1989 was in a high-risk category for hepatitis C. The strange thing was that I'd had no noticeable symptoms in all those years except for the elevated liver numbers. No fibrosis or cirrhosis, but it was possible I could face those problems and eventual cancer of the liver if I didn't do something. I went into a kind of training mode. I quit drinking all alcohol and began taking some medicine called Ursodiol to suppress the virus and try to lower the liver numbers.

The amount of iron in my blood was also too high. My doctor had me do some phlebotomies. His theory was that as my body reproduced new virus- and iron-free blood, the number of dead and damaged blood cells would be reduced. All this was leading to a period of six months to a year of taking Interferon, which I'd heard was a little like undergoing chemotherapy with some side effects. The doctor told me it was the only drug that had been found to have any effect on eradicating the virus from the blood. The odds for that were less than fifty-fifty, but would increase if I had near-normal liver numbers, a low viral load, and a strong immune system.

The initial plan was to enter the hospital around the beginning of March. They would hit me with a knockout punch of Interferon, monitor my response for the first three weeks, then put me on a maintenance dose to last for anywhere from six months to a year. If the side effects got too severe, I could always quit and stick with herbs, supplements, and a healthier lifestyle to try to control the virus.

About the time I told Mom and Terri about my hepatitis C and plan for treatment, they got hit by a double whammy. Dick and Dottie were now living in North Carolina. Dick had a salesman job for some electronics company—there'd been a succession of jobs after he lost his pilot's job several years before after a car accident messed up his back and he couldn't pass a yearly physical test anymore—and Dottie was working in real estate part-time. She'd recently been diagnosed with lung and liver cancer, as well as some tumors in the brain. She was sixty-two and the doctors gave her about a year to live. She'd just finished some radiation treatments and was undergoing chemotherapy. Within a few months, she was gone.

The year ended with no major Y2K disasters, but in January FIU calculated that we'd get only about two-thirds the enrollment of the first year, when we'd recruited the maximum number allowed by the Ministry of Education. The board of directors was starting to panic and already considering ways to cut down on expenses, starting with teacher bonuses and perks.

In February, Shi-chan complained of stomach pains and went to the doctor. She was having some complications as a result of her operation. She hadn't been chewing thoroughly. Over a period of time, peritonitis, an inflammation of the peritoneum, the membrane that lines the wall of the abdomen and covers the organs, had taken hold. There was a buildup of fluid in her abdomen and she couldn't eat much without getting full and having a serious stomachache. Her doctor gave her a strict warning about chewing thoroughly and not overeating.

At the beginning of March, I consulted with my doctor and made arrangements to go into the hospital for three days on the twenty-first to have a liver biopsy done. It was mainly to be sure that if I opted for the Interferon treatment, my insurance would pay for almost everything. Interferon was expensive, and the insurance companies wouldn't cover anything unless a biopsy was done first.

The biopsy was not the most comfortable experience I'd ever had. The young doctor who was to stick the needle in my side was probably an intern. I was lying quietly on my back on the operating table. An IV line was placed in my right arm. The doctor was to perform a percutaneous liver biopsy, which involved inserting a thin needle through my abdomen into the liver and removing a small piece of tissue. My biggest fear was that he'd accidentally stick the gallbladder or a lung.

The doctor told me to raise my right arm above my head. He tapped on my stomach and side and made a mark with a pen on the location he'd penetrate. He applied some gel on the location and used an ultrasound to determine the precise target. After wiping the gel off, he sterilized the skin with iodine. Then he said, "Take a breath, hold it, and don't move."

I grabbed the rail behind my head and held my breath. The doctor inserted the needle. It struck a rib bone and hit a nerve. I screamed, "Fuck!" It must've shocked the doctor, but he didn't panic. He pulled the needle out and disappeared into the next room for a conference. A minute later, he returned, smiled at me, and said, "Are you OK?"

I said, "I've been better."

The second insertion went smoothly. When he pulled the needle out with the little chunk of liver in it, he looked at it briefly, then disappeared into the next room again. I heard him say excitedly, "You gotta look at this! You gotta see it! Look at the color! I've never seen one this color before!"

That didn't do a lot for my confidence.

I spent the night in the hospital. I had to lie flat in bed for twenty-four hours. The next day, they gave me a CT scan and I got to look at the pictures. There was a slight tear on the liver where the needle had bounced off the bone, but there was no significant damage. Aside from that, the liver looked good. My side was a little tender, but the doctor told me I could start swimming again in a couple of days. My back was stiff for a short time, but once I left the hospital and started walking around more, it loosened up.

For the previous few months, I'd been studying about the world of e-publishing. I sent *Looking for the Summer* and *Toraware* out for possible publishing by an e-publisher I found called Dead End Street. I thought they'd be right up my alley because they specialized in "alternative literature." Most of the other e-publishers focused mainly on romance, science fiction, and fantasy. I owned the electronic rights to my books, so there seemed no problem having one publisher do the print version and another do the electronic version, which included versions on a CD-ROM, on a floppy disk, or on a downloadable PDF file from an online e-bookstore or e-publisher.

I queried Dead End Street. The acquisitions editor wrote back saying they'd be interested in looking at my books. I had to contact their lawyer about any potential legal problems concerning books that were already in print, but none were found in my case. I got the lawyer's go-ahead to submit. Once the documents arrived on the other end, the same process of dealing with a regular publisher would take place. The manuscript had to go through two sets of editors to get approval. If they liked the story, they'd send editing suggestions. The writer either had to make the changes or explain why he wanted the manuscript unchanged. It could be a few months before final decisions to publish or not were made. Contracts had to be drawn up, advance reviews garnered, and distribution outlets contacted.

After about a week of e-mail negotiations, I agreed to sign the contract with Dead End Street to do the e-book version of *Toraware*. They passed on *Looking for the Summer*. The contract was eleven pages long and quite complicated, but I found all the little "small print" areas and held out for what I wanted. I got concessions on nearly everything and the royalties were nearly triple what was offered in the beginning. One of the reasons I got what I wanted was that the story didn't need much editing, so the expense on the publisher's side for that would be minimal. Touka Shobo had to cease publication and distribution as Dead End Street wanted all the publishing rights, not just electronic rights. Touka Shobo agreed. They weren't a big enough publisher to maintain an overseas presence. They'd continue to put out a limited print edition of *Looking for the Summer*. I queried Jacobyte Books, an Australian e-publisher, about doing an electronic version for that book.

In the middle of June, my doctor and I decided on some definite dates to begin my treatment. I'd start July 1 with an aggressive program of phlebotomies combined with a drug called Desferal to get my iron level down. I'd go to the hospital every other day for a month of that treatment. I'd then enter the hospital August 2 for three weeks of KO-punch doses of Interferon that would be followed by at least six months of maintenance doses if my body responded well while in the hospital. I'd be able to cover a good portion of the expense with my insurance because I had the liver biopsy in March. I was thankful I belonged to a good union.

Shortly before I was to start the Interferon treatment, Shi-chan had her biannual checkup. It showed that almost all the fluid in her abdomen was gone and all her numbers were in the healthy ranges. She was feeling better than she'd felt in a long time. She had a good appetite and was eating well again. Her persistence was paying off. I was proud of her.

I entered the hospital the day after FIU's semester ended. Before the actual Interferon treatment started, I had to go through a battery of tests where they poked and probed nearly every orifice in my body, stuck me full of needles like a living voodoo doll, and jammed a stomach camera down my throat to look at my insides. They let me out of the hospital for one day because I told them I still had some work to finish. I guzzled one last cold beer before returning. I did a check of e-mail and learned that Jacobyte Books had published the digital version of *Looking for the Summer*.

For the first two days, I had some flu-like side effects—a slightly high fever around midnight, some headaches, and stiff muscles, but no nausea or diarrhea. I couldn't sleep well because of an alternating chill and high body temperature at night, but I was able to eat breakfast and lunch. I walked for a while in the mornings before doing some stretching, which helped me take naps afterward and lower my temperature. Shi-chan visited in the afternoons.

For the remainder of my three-week stay, I had no fever or headaches. I might've been a rare case. All the other patients on my ward who'd received or were receiving Interferon treatments told me about the nasty side effects that they had. They couldn't believe I was up and not showing any side effects except for the first two days. In my research before entering the hospital, I'd read that in the United States many patients called the drug "inter-fear-on" because the side effects could be so terrible that some even had to stop the treatment. My main problem appeared to be boredom.

The fall semester started and things went smoothly. For the first few weeks, I handled the three-shots-a-week Interferon treatment well. Once in a while I'd get a slight fever and stiffness a few hours after a shot, but that would be gone the next morning. The worst part was feeling like a human pin cushion. I requested the nurses to rotate the shots back and forth between the left and right arms, but I could still feel where I'd been stuck in the muscle of both arms when I lifted them over my head. I wrote Mom and told her I'd consider switching over to taking the shots in the butt, but if I bent over, I'd get flashbacks to the time in Jacoby Creek I burned my butt on the wall heater and cried when anybody looked at me crossways. I wasn't about to show the nurses my precious bum yet.

The Grim Reaper was busy during this time. Not long after Dottie died, Mom's Uncle Tommy passed. On the heels of that, Uncle Dick had a heart attack and died not long after. I was glad that he and I'd mended our fences years ago. He'd even bought a few copies of *Looking for the Summer* to give to some friends. Mom had also put the past to rest with him.

The final blow in this dark streak occurred at FIU. One of the boys—only twenty years old—in my homeroom class jumped off the top of a tall apartment building. I was the last teacher to see him. He'd come by my office the previous week to get my signature for some paperwork for dropping out of school. We talked about life for about thirty minutes, and he seemed a bit encouraged. He said he'd have a job interview in a few days. He got the job, but killed himself three days after he started. He'd done well in school for his first six months, but over the last two years he hardly came to school at all. The last words I said to him were "Good luck and know that things will always work out for the best in the end." The police found a diary in his room. The last words written in the diary were "I visited thirty more homes today, but still no sales." For a long time after that, it was hard to be in front of a classroom and not see his face.

Dick began calling Mom collect almost every day, demanding attention and help from her. I had a bad feeling that this could be the start of a steep descent for Dick. He then made a trip to Portland. For the next month, Mom kept us informed almost daily by e-mail about their activities, conversations, and ups and downs. Dad and Linda D. decided to take a trip to White Salmon around the same time so she could see where Dad grew up. Dick planned to go to White Salmon to see Connie and her husband Gene, so Dad hoped to spend some time with Dick and take him to White Salmon in his car. Everyone hoped that spending time with various family members would help Dick a little in recovering from Dottie's death.

Mom's e-mails covered only the basic information. The details came with the long letter she wrote after Dick returned to North Carolina. In it, she gave detailed descriptions how heavily Dick was drinking and how his attitude toward people and life had radically changed. He was verbally abusive to everyone he saw, accused Mom and all his family of not loving him and of conspiring against him. He demanded money that no one had to give. Mom ended the letter with a warning that he would probably come to me begging for more money. She was scared he was becoming a monster.

When I finished reading the letter, I thought, "Man oh man, this isn't so different from what Mom went through with her brother in the last year of his life." I wrote her an encouraging letter the following day. I finished my six-month Interferon treatment in February. Although the numbers on my blood tests were greatly improved, the treatment hadn't killed the virus. The only thing I could do was to resolve to maintain those numbers. Maybe in two or three years if a new treatment came to Japan, I'd give it a try. For the time being, I needed an Interferon break.

18

Let's Go to Ireland

FOR the next two and a half years, the vicissitudes and drama of Dick's life constituted a large portion of the correspondence between Mom and me. At one point, he would end up on the streets. It was probably as stressful a time in Mom's life as she'd ever experienced. She was increasingly torn between two extremes of emotion. On one hand was her family loyalty and love for her children. On the other was her need to avoid a repeat of what her brother had put her through. She was already financially strapped after having worked off Herb's gambling debts and now taking on the responsibility of caring for Terri. She also had her own medical issues to deal with and, at seventy-four, was still working full-time in a high-pressure job. She was a rock, but there was a limit to her strength.

I did my best to give as much emotional and financial support as I could. When her frustration would spill over into thinking Dick's problems were her fault as a failed mother, I'd respond as well as I could to assuage her guilt and fears and let her know she wasn't at fault, that he was no longer a teenager, and that he was responsible for creating his own karma. Knowing what buttons to tickle, I often made her laugh by appealing to her sense of the absurd.

The terrorist attacks of September 11, 2001, caused a shift in our attention. It made me reflect on the time I'd spent in Afghanistan with Ataullah and his brothers. I wrote a short piece about those memories of Ataullah and sent it to both Dad and Mom.

Shi-chan and I tried not to obsess about the war news and instead concentrated on our jobs. FIU was having a tough time recruiting students. Several of the professors who'd been hired for the first four years of setting up and getting the university rolling retired. The board of directors decided not to hire anyone new. A new Digital Media Department would start up the year after next and I'd be responsible for teaching some different classes, including Introduction to Electronic Publishing. Starting with the new semester in April, I'd have to teach a class on American culture and society. I had my work cut out for me. There was no English major at the school, so I'd have to teach the class in Japanese.

Throughout much of the rest of the year, the TV news became increasingly worse. A patriotic fervor swept throughout the U.S. It seemed the Bush administration was intent on connecting Saddam Hussein to al Qaeda and invading Iraq. The American news programs we watched focused almost entirely on Saddam's alleged buildup of weapons of mass destruction. Supporters of this view were interviewed at length. Critics, if they appeared at all, were limited to just a minute or two. These news programs always had the American flag waving in the background and patriotic music blaring. Online stories by major news services pushed a buildup to war. To me, most of the media were little more than cheerleaders for an administration hungry for revenge and war. The Japanese media followed in lockstep.

Wherever we went, we saw a lot of glum faces.

Inveterate optimist that she was, Mom would always find ways to suppress any sadness or depression by making plans for something or starting a new project. This time she came up with a doozy that would get us up off our butts and moving collectively toward a positive and exciting goal.

In an e-mail to Mom, I mentioned in passing that after watching some golf from Ireland on TV, I thought it would be a fun place to visit. Mom wrote back that she'd been yearning to go to Ireland since she was in high school. She had a small investment that she was thinking about cashing in and the idea of using it for a trip had come to her. A couple of her friends took a trip to Ireland a few years before and actually found and visited the old homestead of Mom's father's ancestors in County Mayo. Mom wrote:

> Life is so tentative right now. What do you think about the three of us meeting in Ireland and taking a jaunt up to the old homestead? By next year when you two could get away, I would have enough vacation time saved. I think it would be an incredible experience!

Shi-chan and I loved the idea. We wrote back immediately telling Mom the best time for us was the next August. I'd get about a month off in March but might have to take another homestay group somewhere. Shi-chan always kept her school running in March and took the whole month of August off. Also, in late March, I'd have a graduation ceremony to attend, so I wouldn't be able to take off as much time then as I could in August.

I told Mom I'd go anywhere she wanted to see. I had no special preference as to specific places. Anywhere to me would be an adventure. It was the people you met rather than the places you saw that provided the best memories.

Over the next few months, we became occupied in preparation for this "trip of a lifetime." We studied about the history, culture, and people of Ireland. We made potential travel itineraries with intricate possibilities, threw those out when a better idea or item caught our fancy, made new plans, and exchanged ideas and information via e-mail and telephone. It gave Mom a burst of enthusiasm and pure joy that pushed aside the frustrations of the onslaught of age, her physical aches, and her anxiety about her children and other family members. The tone of her letters and e-mails, as well as the sound of her voice when we talked on the phone, exuded excitement and enthusiasm.

On the book front, I had some good results from promotional efforts. A group of students in Okinawa used *The Many Roads to Japan* and had a great response to it. Their teacher invited me to give a presentation at the local English teachers' association in April. They'd pay my airfare and hotel, as well as about a fifty-dollar stipend. In early February, Chikushino City Hall asked me to give a two-hour talk in Japanese about life for a foreigner in Japan to a group of about two hundred people. They'd pay me a hundred and fifty dollars. I queried some peace museums over the previous few months, and some bought my books. One even sent out a recommendation including an order link in its newsletter that went out to two hundred peace museums and libraries worldwide. The woman who ran a peace museum in the city of Kochi on the island of Shikoku planned to use *The Many Roads to Japan* as a textbook in the university class she taught.

At the beginning of February, the space shuttle Columbia exploded just a few minutes from landing, spreading debris over a wide section of Texas and Louisiana. The drumbeat to war grew louder. Secretary of State Colin Powell appeared at the United Nations on February 5 to make the case for attacking Iraq, claiming Iraq had vast stockpiles of weapons of mass destruction. At the end of March, the invasion of Iraq was underway.

FIU kept me busy. After all the second-semester classes and final exams were completed, I had to help proctor some entrance exams. There were many emergency meetings to attend. In March, I had to visit some high schools in different parts of Kyushu to give demonstration lessons and try to convince those students that our university was where they should go. There was a growing feeling of desperation at the university. Enrollment had dropped considerably since the first year. I hoped the school would stay afloat at least until I could retire.

When all the entrance exam results were finished and the deadlines for tuition payment passed, FIU ended up with around two hundred new students, which was an improvement over the one hundred fifteen of the previous year. Everyone breathed a little easier, thinking maybe we'd hit the bottom and were gradually pulling ourselves up. The board of directors yielded to the faculty's request to allow more foreign students. We accepted over eighty Chinese student applications. This portended a huge difference in campus atmosphere. Although the university carried the word "international" in its name, the truth was we'd never had more than a handful of overseas students. Now bunches of them were coming. A special committee was set up to deal with the situation. As a foreigner, I was put on the committee and expected to be heavily involved.

When the Bush administration launched its attack on Iraq, I felt sick. I feared the consequences would reverberate for years. Shi-chan and I subscribed to a cable TV server so we could watch the news from different countries. We were amazed at the variety of ways the war was portrayed in different parts of the world. Shi-chan often flipped through the channels, consulting her dictionaries, and writing notes furiously. In the end, we tried to take every bit of news with a grain of salt and expose ourselves to a variety of viewpoints before making any assumptions on what was really going on and what the ramifications were of each military and political decision made.

We looked forward to Mom's e-mails. They were peppered with heartfelt expressions: "Ah, yes, Ireland. Just the thought and anticipation of the 'trip' of a lifetime brings a smile to my face." "I'm so excited. Can you tell?" "Oh dear, do I sound excited?" "Wow! This is truly a dream come true. Just shows if you live long enough, stay optimistic, dreams do come true!" "Well, kids, think green, think Ireland. I really cannot believe that a lifelong dream is going to come true." "Am I getting excited? That's probably a great understatement. I've been walking on air for weeks." "This is going to happen—the Good Lord willing and the creek don't rise." Her zeal was infectious.

Spurred on by the thought of her father's desire that she see Ireland someday because he'd never been able to, Mom went to great lengths to find information about ancestors and contact anyone who might have even a remote connection to a possible current relative still living there.

Mom knew only that our Irish ancestors originally came from Belmullet, County Mayo and suffered through the great potato famine. She wrote to two distant cousins who'd visited County Mayo and had actually seen the original Murphy homestead. She wrote to another cousin who was living in Florida and asked him for some pointers as years before he'd also visited Belmullet and met Mary Murphy, the widow of Seamus Murphy, the great-great-grandson of John Murphy, the founder of the ancestral home. Apparently, Seamus had died in recent years.

Mom wrote to Mary Murphy. She also sent a note to the Belmullet postmaster. A month passed. She hadn't received an answer from either Mary Murphy or the postmaster, but her persistence eventually paid off. Near the end of March, she got a sudden telephone call from a Mary Fernandez from Chicago. Mary Fernandez and her husband had just returned from visiting relatives in Belmullet. She said that Mom's letter to the postmaster had been published in the village newspaper and she had read it. She knew Mary Murphy and was a very close friend of Mary Lavin, Seamus Murphy's sister who lived with her husband, Tony, in County Roscommon. For the next few months, Mom and Mary Fernandez developed a close friendship and often called each other to share Murphy family information. More than anything, Mom now wanted to meet both Mary Murphy and Mary Lavin in person and see the old homestead.

Mom and I began ending our e-mails with a message sending buckets of Irish pixie dust for good luck. We told each other "You gotta keep believing in magic and those Irish leprechauns!"

Three weeks before Mom, Shi-chan, and I departed for Ireland, tragedy struck FIU. One of our Chinese exchange students was killed in a horrible car accident. She was riding a bicycle and didn't stop at a stop sign. A dump truck ran over her. The death hit everyone at the school hard. She was twenty-three and probably the best and most popular of the foreign students. Many people attended the funeral. The student government held a special ceremony and planted a cherry tree in her name on campus.

We were all ready for a break.

Mom flew to Dublin from Portland. Shi-chan and I flew from Japan. We all arrived safely with minimal mishaps. We spent the first few days doing the sights in Dublin, then took a train to Galway. We contacted Mary and Tony Lavin in Castlerea, took a bus there, stayed with them, and enjoyed their warm hospitality. Mary Lavin helped us trace our lineage back six generations.

In Castlerea, we rented a car. Shi-chan drove, I navigated, and Mom smiled in the back seat and took in the scenery. We went about as far west as you can go, to the Mullet Peninsula, spent an afternoon visiting with Mary Murphy, found the original Murphy house still standing, and in an unmarked cemetery found three graves belonging to cousins who'd died in the last fifty to sixty years. After that, it was on to the northern part of Ireland to Sligo, back to the Lavins' place for two more days, and finally back to Dublin for another two days. All told, we spent three weeks that were full of fun, surprises, adventure, laughter, magic, and memories to last the rest of our lives. Shi-chan found her English almost on a par with native speakers. Mom found her youth. I found a couple of independent bookstores that agreed to buy copies of my books to put on their shelves.

Several moments of our pilgrimage remain firmly fixed in my memory. They're an integral part of my mind movie. I return to them often when I'm in need of one of Mom's joyous smiles. One is visiting the Murphy ancestral home. Mom's eyes fill with tears as we approach the old home. It's about two hundred years old and was lived in up to 1995. At the front gate, Mom bends down, touches the ground with both hands, and says a silent prayer. We're sure Grandpa Pat is smiling down upon us.

Two days later, we leave Belmullet and drive along the Wild Atlantic Way heading toward Ballina. The cliffs are spectacular. There are fields and fields of peat bogs along the sides of the road. Men are gathered in the fields, throwing the peat in trucks by hand. We see a lot of abandoned rock houses without roofs. We stop at Downpatrick Head. We follow the signposts to a gravel car park. From there, it's a short walk on an incline across rough grass to the cliffs. A strong wind is blowing. We come across a large sinkhole. Just beyond that are the remaining stone walls of a church founded by Saint Patrick. Inside the walls is a life-sized statue of Saint Patrick standing on a large base.

Mom sees the statue before Shi-chan and I do and walks quickly ahead of us. When we catch up with her, she's looking up at the statue, her hands firmly against her sides, and speaking to the statue. When she finishes, we ask Mom what she said.

"I apologized first for being a bad Catholic," Mom says. "Then I thanked him for taking care of us so far on this trip to realize my dad's dreams. I told him to please keep sprinkling that pixie dust down on us and we sure appreciate all the great luck and guidance he's given us. And I told him he'd better take care of my dad or else he'll have to contend with me when it's my turn and I'm sure he doesn't want that!" Mom has the widest grin I've ever seen.

We then move up to the edge of the cliffs and look out on the Dun Briste sea stack. None of us speaks for a few moments. I see tears on Mom's face.

The day before we return home, we go out to dinner in Dublin, then walk down one of the main streets to see if there are any musicians performing. Sure enough, there's a young French jazz group playing. They have a guitar case open for people to toss coins into. I hand Mom some money, nudge her forward, and say, "Go on, Mom. Put this in their guitar case. Go for it." There are probably about seventy people watching and tapping their toes to the music. Mom struts her way to the guitar case. In a flash, the entire group of musicians surrounds her. She kicks up her heels like she's eighteen again and in the spotlight. One musician lays down his trumpet and starts dancing with her. The crowd whoops it up and cheers. The grin on Mom's face is the epitome of joy. Shi-chan's frantically taking pictures. When the song is over, the crowd gives Mom a standing ovation.

Mom has to get up at three in the morning of our final day. The taxi comes right on time. Before Mom has a chance to tell him about her father, the driver introduces himself as Patrick Murphy. When they get to the airport, he won't let Mom pay him. He says, "One Murphy cannot charge another Murphy this early in the morning." He also spends one euro to get a cart for her to put her luggage on.

I've often wondered if that was Saint Patrick's way of responding to Mom's talk.

19

TV and the Dean of Students

W E'D been back from Ireland for just a couple months when I got an unexpected e-mail from a Shinichi Asabe, the director of a television series on the local RKB television station. He was looking for someone to do a documentary on and found my homepage while searching on the internet. He was interested in doing a documentary on my life, books, and peace activities. I agreed to talk and invited him for dinner.

A week later, Asabe showed up at the door bearing a six-pack of beer and a bottle of red wine. A little on the plump side, pasty-faced, and weary-eyed, he had the look of a person who drank regularly and was overworked.

He launched into his idea for a documentary. We also talked a lot—or rather he explained a lot—about Makoto Oda and *Beheiren*, the group Oda organized in the 1960s to help resisters to the Vietnam War find refuge in other countries. My old *senpai* Ichikawa told me about Oda a few years before. Oda had written over a hundred books and was a hero to Asabe.

His idea was to do a documentary with an anti-Iraq War stance. He wanted to focus the documentary on three parts: (1)

my having written a textbook about my conscientious objector experiences during the Vietnam War and using it in Japanese university classes, (2) a dialogue with Oda in Kobe discussing our separate experiences in the 1960s and '70s, and (3) going to Vietnam and meeting some people who were affected by the Vietnam War.

Asabe seemed an intelligent, thoughtful man. Shi-chan was impressed that he treated her as an intellectual equal, responding to her questions and explaining his views to her. "He's not chauvinistic, like a lot of Japanese men," she said. He'd ordered my two novels and read the online version of *The Many Roads to Japan*. I agreed to do the project.

Asabe said he'd draw up a plan and submit it to his superiors. We'd need permission from FIU for the TV crew to film in my classes. RKB would pay for travel to Kobe to meet Oda and possibly for a three-day visit to Vietnam the following summer.

Throughout the night, we spoke mainly in Japanese. It was an intellectual challenge with the conversation going in several political, historical, and philosophical directions. I did my best to hang in there, but there were times when I was a bit lost as the level of these topics was beyond what I usually dealt with in daily life.

After Asabe left, Shi-chan said, "It's unbelievable the way they just come to you. You don't have to go looking for them." She also warned me, "If you meet with Oda and are filmed, you should insist on using your own language. That way, you'll have some control over how it comes across. This could be dangerous as well because you'll be exposing yourself, and if you try to do it in a second language, there are certain nuances that could be misinterpreted."

Two weeks later, Asabe sent me an e-mail saying RKB had

decided to broadcast the documentary program in its "Move 2004" series, which was a thirty-minute documentary series aired every Saturday night in Kyushu, as well as in Yamaguchi and Okinawa Prefectures.

Over the previous year, I'd exchanged some e-mails with Kazuyo Yamane, a peace activist who taught a peace education class at Kochi University, worked at the Grassroots House Peace Museum in Kochi, and edited its monthly newsletter. She used *The Many Roads to Japan* in her university class. The students responded positively to the textbook and its discussion questions. I received e-mails from many of them and answered their questions. Yamane invited me to come to Kochi and do a lecture and informal question-answer session with the students, members of the peace museum, and anyone else who wished to attend. She couldn't guarantee that I'd get paid, but I told her not to worry. I also asked for her permission to allow a small TV crew to come along to film the interaction.

Yamane replied the next day and was enthusiastic about the documentary project. She'd make the arrangements for securing a place for the lecture, some entertainment afterward, and a tour of the Grassroots House Peace Museum the following day. She offered to book motel rooms for me and the TV crew if we needed that, too.

I sent an e-mail to Asabe to get his thoughts on filming the lecture and other activities for use in the documentary. He agreed the activities in Kochi would be an important part of the program.

I flew to Kochi with Asabe and a crew of three on the day of the lecture. About forty people showed up, mostly Yamane's students and a few local citizens. A Kochi TV station also filmed it. A local reporter was there, too. I gave an hour-and-a-half lecture in both English and Japanese. There was a nice response from everyone.

After the lecture, we went to a place called Peace Cafe, where about thirty young musicians, activists, and students were hanging out. They'd prepared a dinner. A few people got up and spoke. A rock 'n' roller, a folk group, and a drummer gave separate performances of their own songs. The folk guitarist then strummed some bars of Bob Dylan's "Blowin' in the Wind," and I sang a bad rendition of the first stanza. We capped the evening off with me telling stories about my journey through Iran and Afghanistan. I sold twenty-six books, thirteen each of *The Many Roads to Japan* and *Looking for the Summer.*

The next day, Yamane gave us a tour of the Grassroots House Peace Museum and some peace monuments. After lunch, we attended an antiwar rally. Many people were out protesting the dispatch of Japanese Self-Defense Force members to Iraq. Everything was filmed. There was a story about the lecture in the morning paper, and apparently that night there was a bit about it on the Kochi TV news.

The weekend was a special experience. I was particularly impressed by Yamane's students. They were eager, enthusiastic, serious, and attentive. It was as if they were the ideal students I was thinking about when I originally wrote the book and the discussion and essay questions for the end of each chapter.

I was especially pleased when Yamane followed up with an e-mail after her final class, in which her students wrote their impressions of the textbook and lecture.

The meeting with Makoto Oda took place the last weekend of February. This time, Asabe, the crew, and I traveled to Kobe by bullet train. From Shin Kobe Station, we took a taxi to Oda's apartment in Ashiya. It was the only apartment on the top floor of an eight-floor apartment building that overlooked the beach and ocean. Oda greeted us at the door and led us into the living-dining area, which had a sofa, two large armchairs, and a coffee table. His wife's paintings hung on the wall. Behind the sofa were two more rooms. One was Oda's workplace. It was stacked with bookshelves, a desk, a chair, and a computer. It had the feel of a used bookstore. There was barely room to squeeze through.

The film crew filmed a short clip of Oda pretending to work in his workplace. Then they set us up in the living-dining area facing each other for the interview. On the coffee table was a large aerial photograph of a smoke-filled Osaka taken from an American bomber in June 1945. Oda pointed to a spot on the picture and said, "I was there, inside the smoke. When you look at this scene, in a sense it's beautiful. But if you were there, it's a kind of hell. People died there. I was there. This kind of situation I experienced three times. Two months after that photo, Japan surrendered."

Oda asked me about my experiences as a conscientious objector. He listened to my story patiently. When I finished, he lapsed into long historical asides and a few jokes. When he wanted to make a particular point, his large head jutted forward. He had plenty of thick, white hair. His eyebrows were thick and black. While listening, he leaned back and his eyes rolled back into his head. All I could see were the whites of the eyes. It was a little unsettling, as if he were about to have an epileptic seizure. When he was ready to speak, he leaned forward again, eyes boring into me, and off he'd go on another monologue.

The interview lasted about four hours. One topic that stuck in my mind was about how he'd helped set up a program for German conscientious objector soldiers to perform volunteer community service in Hiroshima and Hokkaido. By the end of the interview, I was mentally exhausted. Oda's strong Osaka dialect had stretched my powers of concentration. He invited me to stay for dinner. Asabe and the film crew returned to the hotel. Oda's wife and daughter spoke English well, so I could relax while eating and conversing with them.

The next day, there was a gathering of *Beheiren* members involved in an exchange program with Ho Chi Minh City in Vietnam. Oda had asked me to attend and speak in the middle for about a half hour. After he spoke for an hour, they showed a documentary on the 1968 My Lai massacre. The documentary was made in 1989 and had interviews with three of the soldiers who were involved and some surviving villagers. It brought back some old memories of Vietnam vet friends who were never able to adapt to regular life again. I had to speak right after the documentary and got choked up in the beginning but managed to muddle through. I had to ask Oda a couple times for help on Japanese vocabulary I didn't know.

At the end of the day, Oda saw us off at the train station. He had a large smile when he shook my hand and thanked me for speaking at the gathering.

On the train ride back to Fukuoka, Asabe told me the remaining parts to film for the documentary would include an interview with Shi-chan and me at home and a meeting at the school with two students who'd go with me to Vietnam in August, provided the first part of the documentary, scheduled to be broadcast in the middle of April, was well received.

Things got hectic at the university. A new president was to take over at the beginning of the school year in April. The previous president had to quit due to bad health. The new one was a member of the board of directors and had been the head of the

Digital Media Department, which was added the year before. He was making plans for who the heads of the various committees would be. He penciled me in as the head of the International Exchange Committee. The job carried a huge responsibility. I'd have to jack up my Japanese vocabulary level in order to deal with the sister-school agreements, the school bureaucracy, the presiding over meetings, and the preparation of a plan for a Study Abroad Information Center in the library. I'd always felt more comfortable as the "outside laborer" who groused about the system, but now I'd be in the system and have to deal with it.

At a faculty meeting in March, he introduced his first round of selections for all the key committee heads. For the two most important positions of dean of academic affairs and dean of students, he nominated an unpopular digital media professor and one of the Japanese English teachers. There was much resistance to the digital media professor. The new president had to come up with a new plan.

He called me into his office the next day and told me he now wanted me to become dean of students instead of head of the International Exchange Committee. My jaw about hit the floor.

Not only would I have to deal with the responsibilities of the Student Affairs Committee, but I'd also have to be a member of six other committees, three of whose meetings I'd have to preside over. I'd have to improve my Japanese to an even higher proficiency to deal with chairing and participating in these meetings, speaking in front of parents and high school teachers from around Kyushu, overseeing the student council, making decisions on school events like the school festival and the student council budget, handing out punishments for exam cheaters, and dozens of other things. I'd also be trying to read and understand all the Japanese school rules, by-laws, scholarship forms, and weekly office mail that was necessary for keeping up to date on what I'd have to know ahead of time for all the meetings and events. Just thinking about all this gave me a headache.

Part of the deal was a promotion to full professor. In order to do that, the president would have to move me from the International Communication Department, which already had too many professors, to the Digital Media Department, which had only one professor. His thinking was that because I'd published two books in electronic form, I could teach the electronic publishing class and eventually take on a seminar class in that specialty. I'd also get a nominal pay raise and a kind of "combat pay" benefit amounting to about four hundred dollars a month. Unfortunately, the number of classes I had to teach wouldn't be reduced. Time management would be key. I'd probably have to work a lot of twelve-hour days and weekends, too, in trying not to fall behind correcting home-work and preparing lesson plans. Weekdays would be filled with classes, preparation for meetings, the actual meetings, which sometimes lasted for hours, and the traditional Japa-nese phenomenon of *nemawashi*—laying the groundwork by meeting informally with people within a group to ask for help and support in carrying out plans and projects. Sometimes these meetings would happen one-on-one, sometimes outside of work, particularly at a bar.

I'd always thought that the people on the board of directors running our school were nuts, but now I knew they were. I felt like Groucho Marx when he said, "I wouldn't want to be a member of any group that would have me as a member." I also knew that I couldn't refuse the assignment if I expected to work at the school until retirement age and that I should take it as an honor that they'd entrust a wayward foreigner like myself with that much responsibility. As far as I knew, I might've been the first foreigner to hold such a university position in Kyushu, if not in all Japan. If there had been others, there probably hadn't been many. I wrote to Mom, saying they were going to get a lot of mileage out of this old plow horse.

To maintain my sanity, I planned to continue a daily regimen of meditation and stretching, as well as swimming two or three times a week. Unlike when I began my job as a full-time teacher at the women's junior college and Ichikawa took me under his wing and guided me through the first few months, there was no one to count on for help in preparing for the duties of a dean of students. I'd been a member of the Student Affairs Committee for several years, but I'd ignored the details of most of what the head people had to do. I'd been content to keep my head in the sand and perform just the menial chores given me.

Beginning on the day of the entrance ceremony and continuing through the first week of orientation activities for incoming freshmen, I'd be expected to attend the overnight leadership training program for the second-year students assisting and guiding the incoming freshmen. I'd have to speak to the new students moving into the campus dormitory, explain about student school life to the parents who attended the entrance ceremony, and give a one-hour lecture to the freshmen on the second day of orientation activities. In the days leading up to the entrance ceremony, I spent hours at a time reading through the "student life" sections of various PR booklets the library had, writing down and memorizing key vocabulary items, anticipating questions I'd probably get, making notes on how to answer them, and writing up and practicing my speeches.

I also had to choose who I wanted on the Student Affairs Committee and contact them to ask if they'd accept my invitation.

There was a mountain of e-mail and paperwork to go through. I got my hands on and read through all the minutes of the previous two years of committee meetings so I could anticipate what items would be on the agenda and what specialized vocabulary I'd need to know and use. The first meeting was scheduled for April 13. Fortunately, Hirashima, the administrative head of the Student Affairs Section, always had a preliminary meeting with the dean to go over what items were to be discussed or reported on, what reference material would be handed out to the committee members, and who would have to explain what. That preliminary meeting, called *uchi-awase* in Japanese, would be on April 9.

The weather cooperated on the day of the entrance ceremony. It was sunny and the cherry blossoms were in full bloom. After the ceremony, six of us teachers and administrators gave our speeches to the parents. At the end, Hirashima did a promotional bit informing the parents about the TV documentary and when it would be broadcast. The next day, I gave my orientation lecture to the freshmen about student life, then proctored an English placement test in the afternoon. The following day, the film crew came to school for their filming of me interacting with students on campus.

At my first committee meeting, I was nervous. I'd been attending committee meetings for over ten years, but I had no idea how to chair a meeting or how to summarize what had been discussed before proceeding to the next item on the agenda. Fortunately, Hirashima and his assistant Izutsu did most of the explaining. Later in the month at the faculty meeting, I was seated to the right of the president and had to report the key points of what was discussed and decided at the Student Affairs Committee meeting. I read from prepared notes and was lucky not to have to defend anything. In both cases, I breathed a sigh of relief in having survived my baptisms by fire.

Two days before the documentary aired, I appeared on a live segment of RKB's news broadcast. The interview lasted five minutes and they showed a preview of the documentary. Again, the ol' Irish pixie dust was swirling around me. I survived the experience without making any major mistakes. Asabe had told me beforehand what questions would be asked.

As all these things were happening, Mom's life, too, was going through big changes. She was now seventy-eight and her body was telling her it was time to slow down and stop being a working fool. She'd done some good financial planning over the last few years. She put her 401(k) plan into an annuity to supplement her Social Security income. She had two other small pensions she'd get for the rest of her life. I'd also sent her money to invest for my own retirement, but told her she could dip into that whenever she needed it. Secretly, I wanted her to have that money, but she was too stubborn and independent to accept it. "Only in an emergency," she said. She figured if she worked part-time a couple days a week, she'd have enough income for both her and Terri to get by.

Mom sent out query letters to some temp agencies and within a week had four replies asking her to call to make an appointment. Then without even looking for it, a part-time job offer for two days a week fell into her lap. A good friend's former boss needed another worker for a new office he was setting up. Mom could name her own days and hours and the pay would be better than the places she'd sent query letters to. The job entailed helping two other women organize the new office and setting up a filing system for a new real estate holding company. The president would be in the office only now and then. Apparently, he used to have all of the Burger King franchises for Washington, Oregon, and Idaho. After he sold them, he started the real estate holding company.

With this new work securely set to begin in July, Mom handed in her resignation letter to the law firm where she'd worked for a long time. Her final day at work was quite emotional. Her boss and others in the office cried when she left, showered her with farewell gifts, and gave her a small severance package, something the firm had never done for anyone before. She and Terri also found an apartment complex that had newer and better facilities than the place they were living in. They completed the move before she started working the new part-time job.

There were times during those first few months as the dean of students that I was so busy I could barely catch a breath, fart, or have time for any thoughts other than focusing on the task at hand. Just the amount of mail in Japanese I had to go through every day boggled my burned-out brain. There were always meetings to attend, a constant stream of students coming to my office, a vast amount of information to absorb, several decisions to make every day, and many people in and out of school to deal with. In the midst of it all, I still had to squeeze in time to prepare for classes. Sometimes this stuck in my craw, but in those moments, I'd create another thought to blot out the aggravation: "If these assholes only knew they were entrusting these kids to an old druggie anarchist, they'd probably shit their pants. Who'd believe that this old hippie *gaijin* who came to Japan on a one-way ticket with no qualifications, no knowledge of the culture or language, and only a hundred dollars in his pocket twenty-one years ago would end up in the upper tier of a Japanese private university hierarchy? How d'ya like them apples?"

I meditated a lot, sometimes twice a day.

Asabe's documentary got good responses from viewers. In the middle of May, however, he informed me that RKB had backed out of their original plan to finance a second part that would send me to Vietnam on a study tour with two FIU students. He thought that most Japanese media were trying to avoid fanning the flames of antiwar dissent and opposition to the dispatch of Self Defense Forces to Iraq. The RKB broadcasting station in Fukuoka was owned by and beholden to the Mainichi Broadcasting Company in Osaka and the Mainichi Shinbun in Tokyo, and it seemed the executives at the home offices didn't like the antiwar stance taken in the documentary. Asabe said he thought they were afraid of corporate sponsors withdrawing advertising money mainly because Oda Makoto, who'd been a thorn in the side of the government for years and was seen as a leftist provocateur, played such a large role in the film. One of the executives told Asabe the only way he could agree to filming a second half in Vietnam would be if I confessed on film that I'd been wrong in my decision to refuse to fight in the Vietnam War. Asabe refused even to try to persuade me. He knew I'd never agree to do that. He apologized for not being able to fulfill his promises. He regretted that RKB owned the rights to all the material he'd already created and he could not use any of it in an independent project. RKB had him by the balls because he was responsible for taking care of his family. He hoped to be able to quit in two years when his two boys would graduate and he could become a freelance journalist again.

I wrote back, telling him it was a shame, but I wasn't too surprised. Corporations always put profit before political risk. I said that if he was able to get a chance two years down the road to work on another worthwhile project, I'd do my best to help out. I added that many people had seen the first part of the documentary and given wonderful comments. I'd even received a few letters from people who saw the program and wanted to buy my books. One was a forty-year-old woman from Kumamoto who wrote, "Thank you for coming to teach and write in Japan." Another was from a professor at Nagasaki University who was teaching and researching about the psychological effects of war. If those people were any indication of how most viewers responded to the program, I'd say RKB's executives were missing out on a great opportunity by not following up with part two. They had no guts; they would get no glory.

As the semester rolled on, I slowly got into a rhythm and gained some confidence in carrying out my duties. The key to survival was time management and staying ahead of the game. That first year as dean of students sticks in my head as a jumble of events, activities, plans, decisions, disciplinary actions, speeches, panel discussions, constant references to the electronic dictionary that never left my side, embarrassing moments of miscommunication, exchanges of business cards, speed reading of Japanese e-mails and school-related paperwork, meetings, more meetings about the meetings, and even more meetings about meetings to come.

Among the things that stick out in memory most are the regional and national conferences with representatives from many schools exchanging ideas on how to deal with student problems. Hirashima attended the regional conference with me and did most of the speaking, but he had to leave early. At one point, someone asked for help in dealing with a sudden influx of foreign students. No one else had any solutions to offer, so I took the microphone and explained how in the previous year FIU had faced the same problem. We'd created a new committee specifically for dealing with foreign exchange students. Over the past year, the committee was able to help our exchange students by finding affordable housing; offering scholarship possibilities based on academic performance, participation in cross-cultural events, and volunteer activities; guidance in visa requirements and laws; guidance in filling out required paperwork for class enrollment; and sending out committee members to check on and issue warnings to those who'd missed more than two classes in a row. In a few cases, a student disappeared. The school contacted immigration and expelled the student. While I was talking, several of those in attendance took notes.

At the national convention, there were representatives from more than three hundred fifty universities and colleges. I was the lone foreigner and stuck out like a sore thumb. At the end of the first day as I was heading out the door of the convention hall, a dean of students from another university walked up to me and asked, "How did you get to be the dean?" I was too tired to get angry. I looked at him for a moment, sighed, and said, "I guess our board of directors was desperate. These are tough times, you know."

In addition to the conferences, I sometimes had to go on the road to visit high school counselors and try to convince them to send some students to FIU. More than once, the counselor told me directly that our school's ranking was too low for him to consider. In other cases, the counselor was also an English teacher, greeted me warmly, and spent a good portion of the meeting speaking in English. One even took me out for dinner and drinks that night.

The local and regional parent-teacher conferences were exhausting, particularly if the parents at the get-togethers afterwards for drinks and dinners tried to weasel their way into a special relationship that would favor their child getting recommendations and introductions for opportunities while job hunting in their senior years. In particular, there was one father from Kagoshima who'd been active in promoting FIU in his prefecture and somehow believed he should be rewarded for having convinced a few kids to come to our school over the past two years. He hounded me with e-mails and phone calls for a full month after his area's conference. I remembered the time teaching at the junior college when one of my homeroom students miscalculated how many credits she had and ended up one credit short of being able to graduate. She would lose the job she'd been promised by a good company. The school's policy was that she had to pay full tuition for one more semester, retake the class she needed, and pass it to graduate. Her parents came to my office and pleaded for me to do something. They even tried to pass some bribe money to me under the table. I refused to take the money. It was an awkward and embarrassing moment. I didn't want a repeat of that, so I finally wrote back to the Kagoshima father and told him to stop contacting me. His son was a good kid and would do fine without any interference.

There were a few cases of student cheating to deal with. During the final exams of the first semester, two students got caught using cheat sheets. We had a system with two teachers on duty during the exams who could respond immediately. Despite the warnings issued before all exams, there were always a few students who took a risk. If they got caught, the teacher who proctored the exam and made the accusation would be interviewed and notes taken. The students accused of cheating would also be interviewed. An emergency committee meeting would be held to discuss the case and decide if the students were guilty. If guilty, they would be called into the dean's office and informed of their punishment, which generally was forfeiture of all semester credits for a first-time offender and expulsion from school for a second-time offender.

This time, both students were first-time offenders and admitted their guilt. My first inclination was to take pity on them. I'd been an anti-authority wiseass for much of my youth. The irony was that now I was the authority figure and, in essence, the judge of their cases. While pronouncing their punishment, I flashed back to my court martial at the age of nineteen and the feelings I had when the Air Force judge pronounced my prison sentence. One of the students broke down in tears. I did what I could to encourage her and let her know it wasn't the end of the world.

Near the end of the year, Shi-chan and I began thinking about what to do when it came time to retire. We'd been lining landlords' pockets with rent money for a long time and didn't want to be doing that when our incomes disappeared. We worked out a budget and decided to look for a home. Shi-chan checked the internet. The first house that came up looked like it was waiting for us to buy it. It was a two-story house with three rooms and a toilet upstairs and a guest room, dining-living-kitchen area, and toilet and bath downstairs. It was in a quiet neighborhood with open space around it and a view of the nearby mountains. Shi-chan could use one of the upstairs rooms as a classroom.

It was a perfect location, about ten minutes by bicycle from FIU in one direction and a ten-minute walk from a train station in the other direction. Most of Shi-chan's students would come by train and walk from the station to her school, but there was also enough parking space for three cars for those who wanted to drive. With the housing market bottoming out, we could get a decent interest rate on a loan. The house was actually built about a year before, but two different families who wanted to buy it ran into financial difficulties and the place was just sitting there.

We had a contractor look at it from top to bottom and there were no problems. Everything had been done to spec. We couldn't have found a better place if we'd searched for a year. We decided to buy it. We'd lived frugally all our years together and had some cash to spare. I plopped down about two-thirds of my savings for the initial payment. We got a ten-year loan on the rest at a fixed interest rate of two point one percent. We still had enough money in the bank to tide us over in case of illness or disaster. My nomad days officially came to an end. This would be our retirement home.

Before we moved and while we were between semesters in March, Mom paid us an eighteen-day visit. Shi-chan's mother and Keiko also came to stay for a week. It was the first time for the two moms to meet. Despite the language barrier, they hugged and laughed and had no trouble communicating with each other. Keiko had a chance to practice her English. I had a lot of meetings and a few school functions to attend but could still spend time with them. Shi-chan was free from her university classes but still had weekend classes at home. Some of our friends stopped by occasionally to share some time and a meal. It was a good, relaxing time for everyone.

One of the highlights of the visit for Mom was participating in the purifying of our new house by a Shinto priest before we moved into it. We went to the new house at 9 a.m. on March 19 to meet the priest. He set up a portable altar in the downstairs tatami-mat room with the *tokonoma* alcove. He placed some vegetables, *sake*, rice, and fish on the altar; recited a prayer; and waved his *harai-gushi* wand to the left, to the right, and to the left again before the altar. He gave both moms, Shi-chan, Keiko, and me a *sakaki* tree branch to place on the altar. He showed us how to do the prayer ritual of bowing twice, clapping our hands twice, and bowing once again. He instructed us to say a brief prayer after doing this. He poured each of us a small *saka-zuki* cup of *sake* to drink.

After we finished our prayers and *sake*, the priest went to each of the rooms and shook the *harai-gushi* wand to drive out any bad spirits. Finally, the priest, Shi-chan, and I went outside to the entrance to spread some salt. Mom was wide-eyed throughout the entire ceremony. Several times, tears streamed down her cheeks.

We all got up early the next morning. Both moms and Keiko had some packing to do as they would head home the following day, which sadly was Shi-chan's birthday. Shi-chan and her mom were in the kitchen cooking and Mom, Keiko, and I were in the living room visiting when the house began to shake. The shaking went on for what seemed a long time. I jumped up from the sofa, ready to shove the living room table so Mom and Keiko could get under it. I shouted to Shi-chan to turn off the stove, but her mom had already done so. Just when it seemed the house would collapse on top of us, the shaking stopped. We thought of the 1995 Kobe earthquake. We felt fortunate the shaking hadn't continued any longer.

There was no damage in our immediate area, but when we turned on the TV news later in the day, we found out the earthquake was recorded at magnitude 7.0. One person had died, several hundred were injured, and there was a lot of structural damage in the downtown part of Fukuoka and nearby areas. Some of the main highways were closed and some train lines were shut down so officials could check for damage. The hardest hit area was Genkai Island, which was about twenty kilometers from Fukuoka and accessible only by ferry. About a hundred twenty older, traditional Japanese houses were destroyed and fifty-five others partially damaged. I took a bicycle ride that day to see if there was any damage to the house we'd just bought. Fortunately, there was none.

Later in the day, one of Shi-chan's friends came over. All of us went to a hot springs to calm our rattled nerves. When Mom got in the big tub with the other women, she leaned back and her breasts bobbed to the surface like two buoys. All broke into stitches over that sight. We rearranged the furniture that night just in case there were aftershocks that could knock things over. There were a couple small aftershocks. No one slept soundly. When we took our moms and Keiko to the airport to see them off, we joked about all the excitement they created whenever they took a trip. Mom promised that even though her next birthday would be her eightieth, she was intent on making at least one more trip to Japan.

20

The Dean's Second-Year Grind

THE new semester started before we had a chance to move in the new house. The shift to the reality of job demands began with three solid days of meetings with the student council and training for the students who'd help out with orientation. That was followed by a meeting with the part-time teachers and an orientation meeting with the dorm students and their parents. Next was the entrance ceremony and three days of orientation filled with speeches, meetings, English placement tests, and registration of classes.

The top English teacher who'd been the dean of academic affairs for the previous year quit after finding another job at a national university in Kagoshima, so now, in addition to being the dean of students, I was also the de facto head of the four English teachers and responsible for coming up with a plan for a four-year English course. We didn't have a true English department; there were just first- and second-year general education English classes. The board of directors thought a revision of the entire curriculum was needed to recruit more students.

Japan's eighteen-year-old population had dwindled so much that there were predictions that by 2007, there'd be more university seats available nationwide than there were students to fill them. Essentially, everyone could get into university, so competition was fierce. Many schools were falling by the wayside. FIU's student population was at the fifty-one percent capacity level. If we fell under fifty percent, we'd lose the financial aid we were getting from the Ministry of Education. Without that aid, the school would go bankrupt.

Paranoia swept the campus. There were rumors of a rich school coming in, buying the place, and setting up their own courses and curriculum. Even if that happened, it would be three or four years down the road. A lot of people would lose their jobs, but I was sure any new owners would keep the Digital Media Department and the English classes. Those seemed the key to any school's survival. I believed my own position was secure. As long as I continued to receive a salary, I'd work for anyone.

On the plus side, I'd managed to make it through the first yearly cycle as the dean of students without making a shambles of it. For the most part, I could now anticipate what was coming and plan for it on a daily basis rather than having to react to everything as it happened. I also had the challenge of a new class to teach: Introduction to Electronic Publishing. As part of the preparation for the class, I set up my own little publishing company through an online site. If things went well, I'd have the students publish their own books in PDF and paperback, or at least a newsletter or magazine in PDF and HTML. The coming year looked to be problematic, but that was true every year. When I saw the students' smiling faces, everything else fell into place. The cherry trees were blossoming. That always lifted the spirits.

We moved into our house on April 25. After the earthquake, there were a few strong aftershocks, but the house held up and suffered no damage. For the first month, Shi-chan and I were so busy that we were living out of boxes. Shi-chan did almost all the work in getting the house organized, putting knick-knacks here and there, and creating space where none seemed to exist. She arranged and rearranged her classroom several times until it was just the way she wanted it.

As we entered the rainy season of June and July, classes were going well, but the grind of twelve-hour weekdays and almost every weekend was wearing me out. Weekdays had me running from classrooms to meeting rooms to the mailroom, where numerous documents that demanded my attention were always piling up. Many hours were spent at the computer in my office reading and responding to office e-mails. Weekends were spent preparing lessons, checking homework papers, studying the minutes of committee meetings, and copying phrases and key *kanji* vocabulary to practice. I would try to convert the phrases and *kanji* from passive knowledge to active knowledge by using them in e-mails and work conversations as soon and as much as possible. Ten years before when I'd been a low-ranking lecturer with few responsibilities other than my own English classes and the minimal requirements of being on the library committee, I might've been ranting and raving, but now in my fifties with loads of responsibilities, I was simply too tired to blow up. That's how the system always got you: worked you to death so you couldn't rebel. I sometimes reminisced about being that nineteen-year-old hippie in the Air Force thumbing his nose and flipping the finger at the military establishment.

If nothing else, my Japanese had improved by leaps and bounds over the past year, particularly in the area of reading.

My American Culture and Society class was for non-English majors and had ninety-one students, some of whom were Chinese and Korean. That class and my electronic publishing class both had to be done in Japanese. Checking student papers and essays in Japanese was a challenge, but I was reading faster and comprehending more. That was one area of Japanese study I'd neglected previously, but the essays and papers and all the documents and e-mails related to my job became my textbooks. Whenever I felt overwhelmed, I tried to remember that, in essence, FIU was paying me to learn Japanese.

Studying the language was one thing; mastering it was something else entirely. Saint Francis Xavier, the sixteenth-century Jesuit missionary, once said that the Japanese language was created by the devil to prevent the spread of Christianity in Japan. In particular, comprehension and production of long sentences had always been problematic for me. The most difficult thing was relative clauses. In English, relative clauses usually came after the head noun they modified. In Japanese, these clauses came before the head noun. To a certain degree, you had to be able to think backwards. If you tried to think in English and translate into Japanese, it took too much time and you got lost in the middle. An example of what I'm talking about:

English: The man who is wearing glasses, reading a newspaper, eating an apple, and standing next to the chair is my brother.

Japanese: Glasses wearing, newspaper reading, apple eating, chair next to standing man my brother is.

I was still prone to making occasional pronunciation mistakes that produced looks of surprise, wonder, embarrassment, or even anger among my Japanese coworkers. I had to be careful when speaking Japanese because the length of the vowels was shorter than for English vowels. If my concentration lapsed and my brain veered toward its English side, I'd pronounce some vowels as if they were English vowels and end up saying things like "How is your ugly prisoner?" when I meant "How is your esteemed husband?" or "I lust for your body" when I meant "That's an interesting wind chime. May I see it?" Fortunately, most of the time, my listeners patiently put up with these lapses and we'd have a good laugh about it.

The result of all the hours upon hours I spent just trying to perform my job—which, other than teaching in the English classroom, had to be done in Japanese—was that I was actually beginning to think in Japanese. I was producing longer and more detailed sentences, as well as understanding more without having to guess as much. This was enough to give me the confidence to keep going and not give up. Of course, there was a certain amount of pride that kept me going, too. I wanted to prove to the naysayers that a geeky foreigner could do the job just as well if not better than the traditional head-stuck-in-the-mud, middle-aged-and-older Japanese farts who usually got promoted to top positions by not rocking the boat or taking any risks.

I was not so naive as not to be aware that Japanese universities were turning into desperate competitors who'd do anything and expend incredible amounts of energy trying to lure a rapidly dwindling young population into their schools. As a foreign dean of students, I was a major chess piece to be manipulated and used for promotion. Although the board of directors hadn't reduced my teaching load, they were paying me extra for the privilege of my position. The money was nice, but I knew I couldn't maintain the same working pace for much longer. I looked forward to a short summer vacation in August, to just lying around and enjoying our new house.

Before that could happen, however, there were still a few incidents to deal with. On the lighter side was a case where two students in the final hour of the final day of the end-of-semester testing period got caught cheating. Just when all the committee members thought they were free to go on summer break, emergency meetings had to be called, all the evidence presented and discussed, and a verdict given. As before, the students pleaded guilty and lost all semester credits.

On the heavier side was a case of student violence that involved drinking. One freshman named Oda was out drinking with some friends when he got a message on his cell phone from another freshman named Kumatani in his homeroom class inviting him to come have a good time. A few minutes later, Oda got another call from Kumatani telling him if he didn't show up, he'd get his ass kicked.

Oda left the party he was at, met Kumatani at a nearby parking lot, got in Kumatani's car, and went to Kumatani's apartment. Another freshman was in the passenger seat. At Kumatani's apartment, the three had a drink. Kumatani pulled out his cell phone, showed a list of phone numbers from an online dating site, and said, "I'm gonna phone some girls. Tell me which one you like."

Oda picked out one girl. Kumatani called the girl and said, "We'd like you to meet up with three of us."

Oda got frightened, told Kumatani he had to go back to the party with his friends, and left. A few minutes later, he got another call from Kumatani, who said, "If you don't get your ass back here, I'm gonna mess you and your friends up bad!"

Oda went back to Kumatani's apartment but first sent a message to one of his friends that he was in serious trouble. That friend contacted the police. When Oda got back to Kumatani's place, Kumatani said, "Why the fuck did you leave after I went to the trouble of calling that girl? Get your ass outside!"

They went outside. Kumatani had a baseball bat and hit Oda with it five or six times, twice on the head. A neighbor man heard the racket and came running to the scene. Kumatani told Oda to apologize. Oda threw himself on the ground and begged forgiveness. Kumatani asked the neighbor not to call the police. He turned to Oda and said, "You can go."

Oda ran back to his friend's place, where the police were talking to everyone who was at the party. The police questioned Oda, took some notes, and called an ambulance, which took Oda to a hospital. He was kept overnight for observation. The next day, Oda and his father spent nearly all day with the police and filed a report. Oda waited almost a week before reporting the incident to the school.

I called an emergency meeting for the Student Affairs Committee to discuss the issue. We decided that first Izutsu and I would conduct separate interviews with Oda and Kumatani before making any decisions on how to proceed. During the interview, Kumatani admitted he'd hit Oda with the bat, realized he could've killed him, and said he had no excuses. Another committee meeting was held. We decided that since Kumatani would be punished in some way through the legal system, we should wait to see what happened and decide in September whether or not to expel him.

The last incident was the most painful. A senior who'd been an excellent student, had taken classes from both Shi-chan and me, and wanted to be a teacher was killed in a car accident on his way to a job interview in Fukuoka. Just four days before the accident, he'd come to our place for a barbecue dinner, and we'd spent a few relaxing hours talking about his future and our own experiences when we were his age. His death hit everyone hard. I couldn't attend the funeral because other duties at school prevented me, but many teachers and students went. Shi-chan went and said the mother was really appreciative. The grandmother couldn't stop crying for two days.

The *Obon* holiday break in mid-August was a welcome relief. I was thoroughly exhausted. Shi-chan and I just hung out for a few days in the main living-dining area with the air conditioner running. We summoned up enough energy for two barbecue dinners, then collapsed again. I went up to my office one day to take advantage of the empty campus and do some cleaning. When finished, I sat at my desk for a while, gazing out at the Dazaifu mountains and reflecting on everything that had occurred during my time as the dean. I had only a few more months before my two-year term was over. I hoped it would be incident-free, but I knew that was wishful thinking.

During the break, we found out that FIU had lost its support money from Japan's Ministry of Education for the next two years. Things didn't look good for recruiting a large number of students in the coming year. Our annual August Open Campus events where high school students could tour the campus, meet with faculty and current students, and attend sample lessons saw fewer numbers than in previous years. The board of directors had no plan other than reducing the number of teachers to cut costs. From a peak of forty-five full-time teachers at the beginning in 1998, FIU now had only thirty. Most of them were over fifty and heavily saddled with committee and administrative responsibilities. The administrative staff was also understaffed and overworked, many like Hirashima forced to take on multiple positions in trying to work for both the university and the women's junior college. There was no system to integrate the two schools. Only a few graduating junior college students had continued on to the university. The overall atmosphere was despondent.

The revision of the entire curriculum was now crucial for the school's survival. We English teachers doubled our efforts to hammer out a proposal for a concentrated and comprehensive four-year English program that would result in higher levels of proficiency and more jobs for graduating students. Heading up our effort and setting the agenda for what items to discuss, what paperwork to prepare for our meetings, what strategies to use to convince the entire faculty of the validity of our proposal, and how to justify the allocation of limited resources other courses also wanted turned out to be one of the most difficult jobs I took on at the university. It required not only all my teaching and learning experiences, but also a detailed knowledge of the entire school's curriculum, where credits came from, how they were distributed, and what each teacher and administrator had to do. My experiences as the coordinator for the Matsushita language program back in the late 1980s came in handy.

At the end of August, I got a letter from Dead End Street, returning all *Toraware* rights to me and discontinuing its publication. Jacobyte Books had also returned the rights of *Looking for the Sumer* two years before when they culled from their catalogue the books that hadn't sold well. I formatted both books so I could keep them alive through my little online publishing outfit.

Shi-chan was stricken with a persistent bladder infection that kept her down for almost a month. She went to the doctor, got some antibiotics, and was back on her feet by the time second semester classes began. Some of the students at her own school had to quit for one reason or another. The number of her students fell to eleven from a peak of twenty-three. She was trying to design and put up a new homepage for advertising purposes. At least her three part-time university classes were reliable. She could count on the income from those, but not from her own school.

Although autumn semester classes didn't start until September 26, I had a full-on schedule for the entire month. There were many meetings with the student council, which was preparing for the annual school festival. The Fukuoka parent-teacher conference had about a hundred parents coming. The school president, the heads of the two departments, the head of the jobs committee, the dean of academic affairs, and the dean of students all had to speak. There was a question and answer period afterward, but most of the parents were concerned about job prospects for their kids, so I didn't have to answer any questions.

The regional parent-teacher conferences were a different matter. Only administrative staff, the two deans, and one or two teachers from the academic affairs committee had to attend. Fewer parents went to these conferences, but they always had serious questions. I was responsible for chairing the meetings in the Kagoshima and Kumamoto areas. The meetings went well, but I was worn out from having to concentrate so much in difficult Japanese. The professor I went with told me afterward that he was amazed at how much my Japanese had improved in the last two years. That gave me the motivation to keep going.

At the September faculty meeting, it was officially announced that we'd have to cut our student capacity number from three hundred to two hundred in a move to try to regain support money from the Ministry of Education. That meant the number of classes available for part-time teachers would also be reduced. In the past, the English conversation classes had seven levels decided by a yearly proficiency exam and the reading, writing, and listening classes had five levels. At another English teachers meeting, we had to decide how many levels and classes to cut. That plan would be brought up at a department meeting. The Digital Media Department asked me to take on an electronic publishing seminar class. The department was going into its fourth year and, as a professor, I was required to have a seminar class that included graduation papers and projects for students to complete. I had to give up one of my English classes.

It was also announced that we'd be conducting ninety-minute classes and have the same class periods as the junior college. That would make it easier for teachers from both schools to teach classes at the other school. The boat continued to sink. More part-timers were let go.

The week after the regional parent-teacher conferences, I was sent to Fukushima to represent FIU at the national conference for people responsible for student affairs. Around four hundred people attended the three-day event. The level of Japanese used at the morning lectures and afternoon buzz sessions combined with the concentration required to participate actively left me panting.

On the last weekend of October, I had to be at the school festival until late for each of the three days it ran. That duty was somewhat refreshing after the intensity of everything else the last two months. There were a lot of dancing and singing events scheduled on the outside stage. The student council kids put a lot of planning and work into the event and a lot of people attended. I gave an opening greeting from the main stage, then later was one of the judges in the foreign students' Japanese speech contest. Our baseball team, despite having no ground to practice on and only nine members, won their league and advanced to the All Western Japan tournament in Hiroshima in the middle of November. Despite the numbers dwindling and all the negative news, our students were doing well in different areas.

At the beginning of December, there was an extortion case involving two of our freshmen students. The amount of money was not exorbitant, but the fact that one kid took advantage of a weaker student for personal gain was something that had to be dealt with. Izutsu and I had a hearing with each of the two involved that lasted from 3 p.m. to 7:30 p.m. Again, it left me exhausted from the strain of having to pay so much attention to detail and trying to read between the lines of what was truth and what was a lie. The Student Affairs Committee met on November 13. We decided to boot the perpetrator out of school.

The semester classes and final tests finished up at the beginning of February. I had just a few more meetings to attend before my two-year dean stint was finally over. Then came the worst shock of all. Around 6 a.m. one morning, Hirashima collapsed at the school, was rushed by ambulance to the hospital, and died. The doctors said it was from a heart attack, but in my mind it was from overwork. He was the same age as I. He'd been working long, long hours for the last four years. His family certainly had the right to sue if they chose to do so.

I'd known him for nearly eighteen years. He'd been a great guy from the start, always giving of himself to other people, to the students in particular. He was the head of both the academic affairs section and the job-hunting section for both the university and the junior college. He had his own band. He was the lead singer with a fantastic voice and sang many Beatles songs. I'd worked with him for several years on the student affairs committee at the junior college, and for my first year as the dean, he was the head of the university student affairs section and my guide and conscience.

I felt as if the board of directors had killed him. During all his years at the school, the students loved him more than any other teacher or staff member. He was the main man. Now he was gone. I thought this might be the beginning of the end of FIU.

The wake was held on a Saturday and the funeral on the next day. I attended both. Of all the funerals I'd seen in my life, none came close to the emotional impact of this one. Hundreds of people came from near and far to say goodbye. About three hundred mourners packed into the temple. When it was all over and we departed the building, we saw a line of hundreds who'd stood outside in the cold just to hear the services over a loudspeaker and go inside at the end to see Hirashima's face one final time. People wept and shook uncontrollably.

There was a teachers' memorial for Hirashima a week later. His family attended. I spoke as the teachers' representative. I made it only partially through the speech before choking on my words.

21

Post Dean Life at FIU

I HAD about a month remaining in my term as the dean of students. There was still a lot of work to do. Much of that involved my position as the de facto head of the English teachers. The first worry was that only seventy-five freshmen students would be enrolling. It was the lowest total in our short history. When word of that got around, high school counselors and parents wouldn't recommend their kids to go to a dying school. We had an urgent responsibility to show that we were doing something to save the school, namely, offering a unique program that no other schools had and could help the students get jobs when they graduated.

At a special International Communication Department meeting in early March, I handed out some prepared paperwork to the department teachers and outlined the English teachers' English course proposal. Although I officially belonged to a different department, it was no problem to take charge of this project and effectively be working for both departments because I believed the plan for a new curriculum was the most important priority our school had. The meeting lasted three hours, but the proposal got everyone's agreement, provided we made a few administrative adjustments.

My final responsibilities as the dean of students were meeting with the student counsel and orientation committee students to prepare for the new semester's orientation week and giving some speeches during that week.

All my classes started out fine, but I was disappointed to catch five students in the American Culture and Society class cheating on papers they handed in. They'd copied word for word from the internet. Despite my warnings at the beginning of the semester, many students just didn't understand that although it was easy for them to copy and paste, it was also easy for a teacher to find the exact place they copied from. If I suspected the writing style and the *kanji* being used was way too high a level for any student, all I had to do is take a sample expression or sentence, feed it into a Yahoo or Google search engine, and the page they copied from would come right up. This rash of plagiarism prompted me to do some research on how other schools and teachers dealt with it. I thought my own research paper might be worth doing.

Throughout July and August, Mom and I exchanged several messages. We made plans for her to visit in October, which got her reminiscing about her first time to Japan and how she'd always had a bit of the wanderlust in her. She said she'd always felt there was something "out there" that she needed to find out about. She was still searching. She closed her reminiscence by expressing how life had been good to her and how she'd loved watching me grow up as she saw so much of herself in me at times—the rebel part of my personality.

Mom arrived safely in the middle of October. We had great weather almost the entirety of her two-week stay. We were all tired from work and life, so we mostly spent quiet time together reminiscing, sharing stories and laughs, cooking simple meals, and watching some videos. Mom had some bad swelling in her ankles. Shi-chan took her to a clinic. The doctor determined Mom had a case of economy class syndrome and prescribed a diuretic.

Mom attended and participated in some of Shi-chan's classes, both at home and at FIU. I also asked her to be a special guest lecturer for one of my classes.

To prepare for Mom's lecture, I asked the students two weeks earlier to prepare a list of questions they'd like Mom to answer. These questions included:

- What surprising things have happened to you in Japan?
- Based on your own life experiences, what advice can you give us for our futures?
- What stereotype images did you have of Japan before you came here for the first time?
- What are your thoughts about Mr. Norris living and working in Japan?
- What are your impressions of Japanese students?
- Please talk about food in the U.S. and changes you have noticed in Japan in the last 20 years.
- Please tell us about your son's childhood.
- What do Americans think about the war in Iraq?

Mom looked over the questions and prepared a rough draft, which I then checked and made a list of vocabulary and phrases that I thought the students would have trouble understanding. I translated each of the items on the list and made copies to hand out. Students could use the copies to make their own notes while listening. I also asked one of the digital media teachers and two students to film the lecture and make a DVD.

The students listened attentively and took notes. After about an hour, we had a question and answer period based on what the students had heard and understood. Everyone had a wonderful time. I was proud of Mom. Later, she said it was an incredible, thought-provoking experience for her. She looked forward to seeing the DVD so she could see what mistakes she'd made and how she could improve for the next chance.

Mom's ankles were still swollen after she returned to Portland. She went to her doctor to have them checked again. He told her he wasn't too concerned as many people experienced economy class syndrome, but he was surprised at how long Mom's case lasted. Mom had also been experiencing shortness of breath for a few months, so the doctor took a chest X-ray and did some blood work.

As usual, Mom didn't like to dwell on her own medical issues. She summarized her situation by saying she was feeling better and "you can't keep this ole Irish lady down for long." The more important thing for Mom was telling us about Terri's appointment with her neurologist and going to the MS clinic to be tested. She went to the clinic about every six months. She was always put through a lot of tests for flexibility, walking straight, and cognizant understanding. This time, she tested higher on all of the tests than she had for the past eight years. Her neurologist told her he was ninety-nine percent sure her MS was now in remission. It seemed like a miracle after nearly ten years of coping with intense pain, exhaustion, and taking huge amounts of medication. Mom was sure that Terri's positive attitude had a lot to do with this good news. The neurologist told her the same thing. She didn't have to go back to see him for one year unless something unexpected like severe muscle spasms happened.

The year ended on a positive note. There was a faculty meeting on Christmas Day. The school president announced that for the first time in three years we'd be able to get enough students to qualify for support money from the Ministry of Education. The coming year would be tough as the board of directors demanded we reduce the number of part-time teachers by thirty percent and all full-timers take on additional classes to cover the loss of manpower. Instead of grumbling about the extra work, I remembered all my years of wandering and working minimum-wage labor jobs.

During the winter vacation from December 26 to January 4, I had to concentrate on keeping ahead of the game with my first senior seminar class. I'd had them produce a book of student essays and stories in different formats (print, HTML, PDF, Word, and a short, recorded audio book). The final part of the seminar class was the thesis paper. I had ten students—five Japanese and five Chinese. I had them write a ten-page paper with three chapters: (1) a summary of the history of publishing, (2) a summary of their experience of the previous two years (they'd also taken my Introduction to Electronic Publishing class), and (3) a prediction of how publishing would change in the future. The papers were written in Japanese and the rough drafts had to be handed in before the winter vacation started. There were two more classes in January and I'd have to spend time with each student explaining what needed to be rewritten and how it should be done. Again, time management was crucial. I also had to do a two-page English translation for the narrative part of a DVD on the history of Dazaifu City that another seminar class was producing. They were doing the DVD in Japanese, Korean,

Chinese, and English. The three-minute video files would be shown on Dazaifu City's homepage and could turn out to be good advertising for the school.

During the spring break, I started a new academic paper. I hadn't written anything in about three years, so I was a bit rusty, but the issue of plagiarism had been on my mind for a few years. I'd done some research, but most of what I found on academic plagiarism that was available in English dealt with English writing done by native and non-native speakers. Very little had been done by native English speakers who were teaching in a foreign language. I decided to document my own case as an American professor teaching at a Japanese university. I finished the rough draft of the paper and, thinking it deserved an international readership, submitted it to the British journal *East Asian Learner*. They wrote back, saying their editors had voted to publish it, provided I made some recommended changes and additions.

Throughout the spring break, a stronger confrontational atmosphere between management and teachers, as well as between departments, developed. The board of directors cracked down on too many teachers not coming to school in between semesters. We now had to punch in by 9:30 a.m. every day and if we didn't, we'd lose that day's salary. The faculty meetings were argumentative, and some International Communication Department teachers were calling to terminate the Digital Media Department.

Among the causes of the sour mood was the school president, who'd started the previous year. In terms of incompetency, everyone thought he put the previous three presidents to shame. He was another in a long line of former Kyushu University agricultural department professors who took advantage of an old boy network that went back to the original head of the board of directors. Through the years, many of the board at our school were scooped up after retirement from Kyushu University and turned into board members or school presidents. All the heads of the board of directors for the past forty years had been from that network. Most were totally removed from the realities of running the school. They had no vision for the school's future. Neither the junior college nor the university had ever had anything resembling an agricultural department.

Nearly all the teachers and administrative staff members thought this president was just a lame errand boy for the board of directors. As the president, he was supposed to represent the teachers at the board meetings but hadn't done a thing other than draw a good salary for sitting on his ass and trying to reshuffle the heads of committees so there'd be no progressive voices or opponents to deal with. The school was stuck in an administrative quagmire.

With a new school year starting soon, we still had no dean of academic affairs or chair of the International Communication Department. The teacher who'd been tabbed to be the dean of academic affairs got his name and reputation dragged around at a recent faculty meeting, so he refused to accept the president's nomination. The teacher who'd been named to take over the International Communication Department chair's position decided he couldn't handle the responsibility. At a gathering with the part-time teachers, the president handled the dean of academic affairs' responsibilities for explaining the school's academic policies and rules. There was a rumor that he'd take on that job permanently in addition to being the president. Cynical teachers remarked that that was one way to get rid of a dissenting vote in the management committee, which was comprised of the president, the dean of students, the dean of academic affairs, and the two department heads. A sixth emergency faculty meeting in March was called to resolve the issue but was mysteriously cancelled for no reason. None of the committees could move until all positions had been approved. This was especially frustrating because there were many administrative and educational projects that had to be completed before the school year started.

In the midst of this drama, the president asked me to take over the International Exchange Committee. The previous head of that committee was a digital media teacher who got stressed out easily and had too quick of a temper to handle the pressures and complicated human relationships involved in the job. I shrugged my shoulders and agreed to take on the two-year job. My feeling was that there was no escaping responsibility in the Japanese educational racket once you hit your fifties and got promoted to professor. It sometimes seemed more a curse than a blessing.

The one advantage was that I could appoint myself as the chaperone for the month-long August homestay-study program at the University of Victoria in Victoria, British Columbia. We'd been sending some students to that program for a few years. Victoria was close enough to Portland that I could probably sneak away for a weekend visit with Mom and Terri. I'd still have my homework to do to get caught up on all the legal conditions to the exchange agreements we had with other schools, mainly in China and South Korea, as well as another level of specialized vocabulary to learn and use.

On the positive side, we managed to get a hundred and eighty-seven new students, more than we'd gotten in the previous two years combined. Fifty-five were third-year Chinese transfer students from two universities in Dalian. Another nineteen were second- and third-year transfer students from a local university that closed down a year before. That was a one-time lucky draw that wouldn't be repeated the next year, but it still was a big help in getting much-needed support money from the Ministry of Education. The rest were first-year Japanese students. A large number of them were from the autumn entrance exams for high school kids with good grades. The English teachers hoped they would be a serious group as we needed them for the new four-year English course. Also, all the foreign teachers got five-year contracts for the first time. Personally, I wasn't sure whether to celebrate after getting mostly one-year contracts for fifteen years or to feel as if it was a kind of prison sentence. I was feeling drained. In my mind, it seemed prisoners worked fewer hours a week than I did. I tried to look forward to the new semester as at least then I'd have to deal mainly with just the students.

As the semester wore on, I ignored the school politics and concentrated on my classes. I was pleased with how they were proceeding. To my mind, the new students comprised a new generation that was more serious and studious than previous generations I'd taught. They just needed to be guided in how to study. They wanted to, but didn't know how. Part of that problem was the education system in Japan, which to me still aimed at throwing a lot of information at students and expecting them to memorize it. There was not much guidance for critical thinking and helping students form their own opinions. When a teacher like me came in the classroom, introduced things the students had never seen or considered before, then asked them, "So, what do you think?" they weren't sure how to react because few teachers had asked them for their own opinions before. It was important to show patience and encourage them to trust their own ideas. It usually took some time for them to realize that sometimes there were no set rules or answers and that it was OK to take a risk and think for themselves. My experience had always been that once they realized they had the freedom to explore and discover their individual thoughts, they'd invariably become more active by the end of the semester.

I didn't run into any serious problems as the head of the International Exchange Committee. The committee members responsible for most of the work dealing with agreements between FIU and some Korean and Chinese universities were reliable and hardworking teachers, so I didn't have to worry much about that end of things. My immediate concern was the possibility of not being able to recruit any students for the summer homestay-study program in Canada.

The yen-Canadian dollar exchange rate was increasingly tough on the yen. The Canadian price of the program hadn't changed, but the amount of yen students had to pay had gone up about thirty percent in the last two years. At the end of May, there was only one student whose parents were willing to put up the money. We'd know for sure around the middle of June if any more could go. It'd be hard to rationalize the need for a chaperone for only a couple of students. I started searching online for a cheaper program on the West Coast. I found two possible places in Portland, Oregon. Of course, I had ulterior motives for choosing Portland. If I could arrange an exchange program or even just an agreement to send some students to Portland, I could possibly get the school to pay for me to visit Mom and Terri once a year. I submitted a proposal that outlined the importance of continuing an overseas English homestay-study program as a key part of the new curriculum—particularly as a recruiting tool for the English course. The Canadian program was now too expensive. We needed to find a reputable yet affordable program to replace it. I could kill two birds with one stone by chaperoning even one student to Canada, wait a week until the student settled into a rhythm and became more independent, fly to Portland, spend a few days checking facilities and negotiating with school administrators about their programs, and return to Japan with a report on each school and a recommendation. The board of directors approved the proposal and freed up some money for my plane ticket and a per diem for room and board for two weeks.

We ended up with two students. The first week in Victoria went smoothly, so I flew to Portland, leaving the students with Mom's phone number in case of any trouble. I spent a busy nine days visiting Portland Community College and Everest College, a two-year business school with an English as a second language program that would soon go independent under the name of Portland English Language Academy. Terri felt good enough to drive me around. I took extensive notes, collected a lot of material to take back to Japan, and worked on a rough draft of my report. Mom was tired much of the time during my visit and complained of being constantly short of breath. She planned to have a complete checkup after I left.

After returning to Japan, I wrote up the report of my discussions with the two schools in Portland and my recommendation for setting up an agreement with PELA. Their English Plus Volunteer program gave eleven hours of classroom instruction a week, three hours of language lab, four hours of volunteer experience, and four hours of additional activities. Volunteer work included working in an office, working at free markets, doing cultural exchanges with local groups, helping out at elementary and international schools, and many other activities. Additional weekly activities included standardized proficiency test instruction, observing Everest College classes, conversation classes, and more volunteer work.

The key points of my recommendation outlined the cheaper cost of the program compared to other schools in English-speaking countries we had either dealt with in the past or were currently dealing with; the advantage of having homestay and volunteer services in addition to the classroom experience; and the number of starting dates for a four-week course throughout the year, which would allow our students to participate without having to miss any classes or tests in Japan.

After I completed the rough draft for the proposal, I asked one of the committee members to correct my Japanese. The proposal first passed through our International Exchange Committee, then through the faculty meeting, and finally through a meeting of the board of directors. After a series of negotiations by e-mail with the director of PELA, the final agreement was signed by both sides. From that point on, it was a matter of creating a flow chart for recruiting, orientation, and preparation; advertising the program in school publications and on its website; and getting the ball rolling early in the school year with an explanatory meeting outlining the program.

22

Heart Problems, Interferon 2.0

MOM'S shortness of breath wouldn't disappear. For the
next few months, she had a plethora of tests with hospitals, physicians, cardiologists, clinicians, and heart specialists
without receiving any definitive diagnosis or solution. At first,
one doctor said there was no blockage of any kind in her arteries and the lungs were working pretty well. He thought she
had a leaky heart valve, but it wasn't serious. Next, she had a
pulmonary cardiac exercise stress test. Mom's comment was
"that's quite a mouthful, isn't it?" For that, she had to get a refer-
ral from her primary physician and an OK from her insurance
company. Then the pulmonary department at the hospital had
to coordinate a time with the heart doctor. There were too many
bureaucratic hoops to jump through and it was hard for Mom
not to get frustrated and impatient.

Around the middle of December, Mom wrote that her doctor
thought she had a diastolic dysfunction of the heart with an
enlargement of the atria. This meant that her heart had slowed
down and was pumping blood at a good rate to the lungs from
one side of the heart but not at a good rate on the side of the

heart that pumped blood to the body. The doctor recommended a new medication to slow the heart down enough so that both sides would arrive at the correct pumping speed. Mom's comment: "Sound complicated? You should've seen the expression on my face."

About the same time, my own doctor recommended I start another round of Interferon treatment. There was a new generation that was being used with another drug called Ribavirin. The combination therapy was getting better results than earlier treatments had. My viral load was at its lowest in years. The doctor thought I should do this once more before I hit sixty and the immune system started to wear down. The idea was to suppress the virus and decrease the odds of cancer cells developing in the liver in later years. Of course, it would be great if we killed off the virus, too. I was undecided, but his reasoning was sound.

One night in late November, Dad had pain in his left arm. His wife took him to the emergency room at Saint Joseph Hospital in Eureka, where they hooked him up to machines and tubes and kept him overnight for more tests. A blood test taken in the middle of the night showed he'd had a heart attack, but it was not as serious as it might've been. Dad's doctor said that if Dad had to have a heart attack, he picked a good one because it affected only two tiny blood vessels and he could get along well without them. He was kept in the hospital for observation for two days, then allowed to go home.

Of all of us, Terri had the most encouraging news. She went to her annual multiple sclerosis appointment with her neurologist and specialists from Oregon Health and Science University and passed with flying colors. Her neurologist told her she was still in remission. She'd had such a rough time for years that it seemed miraculous. Mom thought Terri's strength of will and positive attitude had as much as anything to do with the improvement. Terri never lost hope she'd get better. She still had issues to cope with and down days now and then, but overall was handling life well.

Things were quiet for the next two months, but a late February e-mail from Terri gave us another shock. Mom's final diagnosis was that her heart's mitral valve was leaking severely. She needed open-heart surgery.

For the next few weeks, Terri kept Shi-chan and me informed of the results of the surgery and progress of Mom's recovery. During the surgery, two of Mom's ribs were cracked. It was a rough time for everyone, especially the first two days after the surgery when it was touch and go as to whether Mom would live, but Terri's knowledge and dedication, together with Mom's attitude, helped tremendously. When Mom was finally home and able to use the computer for short periods of time, she sent us e-mail notes of her version of the ordeal. From the beginning of April to near the end of May, these notes helped us visualize how she was doing physically and mentally. Her strength and resilience were inspiring. I could only imagine how painful it was. We kept her supplied with tons of pixie dust and prayers. Two of the notes stood out above the others.

> May 3rd: I'm really very encouraged with the rate my recovery is proceeding as each day is just a bit better than the day before. I really feel very fortunate and it's probably a good thing I had no idea what this would involve. With patience and determination, I know I'm going to be in better condition by mid-summer than I have been for a couple of years at least. I'm finding that life is to be "lived" and not just tolerated. Of

course, you kids make all of these efforts more than worthwhile. Grandma Frederick used to say, "If the Good Lord is willing and the creek don't rise, it will happen!"

May 13th: I still get pretty tired by the end of the day, but actually I'm doing great. Still pretty sore, but it takes cracked ribs about as long to heal completely as it does a broken bone. Am driving now and that feels good. Not quite ready to go back to work yet, but I have to remember it hasn't been eight weeks yet since the surgery. Had blood drawn again yesterday morning and the cardiologist called yesterday afternoon to say I can quit taking the Coumadin after this week, so no more doctor appointments or lab tests for a whole month! And think I mentioned I don't have to see the heart doctor for a year. Hooray!

Only two months after major heart surgery and Mom was driving again? At the age of eighty-two? We were gobsmacked! I knew for certain that Mom was well on the comeback trail when she started asking about our work and health instead of describing her own recovery progress. Her voice was stronger each time we visited by video on Skype. We were especially proud of Terri for being such a stalwart. We were proud of everything she'd done during these trying days, how she'd stayed on top of the nurses looking after Mom at the hospital, how she'd taken charge at her own expense and somehow stayed strong throughout.

We were happy to report back to Mom and Terri that Shi-chan's biannual checkup showed her stomach looked fine, all her numbers were in the normal range, and she was now a ten-year cancer survivor.

My turn for a hospital stay was next, but I still had a lot to do before I started round two of my Interferon battles. In February 2008, I was asked by a large peace group to appear as a guest speaker in May. I'd have to do that in Japanese. They'd seen the documentary about me a few years before. They invited a journalist who made a different documentary and me to participate in a round-table discussion. The group comprised the Kyushu branch of a national group dedicated to preserving Japan's peace constitution, especially Article Nine, which forever renounced war as a means of resolving international disputes. I agreed to participate. Several hundred people were expected to show up. The journalist would be the main speaker and talk about the documentary she made on victims of the Vietnam and Iraq wars. I'd then do a ten- to fifteen-minute introduction in which I'd talk about my conscientious objector experiences. After that, the discussion would be held with a moderator, the journalist, and me.

The event was held on May 11. Part of the journalist's documentary was shown before the discussion. It was about how the Iraq War was affecting veterans who returned home and had a difficult time readjusting to life and coping with severe symptoms from depleted uranium sickness. After the hour-long discussion, there was a question and answer period. Later, I went out to dinner with some of the members of the peace group. They even paid me the equivalent of three hundred dollars as a speaking fee.

I managed to complete another academic paper. Motivated by my time with the peace group members, I spent a month doing research and compiling a paper titled "A Comparison of

American G.I. Resistance to the Vietnam War and the Iraq War." It was a time-consuming but satisfying project to complete. It took me away from the little bubble that comprised my life as a foreign teacher at a small Japanese university and made me think more about the outside world and larger issues.

For a while, at least. The realities of that little bubble still had to be dealt with. Adding to the administrative responsibilities I already had, I took on the challenge of running an English speech contest. For the past three years, the public relations committee had done a piss-poor job of running the contest. It had started as a PR ploy to attract high school students and promote interaction with the local community by allowing local citizens to participate. The three native English speaker teachers from the junior college and university were asked to do the judging. The first year drew some interest, but since then none of the committee members put any effort into the contest. The only students who applied were from the junior college and all were from one hard-working Japanese teacher's homeroom class. Their participation earned them extra points toward a better grade. No university students had applied for two years.

One day, the junior college president spoke to me directly and criticized the university English teachers for being lazy and doing nothing for the contest. That got my goat. I decided to show him how wrong he was. Although I was not a member of the PR committee, I told the head of the committee that we English teachers could take over running the contest if he needed our help. He gladly handed over the responsibility to me.

Throughout February and March, I met with the personnel section chief to find out what was needed to ask for funding and facilities. I drew up a proposal outlining why the contest was important for the promotion of the school during a period of

declining enrollment and submitted it to the relevant committees before it was passed up the chain to the board of directors,
who gave their approval. I next did all the schedule planning,
writing of invitation letters to high schools, and behind-the-
scenes arm-twisting to get a good program rolling a lot earlier.
I had enough experience on various committees to know that
our school had a slow-moving bureaucracy that needed to be
pushed and cajoled to get anything done. By May, everything
was moving ahead according to schedule. The plan was to hold
the contest in November, but recruiting some university students
and getting them to hand in and practice their speeches beforehand would take a lot of time and encouragement.

The semester rolled on without incident or disaster. When
August came and it was time to start the new Interferon treatment, I felt I was as prepared as I could be. I was optimistic in
thinking that it would be easier this time around compared to
eight years before because my liver was in good condition. The
most recent CT scan showed no fat and no scarring.

The first three days in the hospital were filled with various
tests, including a colonoscopy. I'd heard many horror stories
about getting one, but I didn't feel anything. It was over in
about ten minutes. Only two small and benign polyps were
found and removed. The actual Interferon-Ribavirin treatment
started on the fourth day. As was done the previous time, they
gave me daily Interferon shots along with the prescribed dosage
of Ribavirin pills. I had no bad reactions, so they kept me there
for only eight days. I knew this was the easy part. The tough
part would be in persevering for the long haul of side effects.
I'd get one Interferon shot a week and take daily Ribavirin pills
for as many months as it took. If we got good results early on,
the treatment might last over a year. It would be a bit expensive,

but I had insurance. As a foreigner with a permanent resident visa, I was qualified to apply for some financial assistance that was the result of a new law that allowed hepatitis patients to get help from the government. This law came into effect when about fifty patients sued the government and won a Supreme Court decision after they contracted hepatitis C through tainted blood products an Osaka hospital used with its dialysis machines. The government had imported the tainted blood and given it to the hospital. Two weeks after applying, I received notice that I'd get help for any drug costs above five hundred dollars a month. My treatment would cost me over nine hundred dollars a month, so that assistance was a big help.

A week after entering the hospital, there was more bad news. Dad had a stroke and was now in the hospital. Linda sent an e-mail explaining that she thought Dad was in the shower for too long the night before, so she called out to him through the door. He tried to respond, but his speech was slurred. She had to push the bathroom door open because he'd fallen against it. She found him on the floor and called an ambulance. His left side was paralyzed. He couldn't do anything for himself. The nurses had to use a patient sling to get him out of bed and into a chair. His doctors said he had a long process ahead of him. He was going to have to learn all over again how to walk, talk, and feed himself.

For the next few months, Mom, Terri, Linda, and Linda D. kept me up to date on Dad's rehabilitation program. Even Dick sent a few brief notes. I did my best to keep up my end of the correspondence by offering encouragement to everyone and giving them details of my own treatment.

Dad was moved to a nursing home for his initial physical therapy. Within two weeks, they'd removed his stomach feeding tube and he was eating three soft meals a day. His therapists said he was becoming more alert and sometimes writing something on a pad for them to read.

After about a month in the nursing home, Dad begged to go home. He wasn't getting good care. Linda sent me a note explaining that one night the nurses gave him the drug Coumadin by mistake and he had severe reactions. He shred his diapers three different times and shook the rail on his bed all night. He tried to yank his useless left arm off and throw it away. The nurses strapped him to the bed that night. They began calling him "Ripper." Finally, about a week later, he was allowed to go home after Linda arranged to have a hospital bed, a wheelchair, and a Hoyer Lift available. She and Michelle took some lessons to learn how to use the different equipment. She also arranged for a therapist to come to the house. His concentration improved a bit and he could speak in a slurred manner for short periods of time.

I wrote back saying I was probably developing a strange gallows humor as the image of Dad shredding his diapers and shaking his rail brought a chuckle out of me. I had an image of a prisoner going on strike. It was unlike Dad's usual gentle nature. I was sure it was a combination of depression, frustration at not being able to go home, and the drugs they were giving him that caused his reactions. Interferon was doing similar things in messing with my own mind.

That treatment was no picnic. The side effects of the weekly Interferon shots followed a cycle. The first three days after the shot were the roughest with a fever, slight headache, and achy joints and muscles. Those symptoms would generally recede by the fourth day, but a deep lethargy followed. I had no energy. It was difficult to concentrate. I was taking frequent naps, but always woke up feeling anemic and heavy. My viral load dropped, so that was a positive. By October, I'd lost about ten pounds. Unlike Dad, I had a clear viral load target number to shoot for and could look ahead to a distant date when the treatment would be over. His case seemed like a combination of endless prison and torture.

After he'd been home for a few days, we gave Dad a call. Shi-chan and I did most of the talking, but he listened earnestly and made a couple comments here and there. Linda and I talked for a bit and Dad dropped off to sleep. Apparently, he was holding some food down better and had a couple of good bowel movements. We were glad to know there were enough people who really cared around him and were helping take care of him. He'd also made some friends with the Medicare people, who were checking on him frequently and helping Linda by explaining how to use the different equipment and what to watch for.

On the last Saturday of October, we held the English speech contest. All my planning, organizing, and labor paid off. I acted as the M.C. It ran from 1 p.m. until 4:30 p.m. with fifteen speakers, seven from different high schools, three from the junior college, and five from the university. I had one of the digital media students film the event and make a short documentary with interviews at the end. I planned to make a speech contest page to put on the school website and include the video for promotion. I also planned to send a note to the junior college president and rub his nose in the success of the contest. That's the way the Interferon was affecting my brain. My hemoglobin level and white and red blood cell counts were at their lowest. I developed a serious rash that covered most of my body and was driving me crazy. People on the hepatitis C forums called it the Riba Rash. It was one of the worst side effects of the Ribavirin drug. I wrote Mom that I was like a walking zombie, then made a correction: a stumbling zombie. At least, I'd dropped enough of the viral load to see the goal of zero come into focus.

Dad had to be rushed to the hospital again in November. He complained of heart pain, so Linda called the ambulance. At an Arcata hospital, they found his gall bladder enlarged and infected, so he was sent by ambulance to a larger hospital in Eureka. Surgery was performed because his gall bladder was gangrenous. They let him go home a week later, but soon after that, he had to go on hospice care.

We called Dad every week. Even though it was hard for him to talk and swallow, he was alert and his brain was still sharp. He was living on willpower alone. Everyone in his family was constantly around and taking care of him the best they could. He was overwhelmed with love and often cried.

While these events of the past few months were happening, Mom returned to her part-time job. She worked two days a week for just a few hours each day. The work was not physically difficult for her, but she was tired when she got home and still suffered from shortness of breath. She went for walks and did some stretches every day. She said that made her feel better. Her biggest frustration was the nerve pain she had because many nerves were cut or damaged during her heart surgery. She went to a therapist who gave her strong massages on her scar tissue, which was keeping the nerves from regenerating. It was painful, but she thought it was worth it if it worked. Her doctor gave her some different pain medication that made her feel nauseous and dizzier. Mom wrote:

Perhaps I should say "woozier" since I've been kind of dizzy all my life. Stay safe and warm and remember we love you both like the words from an old song—I

love you a bushel and a peck, a bushel and a peck, and
a hug around the neck! I used to dance to this tune
many years ago!

As the new year started, it looked like Dad wouldn't make it
much longer. His family gave him a birthday party on January
22 with many relatives in attendance. Terri made the journey
back to Arcata. I couldn't fly because of my treatment. I promised I'd write a eulogy when it was needed. Linda D. agreed to
read it at the funeral. We all prayed that wouldn't be too soon.

From the different e-mails I was getting, I learned Dad recognized almost everyone but seemed to be in a different era much of
the time. His behavior and words were out of kilter. The nurses
thought he was tying up loose ends, shutting down, and getting
ready to die. He ground his teeth a lot while sleeping. He'd curl
up into a fetal position and couldn't straighten out. He'd remember past events and often spoke about summers water-skiing
at Shasta Lake and how much he loved and missed his brother.

As his condition worsened and the hospice people were giving
him more morphine, his confusion increased. He had occasional
periods of clarity and talked about his logging days, but these
periods grew increasingly fewer. One time, he was staring off
into the distance and suddenly leaned forward with eyes wide
open and said, "It's coming down the chute!" He was probably
reliving a long-ago logging experience.

The end came on June 6, 2009. Dad died peacefully in his sleep.
It was ironic yet fitting that he died on D-Day. After all, he was
one of the fighter pilots involved in the bombing of Normandy
on June 6, 1944. He also provided air cover on June 14, 1944 for
Franklin Roosevelt and Winston Churchill as they crossed the
English Channel on a destroyer. A few days after Dad died, there

was a memorial. Many people came to pay their respects. Linda D. read my eulogy.

The 2009 swine flu pandemic forced FIU to cancel all overseas homestay-study programs. I'd hoped to chaperone a group to Portland, but it was probably for the better that I stayed home between semesters and rested. My treatment side effects were kicking my ass badly. When the spring semester began, the rash that covered my entire body and made me look like a red lizard developed eruptions with pus and even blood oozing out of them in different places. The itching drove me crazy and kept me from getting any sleep at night. During the daytime, I tried to catch some catnaps, but overall I was just exhausted and spaced out. I couldn't concentrate for more than a few minutes at a time. Work was a burden. My appetite, however, was still strong and my blood test numbers were improving each month. The virus was about ninety-eight percent gone, but as I wrote to Mom, that last two percent was like trying to ferret out Osama Bin Laden. I was almost at the half-way mark of the seventy-two-week treatment. Sometimes I wondered how much longer I could handle it, but if it killed off the virus in the end, it was worth the suffering.

Things got even worse, however, when shortly after the semester began, both knees developed knee effusion. I couldn't walk for three days and stayed home from work. I finally went to the hospital, where a joint specialist took some X-rays and drained a massive amount of fluid from both knees. First, he cleaned the right knee before using a hypodermic needle to put a port in the knee. Next, he took a large syringe and hooked it up to the port to extract the fluid, which poured out in a yellow stream and filled up the syringe. The doctor yelled out to a nurse, "Get another one!" twice before draining the entirety. He repeated the process on the left knee, which had less fluid and used up only one syringe. He put an ACE bandage on both knees and told me not to do any physical exercise for two days.

After having the knees drained, I could get around somewhat with a cane. I returned to work but tried to stay off my feet as much as possible. I had the knees drained again three weeks later. It was still painful to get around, but I didn't miss any work after that. I started taking some diuretic water pills. They made me piss more and, combined with Shi-chan's leg massages, helped greatly. The swelling almost disappeared. I could bend both legs enough to get out and ride my bicycle to work and to the markets. I started a long-term relationship with a cane.

The virus finally became undetectable. I talked my doctor into reducing the amount of Interferon and Ribavirin I had to take. I figured now that we had the virus on the ropes, I didn't need the KO-punch amounts I'd endured from the beginning. Soon after, the severity of the side effects lessened. Anemia was still a constant. I wanted to get back to swimming again. My muscles had nearly disappeared and I'd have to start from zero to get back in shape physically. Before starting the treatment, I'd been swimming an hour three times a week. The first time I returned to the pool, I tried swimming some laps and had to give up after five minutes because my muscles were so weak and I was out of breath.

For the first time in my life, I felt old. Dad's death and Mom's brushes with it brought home the reality of mortality. My thoughts turned toward retirement. FIU was still barely surviving. There were only about half the number of full-time teachers we had just a few years before. Those of us still hanging on saw our workloads radically increased while having our salaries slashed. In the good ol' days, eighty percent of my job was educational and twenty percent administrative. Now it was reversed. I was on five committees, and it seemed all I did at school was run from meeting to meeting. Job satisfaction was at an all-time low.

I calculated ways to retire early without going to the poor-house. I figured if I could survive five or six more years—about the time we'd have our house paid off—Shi-chan and I could probably semi-retire if we continued to live a frugal life. I was lucky that I qualified for both Japanese and American Social Security. I'd also get a decent lump-sum retirement payment from the teachers' union.

I was relieved when August finally came. I could sleep late sometimes and not have the pressure of getting a lot of things done under strict deadlines. For about a month, there wasn't much work pressure to deal with. At the end of the semester, I'd been running on empty, and my concentration power disappeared. I had several Interferon-Ribavirin "brain fog" moments at work. A few times someone said something to me and within seconds I'd completely forgotten what they said and stared at them uncomprehendingly. At other times, I made a comment that stopped everyone in their tracks and had them staring at me with a look that said, "What the hell are you talking about, boy? That has absolutely nothing to do with the issue at hand." All I could do was shrug my shoulders and grin sheepishly.

I drew what little strength I had from Mom's supporting e-mails and words of encouragement. Such comments as "My heart aches for you"; "Again, I have to say how proud I am and how much I respect you for sticking with this long, long treatment"; "I'm so sorry you are still going through a tough time with the treatments; you've been a brave soul to stick with it"; and "Perhaps you've inherited some of those *go get 'em* genes from Grandpa Frederick, Grandma Murph, and your ole Mom here" kept my spirits up and head above water. My favorite was "I wish I could do something to help, but alas, here I am miles and an ocean away from you both and as that old, old saying goes: 'If wishes were horses, beggars would ride.'"

Mom kept having shortness of breath with any kind of exertion. She had several doctor's appointments to try to find the root of the problem. At first, her doctor thought a heart muscle that helps the heart beat wasn't functioning as it should. He thought perhaps it was bruised during Mom's heart surgery, or maybe it was just dying. Mom told him absolutely no more surgery. She was frustrated with the lack of complete recovery from the previous surgery over a year before. Her conclusion was that although she'd escaped it for a long time, old age and arthritis were taking over her body.

The next step was to have an echocardiogram. The results showed the heart and the repaired valve were working well. More tests were scheduled. There seemed to be something blocking the oxygen from getting into her blood stream, but they couldn't figure out what. Mom said at least she was able to work part-time and drive. Two weeks later, Mom went to a pulmonary clinic, where the doctor said he thought her lungs were probably injured during her heart surgery. He gave her an inhaler to use a couple of times a day in the hope it would help the lungs work better. The little polyps in the lungs that were found a year before had not increased. The biopsy they took—with what looked like a horse needle, Mom wrote—came back benign.

Shi-chan and I looked forward to visiting Mom and Terri in March. My treatment would be over by then and the spring break homestay-study program in Australia was canceled, so I wouldn't have to chaperone any students.

I had my final Interferon shot on December 29. A week later, I took my last Ribavirin pill. It was a relief to finish that torturous treatment, but there would still be a few more weeks until I regained my weight, strength, and stamina. I took a perverse pride in having managed to continue working the whole time. My students probably felt differently.

Mentally, I was raring to go in my rehabilitation, but I hadn't anticipated what the withdrawal symptoms would be. Like that of a heroin addict going cold turkey, my body reacted violently when deprived suddenly of the strong drugs it was used to. For a few days after taking the final pill, I had a fever of a hundred and two. Both knees swelled up so badly I couldn't walk for a while. I had them drained again. My cane was my constant companion. The skin rash and itching, however, eased up considerably.

I felt a lot better when my first post-treatment blood test showed my basic numbers in the normal range. That was a first. When the detailed results came back from the lab a week later, the virus was undetectable. My doctor, Shi-chan, and I were ecstatic. I told Mom that the year and a half of misery was worth the fight and the ol' Irish stubbornness had saved the day. It looked like I'd beaten the sucker after battling for nearly ten years.

23

Portland Calls to Me

B OTH Shi-chan and I needed an extended rest. She'd been teaching part-time at three universities for two years in addition to her own school's weekend classes. Trying to take care of me sapped her of what remaining energy she had. The three weeks we spent in Portland with Mom and Terri gave us a much-needed escape from our jobs and responsibilities.

We spent a lot of time at the kitchen table drinking coffee and listening to Mom's stories, several of which I recorded on a portable audio recorder. Shi-chan taught Terri how to cook *okonomiyaki*, a popular Japanese dish with shredded cabbage and sliced meat. I gave Mom a few basic lessons in Japanese. This was the start of a new pursuit that could occupy Mom's mind and divert her from her pain and physical decline. It was also another means for our communication. We agreed to continue the lessons after I returned to Japan. I'd send her homework to do, check what she'd done, and send her feedback. We joked that it would help delay the onset of dementia.

Revitalized by the Portland vacation, I returned to work fully motivated. I was no longer the head of any committees, so I could focus on improving the speech contest and promoting the Portland overseas-study program. If nothing else, my experiences as dean of students and head of the International Exchange Committee taught me the importance of planning ahead, preparing in detail, and constant promotion in trying to ensure the success of anything in FIU's bureaucracy.

I set about creating a speech contest page to be placed on the FIU website. I was the only English teacher who had any idea how to do that. During the previous speech contest, I had a student videotape all the speeches. I got those students' permission to put the videos on the YouTube site. I'd also put together a program for that speech contest with Japanese and English scripts so the audience could follow along with the speakers. I still had those files. I made a basic webpage with an explanation of the details of the next contest and links to the videos and program files. I called for a meeting of the English teachers from both the junior college and university, got their OK to submit the webpage for the administration's approval, and hammered out the details for the current year's theme and guidelines for writing the speeches, the dates of the speeches, and the wording in the invitation letters and other documents.

Among the documents I needed to prepare to send through the different tentacles of the school bureaucracy were a guideline outlining the contest theme, rules, deadlines, and contact names and numbers; an invitation letter to selected high schools; a proposal to the board of directors with a detailed request for funding and resources; an entry sheet; a flyer for advertising on campus; a permission form for using student scripts and videos on the school homepage; a timeline for steps to be done; and a list of high schools to invite. Since the contest included participants from both the junior college and the university, all this paperwork had to be sent not only to the university personnel department but also to several layers of junior college committees for their agreement and rubber-stamping, too.

When doing all this *nemawashi* greasing of the wheel to get everyone's understanding and approval, my main explanation of the aim of the speech contest was the promotional aspect. University and junior college recruiting efforts—including summertime Open Campus events and free sample lessons to high school students—over the past few years had done little to attract new students. We had to do something to improve the reputation of both schools. Getting high school teachers and students to come to our campus and become interested in either school was critical for survival. We had to eliminate the rivalry and competition that existed between the two.

In the past, the university committee running the contest sent out invitations to only local high schools. As a result, the highest number of high schools that responded was only three. I insisted we send out invitations to all high schools in Fukuoka Prefecture that had English language programs. Almost everyone whose arm I needed to twist agreed, but that agreement always seemed conditioned on their not having to work any harder than they already were. I'd anticipated that and was prepared to do most of the paperwork myself.

At the end of May, the speech contest page was up on the FIU website. We got permission for an increased budget. Invitations to all the listed Fukuoka Prefecture high schools were sent out. I put flyers and entry sheets in all our teacher mailboxes, announced the details at the faculty meetings, and started recruiting our own students.

Next on the project list was an active promotion of the Portland homestay-study program. This also required a lot of behind-the-scenes legwork, which started at the level of explaining to the members of the International Exchange Committee what needed to be done. My plan included a specific date for an explanatory meeting with interested students and a general timeline of deadlines for applying, getting a passport, and making payments.

The International Exchange Committee set up a general explanatory meeting on May 20 for the China, Korea, and Portland summer homestay-study programs. Of the seven students who attended, only two were interested in Portland. The first meeting for focusing exclusively on the Portland program was held on June 5. Twenty-five students came; three committed to go.

The next day, I sent an e-mail to the director of PELA reporting that three students were committed to attending the English Plus Volunteer program running from August 2 to August 27. I requested three things. First, we needed a delay in arrival for the scheduled July 27 orientation and placement exam. FIU's semester final exam testing schedule required the students to take exams until July 29. A July 30 departure from Japan would have no conflict with the testing schedule and allow us to take advantage of cheaper airline tickets up to August 1. Second, we needed the bank account number for PELA so we could wire transfer all fees. Third, we needed an answer to how early the housing placement fee, airport pickup fee, and housing deposit had to be paid. I anticipated our students would have all their passport information, in-school application forms, and parents' permission forms completed by June 17 to start the online PELA application process. I explained we'd also get a definite schedule and detailed estimate from the travel agent by June 20.

PELA responded two days later. It was OK for our students to miss the July 27 placement test and orientation. They could start classes on August 2 and take the placement test in the morning. The host families could pick the students up at the airport on any day. PELA would send an invoice for the whole amount of tuition and housing fees. Nothing needed to be paid in advance, but they requested we send the travel schedule once it was decided.

Money was so tight that sending a chaperone was seen by the board of directors as an unneeded and expensive luxury. I sent a proposal in Japanese to the head of the board to try to get permission to loosen the strings on the board's purse. I explained a chaperone was needed because it was the first time to send our students to PELA. In order to guarantee a good experience for the students and maintain the quality of FIU's education, it was important to check in person on the types of volunteer activities, the homestay conditions, the quality of the classes and teachers, and how to deal with the mass transit system. Three days later, I got his reply. He allocated enough money to cover the chaperone's travel and daily life expenses. The catch was I had to be back within two weeks in order to give a mock lesson at one of our Open Campus recruiting events. Near the end of June, the three students completed their PELA online applications.

At the beginning of June, Mom got laid off from a job for the first time in her life. She'd had a feeling earlier that the business where she worked part-time was having financial problems. She heard rumors they were going to close. She was upset because they gave her only two days' notice. She wasn't shy about letting them know how disrespectful and rude it was that they hadn't had the courtesy to give the usual two weeks' notice. She worked the final two days, cleaned out her desk, and finished two projects she was working on. The other two ladies in the office took her to lunch. She was told after lunch that the office manager had called their boss and told him she also thought the way they'd let Mom go was a lousy thing to do. The boss apologized and gave Mom a small bonus. Mom summarized the whole affair by writing, "I guess I'm from the 'old school' of employee/employer relationships."

Mom cheered up when I told her I got permission to chaperone our kids to Portland for two weeks in August. She gave me one of her special smiles when I told her in a Skype call how great she was doing in her Japanese study and now that she was unemployed for the first time in her eighty-four years on this planet, we'd be able to spend even more time on Japanese verb conjugations, transitive and intransitive verbs, grammar markers, the different types of adjectives and how to convert them into adverbs, and how to say "I'm proud of my son" and "I love to study Japanese." I loved it when she giggled.

I arrived in Portland on July 30 with the three FIU students. The time in Portland passed quickly. The students had few problems. They returned to Japan safely two weeks after I did.

Mom had had arthritic pain for a long time. Now her right knee was also giving her problems. Shortly after I left Portland, she wrote, "I took a bit of a tumble and feel like a truck ran over me, then backed up and ran over me again. I'm fine—just stiff and sore, but that will go away."

For a full month, Mom was down, not feeling good at all, having lots of pain, and exhausted all the time. Many more tests were done. Finally, her doctor came up with a diagnosis. He thought she had a type of rheumatism called polymyalgia rheumatica. He put Mom on a low dose of the drug Prednisone and some other pain medication in the hope of helping her start functioning again. Mom was concerned that I'd probably be prone to the disease as her mom, Grandma Frederick, and some of her mom's siblings had a lot of arthritis in their later years. Mom wasn't happy about being put on Prednisone because of the many possible side effects, but she agreed to follow her doctor's recommendation. Relieving her pain was the main priority.

That pain was persistent—sometimes severe, sometimes tolerable. On her good days, Mom reviewed her Japanese lessons and the notes I'd sent her with my corrections. Her frequent bad days of severe pain made it difficult to maintain motivation, but she tried to keep plugging away because "keeping the mind busy is surely the best thing to do."

I hoped to brighten her day by sending an e-mail detailing how we'd had more speech contest applicants than ever before. We had to cut over half of the applicants. In the end, the contest was a big success. A few days later, Terri wrote to us that Mom was back in the hospital again, this time with pneumonia and the beginning of sepsis.

We thanked our lucky stars for Terri's presence, medical knowledge, and love of Mom. She wrote us daily reports of Mom's condition and recovery. We also had a few Skype calls when Terri wasn't running back and forth from the hospital. From the beginning of the crisis, Terri was convinced that Mom would rally. She wrote, "Mom always does this—scare the hell out of us for a week or so, and then rebound and start racing to recovery."

On the second day after being rushed to the hospital, Mom was out of the ICU. The sepsis was responding to antibiotics. She was given an MRI on her neck, spine, and the shoulder that had been bothering her. The doctors also determined that Mom didn't have polymyalgia rheumatica after all. When Terri arrived at the hospital on the third day, she found Mom going for a walk. She reported that Mom was "so loopy on the pain meds right now that she's a riot. Funnier than ever!"

Two days later, Terri took our e-mails to the hospital and read them to Mom, who was now eating on her own again. She was moved back to the floor for recovering patients. Mom's orthopedist said that Mom had torn her rotator cuff at some point. She was getting more aggressive respiratory therapy and would soon start physical therapy, which would help stimulate her appetite. All was moving forward at a good pace. The sepsis was under control. X-rays showed the pneumonia spots getting smaller.

Terri began preparations for bringing Mom home. She bought a special hospital bed to put in Mom's bedroom. Mom would be hooked up for a while on an oxygen tank and would need special breathing treatments, so Terri got a pulse oximeter for measuring the oxygen in Mom's blood. She said she didn't want Mom going toxic on her or have the oxygen level drop when Mom had to be active. Terri also got her hands on a stethoscope and a manual blood pressure cuff. Mom would also need nebulizer treatments for her difficulty in breathing. In many cases, Shi-chan and I had no clue of what Terri was talking about. We needed her to explain in detail what the various equipment and drugs were for and what they did.

Mom's return home was delayed for a day. Her adrenal glands were suppressed and not waking up as fast as the doctors wanted. She was given medication to help get the adrenal system running. She was still dehydrated and her legs were showing some edema. A deep venous ultrasound was done to make sure she wasn't getting blood clots.

Finally, Mom was allowed to go home. She had a lot of therapy to undergo. Terri had her hands full, but put all her efforts into making sure Mom would get better. A typical day included pills at certain times, breathing treatments, breathing exercises, physical exercises, blood pressure taken several times, and Terri listening to Mom's lungs through the stethoscope. This regimen continued through the day. Terri joked that finally she had Mom on a leash. She figured that by the first of the year, Mom would want to strangle her. That was fine by Terri. It would mean Mom was well on the way to recovery.

It took about two weeks before Mom could have any visitors. Her breathing exercises were difficult for her and would continue to be until her pneumonia cleared completely. Terri reported that Mom was starting to move around the apartment quite well considering what she'd been through. Her strength was coming back gradually.

As Mom continued to get better, we made more Skype calls. It was good to see her smile and hear her voice. Terri came up with the idea of getting a Japanese brush kit, inks, and calligraphy paper for Mom's Christmas present. I wired some money to our joint account.

Mom's recovery period became a time to reflect on her life and which projects she could do going forward now that she had severe physical restrictions. She'd spent her entire life dealing with obstacles of one kind or another. Artistic pursuits always played a role for her in overcoming them. She always had some project going on. She was an artist who needed to create to feel alive. Now more than ever, she probably felt the pressure of limited time.

She wrote some stories about Granddad and Grandma Frederick. She planned to make a book for two cousins who grew up without knowing anything about that part of their family. This project kept Mom occupied for a few months. She also started painting nature scenes and birds with her Japanese ink brush set.

When not engaged in these two activities and her rehabilitation sessions, she returned to writing poetry. One day, she set her thoughts down to remind each of her three children how much joy and happiness we'd given her throughout her life. Her poem to me was an arrow to my heart.

TO THE MAN MY SON HAS BECOME

I watched through loving and tear-filled eyes as you stepped out of your childhood skin into another time of uncertainty.

I watched your face as you began to show concern for the world around you and the wonder of which road to take to fulfill your dreams.

I carried you as far as I could—for seven long months—hoping you would become the man I see today.

It is as if you floated through a symphony of space, moving above the clouds and finding your own path to the future.

As you trudged over and beyond that uncertain bumpy path, you learned to stand tall and firm and strong—for there seemed to be an unspoken language that told you it was time to transform into a competent, loving human being.

I am thankful that you are comfortable within the rhythm of your own heart, showing you are a complete being with emotions and feelings that flow through you, so much like a river, never ending, only bending.

I know you have been brave enough to follow your heart as you stand firm and are now defining your strength and masculinity, which allows me to see, through the eyes of a loving mother, the man inside this boy I brought into the world.

Please know how pleased and proud I am of the man you have become and how much unconditional love I have in my heart for you.

—Mom

24

Fukushima, Fractured Pelvis, and Other Woes

MOM'S miraculous return from knocking on the door of the pearly gates gave us hope for a good 2011. In January, I turned sixty, the age when Japanese celebrate *Kanreki. Kan* means "return" or "cycle" and *reki* means "history" or "calendar." *Kanreki* is a time to celebrate being reborn and entering your second childhood, a time for reflection, and an opportunity for a new beginning. I liked the idea of passing on responsibilities and duties to the next generation. Mom turned eighty-five.

Each e-mail and Skype call brought news of improvement. One day in early February, Mom went all day and night completely off oxygen. She shouted "hooray" and called it another big step forward. Not long after, she and Terri went to a beauty parlor, stopped at a pharmacy, and did some shopping, all while not on any oxygen and not having to use a walker. Mom beamed when she told us.

March 11, 2011, brought an abrupt end to this streak of positive steps. I was in my office for most of the day. It was a Friday. Shi-chan had an evening class at home. When I got home, I started cooking dinner and didn't turn on the TV news until after 7 p.m. An earthquake reported as magnitude 8.9 had struck near the northeast coast of the main island of Honshu. We didn't feel anything in Kyushu. Words like "apocalyptic," "Armageddon," and "dystopian" came to mind but couldn't describe what was on the screen. Shi-chan finished her lesson around 8:30 p.m. She came downstairs and her jaw dropped when she looked at the screen. We sat transfixed in front of the TV until the early hours of the morning.

Aerial scenes shot from news helicopters were shown repeatedly: a thirty-foot tsunami wave crashing over a sea wall in Miyako City, Iwate Prefecture; natural gas storage tanks burning and sending off plumes of black smoke at the Cosmo oil refinery in Ichihara City, Chiba Prefecture; another massive tsunami wave engulfing a residential area and sweeping burning houses out to sea in Natori City, Miyagi Prefecture; a tsunami wave tossing about cars and planes and everything in its path at the Sendai Airport in Natori City.

We spent all day Saturday watching the news. It was the strongest earthquake ever recorded in Japan. The death toll at that point was in the hundreds, but the news media quoted government officials as saying the number would rise to more than a thousand. About two hundred to three hundred bodies were found along the waterfront in Sendai. Thousands of homes were destroyed. Many roads were impassable. Trains and buses were not running. Power lines were down. The JR rail company said three trains were missing.

Japanese officials issued evacuation orders for people living in the vicinity of two nuclear power plants that experienced breakdowns in their cooling systems. The officials warned that small amounts of radiation could leak from both plants.

All day long, the news showed scenes of survivors calling for help and rescuers searching for people buried in the rubble. Self-Defense Forces were on the scene and helping firefighters evacuate people. On the rooftop of Chuo Hospital in Iwanuma City, doctors and nurses waved flags and umbrellas. They'd written "Help" in English and "We need food" in Japanese on the roof.

The disaster took on a more ominous tone when, two hours after Cabinet Secretary Edano stated in a press conference that no radiation had leaked from the nuclear plants, Prime Minister Kan declared a nuclear emergency and the government issued evacuation orders for the thousands of people living within a three-kilometer radius of Fukushima Daiichi Nuclear Power Plant. According to the news, a thirteen-foot tsunami wave hit the plant but was deflected by a wall built to withstand waves up to thirty-three feet high. A few minutes later, a fifty-foot wave breached the wall, destroying seawater pumps, drowning power panels that distributed energy to water pumps, and surging into basements containing backup generators. Power was lost in five of the six reactors. Without power, water pumps couldn't provide a steady flow of cool water to the reactors' cores. A meltdown was inevitable.

Early the next morning, the evacuation zone was expanded to ten kilometers. In the afternoon, a news camera captured a hydrogen explosion that blew the roof off the Number 1 reactor. The concrete walls collapsed. All that remained was steel framework. Some workers were injured in the explosion, which also damaged cables that were being laid for restoring power to the Number 1 and Number 2 reactors. The evacuation zone was expanded to twenty kilometers.

On March 14, a hydrogen explosion at the Number 3 reactor

destroyed the upper part of the building. The next day, there was another explosion at the Number 2 reactor. Knowing that the media broadcasts in Japan were being heavily controlled and censored, we checked other sources such as Democracy Now, the BBC, and Al Jazeera, hoping to find some objectivity and truth in what information was coming out. How bad was it exactly?

The first Democracy Now headline we saw online was "This Could Be Chernobyl on Steroids." Nuclear engineers, physicists, and other guests on the different news sources we read and watched believed that if the wind had been blowing the other way when the reactors exploded, across the island instead of out to sea, Japan would've been cut in half and destroyed. They also thought that there'd be as many as a million cancers over the next thirty years. It was hard to know what to think.

During the first few days of the crisis, we were flooded with messages from people worried about us. Mom also had many friends and relatives expressing their concerns. We spent a lot of time writing detailed e-mail messages and making telephone calls to thank everyone and let them know we were far from the devastation and doing fine.

Life continued and the new semester started. I was now assigned full-time back to the English course in the International Communication Department. The board of directors eliminated the Digital Media Department because it had too few students. The students who'd already entered the department would be seen through to graduation. After that, most of the department teachers would be let go. Dwindling enrollment and the increasing inability of many families to pay tuition fees were threatening to close not only FIU but also many schools throughout Japan. At the April faculty meeting, the head of the board of directors sounded the death knell and told us university teachers that if we didn't recruit the required number of students within the next two years, the doors would be slammed shut.

At least I was back in the English course, where I belonged. I could concentrate on what mattered to me—the PELA program, the speech contests, and my new senior seminar class. Shortly after the semester began, we held an explanatory meeting for the homestay programs in Portland, China, and Korea. A few students attended, but no one signed up for any of the programs. The influence of the nuclear disaster was still too close.

Progress on the speech contest went well. I talked the English teachers into trying to hold two contests, one for high schools and one for our own university and junior college students. We requested more budget money to send invitations to high schools in four Kyushu prefectures rather than just Fukuoka Prefecture. I prepared all the paperwork for the junior college promotion committee and the personnel section. I also converted the 2010 speech video files, put them up on YouTube, created PDF files of those speech scripts, and put everything on a speech contest page to be added to FIU's website. At the beginning of April, I met with the relevant junior college committee members to explain the paperwork and negotiate speech contest dates. When everything was agreed on, I gave the files for the speech contest page to the person in charge in the promotional section and asked the personnel office to send out invitation letters to about three hundred fifty high schools.

When the June 6 entry sheet deadline came, we had submissions from nineteen high school students and a combined thirteen students from the university and junior college. I wrote a thank-you letter to all the high schools that had sent entry sheets. Throughout the remainder of the semester whenever I ran into our students who'd submitted entry sheets, I gave them continuous encouragement.

My first senior seminar in the English course was an interesting challenge. The theme of the seminar was studying American culture through movies. I prepared a recommended movie list that had forty stories based on famous novels. The students had to pick a movie, do background research on American history of the period the story was set in, and write a minimum five-page paper divided into five parts: (1) the historical background; (2) a summary of the story; (3) impressive scenes from the story; (4) what they learned about American culture, history, and society from this project; and (5) what they thought the original author's message was and why. I required them to do a reference section to show the sources for their historical research. The paper had to be written in English. The students had to schedule at least two meetings a month with me in my office so we could go over how they were progressing. Writing an academic paper wasn't a strict requirement in Japanese universities, so this would be a first-time experience for these students. They'd need a lot of guidance in how to organize and write the paper. These meetings would also allow me to nip any potential plagiarism attempts in the bud.

Many of our senior students had a hard time finding jobs. Few of the big companies were hiring. You could see the discouragement on student faces. I was tempted to remind my own students that in my life, I'd worked nothing but part-time jobs with no benefits until I was forty-one and that it was important to hang in there and sometimes be satisfied with less than an ideal job. I wanted to encourage them to do their best to get as many qualifications as they could, be patient, and have faith that things would get better.

In the end, however, I learned it was better just to be a good listener. It wasn't always necessary to offer advice. Reflecting on how I'd talked to students over the years, I realized that for a long time nearly every other sentence that came out of my mouth was "What you gotta do is . . ." or "If I were you, I'd . . . ." That kind of advice didn't seem appropriate anymore. Maybe what the students were looking for was not so much an answer to any of the mysteries and confusion that plagued them, but just an acceptance and an understanding that it was OK to be confused. In the wake of the earthquake, tsunami, and Fukushima nuclear disaster, there were a lot of students who came to my office to get a load off their chests. If I could listen and respond with a remark that made them smile, I felt I'd done more for them than trying to "guide" them. The truth was I had no definitive answers.

I thought increasingly about retirement. Even if FIU closed its doors, the new students would have to be taken care of for four more years. That would carry me to sixty-five, when I'd have to retire anyway. My retirement package from the teachers' union was safe. My name was registered in the computers of Japan's version of Social Security. I was fairly confident I could count on that. Our house would be fully paid off in three years. Shi-chan's school at home was getting by and we could write off much of our utilities as school operating expenses. All in all, we'd planned and saved and lived frugally all these years. We thought we were prepared, come what may.

In the midst of natural disasters and economic doldrums, however, not every day lent itself to positive thinking. Around the middle of May, I had another biannual blood test. The results were a blow to the gut. Despite my liver numbers being in the normal range and the virus amount next to zero for over a year after the Interferon-Ribavirin treatment ended, the virus was back at the same level it was prior to the treatment. I had to accept it would probably be my dancing partner for the remainder of my life. All the suffering of those side effects—some of which still lingered in the form of fatigue, occasional skin rash outbreaks, and a foggy brain—had been for nothing. I didn't tell Mom. I didn't want to burden her with more worries.

My old cynicism returned. I even started making notes for a new novel. The basic story was this: An over-the-hill, long-time foreign professor at a second-rate Japanese university that is going through its death throes faces a series of mini-calamities that in the end pushes him over the edge. The first chapter starts off with the guy gritting his teeth and getting out of bed with all sorts of pain in his hips, knees, and ankles. He hobbles downstairs, makes a cup of coffee, puffs on a cigarette, and is lost in foggy thoughts. The doorbell rings. He limps to the door with a bad attitude. He opens the door to find some Japanese Jehovah's Witnesses. He tears into them. Next, he heads to a doctor's appointment (riding painfully on a bicycle), where he finds out that his hepatitis C is back and rampaging again. That sends him out the door angry and depressed. On his way home, he's stopped by two rookie cops. They suspect he's stolen his own bicycle because the lock key is missing. This sends him on a rant that almost lands him in jail.

I thought it had potential for some good dark humor. I'd keep piling on one thing after another until the foreign professor finally lost his mind. My tentative title was "You Can't Fix Stupid." That was as far as I got. My fog brain was incapable of carrying the idea further.

A package from Mom brought a smile back to my face. She'd finished her book project on her memories of Grandma and

Granddad Frederick. It turned out beautifully and included some of my favorite family stories of her childhood. Along with the hardcover book, she sent us her first attempts at Japanese ink brush painting. They were mostly small paintings of birds, flowers, and mountains. We thought they were great.

Mom returned to her Japanese study with a vengeance. It seemed at times an obsession. Over the last two years, I'd set up a series of homework assignments for her that involved verb and adjective conjugation patterns and vocabulary acquisition. I figured having Mom try to learn the *kana* alphabet was too much, so I had her use Romaji spelling to create simple sentences that came to her mind. She'd send me the sentences. I'd correct them and make some comments. We'd go over everything in detail during our bimonthly Skype calls. What started out as a trickle now turned into a torrent. Mom was sending sample sentences every week, sometimes twice a week. We enjoyed these sessions.

Mom's health continued to improve. She'd been using an Advair inhaler twice a day for almost a year. Terri tested her breathing every morning to see how much oxygen was in her blood. Her pulmonary physician was so pleased with her progress that he told her she didn't have to take the Advair anymore unless she had a problem breathing from asthma or a bad cold. Her next goal was to work on getting off the oxygen at night. Her torn rotator cuff on her right shoulder was still very sore, but she'd decided not to have surgery as she was functioning OK and was on a low dose pain medication. Her doctors told her she wasn't the best candidate for surgery right now anyway. Her blood pressure and cholesterol were normal again, so they took her off the medications for those ailments.

Mom was so thankful that she wrote a long letter detailing

her feelings of gratitude of still being alive and in one piece, while realizing that the most difficult thing for her to adjust to was having to slow down.

Despite all the political drama at FIU, things were going smoothly for the English course. Both the in-school and high school speech contests went well. I took all the video files we recorded and turned them into DVDs. It was a time-consuming process. There were a lot of file conversions and editing to be done, but the more I worked on the project, the faster I got with fewer mistakes. I gave all the in-school participants and the participating high schools a copy. I sent Mom and Terri copies of the DVDs and the printed programs.

The years from 2012 to 2016 flew by. That period was basically a countdown to my retirement and FIU closing. At the end of November 2012, Shi-chan's father passed away in his sleep. He was eighty-seven and didn't suffer too much. He spent the final month of his life in the hospital and surrounded by family members.

Shi-chan and I went back to Yuasa for the Buddhist wake, funeral, and cremation. At the crematorium, as family members and I watched the corpse being shoved into the giant furnace, Shi-chan punched my arm lightly and whispered, "Did you see that?" I didn't know what she was talking about. Later while we waited in a separate room for the body to burn completely, Shi-chan said that in that moment before the furnace, she saw her father's ghost depart the body, stop for a second hovering above the body, and with a large grin look at her and say "Goodbye!" in English. I didn't know how to react. I said, "Really? Wow."

When the cremated body was ready, family members returned to retrieve the ashes and bones, which were very white. The crematory operator said Shi-chan's father must've eaten a lot of calcium in his life to have such strong bones. Seeing the cremated body and using two large chopsticks, one bamboo and the other willow, to pick out a bone to put in the family urn was a new cultural experience for me. It was surprisingly clean and made me think it was the way to go, rather than being thrown in a hole in the ground and have worms devour your corpse.

Mom wrote back to give her condolences immediately after receiving my e-mail informing her of the death. She recalled that on one of her visits to Japan, Shi-chan's father called and the two of them sang a duet of "When Irish Eyes are Smiling" on the phone—Mom in English, Shi-chan's dad in Japanese. Despite not understanding each other, they'd laughed and communicated. Mom said it would always be a special memory.

These years were a rough time for Mom and Terri. Mom's body continued to deteriorate. Terri's MS had returned, and her battles with its symptoms were constant. The one thing that amazed me during this period of "one thing after another" was how Mom never lost her ability to see the positive. There were moments when she faltered and a certain attitude of fatalism mixed with cynicism appeared, but she always suppressed that and gave thanks for the blessings she had, especially concerning her family.

None of us knew just how badly sepsis could weaken the body. Mom's immune system was severely compromised. She became increasingly susceptible to infections and viruses. Starting with an infected toe in the summer of 2011, she dealt continuously with migraines, the flu, yeast infections, suspected cancer lumps on her chest and back, sleep apnea, vertigo, wild fluctuations of blood pressure, and overall fatigue. How she managed to soldier on was a mystery and a miracle to us. We were lucky Terri was there to care for her and know what to do at the exact moment it needed to be done. Even Mom's doctors marveled at Terri's knowledge and ability. They often told Mom she'd probably be dead if not for Terri.

But Terri, too, suffered greatly from her own afflictions. During this time, she dealt with bladder and kidney infections, MS exacerbations that affected her eyes, pre-cancerous polyps in her colon, a benign tumor on her esophagus, muscle spasms and cramps, nerve pain, crippling knee pain, and dental surgery requiring removal of all bottom teeth due to soft bone tissue. Her doctor said she needed a knee replacement, but that couldn't be done because her MS ruled her out as a candidate for surgery.

The strength of the two of them working together to carry on was inspiring. Remarkably, they seemed to alternate between who was down and who was up. Rarely were the two of them down at the same time. More than anything else, a combination of grit, determination, and a sense of the absurd helped them through each crisis. Mom often wrote how important our Skype calls and e-mails were in helping them keep their spirits up.

Of all the episodes, the biggest scare occurred when Mom fractured her pelvis and was hospitalized again. For almost a month, a flurry of e-mails and Skype calls with Terri kept us informed of the details.

On April 4, 2014, Mom was sitting at her dining table and turned to reach for something on the chest behind her. Her pelvic bone fractured suddenly, but she didn't fall. She was in great pain, so Terri took her to the hospital. The doctors did a CT scan and, in addition to the fracture, found some stones in her liver. Her bile duct was clogged. They decided to manage her pain with medication and put her on physical therapy. Three days after she entered the hospital, a doctor performed a liver procedure to try to remove the stones. Some of the stones were too big. The doctor put in a stent so the stones would bounce against it and break into smaller pieces. The procedure would have to be repeated in six weeks, at which time the stent would be removed.

The day after surgery, Mom was doing OK but had a slight fever and some abdominal pain. She was given antibiotics. Terri reported that Mom's liver was hurting worse than the fracture. Before moving Mom to physical therapy, the nurses gave her exercises to do in bed. They also walked her a little. The next day, a CT scan showed that everything was working, and the stent was perfectly placed. She still had liver pain and nausea when she ate. Terri was satisfied, however, with the care Mom was getting. The hospital staff fell in love with Mom.

On April 11, Mom transferred to a rehabilitation facility, where she started both occupational and physical therapies. Within two weeks, she was walking around on her own with a walker. We were able to connect a few times via Skype. It was encouraging to hear her describe her progress, talk about her daily goals and how she was doing everything she was told to do, and see her smiling. She was released on April 29. The nurses told her she was the shortest-term patient they'd ever had with a pelvis fracture.

Mom sent us an e-mail the next day telling us how great it was to be home and thanking us for the Skype calls. She was especially grateful to Terri, who kept detailed notes on all the medications, what they were for, and precisely when they had to be taken. It was a strict schedule, but Terri made sure Mom followed it to the letter. Mom wrote that her head was dizzy from trying to keep track of all the doctor appointments, therapies, and medication. Even so, she was already working on some new sentences for her Japanese study.

Mom worked hard at her rehabilitation at home. Every day, she went for walks using her walker, increasing the distance each time. Her therapists instructed her to take just one walk each day the first week she was home and to do their suggested exercises. She did them all and was feeling a little stronger each time. She decided she wouldn't drive anymore for fear of turning or twisting and fracturing her brittle bones again. I felt certain she was once again, at the age of eighty-eight, on the comeback trail when she closed her e-mail with "I've been thinking about several projects I want to try. There are many interesting challenges out there and all we have to do is *try!*"

Just before I was scheduled to come to Portland with another PELA homestay-study student, there were more setbacks. First, Portland went through a bad heat wave. Temperatures were near a hundred degrees Fahrenheit with high humidity. Mom spent a lot of time in the bathroom vomiting, didn't sleep well, and felt woozy because of the slow flow of oxygen in her system. About the same time, she tripped and injured her left wrist. Two doctors thought she'd fractured it; two others thought it was a severe sprain. They put her in a splint. When Mom reported this news, she capped it off with "Other than all of this, life is just peachy keen!"

25

Retirement on the Horizon

W HEN the student and I arrived at the airport, Terri and Mom were waiting for us. I was surprised Mom had the strength to be there. She'd aged a lot from the previous year and looked very tired, but her eyes shone brightly and her hug was as great as ever. For the entire time I was in Portland, there were no problems with the student, so Mom, Terri, and I were able to spend quiet time together at the dining table telling stories and reminiscing about the past.

I self-medicated to my heart's desire. Over the past ten years, I'd corresponded off and on with Hammond Guthrie, a painter and writer who wrote a memoir titled *AsEverWas: Memoirs of a Beat Survivor* about his many adventures around the world and befriending such Beat artists and authors as Lawrence Ferlinghetti, Del Close, Gregory Corso, Allen Ginsberg, Richie Havens, and William Burroughs. He'd created and edited an online literary journal called *The 3rd Page: A Journal of Ongrowing Natures*. It contained a lot of antiwar material. In 2004, I submitted an article titled "Where Have All the C.O. Soldiers Gone?" and he published it. He'd recently moved to Portland. I asked him for advice on how to get a medical marijuana card. He told me not to bother with bureaucratic hassles and just come visit his house. He'd be glad to turn me on to some excellent stuff.

Two days after arriving in Portland, I gave Hammond a call and set a time to hook up. I took a city bus and got off at the nearest stop to his house. He was taller than I, had soft, blue eyes, and wore a trimmed, white goatee. He greeted me with a warm smile and a cup of French roast coffee. Over the next three hours, we sampled such brands as Ice Queen, Blue City Diesel, Crazy Train, Casey Jones, and White Widow. He showed me several of his recent paintings. We exchanged life stories and listened to Bob Dylan's *Modern Times* album. When I left, I was thoroughly stoned and equipped with more than enough buds of Ice Queen and Blue City Diesel to last far beyond the two weeks I'd be in the area. I was blessed. And blissed.

My days at Mom's apartment fell into a relaxing routine. I'd get up in the morning, prepare a cup of coffee, head outside to the carport area and smoke a few bowls of Ice Queen, study Japanese with Mom for an hour, do a half hour of stretches, go outside for a few more bowls, visit some more, take a nap, spend some time online checking news, write e-mails and reports back to FIU, have a delicious dinner cooked by Terri, toke a few bowls of Blue City Diesel for a lazy evening buzz, sip on a couple bottles of alcohol-free beer, exchange stories with Mom and Terri until they went to bed, and read until I fell asleep.

Our chats covered every aspect of our lives. Mom had done a lot of reflecting on her life over the past few months. Her stories this time were filled more with a feeling of appreciation for the joys and experiences she'd accumulated than with the humor that filled her stories of years ago.

Sometimes we talked about the troubles at FIU. She worried

about the school going downhill and my taking on too many responsibilities, about my health and having to use a cane to get around, and what the future held for Shi-chan and me. I told her how our board of directors threatened to slam the door to enrollment shut three years ago if we didn't hit the target number over the next two years. We didn't. With our tails between our legs, we teachers went begging in March 2013 for a one-year extension. The board agreed, but a twenty percent cut in salary and no bonuses were part of the deal. That year passed and the enrollment numbers were even worse. The inevitable happened in April. The board closed the school to further enrollment. Just before the announcement was made, six teachers either retired or jumped ship to a different school. We'd have to face the next two years with only eighteen full-time teachers, down from a peak of almost fifty a few years before. We'd still have to see the freshmen class through to their graduation, but the future didn't look bright for the younger teachers and staff members.

I reassured Mom that as far as my own retirement package and pension went, I was in good shape, but the mood on campus was grim and much of the fun had been taken out of the job. I told her I couldn't complain because it'd been a good gig for a long time and would allow me some money to live on in my retirement.

Concerning my health, I said that although I had to use a cane to get around as my ankles, knees, and left hip were arthritic, my daily regimen of stretching and frequent swimming at a local city pool helped keep me somewhat flexible and out of a wheelchair. Shi-chan was doing great. Her interpreting-translating school at home was surviving and she still had three part-time university teaching jobs, although the class for sophomores at FIU would disappear in a year. She wanted to keep working for a few more years. Our home would be paid off in another year, so we'd be able to have food on the table and a place to lay our heads for a good long while. Shi-chan had also discovered the benefits of yoga breathing and stretching and had kept at it for over a year. We did all of our own cooking and ate healthy food.

Mom looked relieved as I explained this, but when I gave her the details of all the work I had to do, she said she worried I was working too hard. In addition to the PELA program, the speech contest, guiding my seminar students through their graduation papers, and the wear and tear of pushing an aging body to keep moving in the classroom, I was also now the head of two committees. There wasn't much work involved in heading the library committee, but heading the editorial committee for publishing the school journal was a challenge. With so few teachers remaining, it appeared we wouldn't be able to recruit the three or four articles needed to justify publishing the first-semester edition. If we missed publishing one issue, we'd lose half the budget money for the following year. I didn't want the journal to sink on my shift, so I pulled up my britches and put together the first of a two-part series of academic papers about teaching English discussion and critical thinking skills to Japanese university students. That paper turned out to be the one that kept the journal alive for two more years.

Mom shook her head as if to say, "See what I mean?"

I said, "Well, you know, Mom, I inherited that trait from you." We grinned at each other.

Before returning to Japan, I talked to Terri about the possibility of her getting a medical marijuana card. For years, she'd been taking a multitude of painkillers and other medications for her MS symptoms. The side effects they caused were worse than the symptoms. She couldn't tolerate smoking weed, but I thought she should at least try some of the edibles to see if they'd give her some relief. She agreed to give it a try. I gave her the few buds from Hammond that I hadn't smoked. She could use them to cook with some butter for making brownies.

Not long after, Terri wrote to say she'd tried some brownies before going to bed and woke up with no spasms and less foot and body pain. That was enough to convince her. She went through the application process and got her card two months later. As she started using edibles regularly, she noticed more changes. She'd had GERD acid reflux problems for a long time. She had to be careful about what she ate and was taking a powerful heartburn drug called Prilosec twice a day. She reduced that to once a day and her stomach trouble got better. She still had nighttime spasms, but they didn't make her get out of bed and go walking in the middle of the night to get rid of them. They'd start to come on but wouldn't turn into gut-wrenching, knock-you-on-your-ass spasms. Most of her neuropathy in her feet and hands went away. She said she was sleeping well for the first time in years.

Mom's condition, however, didn't get any better. Life was still kicking her hard. Her tenacity in battling sepsis was inspiring. Her doctor put her on a stronger medication for two weeks to try to bring her blood pressure fluctuations under control. Her headaches, vertigo, and overall fatigue got worse, but the medication worked for a short while. While on the medication, she didn't have the energy to do any Japanese study. She apologized for that in one of her e-mails: "I'll get back to the homework soon. Today is another one of those 'dizzy' days and I'm trying to outrun a darn headache that is trying to catch up with me. And I'm going to win!"

The next few months followed a pattern. Mom would rally

for a few days, then her blood pressure would fluctuate wildly again. Her doctor would try a different medication, which always produced more vertigo, nausea, and fatigue. When Mom's best friend's husband fell victim to cardiac arrest, was hospitalized, had by-pass surgery, and faced a long rehabilitation process, Mom fell into a depression. She also suffered from what she called "a flu that never seems to go away." Despite everything, she still churned out a few Japanese sentences a week for me to check. We continued our bimonthly Skype calls and lessons, which seemed to provide a morale boost for both Mom and Terri. At the end of one of those calls, Mom said, "Honey, we love you two to the moon and back. I'm sorry if I look like a country farm mule kicked me when I wasn't looking, but I feel better now after talking to you kids."

Spring arrived. I thought about retiring a year early but made a deal with the new school president when he asked me to teach another year. I agreed to work one more year as long as I didn't have to be the head of any more committees. I also got the OK to get funds for one more speech contest, this time for FIU and junior college students only, and one more chaperone trip to Portland with the homestay-study students.

Five students committed to participate in the final PELA program. I was pleased when Linda D. wrote to say she thought she could spend a couple of days in Portland while I was there. She'd started writing a few years before and published a series of medieval and fantasy novels she titled *Crowns and Kingdoms.* I helped her with the editing of three of the five novels. She and her husband had three girls, who were all now nearly grown up. Although we'd corresponded for years, we hadn't seen each other in person for probably fifteen years.

Portland had a bad heat wave for two weeks in July that

knocked Mom flat with heat prostration. Terri notified us Mom had diarrhea, nausea, and actual vomiting for two days. She said she needed to keep the apartment cool for the rest of the summer so Mom wouldn't have another reaction. She wasn't sure if Mom would be up to greeting me at the airport when I arrived as the crowds and the heat were too dangerous for her.

Mom was mostly recovered when the students and I showed up. She came to the airport with Terri, gave me a big hug, greeted the students before they left with their homestay families, and curled up quietly in the back seat of the car while Terri drove us home. Linda D. flew in from San Francisco two days later and stayed in a hotel near Mom's place.

We hardly went out at all during those two weeks. We spent lazy days preparing meals, telling stories of our current lives, and reminiscing about the old days. Linda D. and I had good discussions about writing and her family. I made one Skype call to Dick. It was an awkward conversation. We spoke mainly in platitudes. He was glad to be out of Humboldt County and back in Houston, where the Veterans Association had helped him find a room and a part-time job. He didn't give any details about his medical problems. He chain-smoked four cigarettes before we said goodbye.

Taking advantage of her new status as a qualified medical marijuana patient, Terri had stocked up on some good buds for me. My head was kept in a good place. There were no student emergencies to deal with. Time passed quickly. As Mom wrote later, "It seems like you just came in the door and before we knew what happened, you were packing up to return to Japan."

Immediately after returning to Japan, I contacted all the speech contest entrants to set up meetings to go over their speeches with them. Somehow I got all the entrants to come to appointments, write their drafts, rewrite them a couple of times, translate them into Japanese, and send them to me. The next step was to put together all the files for the speech contest program. That involved formatting them to make sure they all had the same font, spacing, and margins before putting them inside a simple cover. I planned to print up sixty copies to hand out at the contest on November 14. I'd save one copy for Mom and Terri.

Near the end of October, life dealt me another gut punch. Shannon Kelly passed away in his sleep. We'd shared many laughs on the phone just a few weeks before at Mom's. I reported the news to Mom and Terri and asked them to say a prayer for him and think of all the laughter he brought during his life. They responded quickly with words of condolence and special memories they had.

Later that week, Mom stopped by a small Catholic church when she and her best friend were out for a cup of coffee together. She asked the priest to say a mass in memory of Shannon from Mom, Terri, and me.

When Mom asked me if I was going to sign an online memorial page, I told her I hesitated to sign anything. Online messages seemed too public to me. My relationship with and memories of Shannon were more private and special than that. I preferred to keep them that way rather than broadcast them to the whole world. I'd already constructed a little shrine for him in my head, where I could go anytime to reminisce, have a laugh, and share whatever might be on my mind.

Once again, we were on the same wavelength. Mom's response:

> I loved the latest e-mail you sent on the 17th, especial-
> ly the short paragraph telling about your thoughts
> of signing a memory page for our dear Shannon. I

feel exactly the same as you do, Bob. We have our own interpretations of our own memories of times spent with Shannon. I think the deep feelings about those we love and the private shrines we keep in our minds for those we love are meant to be very private for our own comfort and acceptance of the fact they have left us. This way we do not actually lose them. I feel this way about you, my son, knowing the bond we have between us will never be broken. That bond is too strong, too precious. I will always be with you even though my time here is flying by too fast. Any memories we have of time with each other will never be gone or lost. I know you feel the same.

Our final speech contest went off without a hitch. The girls who took on the M.C. and video camera jobs performed well. The fifteen speakers did their best. Everyone had fun at the party afterward. After the party, I took the M.C. and video camera girl out to a grilled chicken restaurant to pay them back for their help. Over the next few days, I put together the DVD, which included the M.C.'s introduction, some goofy scenes of the party, the awards ceremony, and about thirty pictures at the end. As with previous contest DVDs, I sent Mom and Terri a copy. The only big job responsibility that remained was to help my ten senior students finish their graduation thesis papers.

With the countdown to retirement reduced to fewer than a hundred days, I began thinking seriously about what to do in my post-work life. Regaining my health was at the top of the list. Although Shi-chan and I'd almost always returned to Yuasa to spend a few days of the New Year's holiday with her family, I opted this time to stay home. My hip, knees, and ankles just couldn't take the narrow, winding stairs of their place anymore, not to mention all the walking involved in taking planes and trains. For the first time, I thought about getting a hip replacement.

More important than the hip, however, was my hepatitis C. I'd read about some new direct-acting antiviral oral medicines (DAAs) that in clinical trials lasting twelve weeks cured ninety-five percent of the participating hepatitis C patients. There were few side effects compared to the previous Interferon-Ribavirin treatments. Applications by four different companies producing these DAAs were approved by Japan in 2014 and 2015.

I sent an e-mail to Terri's private account explaining I'd decided to go for this new treatment. I wanted to keep it a secret from Mom because I didn't want her stewing over how unfair it was for her kids to suffer like we did. I knew how she could work herself into a bucket of tears over that. An MRI in October found no cancer cells, but my liver was slowly scarring after decades of carrying the virus. It hadn't reached the point of cirrhosis, but if I didn't repress or kill the virus while the scarring was in the early stages, the chances for cancer cells developing would increase. I'd read how a lot of American health insurance companies weren't touching the treatment unless the patient was in the more severe stages of the illness. I supposed they didn't want to be bankrupted by the exorbitant cost of trying to cover half the boomer generation. As far as I knew, my insurance would cover seventy percent of the cost, which meant I'd have to fork over between twenty and thirty thousand dollars. That was a lot of money, but I figured it'd be worth it if I got cured. This could be my retirement gift to myself. My doctor thought I could start the treatment sometime after the start of the new year. The timing would be good as all classes and tests would be finished by the first week of February.

Terri was supportive of my decision. She said she'd keep mum.

Our wedding party in Itami, 1987

Mom and Aunt Louis in hakama, *Itami, 1986*

Honeymoon in Multnomah Falls, Oregon, 1987

Fukuoka Women's Junior College English Department teachers
(Ichikawa on the far left), 1994

The two mothers in Chikushino, 2005

Mom and me on the hill leading to the Fukuoka International University campus, 2006

Shi-chan and her shamisen *teacher, 2006*

In front of our new house, 2006

At a friend's son's wedding, 2014

Terri and Mom, 2016

26

Retirement, Professor Emeritus, and Dick's Last Appearance

THE calendar turned to 2016. I turned sixty-five. Mom turned ninety. My final class was on February 1. After that, all I had to do was correct papers, hand in grades, and attend a few meetings until my official retirement day on April 1. April Fool's Day. It seemed somehow appropriate.

My teaching career was over. As I reflected on the past twenty-four years of teaching full-time at the college and university level in Japan, the feeling that rose above all others was gratitude. Sure, there were all the problems associated with the battles between the teachers and the board of directors, but I was grateful to the school for hiring me at the age of forty-one and giving me the chance to work in a fairly stable job with good benefits. I'd been able to teach without restrictions, do the research I wanted to do, and contribute in many ways outside the classroom. A lot of responsibilities were heaped on my shoulders through the years, but I managed to complete them all without causing the school to collapse. I was able to work until sixty-five, which was rare in an age of corporate takeovers and forced layoffs for many people in their fifties. I'd be getting a decent severance package, as well as a Japanese pension. Shi-chan and I made the final payment on our house several months before, so we had no bills hanging over our heads. Who would've known on that day thirty-three years earlier when I arrived in Japan on a one-way ticket and almost no cash in my pocket that things would turn out this way?

Shi-chan would turn sixty in March. She planned to continue working until she was at least sixty-five. My main role would now be full-time househusband. I also had plans to put together a digital archive of all my books, academic papers, audio recordings, videos of my 2004 TV interview and thirty-minute documentary, and many pictures. Another thing was to get back to exercising. Although I had a daily regimen of stretching and breathing exercises, I wanted to start swimming three or four times a week again.

First, however, I had to go through the hepatitis C treatment. I planned on doing the Harvoni treatment after it became available in Japan at the end 2015, but my doctor introduced me to another option, which was the drug called Viekira Pak, made by the AbbVie company. It was approved in Japan about the same time as Harvoni. It was basically the same type of protease inhibitor and the clinical trial results were as good as Harvoni's. Also, at the hospital I went to, there was a financial assistance program specific to Viekira Pak. The doctor gave me the application forms, which Shi-chan helped me fill out and mail. It took several meetings with bureaucrats and providing a bunch of extra paperwork, but I finally got approved. The program was mainly for Japanese, but I qualified because I had a permanent resident visa and had paid into the teachers' union and insurance programs for twenty-four years.

On the day after my last class, I started taking the daily pills. I experienced some nausea and heartburn, but most of that disappeared after the fifth day. Fatigue was the main side effect, but my joint pain also increased. If I stayed off my feet and did my stretches, that pain receded. About once a week, I got a bad headache. I attributed that to not drinking enough water. It was a strange kind of fatigue, particularly heavy in the mornings. At times, it was almost like being stoned. I'd drift into fog head territory and sometimes find myself staring at the walls for minutes on end without being aware of it. Getting myself to move took a strong effort of will. Throughout the twelve weeks, I slept deeply and had a good appetite. I didn't lose any weight like I had with the Interferon-Ribavirin poison I'd endured. In fact, I had a bad craving for cookies, donuts, and other junk food. I gained about eight pounds. The virus went undetectable in the fifth week. The goal was to have it stay that way three months beyond the end of the treatment. I hoped that finally, after seventeen years of fighting the disease, I'd slain the dragon. The amount I had to pay for the treatment was surprisingly cheap: about three hundred dollars.

I'd barely settled into this new chapter of my life when another disaster occurred. On Thursday, April 14 around 9:30 p.m. while Shi-chan and I were watching TV, we felt a large jolt and our house started shaking. Nothing fell, but we looked at each other and said, "Whoa, that was a strong one." We switched over to the NHK station. There were only quick updates from local stations via telephone. The quake was centered in Kumamoto Prefecture, some seventy kilometers south of us, and estimated at magnitude 6.5. At an emergency press conference, Chief Cabinet

Secretary Suga announced there was no damage to any of the three nuclear reactor facilities located within a hundred and fifty kilometers of the earthquake zone, and that there was no danger of a nuclear incident. About forty minutes after the first quake, we felt another jolt, but the shaking was less severe than before.

We spent much of the next day watching TV news that showed scenes of fires, power outages, collapsed bridges, mud- and rockslides that had engulfed roads and houses, warped rail lines, and large holes in the earth. Two national treasures—Kumamoto Castle and Aso Shrine—were badly damaged. Many people wrapped in blankets sat outside their homes. Others were camped out in rice fields. Throughout the day, there were dozens of aftershocks. Residents near a dam were told to leave for fear of the dam collapsing.

At another press conference, Suga stated there was a need for a constitutional clause that would give the government extra powers during natural disasters. Some media and academics appeared on other channels accusing the Shinzo Abe cabinet of trying to take advantage of the disaster to push ahead with Japan's remilitarization and constitutional reform. An even bigger jolt shook our house at 1:30 in the morning. Both Shi-chan and I sat straight up in bed, ready to dive under it, but the shaking stopped. There was no damage in our house. We found out later that one registered as magnitude 7.3 at the epicenter in Kumamoto Prefecture.

Some of my former colleagues and students were from the Kumamoto area. I managed to get in touch by e-mail with most of them. Fortunately, all were OK, although some suffered damage to their homes and had to be evacuated. The bigger quake caused even more damage and leveled many structures that managed to survive the initial one. Thousands of Self-Defense

Force troops were sent in to help with the distribution of food and water, but for the first few days, the worst areas were nearly impossible to access. Over a hundred and eighty thousand people were evacuated and living in overcrowded shelters. More than four hundred thousand homes were without water, one hundred thousand without electricity. Heavy rains hampered rescue and evacuation efforts. Hundreds of people were spending most of their time in their cars, which was causing a lot of economy class syndrome cases and even a few deaths.

The government insisted there was no danger to the nearby nuclear facilities, but concerns among anti-nuclear political groups and some media continued. At one point, the head of the Nuclear Regulation Agency apologized for the lack of news in the wake of the earthquakes.

Over fifty people died and nearly two thousand were injured, but tens of thousands of lives were displaced or destroyed. It would be years before roads, bridges, buildings, and different infrastructure could be repaired or rebuilt. Once again, we received many letters, e-mails, and phone calls from friends and family worried about us. We said a prayer for the victims every day.

At the end of April, my Viekira Pak treatment ended. The virus was still undetectable. It was tempting to share the good news with Mom, but I couldn't bring myself to do it. For one thing, I hadn't told her the last treatment was unsuccessful. Also, it seemed to me, the amount of suffering her sepsis caused her was so overwhelming that I might exacerbate her misery by bragging about how good I felt.

For the past few months, Mom had dealt with a slew of medical issues. Her doctors were convinced it was all connected to her sepsis. January was particularly hard on her. First, her primary doctor gave her a shot for her hip bursitis and the next day her back went out of whack. She had no tingling or numbness in her feet or legs, so the doctor ruled out a slipped disc or anything more serious. He sent her to a physical therapist for three visits and gave her some additional pain medication.

She developed an ingrown toenail and had to go to a podiatrist. A few years before, she'd also had an ingrown toenail. At that time, the podiatrist removed the toenail, but she then had to fight a bad infection for weeks. Since then, the problem had flared up occasionally. She was half expecting to have to undergo having the nerves around the nail cut out so that it wouldn't happen again, but the podiatrist said that wasn't necessary. He did remove the portion of the toenail that was growing inward. Mom said that really hurt. He told her to keep soaking the toes and gave her some spacers to put between the big toe and the next one on both feet. One of the toes became infected again. The podiatrist ended up having to cut out part of the nerves attached to the toe. I couldn't imagine how painful that was. Mom continued soaking the toes. Terri put ointment and new bandages on each time.

The toe problem was followed by a yeast infection that wouldn't disappear. Mom said the rash didn't itch, but it greatly reduced what little energy she had. The root of this, too, was the sepsis badly inhibiting her immune system. Her doctor told her that not much was known about sepsis because so few people who got it survived. That made it difficult to know what to treat it with and for how long. Her vertigo, erratic blood pressure, and occasional swelling of her ankles were all ongoing. Mom was worn down and feeling enough was enough, but she seemed resigned to dealing with these problems for the remainder of her life. At the same time, she said she was willing to put up with all the tests, the different medications and their debilitating side effects, and feeling like a guinea pig if the research on her case could help just one other person avoid what she had to endure.

Terri wrote me separately that she thought Mom's mental state was starting to decline. She said Mom was showing some signs that things were not quite right but also not quite wrong. For example, Mom's immediate short-term memory. She often forgot some of what Terri had said or asked five minutes earlier. This wasn't happening all the time, but Terri thought there was something almost every day that showed Mom was slowing down. Other than that, Mom was eating well and still got a kick out of life, albeit in somewhat different ways than before. She was now more of an observer of life than an active participant. She was still studying her Japanese and doing some painting. I was glad to hear that.

Shortly after, reality came knocking. For too long, I'd been bragging to others about how tough Mom was and how she'd probably outlive us all. I simply had not wanted to face how old and sick she really was. Always during our Skype calls and lessons, we'd managed to joke about Saint Patrick up in heaven and how he'd better look after us when it was our turn. Maybe I'd even started to believe in pixie dust as something real. Terri's e-mail was a necessary wakeup call.

Terri wrote that at a recent checkup, she'd talked with their doctor about Mom's blood pressure difficulties and her body-brain disconnect. The doctor told her it meant Mom had moved into the beginning of end-stage congestive heart failure. It was no longer a matter of if, but a matter of when. Overall, Mom was doing really well. For now, her water retention, fluctuating blood pressure, and extreme vertigo had subsided. Mom could stay at this stage for days, months, or even years, but her shortness of breath was happening more often, her lack of stamina getting worse, and her general fatigue getting to the point where she'd nod off to sleep for a few seconds or minutes while at the computer, studying, or reading a book.

Terri decided she wasn't going to be very strict anymore about the food Mom ate. She just wanted Mom's days to be full of what she enjoyed. They weren't yet at the point where Mom needed extra care or, for that matter, hospice. She'd promised Mom that she'd do her best to keep Mom out of hospitals. Terri said that Mom wasn't ready to leave us yet, but we should enjoy every e-mail, chat, and lesson while we could.

A week later, Mom took a nasty fall and banged her jaw. Luckily, she didn't break anything, but she had an ugly bruise for a couple of weeks and could eat only soft foods. During a Skype call, Mom said, "Do you think someone was trying to tell me I talk too much?" Her humor was still intact, but gradually it became darker. Her e-mails, too, revealed more of her fatigue and resignation. She kept sending me homework to check. It was as if she didn't do it, she would die.

In some ways, I thought I could understand her thought process. I knew that in quiet moments, she was spending much time reflecting on her life, going through that pentimento process of looking at everything again from a different perspective, feeling perhaps a sharper pain from the regrets and a more poignant joy from the highlights.

My recently completed digital archive project sent me on a similar journey into the past. Throughout my entire working career, I'd always thought ahead, making plans for what was to come, whether it was a lesson plan for a class the next day or a long-term plan for a writing or school project. Since retiring, however, I'd begun to look back on the past, contemplating the multitude of roads traveled and experiences undergone in this life. What had I accomplished? Where had I come from? Where had I gone? How had I arrived at this point in my life? I went through boxes of books, pictures, manuscripts, video and audio tapes, letters, and documents that I'd collected through the years. I organized everything to try to make sense of it all. The result was a huge digital archive, copied on DVDs and USB memory sticks that I sent out to Mom and Terri, Linda D., Alice, Billy, Michelle, and a few special friends.

Basically, the archive was a version of my life story. My thinking was that maybe when Shi-chan and I kicked the bucket, there'd be some niece or nephew who asked, "Who was Uncle Bob? What did he do? How and why did he end up in Japan?" They could check the archive and get a hint about who this character was, where he came from, and what he did with his life. Above all, I thought this project would make a nice present for Mom. I was pleased when Mom wrote back immediately after receiving it. She wrote that despite feeling lousy most of the time, she could now look forward each day to seeing and reading my life story.

The final years of Mom's life are now a blur to me of routines, medical emergencies, brief periods of respite, and a continuation of our correspondence and Skype lessons, which over time saw us repeating some of the same things we'd gone over many times. The frequency of the correspondence didn't change much, but the contents did. There were fewer reports of family gossip and more of the treatment, medications, and pain she was enduring. These descriptions became longer and more detailed, but always capped off with a "that's life" comment. Often she included a statement that her own suffering was nothing compared to what I'd undergone with my

Interferon-Ribavirin treatment torture. That always brought tears to my eyes because I knew the opposite was true. What a mother she was! She always let me know—and I was elated to hear—how proud I'd made her by following my heart and never giving up on my dreams.

Somehow we all managed to hobble through 2017 with minimal problems. There were, however, a few obstacles to overcome. In addition to all the ailments Mom had to deal with, her arthritic right knee bothered her more. Terri's knees, too, were so bad she needed to be fitted for special braces. She also started getting back spasms. She and Mom discussed the possibility of having to get a wheelchair if the braces didn't help. Mom's primary doctor tried having Mom drastically reduce the amount of morphine he had her on, but that resulted in horrible withdrawal headaches, vomiting, and increased pain. Terri got angry and locked horns with the doctor.

My left hip also got worse. I searched the internet for a better cane than the one I had been using. Some shock-absorbing walking aids made in the U.K. by a company called Flexyfoot caught my attention. I ordered a pair and was amazed how well I could maintain balance, have a comfortable grip, and reduce pain when using one of their canes. I recommended the walking aids to Mom and Terri. They fell in love with the canes. In particular, Mom said she was able to "graduate from the walker to the cane." Her posture was better, going up and down stairs was easier, the grip was comfortable with little stress on her shoulders, and she felt more stable. Her improved mobility put a smile back on her face.

Mom kept pumping out Japanese sentences. Sometimes the quality of what she produced astounded me. At other times, it seemed she'd forgotten everything she'd learned. I could see that this was bothering her. I thought that spending too much time on her study might be causing some of her headaches. I suggested she take a break occasionally just to give her brain a rest.

Near the end of August, Mom did a remarkable job on some Japanese sentences she sent me to check. I made extensive notes about the areas she'd covered and sent them along with a long and encouraging e-mail. She had a doctor's appointment the day the e-mail arrived. The doctor told her that he was amazed at what she'd faced and overcome over the past few years. His comment of "Kay, you truly are one fighting Irish woman. I'm so proud of you" left her speechless, a rare event in my estimation. She went home, checked e-mail, found mine, and read it. She was so happy that she wrote back immediately, telling me how encouraging my note was and how proud her doctor was of her.

That high didn't last long. Two months later, Mom got the news that Larry Gernaat, one of her favorite cousins, had cancer of the esophagus. The tumor was malignant and had spread to other parts of the body. Mom was able to talk to him on the phone for about ten minutes. Knowing Larry was going to die devastated Mom. One of the refrains of her life was lamenting how unfair life was and she couldn't understand why bad things and suffering always happened to good people. I had an image in my head of Mom once again having a serious private talk with Saint Patrick. Larry died shortly after Christmas.

Near the end of January, I got some unexpected news that I hoped would alleviate some of Mom's emotional pain. One of the remaining professors at FIU called me at home. He was going to recommend my nomination for professor emeritus status at the next faculty meeting and needed my complete resume. I spent a good portion of the next day putting it together on the correct forms. As I proofread it before sending it off in the mail, I had a chance once more to feel proud of what I'd done. In addition to my tenure as the dean of students and all the committees I'd been a part of, I'd published three novels, one novella used as a textbook, and twenty-four research papers, many of which were cited in other papers and books. I'd also co-authored five reference books and given twenty-one presentations, fourteen in Japanese.

In February, the board of directors approved my nomination. The final FIU group of students graduated in March. The official ceremony for those promoted to professor emeritus status was held on May 10. Six teachers were honored. In total, FIU had nine. According to my certificate, I was number six. It was nice to know that all the work I did, all the research and publications I produced, all the presentations I gave, and all the extra time and efforts I put in for the school and students over the years had not gone unnoticed or unappreciated. The irony was that I was now a professor emeritus for a nonexistent university. At least the junior college was still surviving.

I shared this honor with Mom and Terri and sent them pictures of the ceremony and the certificate. They were elated and sent their congratulations and messages of how proud they were.

A few days after the ceremony, I went to see a hip specialist. An X-ray showed that all the cartilage of the left hip was worn away. Bone was rubbing against bone whenever I moved. The right hip had only about one-third of the cartilage layer left, but there was no pain there, so I could put off dealing with that for a few more years. I decided to have hip replacement surgery at the same hospital I'd gone to for my hepatitis treatments. I liked and trusted the surgeon who'd perform the operation.

I entered the hospital on June 11 and had the surgery the next day. I spent about three weeks of initial recovery and care there before being transferred to a rehabilitation hospital that had an intensive program of daily sessions of special stretches, resistance exercises, and massage before moving on to stationary bicycles, walking treadmills, and weight machines. Neither of the hospitals had Wi-Fi service, so I went digitally cold turkey for six weeks. Shi-chan sent regular messages to Mom and Terri to keep them informed of my progress. I put in a lot of extra work walking with a walker in the beginning and later doing exercises on my own. I was given my freedom ticket on July 26.

Mom's vertigo got worse. The doctors had no answers. All they could do was order different tests and try different medications, which invariably caused her more suffering. The timing couldn't have been worse for Dick and his dramas to reappear in her life.

He called one night and told Terri, "I'm coming out to see you guys. I want to see Mom one more time before she passes." Terri told him it was not a good time and that he couldn't stay at their apartment. He wasn't happy about that, but agreed to stay in a nearby motel for a few days.

A week later, Terri picked him up at the airport and got him a motel room. He looked terrible. His head was stiff and tilted forward because of a neck surgery he'd had. Over the past few years, he'd also had heart, lung, and foot problems. He shuffled rather than walked. His back was ramrod stiff and caused him pain. His eyes were vacant and his skin sallow. He begged Terri to buy him a big bottle of cheap scotch. She did but told him he couldn't drink in Mom's apartment.

Each day was awkward and unpleasant. Terri would pick him up around 11 a.m. By then, he'd already had a few cups of scotch and coffee. She'd help him get in and out of the car and down the steps to the basement entrance to their apartment. He'd sit at the head of the dining table with Mom and Terri on either side.

Mom would try to engage him in conversation by asking about his life in Houston, his job, his friends, or his apartment. He ignored her completely. Occasionally, he picked up a magazine or newspaper, skimmed through it, folded it, and put it back on the table. A few times, Mom reached across the table to pat his hand. He'd yank the hand back with a look of disgust.

Terri would fix a big brunch. They'd eat in silence. Dick would go outside and chain-smoke five or six cigarettes, never bothering to stub out the butts, which smoldered in the ashtray. Around 3 p.m., Terri would take him back to the motel, where he probably drank himself to sleep.

On the final day as Dick prepared to leave, Terri moved the car to a place that would be easy for him to get in. As she got out of the car, she saw Dick at the entrance to their apartment shake his fist at Mom and say something. Mom retreated inside. On the way to the airport, Dick accused Mom of never loving him and causing the breakup of her marriage to Dad. Terri told Dick that was an outright lie and never to come back again. She later asked Mom about the fist Dick made and what he said. Mom told her Dick said, "I could flatten you in a minute." It wasn't the first time he'd threatened her. The only thing he'd done for Mom for the past ten years was to make her cry.

27

Enduring the Final Days

M om's sepsis and vertigo were relentless in their onslaught, which seemed to affect her thinking and understanding processes. More tests were scheduled. She was scared, but wanted some clear answers. Her doctors ordered contrast CT, MRI, and MRA scans of her brain and heart. They thought the blood flow from her heart was uneven. The CT or the MRI would show if there was blockage in any of her arteries.

The tests showed her brain was fine. There were no tumors, no damage, and no sign of strokes—just the normal signs of an aging brain. They also showed Mom had arthritis in her neck, normal blood flow in her brain, and that she'd not had a stroke. The doctors suspected the vertigo was from vestigial migraines or something similar.

The worst test would be the videonystagmography. That was too much of a mouthful, so the doctors used the abbreviation VNG when explaining to her what it was. It had to do with putting a pair of goggles on her that had cameras that would, for the purpose of diagnosing balance or dizziness disorders, track involuntary eye movement. In the end, they called off the VNG because the results would've been invalid anyway due to the pain medication Mom was on and the limitation of movement in her upper body, especially her neck area.

The tests caused a worse dizziness, more vomiting, and bad migraines. Even so, during those two weeks of appointments, panic, and misery, Mom twice sent me a Japanese sentence to check. Seemingly, nothing short of a hard crack to the head would take her away from her Japanese study. With the second sentence, she wrote, "Please bear with me during this tough, painful period. I'm hoping I can still start being *me* one of these days soon. I don't want to cut back on my Japanese study." I felt helpless. There was no end to her suffering. I was overwhelmed by her strength and determination. More than once, the waterworks welled up.

Mom had an appointment to see a neurologist before Christmas. She was hopeful the doctor would have some idea of what could help. Terri thought the problem was possibly loose ear crystals, some strange type of migraine, or her heart. To find the answer, Mom would have to go through more elimination testing, which she didn't want to do. The vertigo also affected Mom's eyesight, making it difficult to read.

When the neurologist checked Mom for the first time, she thought the vertigo was triggered by Mom's migraines. Over the next two months and various tests, she changed her diagnosis. She now believed Mom had positional vertigo and that her arthritic neck was the cause. She recommended physical therapy as the best option for treatment. Mom's arthritis, however, was so bad that even with the physical therapy, the neck might not loosen up. She also thought Mom's eyes should be checked thoroughly and recommended Mom see an ophthalmologist.

Mom started working with a physical therapist at home. Her

insurance covered the cost for as long as the therapist and neurologist thought she needed it. The therapist started slowly as even the simplest exercises were painful. The exercises covered the head, shoulders, neck, back, ribs, and legs. As Mom began tolerating them, others were added. After a month, Mom was getting stronger in her calves, so her balance was a little better. She was turning her head side to side more than she had for several years. Her head still tilted, but Terri planned to have her wear a cervical collar occasionally when the therapy was finished.

About this time, Mom and Terri got another phone call from Dick. He wanted to know my phone number. He planned to come to Japan because he hadn't seen me in many years and he'd never met Shi-chan in person. He supposedly had nine thousand dollars in the bank, but Mom and Terri didn't believe him. They didn't trust him anymore. They changed their phone numbers. They didn't want any more confrontations with him. They were scared of what he seemed capable of doing. They wanted him completely out of their lives. Terri gave me Dick's number just in case I wanted to get in touch with him.

I put a lot of thought into what to do. The more I thought about it, the more it seemed no good could come from Dick visiting Japan. I refrained from calling him in the hope it was a passing whim and he'd realize that a journey like that could spell the end for him. I was afraid if I contacted him, he'd be encouraged to come.

I forgot any problems connected to Dick when I got the next e-mail from Terri. Mom had finally gone to an ophthalmologist. The diagnosis: cataracts were causing her to go blind. The only answer was to remove the cataracts surgically from both eyes. The first surgery was to be done in two weeks. We started doing weekly Skype calls instead of bimonthly calls.

The surgeries went well. Mom's right eye was done first. The left eye was done three weeks later. She sent us a short note saying she'd received the pixie dust and it was working well. She was a little lightheaded and tired after each surgery, but followed the doctor's orders for her recovery. Terri gave her eye drops four times a day and helped her put on an eye patch before bed. Mom was not to bend, push, or pull for two weeks after each cataract removal. At one point about three weeks after the second surgery, they had a scare. It looked like Mom might've gotten an infection in her right eye, but it turned out to be an eyelash stuck in her tear duct. The ophthalmologist removed the eyelash and fitted Mom for new glasses.

A few weeks later, Terri and Mom went over to the eye clinic to have the new glasses checked. On the way out of the clinic, Mom fell in the parking area. She didn't have enough time to call out Terri's name. She went over sideways in less than a second. She landed on asphalt instead of on concrete. Thankfully, she suffered no broken bones, but she was very stiff and sore for a couple weeks.

Just as she was feeling a little better, Mom had another emergency. She woke up one morning and could barely breathe. Terri rushed her to the hospital. The problem was from her sleep apnea. After some oxygen was administered, she started doing better. Terri wrote that actually the trip to the hospital turned out to be a good thing. In the process of trying to figure out what the problem was with her breathing, the doctors found she had a urinary tract infection. She'd had no symptoms except going to the bathroom a lot. It was an issue that could've turned bad if it hadn't been caught.

For the next year, each weekly Skype call became more precious. We'd first talk with Terri for a half hour about how much

President Trump was ruining the country, how Mom was doing, what we were cooking for dinner, and in later months, our concerns about the Covid pandemic and all the riots, protests, and shootings in Portland. Mom would be resting in a chair next to the computer and listening to us. When it was Mom's turn to talk, Terri got up and helped her change chairs.

Mom would rise slowly and settle stiffly into the second chair, look at the screen, smile brightly, and with her head tilted slightly to her left, say, "Hi there, Handsome."

I'd say, "Hi there, Beautiful. How're you doing?"

She'd lean forward with a grin and say, "Let's go to question two."

Shi-chan and I usually asked questions about her childhood and growing up in White Salmon. We could tell she enjoyed telling us those stories again. Sometimes she acted out the characters in the story, gesturing with her left hand, puffing out her chest, making faces, pursing her lips, dropping her jaw, and other movements that helped us visualize the scenes. Halfway through, Terri would bring Mom her pills and a glass of water. Mom would pop a pill in her mouth, take the glass gingerly in her two hands, tilt her head back slightly, and take small sips until each pill slid down her throat. She'd hand the glass back to Terri, wipe her mouth with her left arm, look at the screen, and say something like "These so-called golden years aren't that much fun" or "Don't ever be my age—it's too much work."

A few minutes later, her eyes would fade and she'd lean forward a little bit at a time until all we could see in our screen was her hair. I'd say, "Mom, we can't see your beautiful eyes." She'd say, "Oh!" and lean back with the grin of an impish little girl who got caught stealing cookies. We'd have a good laugh, then say, "Well, I guess it's time to let you go to bed." Our goodbyes usually took another ten minutes.

In the beginning of September, TV news reports and social media postings of natural disasters on both sides of the Pacific had our families scrambling with worry. The tenth and most powerful typhoon of the year caused widespread damage, flooding, and landslides throughout Kyushu. Hundreds of thousands of households lost power. Authorities told over one and a half million residents to evacuate. Sustained winds were recorded at a hundred and twenty miles per hour and gusts up to a hundred forty-five miles per hour. The Japan Meteorological Agency reported that the strongest gusts ever were observed at more than thirty locations.

Through the night of September 5, neither Shi-chan nor I slept much because of all the shutters and windows rattling and the wind howling. We and the house survived. There were no broken windows, no downed trees outside, no loss of power, and we still had running water. By 11 a.m. the next morning, the worst had passed, but there were still strong gusts that continued until evening.

At the same time, it seemed the entire West Coast, from Southern California to British Columbia, was ablaze. Oregon alone had over thirty-five fires burning simultaneously with more than a million acres torched. Two fires in Clackamas County, just to the east of where Mom and Terri lived in King City in Washington County, threatened to merge and were creeping westward. Health experts urged people to prepare for evacuation orders and to stay indoors to avoid inhaling smoke and ash particles.

We stayed in touch constantly by e-mail and, when we could get a good connection, Skype. Mom and Terri told us the sky changed from a deep orange-red on Tuesday, September 8 to yellow later in the week and a foggy white over the weekend. The smoke from all the fires made it difficult to breathe. Terri kept the windows of their apartment closed and the air conditioner running. At one point, both Mom and Terri had difficulty getting a deep breath and had to use Mom's inhaler. They drank a lot of water.

Near the end of the month, the fires were being contained and the air quality was better. Mom and Terri were exhausted but thankful not to have been forced to evacuate. The relatives in White Salmon were also OK.

In the middle of November, I got a short e-mail from Mom that had so many typos, spelling mistakes, and downright weird combinations of keyboard symbols that I thought her mind was going wobbly. I dismissed that thought two weeks later when she sent a heartfelt Thanksgiving greeting. Despite all the problems in the world—the millions of people infected with Covid, the insane challenging of the presidential election results, climate change and the piling of one natural disaster on another—Mom and Terri were appreciative of all they had. Her love was crystal clear.

We continued our weekly Skype calls. All was fine until the call on December 20. Mom saw her doctor for a regular checkup, but he had a different diagnosis this time. He determined she was in the early stages of dementia but wanted to put her on hospice care because of her congestive heart failure. She'd put up a courageous and tenacious battle for a long time, but her body was shutting down.

That call was a tough one. We were blubbering all over the place. None of us could find words to express what we felt. At one point, Mom thrust her head into her hands and said, "Bob,

I'm so scared! I need you here!" A lump came to my throat. It physically hurt to see the fear and sadness in her eyes. I didn't have the courage to tell her that travel from one country to another was impossible. Japan was about to go on a complete shutdown again. I think what Mom needed more than anything at that moment was a real hug. All I could do was say "We love you, Mom" in a high-pitched voice.

Two days later, Mom started on hospice. They determined she could stay at home with Terri as her main caretaker. Mom's biggest fear was that she and Terri would be separated. She didn't want to go to a hospital or nursing home. The hospice people started her on morphine for her pain and Haldol for her anxiety.

We made Skype calls every day. After that first call, Mom was more accepting of her body shutting down. The first three calls contained many stories and much laughter. The characters, locations, and times all changed during these stories. What might start out with her first journey to Japan in 1983 could end up in Humboldt County's redwood country in 1957. We didn't care. Sometimes Mom actually got a second wind when talking with us. Before long, however, her situation began changing almost minute to minute, so each time we were able to connect, we felt grateful she recognized us and was able to communicate one more time.

In particular, there are two scenes from those calls that stick in my mind. Around Christmas Day, one of the hospice emergency medical technicians washed Mom's hair for her. She hadn't had that done in over a year. She was beaming as she looked at the computer screen and talked to Shi-chan and me. Even the complexion of her skin looked great. I said, "Jeez, Mom. That must feel great."

She ran her left hand through her hair and said, "You bet it does. I thought I'd woken up and already gone to heaven!"

We burst out laughing. After the phone call, she told Terri she was happy she'd made us laugh.

The other scene is from the next to last time we spoke to each other.

For the first ten minutes of the call, Mom wasn't responsive. She sat in front of the computer like a zombie, her eyes glassy and looking downward, lost in a distant world. We tried several questions to get a response, but there was none. Finally, I asked, "Would you like to listen to some music? How about listening to some Louis Armstrong? You used to like him." Mom looked up momentarily. Shi-chan found the song "What a Wonderful World" on her iPhone and held it close to the computer so Mom could hear it.

Mom relaxed noticeably and put her head down in her hands, swaying slightly to the music. About halfway through the song, her head still bent forward and her eyes closed, she slowly raised her hands just above her head and held them there as if holding up an offering to a holy person. It seemed she was trying to hold up a memory of great importance. When the song ended, she lowered her hands, opened her eyes, looked into the screen, and said, "That's a beautiful song." As if by magic, she was transformed. For the next ten minutes, we talked about her father accompanying her on the clarinet while she played the piano and Grandma Murph whistled back in her high school days. Then her eyes drooped. She was out of energy. We wished her goodnight and told her we loved her. That was the last time we made emotional contact.

After Christmas, Mom's condition deteriorated quickly. She had a few good days, but most were bad. It was an especially hard time for Terri. On one hand, Terri had spent her whole life preparing for it. All the studying and training she'd done to be a respiratory therapist, the experience of her multiple sclerosis and the different treatments she'd endured in finding out what worked and what didn't in alleviating the suffering, the years of caring for Mom in dealing with heart surgery, sepsis, fractured pelvis, arthritis, and the ordeals of aging had given Terri more skills and knowledge than most professionals got in a lifetime.

On the other hand, she had to deal with the limitations and torture that her MS and practically non-functional knees inflicted on her. Any kind of stress exacerbated those demons, but the stress of taking care of a loved one who is dying and needs special care twenty-four hours a day was almost too much to ask of anyone. And yet she did it.

Mom's slide into full-blown dementia was rapid. She began to get agitated and fiddle with her fingers nervously for hours. Her appetite dissipated greatly. She slept a lot during the day and would be awake most of the night. When Terri put her in her recliner for a nap one day, she got unnerved, saw things that weren't there, thought she wasn't in her own home, and accused Terri of not loving her, being mean, and saying bad things to her.

Mom sometimes fell while wandering around at night, one time smacking her forehead and getting a big goose egg. Terri was not sleeping well, if at all, and her nightly leg cramps got worse. The hospice nurses put Mom on morphine three times a day instead of twice. They also tried using a different medication for Mom's anxiety at night.

We were in daily contact with Terri. She'd let us know if Mom was in good enough condition to handle a call or not. Terri hadn't been able to take any time for herself since the day they learned of Mom's dementia. Her heart was breaking; she had no time even to cry. The hospice people ordered a wheelchair and a bed alarm for Mom's bed. Mom had trouble standing up by herself. Walking was difficult. She became less cooperative when Terri or the hospice nurses tried to help her get up or go to bed.

While sitting in her recliner, Mom occasionally had animated conversations with one of her best friends from her working days, her dad, her brother, me, someone named Harry, and many others. She accused Terri of trying to control her. One time, she got upset with Terri giving her medication before bed. She whispered in Terri's ear that if Terri was giving her drugs, she'd never forgive her. The emotional and physical pain was too much for Terri to bear. She broke down once when eating alone at the dinner table while Mom slept. She pushed her plate away and sobbed until her eyes could produce no more tears. She found herself hoping the end would come soon, but she'd shake her head, buckle up, and face the music again.

There were moments of respite. One night, Mom slept about sixteen hours straight without waking once. The next morning, she was focused. She ate more than usual and drank more water. She didn't sleep much during the day. She had no delusions. Although still weak, she moved and got up with less struggle. That night, however, her agitation returned.

Terri's cramps and lack of sleep got so bad that she had an extra nurse come in as a backup at night. She had a new mattress brought in to try to prevent Mom from her nocturnal wandering. The mattress was scoop-shaped with high sides. Mom slept in the trough area.

Mom fell into a coma on my seventieth birthday. She now showed no signs of anxiety or hallucination. Terri said Mom was calm and in no pain. The only time she had pain was when her diapers needed to be changed. Terri had to roll her completely on her sides to do that.

We called Terri again the next day. She'd set up a Skype account on her Kindle reader. By using that handheld device, she could go into Mom's bedroom and have the conversation there. We hoped Mom could hear us talking and feel good even if she didn't respond. We talked about some of Mom's family stories. We couldn't see Mom, but Terri said she looked sweet just lying there peacefully. We told Mom many times how much we loved her and it was OK to let go.

Two days later, four days short of Mom's ninety-fifth birthday, we got this e-mail from Terri.

January 14, 2021
Subject: It's Over

Bob and Shi-chan,

I am so sorry to have to tell you by email that Mom passed away shortly after 7 a.m. this morning. She was still with us when I woke up and I was on the phone with hospice about a mask for her as she was mouth-breathing only and was told to put her nasal canula in her. When I did, she passed. Hospice is sending someone out, but I don't know when they will get here. I still have to go to the bank and transfer the money and I may still need someone to be here if hospice hasn't been here yet. I don't know what happens now, but please call tonight.

I love you all. Life is too darned short no matter how
long we are blessed to be here. Hugs, Terri

Shi-chan and I read the message. I closed the computer and
slumped forward. Shi-chan put her arm around me. The waterworks flowed for a long time. Later, I went into the Japanese room
with the *tatami* mats on the first floor. We had a picture of Mom
set in the *tokonoma* alcove. I put my hands together and said a
little prayer. At the end, I looked at the picture and said, "When
it's our turn, Mom, we'll meet you on the other side, laugh, and
listen to all those stories again—the Good Lord willing and the
creek don't rise."

THE END

Acknowledgments

I would like first of all to express my profound gratitude to my publisher, Michael Cannings, a consummate professional who from beginning to end provided tremendous patience and support in guiding me through the publishing process. Without his extraordinary copy editing, design, layout, advice, and smooth communication, this book might never have seen the light of print. To Robert Whiting, Rosa del Duca, and Michael Uhl, I want to express my sincere appreciation for giving freely of their time in reading earlier versions of the manuscript, providing invaluable advice for revisions, and giving me the best blurbs a writer could possibly hope for.

I am grateful to David Zeiger for his social conscience and taking time out of a busy schedule to respond so positively to this old conscientious objector's request to look over the manuscript. A special hug and kiss go to sisters extraordinaire Terri Norris and Linda Bloom for their many years of humor, support, and unconditional love. The same goes for Sandra Curtis for being such a longtime, stalwart friend of Mom and pointing out several factual errors in the early stages of the book.

I owe a special debt of gratitude to bosom buddies Bill Cornett and Nick Warren for their decades of friendship, brotherhood, and all-night discussions of great importance about youthful adventures, books, sports, rock 'n' roll, lexicography, and various kinds of nonsense that often were capped off with a final beer and a good punchline.

I'd like to extend my appreciation to the Itami City Sasa Softball Club members for raising me from my first baby utterances of Japanese, teaching me the importance of loyalty and group dynamics in Japanese culture, and overwhelming me with more acts of kindness than I deserved. The same goes for Shigeya Kitamura, whose wonderful friendship, artistic sensibility, and sense of humor in the beginning of my Japan adventure are forever embedded in my heart.

A heartfelt thanks goes out to Tadamitsu "Tad" Kamimoto, Yukiko Hazama, Shinji Fukuda, and Kazufumi "Big Bat" Yamane, all of whom were the best of colleagues and friends during our golden years at Fukuoka Women's Junior College. I can't forget Kuniyasu Ichikawa, the best *senpai* a goofy *gaijin* like me could ever have, and all his years of friendship, encouragement, zany humor, and love of literature, baseball, and good beer. A special word of appreciation also goes to the many colleagues I was lucky enough to work with at Fukuoka International University during our years together.

To the Cady brothers, John and Bill, thank you for a lifetime of friendship and laughter. Finally, I want to express my love and gratitude to my wife, Shizuyo, for sticking with me all these years and giving meaning to my life, as well as the motivation to keep going.

About the Author

Robert W. Norris was born and raised in Humboldt County, California. In 1969, he entered the Air Force, subsequently became a conscientious objector to the Vietnam War, and served time in a military prison for refusing to fight in the war. In his twenties, he roamed across the United States, went to Europe twice, and made one journey around the world. In 1983, he landed in Japan, where he eventually became a professor at a private university, spent two years as the dean of students, and retired in 2016 as professor emeritus.

Norris is the author of *Looking for the Summer*, a novel about a former Vietnam War conscientious objector's adventures and search for identity in Europe, Turkey, Iran, Afghanistan, and India in 1977; *Toraware*, a novel about the obsessive relationship of three misfits from different cultural backgrounds in 1980s Kobe, Japan; *Autumn Shadows in August*, an hallucinogenic mid-life crisis/adventure, and homage to Malcolm Lowry and Hermann Hesse; *The Many Roads to Japan*, a novella used as an English textbook in Japanese universities; and *The Good Lord Willing and the Creek Don't Rise: Pentimento Memories of Mom and Me*, a memoir and tribute to his mother. He has also written several articles on teaching English as a foreign language. He and his wife live near Fukuoka, Japan.

Made in the USA
Middletown, DE
06 November 2023

42007393R00275